IEE COMPUTING SERIES 13
Series Editors: Dr. B. Carré
Dr. D. A. H. Jacobs
Professor I. Sommerville

APPLICATION OF ARTIFICIAL INTELLIGENCE TO COMMAND & CONTROL SYSTEMS

Other volumes in this series

Volume 1   Semi-custom IC design and VLSI
           P. J. Hicks (Editor)
Volume 2   Software engineering for microprocessor systems
           P. G. Depledge (Editor)
Volume 3   Systems on silicon
           P. B. Denyer (Editor)
Volume 4   Distributed computing systems programme
           D. Duce (Editor)
Volume 5   Integrated project support environments
           J. A. McDermid (Editor)
Volume 6   Software engineering '86
           D. J. Barnes and P. J. Brown (Editors)
Volume 7   Software engineering environments
           I. Sommerville (Editor)
Volume 8   Software engineering: the decade of change
           D. Ince (Editor)
Volume 9   Computer aided tools for VLSI system design
           G. Russell (Editor)
Volume 10 Industrial software technology
           R. Mitchell (Editor)
Volume 11 Advances in command, control and communication systems
           C. J. Harris and I. White (Editors)
Volume 12 Speech recognition by machine
           W. A. Ainsworth

APPLICATION OF ARTIFICIAL INTELLIGENCE TO COMMAND & CONTROL SYSTEMS

EDITED BY C. J. HARRIS

Peter Peregrinus Ltd on behalf of the Institution of Electrical Engineers

Published by Peter Peregrinus Ltd, London, United Kingdom
© **1988: Peter Peregrinus Ltd**

ISBN 0 86341 142 8

Printed in England by Short Run Press Ltd, Exeter

Contents

Preface

List of contributors

Chapter 1   **An Introduction to the Rôle of Artificial Intelligence in Command and Control**

       1.1   Artificial Intelligence in Command and Control
              J A H Miles

1.1.1	Artificial intelligence	1
1.1.2	AI spin-off technologies	5
1.1.3	Expert or knowledge-based systems	7
1.1.4	C^2 application issues	13
1.1.5	Concluding remarks	16
1.1.6	References	16

       1.2   Knowledge Representation using Massively Parallel Processors
              S Sharma and T Spracklen

1.2.1	Introduction	18
1.2.2	Exceptions	21
1.2.3	Plan recognition	30
1.2.4	Concluding remarks	33
1.2.5	References	34

Chapter 2   **Uncertainty and Complexity in Command and Control**

       2.1   Uncertainty in Command and Control Systems
              J R Moon, J P Marriette and S P Frampton

2.1.1	Introduction	37
2.1.2	Preliminary concepts	38
2.1.3	Causes of uncertainty	39
2.1.4	Influences on processing function	46
2.1.5	Influence on system architecture	49
2.1.6	Conclusion	53
2.1.7	References	53

2.2 Catastrophes, Chaos and C³I: Toward a New Understanding of Military Combat
A E R Woodcock

   2.2.1 Introduction   55
   2.2.2 Mathematical combat models   55
   2.2.3 The rôle of catastrophe theory   59
   2.2.4 Force multipliers don't always act as force multipliers   71
   2.2.5 Population-dynamical models of insurgent force strength   72
   2.2.6 Chaotic dynamical systems models   73
   2.2.7 Cellular automata can stimulate the combat environment   78
   2.2.8 Summary   81
   2.2.9 References   84

2.3 Reducing Uncertainty and Ignorance in C² Systems
C J Harris

   2.3.1 Introduction to evidential reasoning   90
   2.3.2 Representation of uncertainty of evidence   91
   2.3.3 Bayesian hypothesis methods in data fusion and decision making   92
   2.3.4 The Dempster-Shafer approach to sensor integration   100
   2.3.5 Application of fuzzy logic to C² systems   111
   2.3.6 References   123

Chapter 3 Intelligent Data Fusion

3.1 Toward the Utilization of Certain Elements of AI Technology for Multi Sensor Data Fusion
J Llinas

   3.1.1 Introduction   126
   3.1.2 Multi-sensor fusion in the context of C² systems   129
   3.1.3 Internal details of the fusion process   138
   3.1.4 Issues in the application of AI technology to MSF   150
   3.1.5 Recapitulation   178
   3.1.6 References   182

3.2 Application of Expert System Technology to an Information Fusion System
R B Woolsey

   3.2.1 Introduction   185
   3.2.2 Techniques involved   185
   3.2.3 Description of an information fusion system   197
   3.2.4 Evaluation methodology   201
   3.2.5 References   211

3.3 Battlefield Data Fusion
R T Naylor, A Roth, R A Bromley and S N K Watt

   3.3.1 Introduction   212
   3.3.2 The domain   214

	3.3.3	System components and architecture	214
	3.3.4	Knowledge representation	219
	3.3.5	Uncertain and incomplete information	223
	3.3.6	Data fusion	226
	3.3.7	Implementation issues	228
	3.3.8	Testing	231
	3.3.9	Conclusions	232
	3.3.10	References	233
3.4		Techniques for Knowledge-Based Data Fusion	
		J A H Miles	
	3.4.1	Introduction	234
	3.4.2	Data fusion applications	235
	3.4.3	Data fusion problem decomposition	242
	3.4.4	Multiplatform data fusion	255
	3.4.5	Reasoning with uncertainty	261
	3.4.6	Summary of techniques of data fusion	266
	3.4.7	References	267
3.5		An Object Orientated Approach to Data Fusion	
		S L Rhodes	
	3.5.1	Introduction	269
	3.5.2	The object orientated approach	270
	3.5.3	Data fusion	272
	3.5.4	Signal interface	274
	3.5.5	Object orientated system design	277
	3.5.6	The target functions	279
	3.5.7	Target allocation function	283
	3.5.8	Performance	286
	3.5.9	Instruction rate	290
	3.5.10	Implementing the object orientated model	295
	3.5.11	References	297

Chapter 4   Intelligent Situation Assessment and Planning

4.1		Expert Systems and the Problems of Naval Command	
		D W Cruse and W J Bingham	
	4.1.1	Introduction	298
	4.1.2	The command function	298
	4.1.3	The rôle of expert systems	304
	4.1.4	Naval command aid	308
	4.1.5	References	314
4.2		Knowledge Based Techniques for Tactical Situation Assessment	
		J A H Miles, E M England, H C Faulkner and S P Frampton	
	4.2.1	Introduction	315
	4.2.2	Introduction to techniques	316
	4.2.3	Situation assessment problem	317

4.2.4   Situation assessment by group formation   321
4.2.5   Plan recognition and prediction   327
4.2.6   Resource allocation   330
4.2.7   Summary of techniques   333
4.2.8   Naval situation assessment case study   336
4.2.9   Knowledge acquisition   339
4.2.10   Implementation   340
4.2.11   Discussion   350
4.2.12   References   353
4.3   Intelligent Systems for Naval Resource Planning
      J A Gadsden and W L Lakin
4.3.1   Introduction   356
4.3.2   Information management   356
4.3.3   Demonstrator approach   357
4.3.4   Knowledge-based system attributes   359
4.3.5   What is planning?   361
4.3.6   Planning in command and control   362
4.3.7   Domain examples   365
4.3.8   Why a knowledge-based approach?   365
4.3.9   Flying programme generation   367
4.3.10   The planning problem   371
4.3.11   The interactive planner   372
4.3.12   User interaction   373
4.3.13   Future programme   375
4.3.14   Conclusions   377
4.3.15   References   378
4.4   Navigating through Complex Databases: A Case Study
      B I Blum, R D Semmel and V G Sigillito
4.4.1   Introduction   380
4.4.2   Database technology   381
4.4.3   The intelligent navigation assistant   384
4.4.4   Conclusions   394
4.4.5   References   395

Index   397

Preface

Command and Control (C^2) Systems are the management infrastructure for defence and war or for any other large scale complex dynamic information/resource management system. The first book in this series (Harris & White, 1987) observed that there is no adequate theory for C^2 nor fundamental methodology for its design. This is not surprising, since the higher levels of C^2 are essentially an extension of the basic human decision processes by means of procedures, organisations, equipments, data fusion, situation assessment (or threat assessment) and resource allocation. C^2 systems are amongst the most complex and large scale real time resource management systems known to man; their effectiveness is severely limited by lack of speed, data saturation and the cognitive limits of the human decision maker. Effective C^2 systems are not just decision making processes that select the best option, but also the creation, evaluation and refinement of what the situation is and what, if anything, can be done about it. The majority of practical C^2 systems are action information systems, that is they concentrate upon the acquisition of information, data processing (including correlation, altering and routing) and communications, and physical MMI aspects rather than upon underlying analysis of the tactical decision process itself. The actual process of C^2 continues to remain with the decision maker, in spite of the tendency of modern C^2 systems to become more sophisticated through:

(i)   increasing speed, effectiveness and mobility of modern weapon systems
(ii)   increasing number, diversity and capability of sensors, which together with intelligence is leading to an information explosion problem. This widely sourced data must be interpreted, filtered, correlated and fused in real time to be effective.
(iii)   increasing number of different types of battlefield sensors require complex and adaptive asset management.

It is clear that the rate, complexity, dimensionality and uncertainty of events and the information about them in a crisis situation is rapidly increasing. This coupled with the need for real time decision making will result in high returns for decision aided technology for C^2 systems.

The majority of C^2 systems are complex, ill-defined, generally containing substantial uncertainty, are unbounded and are characterised by non-unique solutions (if they exist at all), frequently with no stopping rule or solution in finite time. At the highest C^2 level man's rôle is as a planner and resource allocator, however he is under stress and is prone to several perceptual decision/planning idiosyncrasies such as conservation, data saturation, self-fulfilling predictions, habit, overconfidence (as well as lack of confidence in other situations), gamblers fallacy and panic. To alleviate this situation Artificial Intelligence (AI) - by which we mean an intelligent computer based system that assists or replaces humans, when they are too expensive, too slow, or the task too dangerous (see Chapter 1.1) - can be used as a decision/planning aided technique that allows the operator to concentrate on the options offered and to determine the most appropriate response. AI techniques and the emerging technology of concurrent processors (see Chapter 1.2) now offer the possibility of real time intelligent decision aids for C^2 systems; AI provides the tools to utilise an expert's (commander) knowledge for effective use in a real time computer based control structure. This offers the potential of an efficient use of a Knowledge Base (KB) of production rules for managing system processing resources, establishment and evaluation of current situation and dynamic problem strategies. A significant feature of the AI approach is that it enables the user to ask for justification and reasoning behind recommendations offered, this is of particular significance in responding to emergency situations when there is insufficient time to analyse all options.

A typical knowledge based C^2 systems architecture needs to accept data from a variety of sources such as physical sensors (eg radar, ESM, sonar, ELINT etc) databases (including encyclopaedic data such as look-up tables on emitter characteristics, aircraft types etc) and other intelligence/information sources; the data is then correlated, combined and fused to produce a single situation picture (picture compilation), which in turn, at a higher more abstract level, a situational assessment is made. Since the purpose of the knowledge base is to provide the user with a set of real time situation assessments, proposed decisions/plans and explanations, incorporation of a model of human decision making at the various stages of the knowledge based system is clearly of critical importance, (ie we need to model the commander as well as the process of C^2 and fully integrate both models). Despite this there are few systematic methods available for eliciting knowledge from experts.

An initial model of the human decision making process that is appropriate to C^2, is the SHORE (S̲timulus, H̲ypothesis, O̲ptions, R̲esponse) paradigm, which may be interpreted in the context of this book as the hierarchy of tasks:

(i)   data acquisition from sensors or intelligence - STIMULUS
(ii)   sensor data interpretation and data fusion - STIMULUS
(iii)   situation or threat assessment - HYPOTHESIS
(iv)   decision plans or goal generation for desired outcomes or resource allocation - OPTIONS
(v)   implementation of plans and monitoring of response/actions to ascertain success through sensor or intelligence [process returns to (i)] - RESPONSE

These activities are increasingly difficult and abstract, and it is therefore not surprising that most research effort, has until recently, concentrated upon AI based multi-sensor data fusion and situation assessment C^2 systems. This is also reflected in the structure and content of this book. As with the first volume in this series on *Advances in Command, Control and Communication Systems: Theory and Applications*, many of the contributions are updated and extended versions of papers presented at the Second International IEE/IERE/IMA/BCS Conference at Bournemouth, UK in 1987; however several sections have been especially solicited for this book to provide a status overview of AI in C^2 systems in 1988. In particular Section 1.1 has been written to provide an introduction to Artificial Intelligence and its potential application to C^2 systems. Here it is recognised that the fundamental problem of C^2 systems is the failure to determine adequate models of the system and the decision maker. In particular the importance of knowledge elicitation (a prerequisite in expert systems) and knowledge representation, together with the sub-problem of explanations and uncertainty in reasoning, is stressed. J Miles describes the prime features of expert systems and associated tools for the uninitiated and makes special reference to the Blackboard Systems architecture widely used in C^2 systems. The section identifies the *bottlenecks* of knowledge acquisition or elicitation, brittleness (or sensitivity to model or knowledge representation) and run time on critical restrictions of expert system methodologies in C^2 systems, and the use for knowledge based systems (KBS) that provide stable and non-brittle/insensitive solutions. Section 1.1 concludes by observing that the conventional approach to developing KBS is through gradually increasing difficulty of problems through prototyping - this is not possible in C^2 - the hard problems have to be addressed.

The near real time requirements, high data inputs and hierarchical nature of automated C^2 systems increasingly require parallel processor architectures. In this context in Section 1.2, knowledge is represented by connections or links between a central processor and primitive elements; in particular a form of the *connection* machine - a parallel processing array with a powerful interprocessor communications facility - is considered to allow representation of ambiguity. The use of these specialised highly parallel computer architectures (one processor per assertion in a large KB) is to achieve fusing of vehicles' detection and tracking and heuristic reasoning of higher level aspects such as determination of vehicle identity/type/intent based upon behaviour patterns, intelligence, tactical appreciation and experience so as to provide optimal tactical pictures.

A major purpose in the utilisation of AI in C^2 systems is to deal with not only systems complexity, data saturation and associated real time decisioning, but also with uncertainty. This presupposes that the sources of uncertainty are understood, it is possible to measure and evaluate its influence, also it is possible to model it adequately, and there exists a mechanism to reduce its effect on the C^2 process, that is, desensitise situation assessment and resource allocation to uncertainty in all its forms. Chapter 2 considers both the sources of uncertainty and some means of representing it in C^2 systems. Section 2.1 presents uncertainty in the process hierarchy of C^2 (cf SHORE paradigm) as:

(i)   **Picture compilation**
        -   positional and quantification uncertainties
            (eg sensor measurement and processing errors)
        -   identification uncertainties
(ii)   **Situation assessment**
        -   uncertainties due to the picture
        -   uncertainties associated with
            equipments/platforms (encyclopaedia data)
        -   tactical knowledge uncertainties
(iii)   **Response/resource allocation**
        -   options and their selection (the outcome of
            implementing any decision is itself
            uncertain).

A full discussion of the various sources of uncertainty and the possible means of dealing with it is provided in this section.

The importance of adequate models of the C^2 process and the commander has already been stressed, it is equally important to model the combat environment in which they operate. The combat environment can exhibit extremely chaotic behaviour, as such it adds a large degree of uncertainty to the planning process. In Section 2.2 it is shown that very simple mathematical models (akin to the Lanchester equations) can describe very complex combat behavioural patterns. The objective of this research is to provide commanders with electronic workstations that support analysis and decision making and specifically:

-   allows top down combat problem solving facility in
    terms of a few key infleunce factors
-   supports cognitive aspects of battle management

- provides combat simulations

The author discusses in detail the rôle of catastrophe theory in C^2 and produces problem solving landscapes that aid commanders to follow combat developments and associated situation assessment and decision making in essentially real time. The theory provides a rigorous framework to support 'top down' analysis of complex systems; the resulting Lanchester type equations may provide insights into multiforce interactions. An alternative approach based upon cellular automata, composed of independent elemental or primitive computing elements (each with a set of internal rules that prescribe simple actions based upon local effects in the vicinity of the cell), is described, by constructing appropriate 'networks', very complex behavioural patterns can be generated. This method is strongly related to learning systems such as finite stochastic automata and neural nets (see Section 2.3).

The first volume in this series on advances in C^2 systems was criticised by one reviewer for failing to include analytical based methods of C^2 modelling and analysis; it is hoped that Sections 2.2 and 2.3 will partially satisfy such readers' craving for mathematics! Section 2.3 provides an introduction to the three most popular mathematical methods of dealing with evidential uncertainty and ignorance in C^2. The Bayesian and Fuzzy Logic approaches are well established techniques and are relevant to both intelligent data fusion and decisioning, whereas the currently popular Dempster-Shafer consensus method is only applicable to multi-sensor data fusion.

Multi-sensor data fusion can be defined as the process of integrating information from multiple sources to produce the most *specific* and comprehensive unified data or model about an entity or event of interest. Multi-sensor data fusion (MSDF) can be viewed as a hypothesis generating process for C^2 assessment and decisioning, that is it precedes option generation, planning evaluation and resource allocation in the SHORE C^2 hierarchical paradigm as well as in practice. The MSDF problem is at least four subproblems:-

(i)   Alignment process and positional data fusion problem
      - checks if sensor data refers to some entity and representation
(ii) association process or comparison problem (pattern matching)
      - checks if two representations refer to same entity
(iii) attribution data fusion problem
      - merges features from two representations into one for same entity
(iv) aggregation into a more abstract representation
      - elementary form of situation assessment.

Chapter Three contains four sections which are devoted to recent research and application of AI to MSDF. Section 3.1 provides a definitive in-depth review of MSDF, providing representative observable sensor pairings of emission characteristics, benefits of MSDF, sensor trade-offs and techniques for optimally combining multiple sensor data (including both analytical - as in Section 2.3, and AI based methodologies). The section categorises the *problems* of MSDF differently as Data Association, Multi-target Tracking, Data Combination and Data Reasoning; these should both be compared with the USA JDL models of three levels of MSDF: Level 1 position/identity estimation; Level 2, situation assessment, Level 3, threat assessment. The JDL model of MSDF is dealt with in some detail; suggesting the rôle limits and applications of AI in MSDF and identifies the need for a data driven expectation model which has a functionally orientated expert system framework that can also deal with uncertainty. The section also describes the manner in which natural language techniques are applied to *message* based MSDF systems, as well as to the more usual MMI systems, drawing similarities between frames that represent situations through data structures and templates used in conventional situation assessment.

Section 3.2, similarly to 3.1, provides an overview of MSDF, and a review of the analytical methods of Bayes, Dempster-Shafer and Fuzzy sets (discussed in detail in Section 2.3), as well as cluster analysis, for use at the lowest levels of data fusion. At the higher levels once data has been categorised, knowledge representation and rules - such as force model templating, semantic networks and frame/scripts methodologies, are considered. Having described the techniques of the fusion process, attention is addressed to the functionality of a specific MSDF system; including surveillance threat, communications, COMINT/ELINT/HUMINT analysis. To evaluate such an approach the section finishes with an interactive training scenario driver that challenges the user to draw conclusions from data and to redirect sensor based acquisition.

Achieving full MSDF on the battlefield is very much more difficult than in the air/sea environments owing to the larger number of entitities, number and diversity of sensors, greater rôle of human intelligence/reporting, and greater complexity and uncertainty of the battlefield. Section 3.3 is concerned with the initial step towards a battlefield expert system based MSDF systems architecture - ECRES-II. It is a blackboard based system that combines a complete terrain representation (types and field of view), a comprehensive database of military knowledge (equipments and formations) and similarly to Section 3.2, a scenario generator or simulator for validation. ECRES-II has the ability to deal with alternative and frequently mutually exclusive hypotheses about the battlefield situation derived from uncertain and incomplete information.   The section concludes with several alternative solutions to parallism, such as distributed co-operating blackboard systems, partitioning, and transputer arrays.

The final two sections of Chapter Three are concerned with the application of MSDF to the less confused and complex Naval environment. The first, Section 3.4, provides an update on the ARE work on MSDF reported in the first volume, however like Section 3.1 is also gives an overview of MSDF and its civil and military applications. An important contribution to the first part of this section is the categorisation of MSDF into *problem domains* of designed worlds, benign real worlds, and hostile real worlds, each being divided into small worlds (e.g. close range sensing for say autonomous vehicles) and large worlds, (e.g. ground air defence or air traffic control). *Multiple* platform MSDF is viewed as a two level or stage process of (i) entity data assembly and (ii) combination of assembled data for each entity to estimate parameters of interest. The correlation ambiguity problem resulting from spatially inaccurate data sources, incomplete sensor coverage, data reception delays, false alarms and variable sensor resolutions is considered in the Naval C^2 context. To limit the number of possible combinatorial correlations produced by multi-sensor, only pairwise correlations are approached in a real time rule based data fusion system based upon a blackboard architecture. Three generic types of hypotheses are required to support the correlation strategy:-

(i)   evidence or reports hypothesis
(ii)   object hypothesis to represent domain system models
(iii)   correlation hypothesis between evidence

To represent uncertainty in the correlation and combination of evidence a reasoning system is reviewed through numerical uncertainty schemes (viable only if there is statistical rich data available), and perhaps more appropriately, symbolic uncertainty schemes such as the theory of endorsements (which translate directly statements about levels of uncertainty into hypotheses).
The final section in Chapter Three on the relatively mature subject of MSDF, is similarly concerned with the Naval environment but is based upon the decomposition of the tactical picture into asynchronous *objects*, which represent attested targets each of which is responsible for increasing its *self-awareness* by evaluating the relevance of incoming data. This object orientated approach has the main advantages of concurrency and limited, precise rule structures that are readily validated. As with the previous sections, Section 3.5 divides data fusion into two functional areas - signal or a data interface and the tactical picture. The interface function is to reduce all track reports to a common format and to prioritise track signals, whereas the target function forms the basic engine of the fusion system - producing the best estimate of position and identity of a specific target. Issues of performance, algorithm execution rate, processing load and requirements (e.g number of instructions required) and

xvi Preface

physical implementation in the so called Sofchip computer
are discussed).

Data fusion is not an end in itself, but as already
observed in the SHORE paradigm, an input to the more
abstract levels of situation assessment, planning and
resource allocation. Chapter Four considers initial
research results in the application of KBS to these latter
areas of the SHORE paradigm to C^2. Section 4.1 is
concerned with the application of KBS to the problems of
Naval Command, however the methodology adopted has a wider
applicability. The section describes the task and
difficulties of a Naval Commander and demonstrates how
expert systems can provide useful command aids, and as such
acts as a scene setter for Sections 4.2 and 4.3.

Section 4.2 provides a substantial overview of the
requirement and the potential rôle of KBS in situation
assessment and presents a *case* study of a prototype system.
This section also addresses the fundamental issue of
knowledge elicitation. Situation assessment, unlike its
input MSDF which is data driven, is *goal* driven with an
output directly related to the decision making or resource
allocation process. The section decomposes the problem of
situation assessment into a series of sub-problems - threat
assessment, defence assessment, mission assessment, action
outcomes, weapon system geometries, rules of engagement,
sensor and weapon coverage plan monitoring and surveillance
- the critical elements in C^2 systems being threat and
defence assessment. Situation assessment itself is
characterised by what is required and what is available,
and the means of reducing the gap. Three complementary
knowledge based strategies are proferred as bridging the
knowledge gap - goal formation of evidence and rules, plan
recognition, and plans (goal driven using stored patterns
or data driven using simulation). The section also divides
resource allocation into two activities with differing time
scales - preplaning resource allocation and reactive
resource allocation. A major contribution of Section 4.2
is the indepth case study of a Situation Assesment and
Threat Evalation (SATE) demonstrator, of particular value
are the observations in respect of the KBS life cycle. An
important element in developing this demonstrator was the
knowledge acquisition from serving Naval experts using
developed scenarios as a focus for system assessment.

At the highest level of C^2 is resource allocation and
deployment of resources, Section 4.3 discusses the use of
KBS technology in this context through the development of
the *Flypast* Naval technology demonstrator. A fundamental
issue to be tested is the assertion that an inadequately
understood problem domain, such as C^2, can be successfully
addressed using an equally imperfect technology such as
KBS! It is hoped that this demonstrator programme will
resolve the basic issues of validation and acceptance of
KBS by the C^2 user. Planning in the Naval context of C^2
can be divided into four categories according to relative
time scales - strategic mission planning, tactical resource
planning, reactive resource planning and autonomous

weapon/sensor direction. The section describes an interactive planner using a constraint-network generator based upon an 'assumption based truth maintenance system, which has been functionally tested against a series of operational naval exercise scenarios as well as against pathological cases designed to test the system's reasoning process.

Whilst much of data fusion is concerned with perishable data whose capture and transmission is critical, some data is of a more static nature and the challenge is identification and integration. Section 4.4 is concerned with applying AI techniques to facilitate access to the USA Army HQ Decision Resource Database (DRD); here of particular importance is the need for an expressive user interface, that enables him to formulate reasonable and accurate queries. Options available include a system teacher or tutorial, vocabulary structure, query formulation and selector.

We might conclude that until the following capabilities in expert systems, knowledge representaion and problem solving/planning have been resolved, AI is still a research/development tool in C^2:-

(i)   the required expert system capabilities of model (rather than rule) based systems, multiple representation, hybrid reasoning about symbolic and numeric information, multiple co-operating intelligent systems and extensive explanation capabilities

(ii)   the capability of knowledge representation for temporal, spatial, qualitative, default, functional, structural and analogue knowledge

(iii)   the capability at the planning level of dealing with dynamically varying goals, conditions, objects and properties; the use of multiple agents; with simultaneous and overlapping events, temporal relations, plan monitors and incremental planners. In addition there still exists serious unresolved fundamental questions concerning the specification, validation and acceptance of knowledge based systems, despite these reservations KBS have a major and expanding rôle to play in future *in service* C^2 systems - much of which will depend upon the work of researchers, such as have contributed to this book.

The views expressed in this book are those of the authors and editor only, and should not be taken as representing the policy or viewpoint of their sponsoring organisations. I would however like to acknowledge the UK Ministry of Defence for permission to publish those sections which are subject to Crown Copyright, as well as to the various UK companies who have supported this and other learned C^3I activities that I have been involved with. A special note of thanks to Lucas Aerospace for their financial support, and to my secretary Sally Mulford

for   fusing   together   an   uncertain   set   of   disparate
information   sources   into,   what   I   hope   is,   a   progressive
account   of   the   current   status   of   AI   in C^2 systems,   any
errors,   omissions   and   imbalances   are   mine.

C J Harris
May 1988

Contributors

S. Sharma
T. Spracklen

Aberdeen University
Dept of Computing Science
King's College
Old Aberdeen
AB9 2UB

J.A. Gadsden
W.L. Lakin
J.A.H. Miles

Admiralty Research Establishment
MOD(PE), Portsdown,
Portsmouth,Hants PO6 4AA,

S.L. Rhodes

Advanced Systems Architecture Ltd
Johnson House
73-79 Park Street
Camberley
Surrey GU15 3PE

J. Llinas

Calspan Corporation
PO Box 400
Buffalo
New York 14225
USA

B.I. Blum
R.D. Semmel
V.G. Sigillito

Johns Hopkins University
Applied Physics Laboratory
Laurel, Maryland 20707
USA

D.W. Cruse
W.J. Bingham
E. England
H.C. Faulkner
S.P. Frampton
J.P. Mariette
J.R. Moon

Ferranti Computer Systems Ltd
Priestowod
Wokingham Road
Bracknell
Berkshire RG12 1PA

R.T. Naylor
S.N.K. Watt

Plessey Defence Systems Ltd
Grange Road
Christchurch
Dorset BH23 4JE

A. Roth   QMC Instruments Ltd
                       Unit A
                       357 Mile End Road
                       London E1 4PA

C.J. Harris   Southampton University
                       Dept of Aeronautics & Astronautics
                       Highfield
                       Southampton
                       Hants SO9 5NH

A.E.R. Woodcock   Synetics Corporation
                       10400 Eaton Place, Suite 200
                       Fairfax, Virginia 22030-2208
                       USA

R.B. Woolsey   Technology for Communications
                       International
                       Information Systems Division
                       34175 Ardenwood Blvd
                       Fremont
                       CA 94536-7705
                         USA

P.A. Bromley   York University
                       York
                       YO1 5DD

Chapter 1

An introduction to the role of artificial intelligence in command and control

Artificial Intelligence and Command and Control

J.A.H. Miles
(Admiralty Research Establishment)*

1.1.1   Artificial Intelligence

Artificial Intelligence is about understanding and creating human faculties which are regarded as intelligence. Command and Control is about the application of human intelligence to the management of resources in a dynamic environment. The link between the two is intuitively obvious, if we wish to understand or assist command and control (C^2) processes then we need artificial intelligence (AI). This introductory chapter addresses the reasons for applying AI to C^2, the state of the art and problem areas.

The term 'AI' is not well defined because intelligence itself cannot be well defined. What is certain is that there is a large research community who refer to their work as AI and this research spreads across a wide variety of disciplines. AI research has shifted its ground in practical terms, because of technological developments, but there have always been two broad objectives:

-   Modelling of human intelligence where the goal is to discover how the human brain works
-   Building intelligent machines to assist or replace humans where they are too expensive, inefficient, slow or the task too dangerous.

This article will concentrate on the second of these objectives because this is where most research towards C^2 systems is currently directed. However, one of the major shortfalls in our ability to build and organise good C^2 systems is the lack of adequate models of the whole system including the human element. It may turn out that attempts to build intelligent machines to perform C^2 tasks will eventually provide such models as a by-product but this is a long way off at present

From the beginnings of practical AI, which started when electronic digital computers became available, an objective has been to build machines which have the human traits which most people describe as intelligent behaviour, for example game playing, understanding language, learning etc. After thirty-five years or so, no machine has yet been constructed with 'intelligence' in the general human sense and there are some who believe it is impossible. True Artifical Intelligence should be regarded as a goal being approached gradually rather than a foreseeable achievement in the near future. While there are resarchers who are striving towards this goal, others are busily trying to apply the techniques so far discovered to useful purposes.

Early AI research showed that making any progress on some of the fundamentals of human intelligence is extremely difficult. There are some enticing shortcuts to AI such as:

- Why not build a learning machine and place it in the world to acquire knowledge by experience and hence become intelligent?
- Why not build a machine which understands a natural language such as English and let it read books?

Both machine learning and understanding natural language have proved very hard problems. Despite years of research little progress has been made particularly on machine learning. Natural language understanding has fared better but is still some way from being a practical method of achieving AI.

As the goal of building a machine with human like intelligence has proved, not surprisingly, too difficult to tackle all at once, AI researchers have concentrated their efforts on particular human traits, some of which have obvious applications. Here are some of the well known subjects:

- natural language understanding
- vision systems
- problem solving
- game playing
- learning
- knowledge representation

1.1.1.(i)   Natural Language Understanding

The goal of this subject is to extract and represent the meaning of spoken or written natural languages, such as English, so the machine can then carry out commands, answer questions or translate into another language either formal or natural. Programs have been written for subsets of English and for constrained domains of discourse but techniques have not yet been found to cope with the variety of language understanding which humans can deal with. If a good solution to this problem were found it would have wide application as an interfacing mechanism to computer systems, for example for querying databases, for machine translation and for instructing the machine to perform actions. In current C^2 organisations there is a great deal of message traffic in natural language form which places huge demands on human resources just assimilating the facts and updating databases. There is therefore a strong incentive to solve the natural language understanding problem for this purpose.

Another important application area is in knowledge acquisition. Putting knowledge into computers is at present a highly labour intensive task and represents one of the bottle-necks in the development of Expert Systems (to be discussed later). As so much knowledge is written down in natural language form an understanding capability could be a very significant step forward in building machines with at least the scale of knowledge to match a human brain.

1.1.1.(ii)   Vision Systems

Vision systems tackle another obvious source of communications and like natural language understanding, aim to extract the meaning from input information, in this case usually a two dimensional image. The research goal is to take two dimensional images from devices such as TV cameras, thermal imagers and synthetic aperture radars, and to create a spatial (3D), temporal and functional understanding of the observed objects. This is a difficult problem because images of the real world are typically very complex; they may contain many complex shaped objects in an infinite variety of configurations; lighting and view point can create totally dissimilar images of the same space. It is difficult to know how the image should be decoded and how the objects should be represented, as macro approximations or fine detail.

Applications for vision systems range from short range sensing for robotics to remote sensing performed by satellites and military platforms. A solution to this problem is not critical to command and control systems but the potential improvement in sensor systems that might result could have a significant indirect effect.

1.1.1.(iii)   Problem Solving

A general theory or method of problem solving was an early objective of AI researchers and some key aspects of problem solving were revealed. But no magic formula was discovered to solve a wide range of real-world problems. Finding general solutions to problems usually involves finding a language in which the problem can be represented adequately. Although new programming languages and styles have been developed which make the solution of some problems easier, no universal language with true general problem solving power has yet been invented. Many researchers now believe that no general formalism is likely to be useful for the wide range of problems which exist and they are now working on specialised methods to suit problems with particular characteristics.

Perhaps the most significant outcome of attempts to find general problem solving methods is the development of Expert Systems. Although a long way from the ultimate goal of problem solving, Expert System techniques have stimulated a considerable number of attempts at solving real problems. As a result, a great deal of practical problem solving experience has been gained to support further research as well as some commercial spin-off. Expert Systems have been applied to a wide variety of problems including elements of command and control. They represent the most exploitable technology to emerge from AI research to-date and as the defence and commercial communities are mainly in the business of applying available technology rather than doing basic research, Expert Systems or Knowledge Based Systems (KBS), as they are often called, are of great interest. They will be discussed in more detail later.

Expert Systems are limited to problems which humans already solve but a general problem solver would have very wide applicability especially to planning problems which have to operate in novel situations. It might also solve problems which currently have no known solutions.

1.1.1. (iv)   Game Playing

Writing computer programs to play games has been a favourite pastime of many AI researchers from the earliest days. The aim is to develop machines which play the more intellectual games, such as Draughts, Backgammon, Chess and Go. Although games have very simple problem domains compared with the real world, they suffer similar problems of explosions of possiblitiies. In theory it is possible to evaluate all the possible moves in Chess (estimated at 35100 (Winston 10)) but no practical machine could do it in a useful time. The aim therefore, as with many AI problems, is to reduce the number of possibilities to be evaluated. Although this is primarily a hobbyist activity which helps to keep AI researchers happy, it is of wider interest because it presents a situation where a human can be pitted directly against a machine albeit in an artificial environment and it addresses concepts of strategy which might have applications in other adversarial situations both civil and military.

1.1.1. (v)   Learning

The goal of learning research is to build machines which acquire knowledge with time and adapt their reasoning to improve their performance at specific tasks or acquire new skills. Newcomers to AI often assume that learning is already a feature of AI systems but in fact it is probably the least understood and most difficult area to progress. A few techniques have been discovered for learning from examples or by trial-and-error for very simple problem domains but generally very little is understood about the subject and AI research seems some way from finding out how to define or express it. Perhaps, like general problem solving, learning is a problem requiring a suitable language.

There would be no shortage of applications for a practical learning system because it would seem to be a requirement of any intelligent system which has to operate in a changing environment. Some problems only change slowly with time so it may be possible to manually update a fixed set of knowledge but true intelligence requires self adaptation.

The solutions to many problems in the real world (as distinct from games or man made environments such as machinery) are not static but change as new information is received or the environment changes. A method is required for incorporating new knowledge and automatically modifying inference rules to deal with new situations. Understanding learning is also important in the development of training systems.

1.1.1.(vi) Knowledge Representation

This topic is not explicitly a feature of human intelligence but it is one of vital importance to AI because it impinges on all the subjects discussed so far. The aim is to find a general way of representing real-world knowledge as a basis for AI systems. The problem is that real-world knowledge is multi-dimensional, highly interrelated, dynamic, much of it is uncertain, and there is a great deal of it. In humans the mention of even a simple concept brings to mind a huge amount of related knowledge so that any aspect of that concept can be considered further with apparent ease. One feature of this ability is known as property inheritance and has been implemented with some success in various forms. Knowledge representation systems have only so far been successful for simple 'worlds' and specific forms of problem solving but no universal scheme adequate for all aspects of intelligence has yet been invented.

1.1.2 AI Spin-Off Technologies

While much AI research continues to address the general problems discussed, there have been two spin-offs which have enabled more application oriented research to take place. These are:

-   AI programming languages and environments
-   Expert Systems and supporting tools

AI has evolved its own programming languages because it is mainly interested in symbolic processing rather than numerical processing. Languages such as Fortran were designed to deal mainly with numbers and do not have very convenient facilities for expressing the symbols used in language or knowledge in general. To allow easy symbol manipulation general purpose AI languages have emerged and are widely used for all aspects of AI. For Expert or Knowledge-Based Systems, more specialised tools have been developed which include languages but also provide special purpose development and run-time facilities. These are variously referred to as 'environments', 'toolkits' or 'shells'.

1.1.2.(i) LISP

The programming language LISP has long been associated with AI and over the years has developed into a highly flexible programming environment. The development of LISP workstations with high resolution, windowed displays and huge LISP source libraries easily accessible to the user, has made programming more of a configuration than a coding exercise. This facilitates the rapid prototyping which is desirable in an exploratory subject like AI research.

LISP Programming Langauge features:

LISP   - List processing language; program and data
         held in lists
       - Declarative language; actions and objects are
         expressed as functions
       - Interpreted language; fully interactive
         programming
       - Some LISP code can be compiled for efficiency

1.1.2.(ii) PROLOG

More recently the language Prolog has emerged as an alternative to LISP. It is based on logic and like LISP, can be surrounded by a good environment for rapid development.

PROLOG Programming Language features:

PROLOG   - Declarative language based on logic; program
           expressed as a set of true relationships in
           no particular order
         - Prolog solves problems by backtracking; it
           has built-in control mechanism directly
           suitable for some Expert Systems
         - Interpreted and interactive
         - Can be partially compiled for efficiency

Prolog provides a quite different style of programming to conventional languages because it does not have the usual control thread running sequentially through the code. This relieves the programmer of the task of ordering statements which for some problems simplifies the expression considerably.

1.1.3   Expert or Knowledge-Based Systems

The terms *expert system* and *knowledge-based system* are often used interchangeably. There is no real difference except that the term *expert system* refers to a particular approach to problem solving involving the acquisition of knowledge from a human expert whereas the term *knowledge-based system* is more general and does not emphasise a particular knowledge acquisition process, but it is a fine distinction. The following description will point out other possible differences.

An *expert system* is a problem solving computer program which:

(a) models the reasoning of a human expert
(b) provides a consultation facility for users (experts or non-experts)
(c) can explain its reasoning
(d) has explicit knowledge

The philosophy of an expert system is to produce a computer solution to a problem by capturing and encoding the expertise of a human expert in the form which the expert and other users will understand. To build an expert system there must be a human expert who can solve the problem. The form in which the knowledge is captured is most important; it must be explicitly stated in a clear language. This makes the reasoning of the system visible to the user and allows the requirement for explanation to be fulfilled. Explicit knowledge and visible reasoning are features which distinguish expert system programs from conventional software systems. Although conventional programs have some knowledge in them, it is usually coded in a form convenient to the programmer and once the function of the system is specified by the users there is no requirement to show how that function is performed at run-time. In contrast the expert system is usually an interactive program which is used on a consultation basis; an expert sytem for medical diagnosis is the archetypal example.

Generally the expertise is in the form of rules, and these rules form the knowledge-base of the system. A controlling framework is used to allow the user to access the knowledge-base in the manner of a consultation whereby the user may volunteer information or the machine may question the user until sufficient evidence is gathered to produce useful conclusions. The user may also ask the system to explain its reasoning so that he may understand how the conclusions were reached.

Other common characteristics of expert systems are:

(f) An expert system is built by a knowledge engineer in consultation with an expert
(g) The reasoning often uses measures of uncertainty
(h) The reasoning works backwards from a number of possible conclusions to fit the evidence - called

backward chaining, or works from the evidence to produce likely conclusions - called forward chaining

(i) An expert system may be built using a standard shell or framework

The term knowledge engineer describes the person who casts the expert's knowledge in the formal language used by the expert system building tools. It is important that the the knowledge expressed in this way is still understandable by the expert to ensure that the knowledge engineer's interpretation is correct and to aid tuning during development.

Several schemes for representing and manipulating uncertainty have been invented. Most are numerical and use probabilistic measures but there are also symbolic methods.

Another important aspect of expert system programs is that the control is usually kept separate from the knowledge. The knowledge engineer can concentrate on expressing the rules and facts without having to worry about constructing a sequence to apply them. Control is provided by the expert system shell or framework software.

1.1.3.(i)   Applications

Expert systems have been developed for a wide variety of problems but many of these fall into the following categories:

Classification:-
medical diagnosis, chemical analysis, fault finding, mineral or oil prospecting

Situation Interpretation and Monitoring:-
industrial plant monitoring, intensive care patient monitoring, tactical situation and threat assessment

Planning and Resource Allocation:-
route planning, system configuration, machine-shop scheduling, military unit deployment and target allocation

Nearly all the early experts systems fell into the *classification* category and the methods for developing this type are well established. They work on relatively static data sets, for example a set of symptoms or test results. The Prospector system typifies the classification form of expert system (Duda (1)). The characteristics of the classification type of expert system are:

- suitable for non-real-time classification problems
- there must be a limited number of goals (conclusions)
- the 'inference engine' attempts to fit the evidence to each goal in turn

- evidence can be input by the user or obtained from a database
- rules may use Bayesian combination or simple logic (AND, OR, NOT)
- reasoning so far or final conclusions can be explained using 'canned' text

The structure of rules in this type of expert system is called an 'inference net', see Figure 1.1.1. Goal states represent the possible conclusions and these are linked to the evidence by the inference net. In a fault diagnosis example, the goals would be various fault conditions and the evidence, measurements or observations of the equipment under test. The lowest level rules operate on the evidence to create inferences which are the first stage in reasoning towards the goals of interest to the user. There will typically be several stages of reasoning to reach the goal states.

Goal States

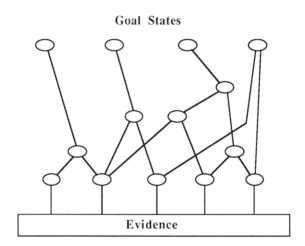

Evidence

FIG 1.1.1   *Example inference net*

The rules have the form, if-conditions-then-conclusion, but where measures of uncertainty are used, the certainty of the conclusion will depend on the certainty of the input conditions and the type of rule. A common method of combining certainty factors is to use a form of Bayes rule.

The components of an expert system, shown in Figure 1.1.2 include:

- Inference Network - the knowledge specific to the particular problem domain.

- Inference Engine - the control program which applies the knowledge in an appropriate manner depending on the consultation the user requires.
- Explanation system - during a consultation the user may request explanations of the reasoning. These are generated by tracing the rules applied so far and by examining the inference net.
- Use Interface - allows the user to interact with the knowledge base and control the consultation. Early systems used just text but graphic are becoming more common.
- Knowledge Compiler - many expert system tools include a compiler to translate the knowledge expressed in a special language into the form required by the inference engine.

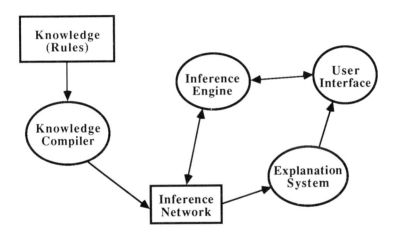

FIG 1.1.2   *Typical expert system framework*

Situation interpretation and monitoring problems generally require a different framework to that of classification problems. The main reason being that the input data set is derived from a dynamically changing environment. Also the number of situations or possible conclusions may be too large to specify simply as nodes in an inference network. A framework which has been used for many problems of this type is the blackboard model. The concept of the blackboard model is of a number of experts who observe and modify the information on a blackboard according to their individual specialisations. Input data are placed on the blackboard and the action of the experts is to create hypotheses to raise the level of knowledge in stages to evolve a solution.

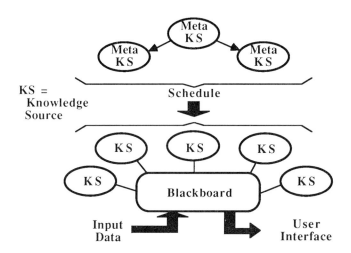

FIG 1.1.3   *Blackboard system structure*

In computer terms, the central component of a blackboard system is the main data structure, 'the blackboard' (see Figure 1.1.3), which represents the current state of the problem including the input evidence and the inferences made from it so far. Sets of rules called *knowledge sources* (ks) represent the specialist experts and these are applied to the data on the blackboard to create further inferences until the required conclusions are reached. In a real-time application every time new data arrive, previous results must be reviewed so there must be a mechanism to schedule the knowledge sources in an appropriate sequence. This scheduling mechanism is also based on rules which are held in *meta-knowledge sources*.

The blackboard model was originally used for speech understanding (Reddy (2)) but has since been applied to signal understanding (Nii (3)) and higher levels of information processing for command and control, see Chapters Three (Data Fusion) and Four (Situational Assessment).

Planning and resource allocation problems have proved less easy to characterise in terms of a common problem solving model. For some applications the selection of pre-defined plans has provided an adequate solution but for more complex problems, especially those involving space and time, recourse has been taken to more basic AI search techniques. The problem is to find a natural way of expressing the knowledge associated with a particular planning domain and then to develop a control framework to perform the search for a solution in a reasonable time-scale.

1.1.3.(ii)   Expert System Tools

Early classification type expert systems were built from scratch using a language such as LISP. In several cases, general purpose expert system shells were derived from these systems by removing the domain specific knowledge and engineering the language and control features. An example is described in Van Melle (4) and Van Melle (5). Many purpose built shells have also been developed. Similar evolution has taken place with some blackboard systems, (see Nii, (6), (7)) and again, some purpose built shells exist (Rice (8) and Vaughan (9)).

Shells provide fairly rigid problem solving frameworks and they are convenient for problems which fit their characteristics. For more complex or less well characterised problems AI toolkits have evolved. These provide a range of AI programming styles which may be used in combination to solve various aspects of a problem. Three well known examples are ART[1], Knowledgecraft[2] and KEE[3].

Toolkits and shells are becoming popular in the commercial world but much research work uses the base languages LISP and Prolog.

1.1.3.(iii)   Development Bottlenecks

There are three important problem areas, sometimes refered to as bottle-necks, with the development of expert or knowledge-based systems:

(1) the knowledge acquisition bottle-neck
(2) the brittleness bottle-neck
(3) the run-time bottle-neck

Knowledge acquisition, the process of eliciting the knowledge from human experts and encoding it using a programming language or expert system tool, has proved a very time consuming and therefore costly process. This is the limiting factor for many expert system projects. For something as complex as a command and control system it may be a considerable problem unless the knowledge can be

---

1   ART is a trademark of Inference Corporation, Los Angeles, California, USA
2   Knowledgecraft is a trademark of Carnegie Group, Pittsburgh, Pennsylvania, USA.
3   KEE is a trademark of Intelligcorp, Pao Alto, California, USA.

acquired over a long period of time, perhaps several generations of equipment. This assumes, of course that the knowledge required is fairly static. Learning systems such as those which generate rules from examples are unlikely to be a solution to this problem in the first generation systems.

Knowledge-based systems suffer from *brittleness*, that is they work well within the strict confines of their knowledge but fail completely outside that knowledge. The reason for this is that the knowledge is captured at a superficial level rather than being derived from any deeper understanding of the subject. In one way this is a strength because the knowledge is at a convenient level to generate explanations for the user. But the lack of deeper understanding and general common sense means that expert systems cannot reason with the unexpected. Researchers are working on knowledge representations which have better understanding capability and on general knowledge bases so there is some hope that this problem will eventually be solved satisfactorily.

Run-time problems are of great concern in the use of knowledge-base systems for time-critical problems such as command and control. Generally speaking the programming methods used for knowledge-based system have proved slow to execute. There is much interest in the use of parallel processing for knowledge-based applications but it is difficult to find efficient mappings between all the layers of software, including the application knowledge-base, the toolkit, the base language, down to the hardware. Many researchers seem to be assuming that the hardware performance will materialise when they are ready to commercialise their systems. It is certainly true that there are still many problems to solve at the knowledge engineering levels before worrying about run-time performance but it is a subject critical to many command and control applications.

1.1.4   *C² Application Issues*

Command and control systems are complex organisations of people and equipments which have to function in a coordinated way to achieve their objectives. Man has already amplified his muscle power by using mechanical systems, his senses by using electromagnetic and acoustic devices, his ability to communicate over long distances by using radio, and his calculating cability by using computers, but thinking is still the preserve of the human brain. This is a limiting factor in several respects; the number of brains that can be brought to bear on a problem is limited especially by cost; the level of experience is limited by the amount of training and the term of service; the communication ability of the brain is limited by fairly low bandwidth input and output; the brain requires a special environment in which to operate and the thinking power of the brain, while impressive, is rather slow. The promise of AI is not to replace the human element, because

C^2 would have little meaning without it, but to augment specific aspects of the brain to improve overall effectiveness.

For all its complexity C^2 has two central functions, situation modelling and resource allocation. Situation modelling is the process of building a model of the world-of-interest as accurately as possible. It requires the fusion of data from all sources and assessment of the fused data to provide a tactical interpretation of the current position. Prediction is also required in order to understand what is likely to happen next as an aid to decision making. Resource allocation is the decision making process to deploy and direct the units under command. Both C^2 functions have to operate in several different time-scales depending on the response time required. For example, deploying a naval task group may take days whereas firing a missile only a few seconds. Knowledge-based systems have already been applied experimentally to subsets of these functions with some success but it will probably be another decade or so before operational systems based on current research are widely deployed.

There are a number of issues with the application of knowledge-based systems to military problems specifically which should be considered. Some of these issues also apply to many large conventional software systems. Firstly there are problems with the basic idea of military knowledge-based system (KBSs).

1.1.4. (i)   Intelligent Machines against Human Intelligence?

If we incorporate knowledge into a computer system to give it some expertise then there may be a danger that an enemy could defeat the KBS using superior human intelligence. Certainly KBSs built to-date tend to be very specialsed and hence brittle owing to lack of general knowledge and will perform poorly if that knowledge is out-of-date. It is important when considering a KBS solution to a problem to make sure that the problem is sufficiently stable to allow the knowledge to be acquired and updated in reasonable time-scales. In applications where a great amount of knowledge is required such as command and control, it is likely that a KBS will take an advisory role and the man will still take an active part in the problem solving (see man's role below).

1.1.4. (ii)   Infinite Number of Scenarios - Infinite Knowledge?

A KBS tries to capture specific knowledge for each situation occurring in the problem domain. In real-world problems such as defence, there is an infinite set of possible scenarios which the system could face and hence is appears that an infinite amount of knowledge might be needed. It is hoped that this problem can be overcome by using more general knowledge but assembling a useful amount of general knowledge is proving a difficult task.

1.1.4. (iii)   Man's Role?

In a simple expert system the user consults the machine by entering evidence until reasonably clear conclusions emerge. The user can request explanations of these conclusions but he cannot add his own judgements to alter the results. This is not too important in non-time-critical situations but where action must be taken in real-time it may be essential for the user to assist the machine with his more up-to-the-minute knowledge. Allowing the user to correct or override the system presents some difficulties which require further research.

1.1.4. (iv)   Explanation - How, What and When?

One of the advantages of KBSs is that they reason using knowlege from a human expert and hence this knowledge is at a level which is understandable to users of the system. By tracing the application of the knowledge an explanation can be generated at any stage in the consultation. This mechanism is fairly easy to provide in non-time-critical situations because the user has time to read details of the reasoning. For time-critical applications explanations are equally important but more care is needed to provide concise information in good time so that actions are not delayed.

1.1.4. (v)   Operational Updating?

For military KBSs is will be very difficult to complete development of the knowledge base in the laboratory or factory because much knowledge will only come to light when the system is fielded. It will also be necessary to update the knowledge base inservice to cope with new equipments or tactics. The question is how to keep the knowledge up-to-date without running the risk of uncontrolled development by independent users.

1.1.4. (vi)   Specification and Acceptance

The recommended way of developing KBSs is through a series of prototypes. This is because there is currently insufficient experience with particular problems to be able to specify, design and implement in the way conventional software is procured. Commercial builders of KBSs emphasise the importance of choosing the right type of problem in order to stand a reasonable chance of success. But in defence there is not such a flexible choice - the hard problems must be addressed.

A KBS consists of a great deal of specialised knowledge which if specified in full would almost amount to implementing the system. If specified only in broad terms then how can the user know that it will function adequately?

Assuming that a satisfactory method of development is found the next question is how to accept the KBS into service. If the system is intended to reason about battle situations then how can we prove that it will be effective or even useful in a future conflict given the difficulty of predicting what is likely to happen. This is more complex than accepting say a weapons system because the characteristics of such an equipment can be much more precisely defined.

We may also want to procure KBSs which have the potential to be 'trained' to perform military tasks over a period of service. In this case a measure of knowledge handling capability is required almost like the procedures used to recruit human resources. This problem has not been addressed yet.

1.1.5   Concluding Remarks

In spite of the problems with knowledge-based systems which still require considerable research, it is inevitable that future command and control systems will be based on this technology in order to meet the increasing functionality demanded by the end users. Conventional software systems have proved successful in data handling and computation but what is now needed is an integration and control mechanism for all the sensing, communications and weapon resources. Because of the complexity of all the elements involved and that of the C^2 task to be performed, a knowledge-based approach seems to offer the only solution flexible enough to handle all the types of processing required while providing the essential visibility to the commanders. Whether the current knowledge-based technology is adequate has still to be determined by the development of more realistic prototypes.

1.1.6   References

1.   Duda, R., Gashnig, J., and Hart, P., 1979, 'Model Design in the Prospector Consultant System for Mineral Exploration', Expert Systems in the Microelectronic Age, Edinburgh University Press, p153-167.

2.   Reddy, D.R., et al, 1973, 'The Hearsay Speech Understanding System: An Example of the Recognition Process', Computer Science Department, Carnegie-Mellon Univeristy, Pittsburgh, Pa. 15213, IJCAI 3, p185-193.

3.   Nii, H.P., et al, January 1982, 'Signal-to-Symbol transformation: HASP/SIAP Case Study', AI Magazine, Vol 3, p23- 25.

4.   Van Melle, W.J., MYCIN, October 1979, 'A Knowledge-Based Consultation Program for Infectious Disease Diagnosis', Int J Man-Machine Studies 10:313-322.

5.   Van Melle, W.J. et al, EMYCIN, 1981, 'A Domain-independent System that Aids in Constructing Knowledge-based Consultation Programs', Pergamon-Infotech, New York.

6.   Nii, H.P., Summer 1986, 'Blackboard Systems: The Blackboard Model of Problem Solving and the Evolution of Blackboard Architectures', The AI Magazine.

7.   Nii, H.P., August 1986, 'Blackboard Application Systems, Blackboard Systems from a Knowledge Engineering Perspective,' The AI Magazine.

8.   Rice, J.P., 1984, 'A Framework for the Development of Blackboard Systems', Proceedings of the Third Seminar on Applications of MI to Defence systems, RSRE, UK.

9.   Vaughan Johnson Jnr., M. and Hayes-Roth, B., July 1987, 'Integrating Diverse Reasoning Methods in the BBI Blackboard Control Architecture', Knowledge Systems Laboratory, Stanford University, AAAI.

10. Winston, P.H., 1977, 'Artificial Intelligence', Addison-Wesley Publishing Company, Inc. ISBN 0-201-08454-6.

Knowledge Representation Using Massively Parallel Processors

S. Sharma and T. Spracklen
(University of Aberdeen, Department of Engineering)

1.2.1   Introduction

Aberdeen University, Department of Engineering have for several years been involved with the Admiralty Research Establishment in such areas as real-time signal processing of digital radar information and advanced architecture local area networks for intra-ship communications (Spracklen and Smythe (17-21), Cowan et al (3)). Such work has given Aberdeen researchers an ideal opportunity to appreciate the data processing problems facing the modern Royal Navy.

One of the most critical and challenging activities undertaken in the Operations Room of a modern warship is to construct and maintain the best possible assessment of the tactical situation in the ship's area of interest. This implies not only locating, tracking and classifying all objects which might contribute to that situation, but also doing so quickly enough to react to any aspects which may pose an immediate threat to the ship or to other vehicles under her protection.

The information on which that assessment is based is derived from a wide range of disparate sources such as own-ship's sensors, radio datalinks, signals, intelligence and tactical plans. The data is generally incomplete, inaccurate, ambiguous, conflicting and subject to deliberate interference and deception by the enemy. The techniques employed in the analysis, evaluation and correlation of this information include both algorithmic processing, operating largely on lower-level aspects of the problem such as vehicle detection and tracking, and heuristic reasoning for higher-level aspects such as the determination of identity and intent, based on behaviour patterns, intelligence and tactical appreciation and experience. It is the objective of this chapter to discuss the problems of how to 'fuse' together all of this data so as to provide the best possible tactical picture, and how to encapsulate as much of this solution as possible in a computer.

1.2.1. (i) Massively Parallel Processors

It is proposed that this should be accomplished by the use of specialised, highly parallel computing architectures - with enough processing elements that we can assign a separate processor to every assertion in a large knowledge base. For a large class of problems involving searches and simple deductions in this knowledge base, the available processing power grows at the same rate as the problem. Thus the time required for such operations is constant, or nearly constant, regardless of the size of the knowledge base. This is important in the naval context where the problems are continuous and real-time and where solutions are required rapidly to complex situations involving information at many different levels. Traditional AI approaches, using Expert Systems, involve a *rule based* approach that attempts to encapsulate the expertise of a human operator into a series of rules that form the knowledge base of the system. In most situations this knowledge base does not change or, at least, *it is not changed by the information received by the system*. Thus the system does not change its view of the world around it on the basis of information it receives - it does not learn by experience, since it cannot modify the rules on which it bases its decisions. Furthermore, the time taken for such systems to reach a decision grows almost in direct proportion to the size of the knowledge base used (ie the number of rules) because their processing power is fixed (usually in some central, mainframe computer). Much work in this area has been carried out by scientists at the Admiralty Research Establishment (ARE), Portsmouth (Gadsden (8)).

The use of highly parallel architectures has been proposed by many authors (Falhman (5,6), Hinton (9,10)) and it has been suggested that these split into four main categories:- Marker Passing, Value Passing, Message Passing and Boltzmann Machines with ever increasing complexity as one moves through the list. These are based, in general, on the semanatic memory network proposed by Quillian (13) where each primitive concept in the memory is a very simple hardware device. These communicate with a central computer (of the conventional kind) via some type of bus arrangement (involving data and addresses of the conventional type, i.e. each primitive processing element is viewed by the central computer (say, a microprocessor) as a peripheral element of some type). Each primitive element has access to a number of bits of internal memory that can be set and cleared by commands from the central processor. Some of these bits can be considered to be write-once bits, insofar that they represent some fixed information about the processor - i.e. whether it is representing an individual or a class etc.

Each assertion in the knowledge base is represented by a *hardware link*. This link is also a peripheral of the central computer (i.e it communicates over the same address and data buses that connect the central computer to the primitive processing elements). To represent an assertion in the knowledge base the central computer must locate an unused *hardware link* and use it to connect two primitive elements together. A third wire from the *hardware link* is used to connect to a primitive element representing the type of relationship and a fourth wire is used to connect to an element representing the context in which the assertion is stated to be true.

These connections represent the *knowledge* of the system. Should the links become broken, the system *forgets* the knowledge associated with that link. These links carry information, in the form of markers, values or messages and are set up by a switching network, similar to that employed by a telephone exchange *except* that *all* lines are private wires. Therefore such a system consists of a central computer connected to a *very large* number of primitive elements and hardware links.

The small amount of memory that each primitive processor contains can be set or cleared by either the central processor or the primitive processor. Therefore, such memory may be used to mark membership of sets. This allows such systems to perform set intersection in a single cycle, or transitive closure operations in a time proportional *only* to the length of the longest chain of links. In addition to intersection and transitive closure it is possible in such an architecture for a marker to gate the flow of other markers through the system. This parallel gating mechanism gives us a way of dealing with complex sets of overlapping contexts, each with its own set of assertions.

The limitation of such marker systems is that only a small, fixed number of markers are available, and it is impossible for an individual marker to record where it came from, or what path it followed through an artibrarily complex network. This means that some apparently simple operations cannot be done in parallel. To overcome such problems many authors have suggested an extension of the simple marker passing mechanism to either value or message passing. Unfortunately such systems involve a considerable increase in the complexity of the hardware as well as involving serial processing at each of the elements in the system - removing much of the attraction of this type of architecture. These problems have been discussed extensively in the literature in the references given earlier.

Falhman (6) from Carnegie-Mellon University has suggested a practical design for a million element marker passing system called NETL, but so far no such system has been constructed and no large scale simulation has been performed. The research has, however, led to the construction of the 'Connection Machine', a parallel processor array with a powerful inter-processor communication facility. This chapter discusses a knowledge representation scheme that could be implemented on such a machine. In particular, we have chosen the representation of 'exceptions' (i.e., information that seems to be in

conflict with other knowledge) and 'tactical plans' (i.e.,
sequences of events that form part of a strategy). The
detailed discussion of these two types of knowledge
highlights the basic techniques used in a massively
parallel marker-passing machine.

1.2.2   *Exceptions*

Dealing with 'exceptions' in a Knowledge Representation
formalism is an important task which can become fairly
complex, expecially when we want to maintain efficiency in
a parallel implementation of the knowledge base.   Some
systems avoid the issue by dis-allowing "the cancellation
of inherited components of a concept to represent
'exceptions'".   (Brachman and Schmolze (1)).   However, any
representation scheme for 'real-world knowledge' must, at
some stage, allow for the possiblity of exceptions to
general statements about concepts.   In this paper we
present algorithms (for a parallel marker-passing network
of the type described in (5) to find, in the presence of
such exceptions, 1. all concepts subsumed by some concept
"X",and 2. all concepts that subsume some concept "X".
Before doing so, however, we make some remarks about
redundant links and ambiguities in semantic networks.   In
particular, we find it hard to accept the argument given in
(Touretzky (22)) as one that shows the shortest path
algorithms fail in the presence of redundant links.   Like
all other work on cancellations that we have seen, we also
confine our remarks to the cancellation of inherited class
membership and subsumption.The NETL system described in (5)
provides a cancellation scheme that can handle only the
simplest cases of exceptions.   The failure of this scheme
in non-trivial situations was recognised and a new solution
was subsequently described in (Falhman et al (7)).   It was
felt necessary to introduce some amount of serial behaviour
into the operation of the network.   In fact, the work of
Etherington and Reiter (4) suggests the "unfeasibility of
completely general parallel architectures for dealing with
inheritance structures with cancellation [cf NETL]."
However, Cottrell (2) argues that the problem is not in the
parallelism of the machine, but in the "one pass" nature of
the marker passing.
The new solution referred to above relies on the
network being maintained in a "legal" state, where all
information is consistent and unambiguous (the other
aproach being to resolve an ambiguities at the time of
retrieval).   Each time the knowledge in the network is
changed, any resulting ambiguities are resolved by using
either an *UNCANCEL link or an *UNEXCLUDE link, depending
on the nature of the ambiguity.   An *UNCANCEL link is used
to remove the effect of a previously used *CANVC (Cancelled
Virtual Copy) link, i.e. to reinstate a 'virtual copy'
relationship between two concepts.   The purpose of an
*UNEXCLUDE link is the same but has been introduced to make
the downscan algorithm work (i.e. to find all concepts that
some "X" subsumes).   The use of *UNCANCEL and *UNEXCLUDE

links as described in (7) is illustrated in Figure 1.2.1. Without these links it is ambiguous whether concept B is subsumed by concept F or not. In both cases shown in Figure 1.2.1, the ambiguity has has been resolved by explicitly stating that "B is-a F" using two different links. If, on the other hand, B is not an F, a *CANVC link would be placed from B to F.

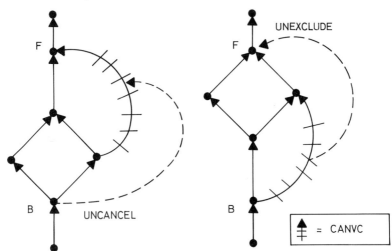

FIG 1.2.1   *Using *UNCANCEL and *UNEXCLUDE links to implement exceptions*

During scans, each *CANVC link can cause a node (head-node for upscan, tail-node for downscan) to get 'blocked' (i.e., prevent the pasage of markers through it). However, the effect of an *UNCANCEL or *UNEXLCUDE link is to 'unblock' such a node connected to its *CANVC link. Therefore, before each propagation step ('prop-up' or 'prop-down') in a scan, all blocked nodes are checked (in parallel) and any 'unblocking' is performed. Only *UNCANCEL (*UNECLUDE) links with the activation marker at their tail (head) can cause a cancellation marker (i.e., blocking) to be removed.

The solution above is a variation of the 'shortest path' heuristic, but haɔ to introduce two new marker passing devices (i.e, *UNCANCEL and *UNEXCLUDE links) to make the algorithms work. The solution we propose is a modest sequel to this work. It is a shortest path algorithm and also assumes a 'restricted' network. However, no new marker passing devices are introduced. Ambiguities are resolved using ordinary IS-A (i.e., *VC) links and *CANCEL links.

Shortest path algorithms have been widely criticised. Most of the arguments and examples given, however, apply not to the shortest-path heuristic per se, but to its suitability to a particular network formalism. Indeed, the arguments may well be looked at as weaknesses of the representation formalisms. The representation we use seems to be more suitable for shortest-path methods.

In (22) it is claimed that shortest path methods fail in the presence of redundant links. This, obviously, is an undesirable feature. Before we describe our solution, we would like to make some remarks about redundant links and ambiguities in semantic networks. In particular, we believe that what is claimed to be a redundant link is not necessarily a redundant link.

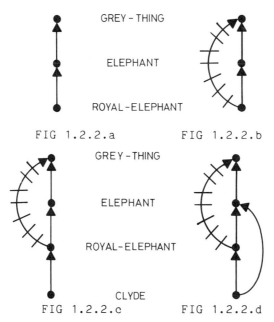

FIG 1.2.2.a   FIG 1.2.2.b

FIG 1.2.2.c   FIG 1.2.2.d

FIG 1.2.2   *Ambiguity in semantic networks*

Consider Figure 1.2.2.a above. This represents "a typical ROYAL-ELEPHANT IS-A typical GREY-THING". Now what if we say "typically royal elephants are not grey". That is, we add a CANCEL link as in Figure 1.2.2.b. We are explicitly changing the relationship between a 'typical royal elephant' and a 'typical grey thing'. But what about the relationship between a typical ROYAL-ELEPHANT and a typical ELEPHANT? Is a typical ROYAL-ELEPHANT still a typical ELEPHANT? We believe that it is not. This is because it no longer inherits all the properties of a typical elephant. The information changed by the addition of the CANCEL link is - a typical ROYAL-ELEPHANT is not grey, and a typical ROYAL-ELEPHANT is an 'exceptional' elephant, not a typical elephant. This is true for CLYDE in Figure 1.2.2.c who is a typical ROYAL-ELEPHANT. Whether or not this fact ought to be stated explicitly (e.g., by placing some flag on the *VC between ROYAL-ELEPHANT and ELEPHANT) is a question we do not address in this paper (the inadequacy of IS-A links has been suggested in (Hussman

(11)). The inheritance algorithms we present do not need
this to be stated explicitly. Another point that fits in
here somewhere is the following: in NETL, when we do a
downscan, from some concept 'X', we are answering the query
"Find any concept 'C' such that C is an 'X' of any kind",
and not "....such that 'C' is a typical X". A downscan
yields typical X's along with any 'exceptional' X's.
Similarly, an upscan from 'X' yields all concepts, 'C' such
that 'X' is a 'C', typical or exceptional. To implement
scans that yield 'typical' X's or C's only, we would have
to take into account the effect of CANCEL links in a way
that hasn't been done in NETL yet.

Back to Figure 1.2.2.c! Now if we add a direct IS-A
link from CLYDE to ELEPHANT, Figure 1.2.2.d, we are saying
that CLYDE is a typical elephant. This is new,
contradictory information. Before the link was added CLYDE
was not a typical elephant. We, therefore, conclude that
the IS-A link from CLYDE to ELEPHANT adds new information,
and is not a redundant link as claimed in (22).
Consequently, we find it hard to accept the argument given
in (22) as one that shows that shortest path algorithms
fail in the presence of redundant links. The addition of
the direct IS-A link from CLYDE to ELEPHANT makes the
previously consistent network ambiguous. The argument
given in (22) however, is suported by the study of
interacting defaults done in the domain of default logic,
(Reiter and Criscuolo (14)). Knowing that CLYDE is a
typical ROYAL-ELEPHANT, and nothing else (because we
haven't seen the CANCEL link yet!), it is consistent with
what is known to assume that a typical ROYAL-ELEPHANT is a
typical ELEPHANT. When we deal with the CANCEL link (i.e.
apply another default theory) we infer that a typical
ROYAL-ELEPHANT is not a typical GREY-THING. However, this
does not cause further inferences leading to the belief
that something that is definitely not a typical GREY-THING
cannot be a typical ELEPHANT and hence, retract the
previous ingerence that a ROYAL-ELEPHANT is a typical
ELEPHPANT. We cannot help feeling that somewhere,
something is missing!. Maybe we need default
representations in which the prerequisites are negations,
e.g., "if ¬A(x) is known, and it is consistent to
believe.......". This idea has been used in the
connectionist inheritance model decribed in (2). We have
not looked into the kind of default representations needed
to deal with interaction of defaults (see (14)), and a
discussion on the subject would be beyond the scope of this
paper. One possible outcome of such a disussion may show
the need to distinguish between properties that define a
concept and those that 'happen to be true' for a concept.

1.2.2. (ii)   Abiguity in Networks

An ambiguity in a network refers to a state in which
two conflicting inferences can be made about a concept with
no reason to select one and discard the other. Several
inheritance systems cope with ambiguity by explicitly

stating one inference to be the preferred one. This has been done, for example, by changing default theories (4), or using appropriate certainty factors (Rich (15)). This 'disambiguation' of the network has also been referred to as "patching" (14) and "conditioning" (22).

The two basic approaches to dealing with ambiguities, as noted in (7), are (i) identify them and correct them (or take any other action) every time the network is modified. This is the 'pre-processing' approach; and (ii) do the same as above, but at retrieval time. The former approach allows the more efficient shortest-path algorithms to be used, but these do not work for an ambiguity that has not been cleared (for whatever reason) by the pre-processing stage. The inheritance scheme described in (7) uses this approach. The latter approach can cope with ambiguous networks, but the inheritance algorithms are generally inefficient. The scheme, using "inferential distance", given in (22), is based on this approach.

An algorithm for finding ambiguities in a NETL-like system (by finding what are referred to as "merge-points") is given in (7). A merge point is a node that can be reached along two different paths, one representing its inclusion in the scan, the other its cancellation. Such an algorithm could be used (possibly several times) at retrieval time (to be able to cope with ambiguous networks) if we did not want to use the pre-processing approach. The main argument for not using the pre-orocessing approach is that there may not be enough time, for example, to complete the consistency checking. The demands on the network however, may be such that it is 'useless' if it cannot provide a response within a certain time. It somehow seems unfair, then, to assume that there may not be enough time to deal with ambiguities at storage time, but there will be enought time at retrieval. The following assumption may be just as reasonable- "At storage time, it may not be possible to *correct* an ambiguity, but we can always detect it". In such cases, we believe the system should *unambiguously* state that there is an ambiguous relationship between two concepts, without trying to clear the confusion; if the system is subjected to too much information arriving too rapidly, it could behave like humans do - i.e., discard information that cannot be 'buffered'. Thus we always have an unabmiguous network, even in the presence of ambiguous information! A similar need for 'unambiguity amidst ambiguity' has been expressed in (Woods (23)). The best way to represent such an ambiguity is not immediately apparent. After presenting our inheritance algorithms, we state just one possible way for a NETL-like system, without trying to discuss its merits or demerits.

NETL-like inheritance hierarchies with exceptions have been formalized in (4) using default logic. Referring to such networks, to which our inheritance algorithms below also apply, it is noted that "there may be severe limitations to this approach". For example, correct inference requires that all conclusions share a common

extension".   The   network   shown   in   Figure   1.2.3.   below   is
'legal'   and   unambiguous   according   to   our   scheme.

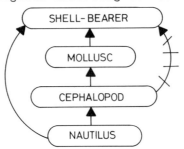

FIG 1.2.3   *A network that does not allow correct inference by default*
             logic (see (4)).

When   we   consider   the   corresponding   default   theories
however,   a   Cephalopod   not   known   to   be   a   Nautilus   gives   rise
to   two   extensions,   because   Cephalopod   has   not   been
explicitly   represented   as   an   exception.   Therefore,   in
default   logic   ((4))   this   representation   does   not   allow
correct   inferencing.   The   fact   that   the   corresponding
default   theory   of   a   'legal'   network   in   our   scheme   has   more
than   one   extension   does   not   cause   problems,   we   believe,
because   we   are   not   using   default   logic   to   perform
inferencing.   The   'ambiguous-ness'   of   a   network   clearly
depends   on   the   inference   procedure   used.

1.2.2. (iii)   Alternative Solution

The   algorithms   for   upscan   and   downscans   proposed   below
are   similar   to   those   given   in   (7)   in   that   they   are   also
based   on   maintaining   the   network   in   a   'legal'   state.
However,   all   occurrences   of   both   *UNCANCEL   and   *UNEXCLUDE
links   are   replaced   by   ordinary   *VC   links.   The   way   *VC
links   are   used   instead   of   *UNCANCEL   and   *UNEXCLUDE   links   in
(7)   is   as   follows:

a.   Instead   of   an   *UNCANCEL   link   from   a   node   (say   N)   to   a
     *CANVC   link,   we   place   a   *VC   link   from   node   N   to   the
     node   at   the   head   of   the   *CANVC   link.
b.   Instead   of   an   *UNEXCLUDE   link   from   a   *CANVC   to   a   node
     (say   D),   we   place   a   *VC   Link   from   the   node   at   the   tail
     of   the   *CANVC   link   to   node   D.

Figure   1.2.4   shows   how   the   information   in   Figure   1.2.2
is   represented   under   the   new   scheme   using   *VC   links.   The
scheme   in   (5)   failed   because   of   certain   'problem'   nodes   in
which   the   'wrong'   kind   of   marker   reached   before   the   'right'
one!   the   two   kinds   being   -   activation   and   cancellation
markers.   In   (7)   it   is   noted   that   (in   order   to   override   a
*CANVC   link)   we   cannot   just   add   an   IS-A   link   ....   (e.g.
from   B   to   F   in   Figure   1.2.1)   ....   since   the   *CANVC   link
takes   precedence".   In   our   scheme   we   use   only   IS-A   (i.e.,
*VC)   links   to   reinstate   a   virtual-copy   relationship   but

this does not cause problems because *CANVC links do not, as a rule, take precedence over *VC links. At each step in a scan, propagation of the activation marker across *VC links is preceeded by the placing of cancellation markers. In this sense, the *CANVC links do take precedence. However, an activation marker on a node prevents the node from being blocked by a cancellation marker. Therefore, the rule would be - "whatever gets there first, takes precedence".

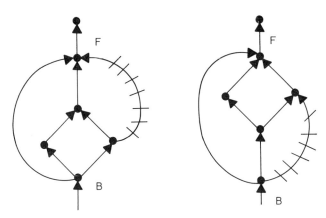

FIG 1.2.4   *Replacing *UNCANCEL; and *UNEXCLUDE links by *VC links to implement exceptions*

     It is up to the 'digestive processes' to make sure that there are no ambiguities in the network that could cause the scan algorithms to fail. Luckily the 'problem' nodes pop-up as ambiguities when looking for "merge points" (7). We must note though, that all merge points found by the algorithm in (7) will not represent ambiguities according to our scheme. Consider Figure 1.2.3 again. Nautilus will emerge as a merge point. However, it is not an ambiguity because there is a direct link from Nautilus to Shell-bearer; this clarifies the ambiguity. In essence, this is the "subclass overrides subclass"! The idea behind our solution is to use either a *VC link or a *CANVC LINK, as appropriate, to ensure a shortest path (i.e, a single link) for the 'right' marker mentioned above. Therefore, the right marker always gets there first!
     Since *UNCANCEL and *UNEXCLUDE are links between a node and another link, the scans described in (7) require markers to be placed on the *bodies* of links. This is a feature not required in our algorithms becasue we do not use these links.

1.2.2.(iii)   *The Algorithms*

(M1 = Activation marker,   M2 = Cancellation marker.)

Downscan

1. Set M1 on X.
2. REPEAT
    a. All *CANVC links with M1 on the head-node and no marker on the tail, set M2 on the tail-node.
    b. All *VC liks with M1 on the head, and no marker on the tail, Set M1 on tail.
    UNTIL no activity
3. Report nodes with M1.

Upscan

1. Set M1 on X
2. REPEAT
    a. All *CANVC links with M1 on the tail-node and no marker on the head, set M2 on the head-node.
    b. All *VC links with M1 on the tail, and no marker on the head, set M1 on head.
    UNTIL no activity.
3. Report nodes with M1.

Note that the algorithm for an upscan (downscan) is obtained from the algorithm for a downscan (upscan) simpy by interchanging "tail" and "head" wherever either occurs.

The algorithms given in (7) do not check for the existence of exceptions before proceeding to deal with them!. As a result, the running time of a basic scan is increased by a "constant factor". This is true of the above algorithms too. However, this may not be a desirable feature. Ideally we would like not to spend any time checking for exceptions when there are none in a particular scan. to achieve this, it seems a good idea to insert the folowing steps (representing a 'fast scan' that ignores all cancellations) before step 1 in the algorithm above.

a. Set M0 on X.
b. Downscan M0. (ignoring *CANVC links)
c. If no *CANVC links have M0 on their head-nodes, Report all nodes with M0 and EXIT.
d. Clear M0 from all nodes.

After step "b", nodes with marker M0 are those which would be reported in the absence of any exceptions. This ensures maximum efficiency in the absence of any exceptions, which, in a 'real-world' knowledge base, will probably include a very high proportion of the scans. Unfortunately, the 'fast scan' gets wasted in scans where cancellations are present. The steps in our scans are simpler than those in (7) mainly as a result of not having to do any explicit 'unblocking' of nodes. In fact, no unblocking is actually done. Nodes that would be unblocked in the scheme in (7), are rendered 'unblockable' by the activation marker getting there before the cancellation marker. A legal network ensures that, in such cases, the activation marker gets the shortest possible path to the 'unblockable' node from any node involved in a relevant ambiguity.

One way to achieve the previously mentioned 'unambiguity amidst ambiguity' would be to introduce an *AMB-VC (Ambiguous Virtual Copy) link. Using an algorithm similar to the one given in (7), we can find the ambiguities (by finding the relevant "merge point(s)"). For example, in Figure 1.2.2.d we come up with the fact that the relationship betwen CLYDE and GREY-THING is ambiguous. The ambiguity is resolved by placing of of *VC, *CANVC and *AMB-VC links from CLYDE to GREY-THING. To place a *VC or *CANVC the user is queried. An *AMB-VC is placed either when there is no time to query the user, or the user is unable to clear the ambiguity. The following step would need to be added as step 2.c in the algorithms:

Downscan - 2.c: If there are any *AMB-VC links such that nodes on both ends have either M1 or M2, then report (for example) "ambiguous relationship between 'tail-node' and 'head-node'", and leave the head-node with only M2 on it. Also, Deactivate this *AMB-VC link.

The corresponding change in the upscan algorithm is obtained by interchanging "head" and "tail" in the above step.

1.2.2. (iv)   The Naked Nautilus

In this section we apply our solution to the "Shell-bearer : mollusc : cephalopod : nautilus : naked-nautilus" problem used as an example in (7). We want to perform upscans and downscans in a part of a network representing the following information:

1. A MOLLUSC is a SHELL-BEARER.
2. A CEPHALOPOD is a MOLLUSC but is not a SHELL-BEARER.
3. A NAUTILUS is a CEPHALOPOD but a SHELL-BEARER too.
4. A NAKED-NAUTILUS is a NAUTILUS but is not a SHELL-BEARER.

Figure 1.2.5 overleaf shows the part of the network represented, first as proposed in (7) , and then using *VC links as we propose instead. Using our scheme, Figure 1.2.6a shows the result of a downscan from SHELL-BEARER, and Figure 1.2.6b shows the result of an upscan from NAKED-NAUTILUS.

Without the *CANVC link from NAKED-NAUTILUS to SHELL-BEARER, NAKED-NAUTILUS would be a "merge point" representing No *AMB-VC link has been used. Instead, we have stated that "NAKED-NAUTILUS is not a SHELL-BEARER". If we did not know whether or not NAKED-NAUTILUS is a SHELL-BEARER, the *CANVC link from NAKED-NAUTILUS to SHELL-BEARER would be replaced by an *AMB-VC link. The markers on each node after the scans would be the same as shown in Figure 1.2.6 but the "ambiguous" relation between NAKED-NAUTILUS and SHELL-BEARER " would be reported.

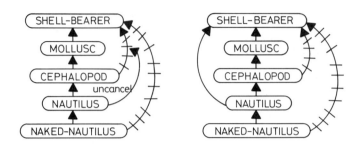

FIG 1.2.5   *Representing the same information in the two schemes: Left*
- [Falhman et al (7)]. Right - New Scheme.

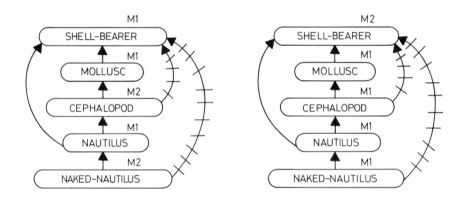

FIG 1.2.6.a   *Downscan from*   FIG 1.2.6.b   *Upscan from*
                 Shell -Bearer   *Naked-Nautilus*

1.2.3   Plan Recognition

One important need in a hostile environment is to be
able to predict the intention of the enemy.   Ideally we
want to be able to predict what a sighted aircraft is
trying to do and how it is likley to try to achieve this.
Such information may often be gathered from the observed
behaviour of a vehicle.

Luckily, the world is not random!   Objects and
activities are bound by a variety of constraints. Assuming
that most activities are, at some level , goal directed,
places another important constraint that enables us to
interpret actions.

Recognising the regularities in a real world
environment allows us to do 'pattern recognition'.   That
is, if a set of observations about an object look 'similar'
to some previous observations on some other objects, the

new object may be said to fit a certain 'pattern'; known information about the pattern may then be applied to the new object. As an illustration, consider what happens when we observe an object with windows, seats and three wheels. The observations resemble the 'pattern' of a 'car' or 'vehicle', and we are reasonably sure that the new object is a mode of transport; uses fuel, etc.

Pattern recognition is not restricted to objects, but applies equally to actions. In particular, sequences of actions form patterns. The knowledge of such patterns and the contexts in which they apply allows us to make inferences in new situations that 'resemble' a known pattern. An observed sequence of events may suggest more than one pattern. Alternatively, none of the known patterns may seem to be relevant. It is important that patterns be defined using more abstract (i.e, general) descriptors so that they may be useful in a variety of situations.

"Scripts" (Schank (16)) are stuctures that have been used to describe a sequence of events. For example, the 'Restaurant' script shown in Figure 1.2.7 below may be used to describe a sequence of events observed in a restaurant.

RESTAURANT
Enter
Take Seat
Order
Eat
Pay
Exit

FIG 1.2.7   *A script based on observations in a restaurant*

In an appropriate context, for instance when someone enters a restaurant, the corresponding script is 'put into action'. As a result, we predict the rest of the activities, i.e. sitting, ordering, eating etc. to take place. Such a representation can be adopted to represent plans in a Sensor-Data Fusion System (see Chapter Two). We now discuss the implementation of tactical plans in a marker-passing parallel machine.

A plan describes a set of actions performed in a particular sequence that a vehicle may use to reach a particular state (i.e., achieve a particular goal). The importance of temporal positioning of events makes the computer representation more complex than that for objects.

Consider the scheme for representing plans illustrated in Figure 1.2.8.a. The figure shows two plans, P1 and P2.

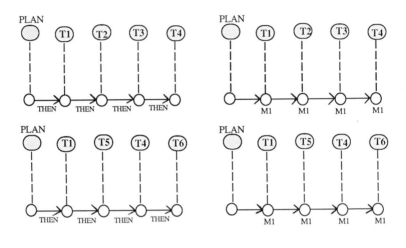

FIG 1.2.8.a   FIG 1.2.8.b

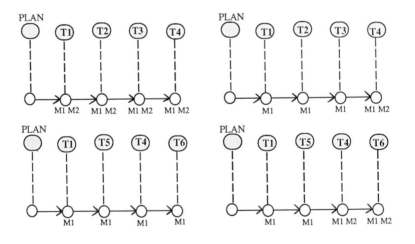

FIG 1.2.8.c   FIG 1.2.8.d

FIG 1.2.8   *Plan recognition in a marker-passing network machine.*

These are familiar sequences of events that the system knows about; there would be at least several tens of such plans in a real command and control system. Plans P1 and P2 are instances of the generic concept 'PLAN'. A plan is represented as a list of events attached to the respective plan nodes. The links betwen the events represent the relative position in time of two events. The nature of each event (e.g., increase in speed, drop in altitude, change in direction, etc.) is defined by linking each event to an event type. In the figure there are six types of events involved, T1-T6. Figures 1.2.8b-d show how marker passing is used to perform plan recognition; this is explained below.

Suppose an event of type T1 is observed. The following activities take place in the marker-passing machine:

1. Mark node T1 with marker M1.
2. Propagate this down to mark all events of type T1.
3. Propagate M1 up all links labelled 'Then'.

The position of markers in the plans P1 and P2 are shown in Figure 1.2.8b. Events in both P1 and P2 are active. The advantage of the parallelism in the system is that the time taken to recognise plans in action is not dependent on the number of plans in the knowledge base. This is very important since it enables us to make calculations (on the response time of the system) which hold even when the size of the knowledge base increases considerably.

After the above three steps we have two candidate sequences of events that represent, for example, the possible intentions of an aircraft. Now if an event of type T2 is observed, the same three steps performed previously are performed using T2 and a new marker, M2. The resulting position of markers is shown in Figure 1.2.8.c. Nodes with both M1 and M2 represent the events that may be expected to follow. Clearly, plan P1 has been activated. A similar process is repeated when the next event occurs. If required, the marker M1 can be released and used again.

The above scenario of events represents, of course, only a simple case of likely events. If instead of an event of type T2, there was an event of type T4, the resulting marker positions are shown in Figure 1.2.8.d. The fact that neither an event of type T2 nor one of type T3 was observed should not reject the possiblity that plan P1 is in action. This allows for more realistic situations in which some events may go undetected.

1.2.4.   *Concluding Remarks*

In this chapter we have presented an alternative solution to the problem of dealing with exceptions in a parallel, marker-passing semantic network of the type described in (5). Before arriving at the above solution, a number of other solutions were tried that attempted to find the required nodes through a process of elimination, i.e. first marking all nodes in a scan irrespective of any cancellations, and then removing all nodes that have been eliminated as a result of some cancellation that has not been 'uncancelled'. The possible advantage of such an algorithm would be that the initial 'fast scan' would not be wasted, whether or not there are any exceptions in the scan. All such 'elimination' solutions tended to get complicated and inefficient and it was decided to abandon that approach after a while.

The two main advantages of our solution appear to be 1. the scans are likely to be more efficient than those given in (7), and 2. a simpler network results from the fact that no new type of link is needed to correct ambiguities resulting from a change in the knowledge base. The use of a minimum number of link types may also be an important implementation advantage. Additions can easily be made to the algorithms so that no time is wasted in the absence of ambiguities. We believe that the 'shortest-path' algorithms proposed do not fail, in a NETL network, because of redundant links. They, however, cannot cope with implicit ambiguities. *AMB-VC links are one possible way of making ambiguities explicit.

This chapter has described the potential applications of Massively Parallel Processor Arrays in the Naval Sensor-Data Fusion and Knowledge representation Environment. It has discussed, in particular, the use of marker passing parallel architectures of the type exemplified by NETL and has concentrated on some of the problems associated with these systems. Such architectures are currently the object of much research within many institutions because of their suitability for hardware implementation. However, their simplicity has led to the belief that they are unable to deal with real-world knowledge. This chapter has demonstrated that many of the problems associated with such architectures can, in fact, be overcome.

1.2.5.   References

1.   Brachman, R.J., Schmolze, J.G., 1985, 'An Overview of the KL-ONE Knowledge Representation System', *Cognitive Science,* 9:ii, 171-216.

2.   Cottrell, G.W., 1985, 'Parallelism in Inheritance Hierarchies with Exceptions', *Proc. IJCAI-85,* 1, 194-202.

3.   Cowan, D., Spracklen, C.T., Scott, M.A., 21983, 'The Integrity of Local Area Networks in Electrically Noisy Environments', *Proc. IERE Conference on Networks and Electronic Office Systems,* IV, 107-112.

4.   Etherington, D.W., Reiter, R., 1983, 'On Inheritance Hierarchies with Exceptions', *Proc. Conf. AAAI,* 104-108.

5. Fahlman, S.E., 1979, 'NETL: A System for Representing and Using real-world Knowledge', MIT Press, Cambridge Mass.

6. Fahlman, S.E., 1980, 'Design Sketch for a Million-Element NETL Machine', Proc. AAAI Conf., 249-252.

7. Fahlman, S.E., Touretzky, D.S., Roggen, W., 1981, 'Cancellations in a Parallel Semantic Network', *Proc. IJCAI Conf.*, 1, 257-263.

8. Gadsden, J.A., 1984, 'An Expert System for Evaluating Electronic Warfare Taking Plans for the Royal Navy', presented at the first conference on AI Applications, Denver, Colorado, 5-7 December.

9. Hinton., G.E., 1981, 'Parallel Models of Associative Memory', Hillsdale, NJ: Erlbaum.

10. Hinton., G.E., 1981, 'A Parallel Computation that Assigns Canonical Object-based Frames of Reference', *Proc. 7th IJCAI*, 2.

11. Hussman, M., 1984, 'IS-A isn't enough: Towards a Taxonomic Framework for Intensional Concepts', *Proc. ECAI Conf.* p350.

12. Poole, D.L., 1985, 'On the Comparison of Theories: Preferring the Most Specific Explanation', *Proc. IJCAI Conf.*, 1, 144-147.

13. Quillian, M.R., 1968, 'Semantic Memory', in Minsky, M. (Ed) 'Semantic Information Processing', MIT Press.

14. Reiter, R., Criscuolo, G., 1981, *Proc. IJCAI Conf.*, 1, 270-2276.

15. Rich, E., 1983, *Proc. AAAI Conf.*, 348-351.

16. Schank, R.C., 1975, 'Scripts, Plans, and Knowledge', *Proc. IJCAI Conf.* 1512-157.

17. Smythe, C., 1983, 'CDMA LAN Solves Contention Problems in Bus Networks', *Proc. FOC/LAN* 83, 131-134.

18. Smythe, C., Spracklen, C.T., 1986, Network Management in a Reconfigurable Spread Spectrum Local Area Network', *Proc. FOC/LAN*, 9-15.

19. Smythe, C., Spracklen, C.T., 1986, *Proc. INRIA Conf.* (France), 403-409.

20. Smythe, C., Spracklen, C.T., 1984, *Proc. IEE Communications 84 Conf.*, Conference Publication 235, 77-81.

21.   Spracklen, C.T., Smythe, C., 1983, Proc. IERE
      Conference on Networks and Electronic Office Systems, IV, 95-97.

22.   Touretzky, D.S., 1984, 'Implicit Ordering of Defaults
      in Inheritance Systems', *Proc. AAAI Conf.*, 1, 322-325.

23.   Woods, W.A., 1975, 'What's in a Link: Foundations for
      Semantic Networks', in Bobrow, D.G., and Collins, A.
      (Eds), 'Representation and Understanding', Academic
      Press, New York.

Chapter 2

Uncertainty and complexity in command and control

Uncertainty in Command and Control Systems

J.R. Moon*, J.P. Marriette and S.P.Frampton
(Ferranti Computer Systems Ltd, UK)

2.1.1   Introduction

Over the last decade the variety and performance of sensors available to force commanders have increased significantly. It is widely recognised that this new capability demands a corresponding increase in processing abilities so as to filter, correlate and fuse the information within a coherent structure. To date, efforts to achieve this goal have largely been directed towards improving the accuracy of sensors and the supporting communications which are used to transmit the data produced to the user. However, more recent research has placed the emphasis on examining the command and control decision process and identifying structures and tasks. Many aspects of C^3 systems have been analysed during recent conferences (e.g. the MIT/ONR Workshop on C^3 Systems series, and AFCEA European Symposia, and the IEE Advances in C^3 Systems series) and a number of them have identified uncertainty as a major factor affecting performance. A typical comment is due to Beaumont (1)

"the challenge is for designers and wielders of command methods to try to narrow the range of uncertainty, to learn to acept and cope with it, and ultimately to gauge it".

It is our view that insufficient attention has been paid to the sources and consequences of uncertainty in C^3 systems and this paper attempts to represent an elementary coherent view of its influence in a command and control system.

*External consultant

2.1.2   Preliminary Concepts

2.1.2. (i)   Uncertainty

Before looking more closely at the C3 process it is appropriate to briefly discuss exactly what is meant by uncertainty. A comparison with incaccuracy would appear a suitable starting point.

The Shorter Oxford Dictionary (2) defines inaccurate and uncertain as follows:

> INACCURATE - not accurate, inexact, incorrect, erroneous
> UNCERTAIN - not fixed in point of time or occurrence; not determinate in amount, number or extent, not sure to happen; contingent; liable to change or accident; not certain to remain in one state or conditon.

Although there is a fair amount of overlap between these definitions, in general it can be said that inaccuracies in sensors are a principal cause of uncertainties in the tactical picture and, perhaps of inaccuracies in the subsequent deductions. To date, the emphasis has been placed on tackling incaccuracy at the sensor level but future efforts in this direction may be profitable only if the handling of uncertainty at higher levels is correspondingly improved.

2.1.2. (ii)   A C3 Model

The discussion in this section is based upon a deliberately simple conceptual model of a C3 system comprising three stages of processing.

(a) Picture Compilation - accumulation and fusion of information to provide a tactical picture (see also Chapter 3)
(b) Situation Assessment - assessment of the situation presented by the tactical picture in relation to the mission (see also Chapter 4)
(c) Response - determination of options and selection of direct action as a result of the assessment.

If this is regarded as a processing hierarchy (Figure 2.1.1), then the type of information being processed and passed on will depend on the level within this hierarchy, with detailed measurements and data predominating at the lowest level and deductions and commands predominating at the highest level. Data will not only flow up this processing framework but feedback paths from the upper to lower levels can also occur; for example the assessment of enemy activity may aid the lower level identification processing.

At the Picture Compilation level an increasing proportion of the processing is being automated; at the higher levels the Situation Assessment and Response processes are still almost entirely performed by the operator, although there are moves towards automation within the C³ research community. These moves are bound to increase in momentum as overall system response times become squeezed by the advancing technology of the perceived threats.

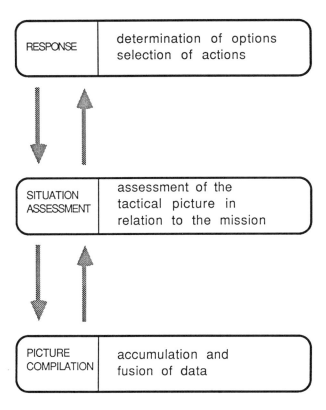

FIG 2.1.1   *Conceptual model of C³ processing*

2.1.3   Causes of Uncertainty

2.1.3. (i)   Uncertainty in Picture Compilation

This processing stage is self-evidently concerned with constructing a picture of the current situation based on information not only from sensors, such as radar and ESM, but also from direct communications, from navigation sub-systems and from collateral sources such as flight plans.

The causes of uncertainty in the perceived picture are illustrated in Figure 2.1.2 and the practical effects manifest themselves in doubts concerning the number, position and identity of contacts.

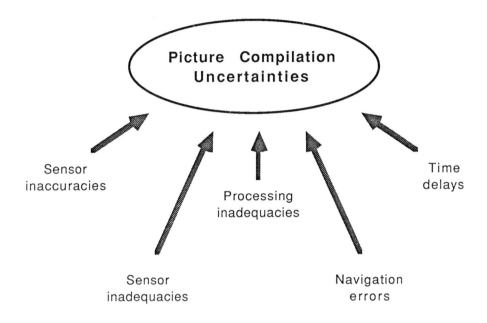

FIG 2.1.2   *Uncertainty in picture compilation*

Positional and Quantification Uncertainties. The most obvious cause of these is the inaccuracy in sensor measurements, and consequently there is always an impetus to develop more accurate sensors and sensors that give more complete information, such as 3-d rather than 2-d plots. However, for sensors providing a long-range surveillance function, the accuracy often has to be compromised in favour of detection performane - it is arguable that this compromise is often not pushed far enough, since the costs associated with uncertainty about a target's presence usually far outweigh the costs associated with uncertainties about its precise position. At shorter ranges the resolution of individual targets becomes an increasingly significant consideration for the related reason that it is important to determine the precise number of targets present. The best compromise between accuracy and detection performance clearly depends on the expected threat environment.

A more insiduous cause of uncertainty in the knowledge of the number and position of objects comes from navigation errors in the platforms responsible for reporting tracks to remote headquarters or fusion centres. These problems are exacerbated when the sensors involved have different resolutions and coverage, and clearly the difficulties expand rapidly with the number of sensors in the network. Perhaps the most notoriously difficult situation from this point of view occurs within the naval C3 environment where attempts are made to net data from a number of dispersed ships and aircraft.

Whatever the sources of data, there necessarily has to be association and correlation processing to consolidate the individual reports into information on discrete real targets, and the efficiency of these processes has an obvious effect on the confidence in the compiled picture - which is the principal reason why correlation processes are still a subject of research after two decades of automatic target data procesing. Current studies are showing that the correlation and data fusion tasks will be amongst the most technically demanding aspects of future ballistic missile defence systems. The problems in such systems are:

(a) Very high numbers of expected objects, perhaps 10^4 or 10^5, including objects designed for deliberate deception of sensors.
(b) Mixtures of ground, air and space based sensors of diverse types.
(c) Sensors with different resolutions, different detection mechanisms and different detection thresholds.
(d) Atmospheric refraction, which affects different parts of the electro-magnetic spectrum in different ways.

It can readily be appreciated that the task of forming a coherent tactical picture in such a system is a major challenge to algorithm designers as well as to sensor designers.

A further significant cause of uncertainty in picture compilation results from staleness of information, which may be the result of intermittent sensor observation or delays in the communication systems. This is particularly true in the case of non-direct intelligence reports from external sources which are often also vague in content and may therefore be uncertain on two counts. It may be possible to perform some pre-processing in such cases, such as applying dead-reckoning or furthest-on circles to a position, but this merely profiles the uncertainty and it does not resolve it. As a last resort such data may have to be discarded.

It is clear that the processing methods have at least as much influence on the uncertainties in the tactical picture as do the basic properties of the sensors. Tracking, i.e., estimation of target trajectory parameters, is one of the most basic processing operations and it still does not appear to be widely appreciated that the Cramer-Rao lower band provides a very useful yardstick for judging the efficiency of tracking algorithms, particularly those involving passive measures, as explained by Moon (12).

Identification Uncertainties. Data from identification sensors is often subjected to a conversion process which itself introduces a further source of uncertainty. An example may clarify this statement.

Consider an ESM equipment able to measure signal parameters such as frequency, pulse length and pulse repetition frequency with a high degree of accuracy. The user is not generally interested in these characteristics per se but in the identity of the emitter concerned. The conversion of the measurements to emitter identity depends on being able to associate all the measured parameters with the known characteristics of a particular emitter. Even if the measurements are highly accurate it may sometimes not be possible to make a satisfactory association and the identity of the emitter remains uncertain. However, if the measured parameters are so inaccurate that they can be associated with a number of possible emitters then an improvement in accuracy may allow the number of possible emitters to be reduced and hence reduce the uncertainty. There will be further uncertainty, due to lack of information on emitter fits to platforms and to lack of knowledge of prior population distributions in proceeding to the inference of either platform type or allegiance from the emitter inferences.

In this case it can be seen that the uncertainty can arise either because of sensor inaccuracy or because of deficiencies in the database supporting the conversion of the sensor measurement to identity. This example illustrates the importance of determining the source of uncertainty.

As well as uncertainty due to factors that are intrinsic to the sensor and the sensor processing, there are a number of other common causes of identification uncertainty. The most significant are doubts about the validity of the association between the sensor that provides the identity information and the radar track, and also doubts about track-to-track correlation when, for example, a track with associated identity moves from the coverage of one radar system into the coverage of another. There is also the uncertainty associated with the interpretation of target characteristics. How do we relate what is perceived of a target to its true identity if trials and observations concerning the characteristics are impossible or inappropriate? A typical example is that concerning an IFF reply solicited from a target; if the reply code is incorrect does this indicate a spoofing enemy or an inattentive friend? Probabilities can easily be used to represent the uncertainty or ambiguity but derivation of such values is bound to be subjective: knowledge or estimates of the likely proportion of enemy spoofers cannot be gained by observation! Uncertainty in the environment (e.g., has an IFF reply not been received because of adverse propagation effect?) and uncertainties in the knowledge of what is likely to be in a particular area will also contribute to the overall doubts about identity. Wilson (3) and Frampton, Marriette and Moon (4) discuss some of these factors in more detail.

2.1.3. (ii)   *Situation Assessment Uncertainties.*

Situation assessment consists of combining observations about the physical nature of the situation with knowledge derived from past experience to develop an integrated interpretation of dynamically changing events. The output from this processing phase consists of a perception of the current situation expressed in terms of intentions and relationships together with predictions of future events.

Leaving aside the acquired expertise an assessor brings to a situation, it is possible to identify four types of knowledge information used in the assessment (Figure 2.1.3):

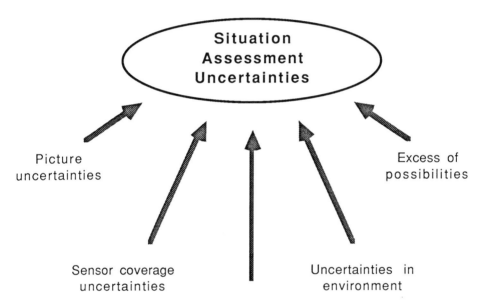

FIG 2.1.3 *Uncertainty in situation assesesment*

   (a) output from picture compilation, typically the estimated location and identity of known platforms.
   (b) details of the capabilities of platforms ·in terms of sensor and weapon fits.
   (c) the contents of tactical manuals.

(d) awareness of factors such as weather, geographical location, own fuel stocks or current emission policy.

The assessment process itself is typically modelled as the generation of successive hypotheses which describe some aspect of the situation such as the postulated relationships between platforms. In the next few paragraphs, an attempt is made to identify the uncertainty associated with each data type.

Uncertainties due to the Picture. The influence of uncertainties in the compiled picture on the assessed situation are not always straightforward. For a start one has doubts about whether the presented picture is complete; in order to resolve this doubt it is important to have information about sensor coverage in time and space, because only then can one make the important distinction between not having a target report because there is no target there, and not having a report because no sensor has looked in that area. This could be a particularly important consideration in battlefield systems, where the terrain has a very direct effect on what can be seen, and also in air defence when the normal coverage is reduced due to ECM, terrain effects or propagation anomalies.

Given that the completeness of the picture can be ascertained, the influence of the uncertainties in the positions of targets on the assessment depends very much on context. For example, the existence, position and axis of a mass raid can be assessed with acceptable accuracy from a fairly approximate track picture. But in other circumstances any uncertainty in the picture will be propagated forward into assessment and may acquire greater signifiance; a naval example might help to clarify this. If the normal operational role of an enemy reconnaissance aircraft is to provide targetting information to a cooperating submarine, and such an aircraft is detected, then the assessment phase may examine the track picture to see if there is indeed a potential cooperating submarine. However confirmation of the existence of this operational pair depends on establishing the position of the submarine with sufficient accuracy to confirm that it could be working with the aircraft, otherwise it remains an uncertain hypothesis. The inference of a missile being launched from an attack aircraft, or the inference of a reentry vehicle being launched from a missile bus, are examples from other environments where precise data is needed in order to make a valid situation assessment.

Platform Equipment Fits. Knowledge of platform equipment fits includes not only which sensors and weapons are on a platform but also information relating to the capability of the equipment. Thus in the case of a weapon details of its range, speed, flight profile, homing mechanism and warhead could be available. Data such as this is subect to rather infrequent changes and is often termed encyclopaedic as a result. As such it might be expected that any uncertainty associated with the data would settle down over a period of time to a relatively low level. Indeed in the case of information on friendly platforms it should be possible to disregard this uncertainty for all practical purposes.

Tactical Knowledge. Typically this data is based on past observations and experience and can therefore be expected to be rather uncertain. For instance, past experience may have shown that a particular type of enemy aircraft usually operates in formations of three but this does not mean that the single unidentified aircraft in an area is not of that type because tactics might have changed. There will always be doubts about the completeness of knowledge about enemy tactics and this cause is irreducible, except by improved intelligence or astute observation.

Other Factors. It also has to be recognised that in many circumstances it is not possible to assess what is happening because there are too few facts to resolve a large number of feasible hypotheses. More and better sensor data may resolve the situation, but this is not necessarily so since the enemy may currently be pursuing a course of action that can evolve in a number of distinct ways. The fact that there can seldom be a definable set of situations that is, in the mathematical sense, both exclusive and exhaustive presents particular algorithmic difficulties and provides a further constraint on the achievable certainty.

2.1.3. (iii)   Uncertainties in Response

Response, the third component of the processing hierarchy can itself be treated as two tasks: determination of options and selection and implementation of one of them. Selection of the optimum decision is a process that must take into account not only the uncertainty of the input data, but also the fact that the outcome of implementing any decision is itself uncertain. For instance, switching on a particular sensor may gather additional information, but it may also reveal the sensor's position to a hostile force that can then take action which may significantly alter the situation.

In deciding which option to pursue, the operator ought to take account of numerous uncertainties including those (Figure 2.1.4) associated with:

- The ability of the picture compilation and situation assessment phases to perform their respective tasks.
- The costs involved in making a right or wrong decision (this topic has received extensive attention within the field of decision theory, but somewhat less in the C^3 environment).
- The current constraints and overall priorities.
- The effect on the situation of the selected action.

A higher level of uncertainty in detail may be tolerated if the options under review are strategic whilst tactical decison making can tolerate much less uncertainty.

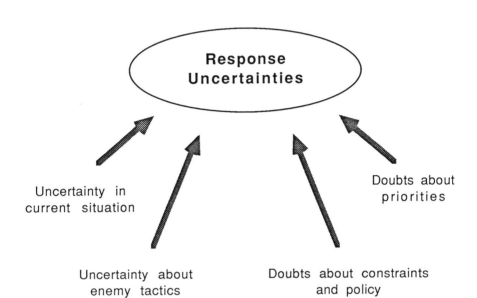

FIG 2.1.4 *Uncertainties in response*

As a slight digression we can observe that the information requirements may also depend on command style- the impulsive decision maker, acting largely on intuition, may not welcome having his judgement clouded by too many facts, so the data accuracy requirements for him are somewhat less stringent than for the commander who wishes to assess carefully all available evidence before making a decision.

2.1.4   Influences on Processing Functions

Having considered some of the causes and consequences of uncertainty we now wish to consider some of the implications this should have for the principal C3 processing functions.

2.1.4. (i)   Picture Compilation

There is not much the Picture Compilation processing can do about detection inadequacies in the sensors, but it has been highlighted that a major cause of confusion in the picture can be due to the difficulties of correlating targets from sensors attached to remote platforms with navigation uncertainties. One way of helping sort out this situation (apart from better navigation systems) would be to use correlation techniques that rely on matching complete plot and track pictures, rather than the one-one or few-few methods that are commonly used at present.

An altogether more intelligent approach to correlation is necessary when dealing with the fusion of track pictures obtained from sensors of different resolution and with radically different detection mechanisms. One is then involved in non-isomorphic mappings and the processing needs to take account of the size of resolution cell and the probabilities that an object will be seen by one sensor and not another. There is still scope for significant advances to be made in this area.

The identification processing could undoubtedly be improved by using methods that depend on techniques of modern statistical inference, rather than the ad-hoc processes and procedures in present use. References 3 and 4 describe a Bayesian scheme, which can rigorously handle most of the previously discussed causes of identity uncertainty. The intellectual case for using Bayesian processing, in conjunction with maximum entropy inferences to represent any unknown prior probabilities, for recognition problems is well presented by Jaynes (13).

2.1.4. (ii)   Situation Assessment

Of course, the Situation Assessment task is fundamentally different to Picture Compilation since it involves expert knowledge of the enemy, his tactics and the environment. This type of knowledge is usually built up by experience and modern techniques of Artificial Intelligence are being researched by a number of organsiations in order to try and improve the quality and consistency of situation appraisals. Also, as mentioned earlier, there are problems for a strictly analytical approach posed by the mathematical incompleteness of the set of possible situations. AI techniques can have a particularly valuable role in controlling the generation of hypotheses in situation assessment schemes.

Research in applying Artificial Intelligence to Situation Assessment by Lakin and Miles (5), Noble (6), Lenat et al (7), Ben-Bassat and Freedy (8) has suggested that the assessor formulates hypotheses representing different interpretations or viewpoints of the situation. The knowledge employed in this task can be partitioned into two types:

(a) control or meta knowledge relating to how hypothesis generation is controlled.
(b) knowldege of the domain, typically expressed as rules which may have a degree of confidence associated with them.

The hypotheses generated by an assessor may represent different views of the same situation; for instance the reconnaissance aircraft in the earlier example may have two postulated submarine partners, represented by two relationship hypotheses, each uncertain to a degree. Once such hypotheses are formed the aim is to reduce, if possible, the uncertainty associated with them; this may be achieved by matching new facts such as a new positions measurement against the hypotheses. The output from the assessment process may thus be composed of the hypotheses whose uncertainty has fallen to a user defined level.

One of the many problems an operator faces during Situation Assessment is in knowing the completeness of the track picture, and we can observe that this task would be made easier if more widespread use was made of calculations and displays of sensor coverage. Wright et al (9) describe one such system for predicting radar and ESM coverage in air defence systems.

2.1.4.(iii)   Response

In discussing response, the third C3 processing component, it is not quite true to imply that no tactical decisions are currently automatic since in some point defence systems entirely automatic engagements can be initiated. However the decision process here is fairly rudimentary. A future extrapolation of this type of decision could occur in ballistic missile defence systems, where rapid decisions about which weapons should engage which targets (and when) will be needed. In this environment a real-time cost analysis of the options may be appropriate, taking into account all of the inherent uncertainties of the situation.

The more complicated type of military tactical decision, involving multiple criteria and many complex constraints, is currently the least likely candidate for automation. However, Wohl (10) presents a strong case for moving towards automated aids for tactical decisions; such a system would operate by prompting:

(a) Awareness of the current objectives and their relative importance.
(b) Awareness of the constraints e.g., rules of engagement
(c) Evaluation of the candidate decision by forcing assessments of costs in equipment and men, and of the potential benefits.

The philosophy is to try and improve the quality of decision making by removing the possibilty of making impulsive and ad-hoc decisions. This type of decision aid would inter alia, place the sources of uncertainty in their correct context.

There is one further point that we would like to make concerning the treatment of uncertainty in response. As a general rule the uncertainty should be propagated forward in the system until such point as a decision has to be made. For example, if a suspect signal is received by an

ESM receiver, then better tactical decisions will be made by assessing (a) the probability that the signal comes from a particular emitter, then (b) the probability that the contact is of a particular type and allegiance. The final tactical decison (e.g., to engage or not) is then best made taking this identity uncertainty into account. If the decision maker is hidden from the uncertainties on identity and any other relevant uncertainties, then there is a greater chance of a wrong engagement decision being made. The generalisation of this example is that sub-optimal tactical decisions will result if black/white decisions are made at each elemental stage in the deductive process.

2.1.5   *Influence on System Architecture*

In this section we consider how the data and inference uncertainties discussed earlier should influence the structure of the hierarchical command, communications and data processing network that lie at the heart of a larage distributed C^3 system, such as might be used for air defence or for land battle management.

If we examine the information, timing and precision needs of different levels in the C^3 hierarchy, then it is apparent (Figure 2.1.5) that the lower levels require timely and precise detail, while the higher levels require the less detailed picture that evolves in a slower timescale.

This pattern of requirement does, of course, evolve from the operational needs that affect each of the hierarchical levels. At the lowest level, the weapon controller is only interested in the target or targets he has to engage, and he requires relevant information to be accurate, certain and quick. This in turn implies that the tasks of radar/target acquisition (of a track possibly notified from a remote sensor), correlation (of local and remote tracks) and identification must also be precise and quick. The data communications structure must therefore allow a rapid dissemination of data at this level.

The intermediate command level is interested in the construction of a track-based picture (the picture compilation function described earlier) which can be used to detect, track and classify individual objecs. This type of picture is useful for threat assessment and sensor or weapon tasking. The accuracy and temporal needs are largely determined by the interface with the weapons systems, but they are not quite as stringent as at the previous level.

The higher levels of command have somewhat different consideration, being concerned less with individual targets and tracks, and more with formations and raid sizes, directions and speeds of approach. This is where there is a need for the situation assessment function. The type of certainty required here is certainty in interpreting the overall track picture which, as we have seen, depends rather less on the detailed accuracy than on its completeness. The track accuracy and timeliness

Increasing
Accuracy and
Timeliness
Requirements

→

Command Level	Information Interests	Reasons
Tactical	General force dispositions	Situation Assessment tactics
Intermediate	Track picture	Threat assessment sensor and weapon tasking
Combat	Isolated tracks	Engagement

←

Increasing Area
of Interest
and Responsibility

FIG 2.1.5   *Information requirements of different command levels*

requirements are less stringent at this level (conversely, the weapon controller at the lower level has little interest in having access to an accurate situation assessment).

So, given the general pattern of spatial and temporal certainty requirements, what is the most appropriate data distribution structure?

Existing distributed command and control systems are usually structured on a tree principle that is orderly and easily controllable, both in the upwards reporting and in the downward dissemination of orders (Figure 2.1.6). Although well-suited to command requirements it is not well-suited to information exchange for a number of reasons:

(a)   it provides high level command with much more detail than is required

(b)   the temporal and spatial accuracy of data sent to the highest level exceeds the requirements at this level

(c)   it can cause unacceptable time delays in passing data between neighbouring low-level units (e.g., units A and B in Figure 2.1.6) because of the tortuous path involved, this path is also very vulnerable to disruptions.

(d)   it causes a very high loading on the data links at the higher levels.

These last two points have very practical consequences. The time delays mentioned above have a direct influence on the uncertainties in correlation and identification and hence, for example, on the chances of successfully engaging a target flying out of one SHORAD area into another. Also high capacity data links are very expensive.

An extended structure with cross-links at the intermediate levels would be much better, since this allows most of the problems of the tree structure to be solved. It enables the overall data flow requirements to be reduced, since it permits higher levels to receive just those aspects of the picture that they are really interested in. Within the planar network that will constitute the communications structure at any particular level, it is clear there will need to be protocols for controlling the spread of information, both within that level and to the adjacent levels. Such a scheme, involving Areas of Interest and Areas of Responsibility, is described by Canfield (11).

Uncertainty considerations can also lead to another means of reducing unnecessary data flows: there is no point in passing imprecise data around the network when precise data relating to the same object is already being disseminated. Obvious examples are a precise radar track, or a very positive identification, both of which can obviate the need for additional spatial or identity information.

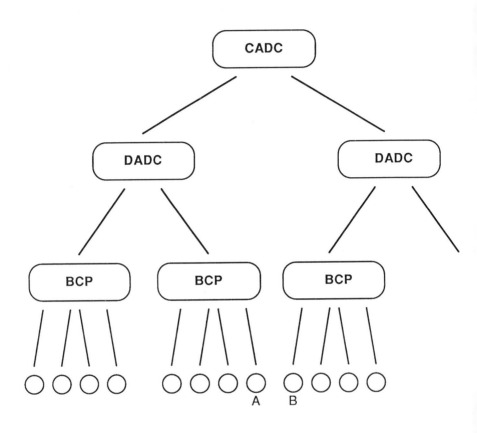

KEY

◯   Batteries

BCP   Battery Command Post

DADC   Divisional Air Defence Cell

CADC   Corps Air Defence Cell

FIG 2.1.6   *Corps air defence command structure*

The above discussion has concentrated on the data processing needs of C3 structures and it is reasoned that a tree structure for disseminating data is far from ideal. However, for disseminating commands a tree structure remains ideal, although it can be pointed out that a tree structure is still a subset of the extended structure and so the concepts are not really incompatible. It is also fair to acknowledge that there are many other practical considerations involved in choosing a C3 structure (such as cost, simplicity, robustness, problems with regional and national boundaries) which may favour one or other of the options we have considered.

2.1.6   Conclusions

This paper has tried to present an elementary coherent view of the influence of uncertainty in C3 systems. The principal points are:

* Uncertainty at the picture level can certainly be reduced by better sensors and better processing methods.
* Uncertainty within the higher-level functions of C3 systems can only partly be reduced by better picture information, since effective fulfilment of these functions depends also on a comprehensive knowledge of the equipment and tactics of the enemy.
* The spatial and timing accuracy needs of a distributed C3 system make a tree structure inappropriate; a more appropriate structure would have cross links at the intermediate levels.

In conclusion it is clear that the design of C3 systems must take uncertainties into account; a system that makes arbitrary decisions wherever uncertainties occur is unacceptable. Techniques that accept and reason with uncertainty are evolving from continued research into applied mathematics and artificial intelligence and these are going to find increasing application within the next generation of C3 systems.

2.1.7   References

1.   Beaumont, R.A., 1981, 'The Tactical Spectrum and C3 State Variance: Accommodating Uncertainty', *Signal 35*, 45-49.

2.   Shorter Oxford Dictionary, 5th Edition, 1964, Oxford University Press.

3.   Wilson, G.B., 1985, 'Some Aspects of Data Fusion', *Proc. IEEE Conference on Advances in Command, Control and Communications Systems*, 99-105.

4. Frampton, S.P., Marriette, J.P. and Moon, J.R., 1986, 'Modelling of Uncertainty in an Aircraft Recognition System', Modelling under Uncertainty Conference, Fulmer Research Institute, UK.

5. Lakin, W.L. and Miles, J.A.H., 1986, 'Intelligent Data Fusion and Situation Assessment'. *Proc. 9th MIT/ONR Workshop on C3 Systems*, Monterey, C.A.

6. Noble, D., 1985, 'A Theory to Guide the Design of Situation Assessment Aids for Decision Making', *Proc. 8th MIT/ONR Workshop on C3 Systems*, Cambridge, MA.

7. Lenat, D.B., Clarkson, A. and Kiremidjian, G., 1985, 'An Expert System for Indications and Warning Analysis', *Proc. IJCAI*, 259-262.

8. Ben-Bassat, M. and Freedy, A., 1982, 'Knowledge Requirements and Management in Expert Decision Support Systems for (Military) Situation Assessment', *IEEE SMC-12*, 479-490.

9. Wright, R.E., Burton, P.F.J., Lambert, C. and Barr, J.S., 1982, 'The Tactical Applications of Microwave Propagation Prediction', *AGARD Conference Proceedings No 331*, 'Propagation Effects of ECM Resistant Systems in Communication and Navigation'.

10. Wohl, J.G., 1981, 'Force Management Decision Requirements for Air Force Tactical Command and Control', *IEEE SMC-11*, 618-639.

11. Canfield, D.J.A., 1985, 'Information Flow Control for Distributed Command and Control', *Proc. 6th AFCEA European Symposium*, Brussels, 162-167.

12. Moon, J.R., 1979, 'Application of the Cramer-Rao Bound to Target Motion Analysis', *Electronics Letters*, Vol 15, 236-237.

13. Jaynes, E.T., 1986, 'Bayesian Methods: General Background', Chapter in 'Maximum Entropy and Bayesian Methods in Applied Statistics', J.H. Justice, (ed) C.U.P. 1986.

Catastrophes, Chaos and C3I: Toward a New Understanding of Military Combat

A E R Woodcock
(Synetics Corporation, USA)

2.2.1   Introduction

While large investments are made to produce and deploy modern weapons systems, relatively few resources have been provided to support studies of the most important area: understanding the nature of combat itself. The recent development of mathematical models of complex physical, chemical, and biological systems raises the hope that these models can provide the basis for a new understanding of military systems. Of particular importance is the fact that very complex behavior can be generated from relatively simple mathematical models (Fiegenbaum (1), Guckenheimer and Holmes (2), Holden (3), May (4,5), Prigogine (6), Thompson (7), Thompson and Stewart (8), Velo and Wightman (9), and Woodcock (10, 11), for example).

A program of advanced military analysis, outlined below, is drawing on research in catastrophe theory, dynamic, stochastic, and chaotic systems including strange attractors, population dynamics, and cellular automata to provide a new understanding of combat (Woodcock and Dockery (12, 13), Woodcock (11, 14), Woodcock et al. (15), for example) (Figure 2.2.1). This program is producing new models of combat which are being hosted on a computer-based facility known as the electronic workbench that can support analysis and decision-making. The combat model-building, testing, and verification activities use the results of on-going research to increase the capabilities and level of sophistication of the models, which are then available for hosting in the workbench environment.

2.2.2   Advances in Mathematics Provide the Basis for New Types of Combat Model

The command and control of modern military forces demands an evolving inventory of at least partially automated decision aids which are much more elaborate than rudimentary data handling, and are based on robust non-linear models of military systems. These aids should also

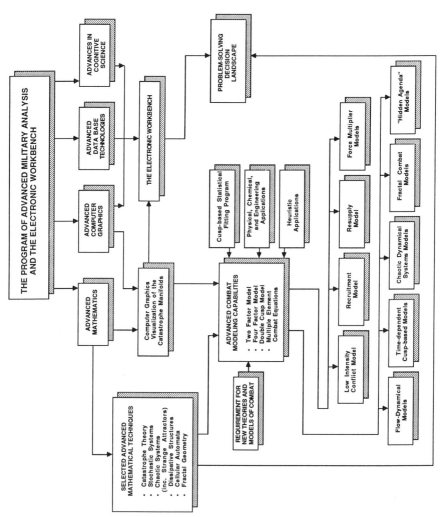

FIG 2.2.1   *A program of advanced military analysis*

be based on cognitive engineering techniques which serve to facilitate perception, cognition, and motor activity by supporting the inherent biological intelligence of the user. In actual combat situations, there is little or no time to perform the lengthy and detailed event-oriented analyses that are possible under other conditions. What is needed are facilities which can give new insights into the behavior of complex military systems by reducing their apparent complexity in a rigorous way. These facilities would:

- Provide a "top-down" approach to problem-solving that allows the analyst, decision-maker, or commander to understand macroscopic combat behavior in terms of the action of a relatively few key influences around which he normally organizes his perceptions of the combat environment
- Support the cognitive and other related aspects of a wide range of decision-making, analytic, and battle management activities.
- Supply a sophisticated form of computer-based graphics interface that can aid the military analyst, decision-maker, and commander in the development of perceptions and in the performance of a range of "what-if" analyses or "thought-experiments."

These activities are being made possible by the application of mathematics to combat modeling and by the development of a electronic workbench facility that uses cognitive engineering, computer graphics, and data base techniques to support the production and use of combat models (13) (Figure 2.2.2). The workbench facility will provide access to a wide range of combat attrition and reinforcement models and combat initiation and termination decision rules that will aid the tactical and/or strategic decision-making process by supporting such activities as situation assessment and impact analyses on an essentially real-time basis.

The more classical types of combat model are inadequate for the task of describing the modern combat environment where complex weapon systems can produce highly non-linear and often counter-intuitive effects. Many of the techniques in current use are based on linear methods which have the effect of suppressing rather than revealing potential non-linear system behavior. Techniques that capture the inherent non-linearity of complex combat-related systems in a manner that can provide insights into the causes and effects of sudden change are clearly needed. If not identified properly, such non-linear behavior can lead to highly misleading and even totally incorrect analyses of a situation of interest with disastrous consequences. Furthermore, the complexity of the modern battlefield has dramatically increased the need for facilities that support the processes of biological intelligence rather than promoting a reliance on artificial intelligence. Applications of artificial intelligence in such areas as medical diagnosis and molecular structure analysis have certainly been successful and other significant advances can be expected (Hayes-Roth, et al. (16), Winston (17), Barr and Fiegenbaum (18), and Fiegenbaum and McCorduck (19), for example). However, we are in danger of being overly confined by prepackaged software products that force us to act in restricted ways about complex and often new and unique problems. For military analysts and decision-makers to rely completely on such electronic expertise in actual combat adds additional dimensions of danger.

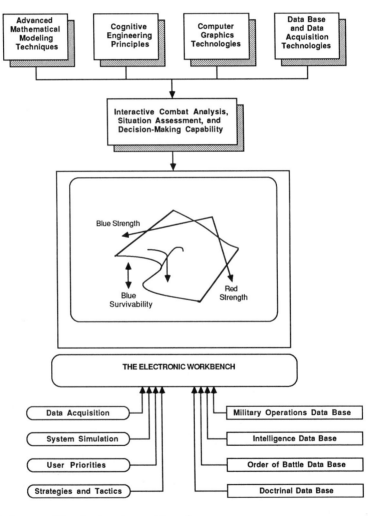

FIG 2.2.2   *The electronic workbench*

Under conditions, such as those associated with the combat environment, in which sudden and unexpected events can occur with disastrous consequences, the human brain must play an increasingly important role since it can generate flexible responses and be adaptable to changing circumstances. Neural activities associated with sensory reception, analysis, thinking, and motor output involve enormous numbers of neurons. Many of our sensory experiences consist of complex patterns in space and/or time. Perceptions involve the interaction of very large number of neurons and very elaborate circuits. Learning is an adaptive change in behavior involving the control of the whole organism by the central nervous system. The structural elaboration of the cerebral cortex of the human nervous system has supported the development of speech and language and has given rise to more adaptable modes of communication and ultimately to symbolic thought (see Ayer (20), Boden (21), Guyton (22), Marr (23), Nowakowska (24), Popper (25), Popper and Eccles (26), Shafto (27), Shepherd (28), and Williams and Warwick (29), for example).

The next generation of decision aids will need to draw heavily on research into human neural functions and related areas to produce sophisticated man-machine interfaces that enhance communication, analysis, and reasoning (see also Chapter 2.3, Neural Nets in C² Systems). Such activities can also be supported, in part, by the use of catastrophe theory and other mathematical techniques.

2.2.3 The Role of Catastrophe Theory

Catastrophe theory deals with sudden changes and can provide geometric illustrations of systems which exhibit discontinuous behavior. Indeed the name "catastrophe", which can be directly translated from the Greek "katas-trophe" which literally means to "turn down" suggests conditions of instability where the "ground appears to fall away from under one's feet!" The theory is particularly useful in those cases in which smoothly changing forces can give rise to both gradual and sudden changes in the same system under different circumstances. Two essential features of the theory are:

• The general framework that it provides for classifying the type of illustration that is available for expressing the relationships between the independent and dependent system variables.
• The mathematically rigorous way that it limits the number of variables needed to capture the essence of system behavior.

Catastrophe theory-based models can aid comprehension and "turn old facts into new knowledge" (Thompson (30)). The theory provides a series of diagrams, known technically as catastrophe manifolds, which Woodcock and Dockery have

called "problem-solving landscapes", that can aid the
military commander and others in tracking events during
combat and supporting such activities as decision-making,
situation assessment, and impact analysis on an essentially
real-time basis. Two-and four-factor models of military
behavior (with control factors that resemble the properties
or "axes" around which a military commander may organize
his perceptions) have been developed (13).
     The elementary catastrophes describe the behavior of
those systems with up to four control parameters (or key
independent variables) and up to two behavior variables (or
key dependent variables) and an associated potential
energy-like property. Woodcock and Dockery have considered
the behaviour of simplifed systems with gradient field
properties as a subset of the more general (and more
complicated) time-dependent dynamical systems and have
concentrated initially on analysis of the stationary (or
observable) states of such systems (12), (13). They have
then put back the time-dependent properties of such systems
in a rigorous mathematical way and have thereby discovered
some new and interesting phenomena. As an example, their
investigation of the space- and time-equivalent
catastrophes (Wassermann (31)) has led to the discovery of
a new type of chaotic behavior, which is described below.
     Additional work in the area of time-dependent dynamical
systems has grown out of initial work applying catastrophe
theory to the analysis of military behavior. This work has
led to the development of a program of advanced political
and military analysis based on catastrophe theory and other
mathematical techniques that provides methods for
investigating the behavior of political and military
systems at many different levels of complexity.

*2.2.3.(i)   Catastrophe Theory can Help Turn Old Facts into New
           Knowledge*

     Invented by Thom in the 1960's, (Thom (32, 33)),
Brocker and Lander (34), Poston and Stewart (35), Zeeman,
(36), Zeeman and Trotman (37), and Woodcock and Poston
(38), for example), catastrophe theory has been used in
many applications in the mathematical, physical, chemical,
life, and social sciences (see Arnold (39), Adelman and
Hihn (40), Beaumont (41), Berry (42), Cobb (43,44), Gilmore
(45), Guastello (46), Hilton (47), Janich (48), Lu (49),
(7), Thompson and Hunt (50), (8), Stewart (51), Stewart and
Woodcock (52, 53), Wilson (54), Woodcock (55, 56), (11) and
Woodcock and Davis (57) for example). Catastrophe theory
has also been used in a series of military applications
((10), (14), Woodcock and Dockery (58, 59), Dockery and
Chiatti (60), Dockery and Woodcock (61), (13), Isnard and
Zeeman (62), and Holt, et al (63), for example).
     Thom called sudden changes in behavior "catastrophes"
and developed a theory (subsequently called "catastrophe
theory" by Zeeman) as a new method for analyzing and
classifying this behavior. Catastrophe theory can be used
to analyze the behavior of those systems which exhibit at

least some of the properties of hysteresis, bimodality, and divergence. The theory also provides a rigorous mathematical framework to support the "top-down" analysis of the behavior of complicated systems such as military systems. As described below, the theory can provide a basis for models of military combat which illustrate the impact of force strength, firepower, and command and control capabilities on military force survivability, for example. These models are then used as the starting point for further investigations and model building activities.

The nature of the elementary catastrophes has been explored in detail (see (38), for example). The cusp catastrophe function V_c, is the sum of germ ($x^4/4$) and perturbation or unfolding ($ax^2/2 + bx$) components and has the form:

$$V_c = x^4/4 + ax^2/2 + bx \qquad (2.2.1)$$

where a and b are the control parameters and x is the behavior or state variable of the function. Stationary states of this function occur when $dV_c/dx = 0$, that is when:

$$dV_c/dx = x^3 + ax + b = 0 \qquad (2.2.2)$$

This equation represents the three (x, a, b) dimensional catastrophe manifold surface which is generated by the stationary states of the cusp potential function (Figure 2.2.3). The elementary catastrophe manifold surfaces can also represent the causes and effects of the behavior of a wide range of different systems and may be used to facilitate problem-solving. When used in this way, the position of a point (referred to as the state point) on the manifold (referred to as a problem-solving landscape) representing the state of a system of interest is determined by the values of the control factors (or input variables). Changes in the values of these factors cause state point movements on the surface of the manifold. The pattern of such movemenmts can be illustrative of system behavior and can involve either sudden (path (p-q-r) or gradual (path s-t-u) changes (Figure 2.2.3).

Thom's theorem implies that the stationary state behavior of all systems (including physical, chemical, biological, and societal systems) with up to four control factors, two behavior variables, and an associated potential-like function, can be described with the aid of one of the seven elementary catastrophes. Subsequent mathematical analysis ((37), for example), has proved Thom's theorem. The use of catastrophe theory to model a particular system, such as that associated with military combat, will require the identification of a suitable set of control factors and behavior variables. Two models based on catastrophe theory which demonstrate the impact of force strength, firepower, and command and control capabilities have been developed (12), and are outlined below.

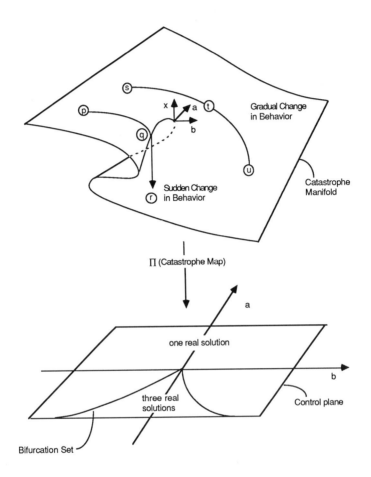

FIG 2.2.3   *The cusp catastrophe manifold and control plane*

2.2.3. (ii)   A Two Factor Combat Model

Catastrophe theory-based macro-level models can provide
a useful type of interface between the military commander
on the one hand and either elaborate computer-based combat
simulations which generate large amounts of data, or the
actual combat environment, on the other (13).   Thus,
Dockery and Chiatti have used a computer program involving
sophisticated   new   statistical   procedures   which   were
developed by Cobb (64) to fit simulated combat data to the
surface of the cusp catastrophe manifold (60).
The two factor model of the combat process involves
consideration of the effect of different strengths of two
military forces (designated blue and red forces here) on
the survivability of the blue force. As a result of Thom's

theorem, this model is based on the cusp catastrophe. Conflicting factors (62) were chosen in the place of control factors for this purpose because they can capture the inherent conflict that exists in the combat environment. The model illustrated in Figure 2.2.4 identifies the conflicting factors and behavior variable as follows: Factor 1, which Woodcock and Dockery have called the blue force strength, represents influences which impose order on a defending (or attacking) (blue) force. Factor 2, called the red force strength, represents influences which impose order on an attacking (or defending) (red) force (13). The behavior variable, called the survivability of the blue force, represents some manifestation of an order-disorder transition in a military combat situation.

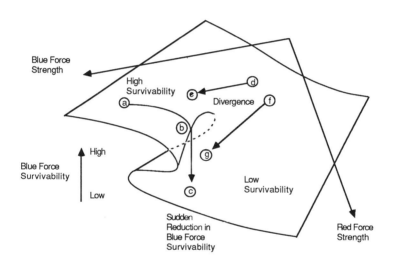

FIG 2.2.4   *A two-factor model based on the cusp catastrophe (After Woodcock and Dockery (13))*

It is possible to identify two areas of the cusp landscape in Figure 2.2.4, which represent two qualitatively different types of system behavior. One area of the landscape, arbitrarily located on its upper surface, represents a condition of high blue force survivability. The lower layer of the surface (below the pleat) represents a condition of low survivability. A number of paths can be drawn on the cusp landscape surface to represent different patterns of military behavior. The path (a-b-c), for example, illustrates rapid attrition of the blue force coupled with a net reinforcement of the red force that leads to the collapse of the blue force.

The paths (d-e) and (f-g) on the landscape are also instructive since both represent a build up of blue forces from a low level. While the starting positions are quite close, the end points are far apart in terms of blue force survivability. On path (f-g), a series of apparently insignificant events and decisions took place which continually underestimated the red force strength. The result, when battle is joined, produces a force at point (g) rather than at point (e) and a commander who has completely underestimated the survivability of his force. However, the commanders at both points (e) and (g) may perceive themselves to be in a strong military position and the fact that the commander at point (g) is in a weak military position can lead to inappropriate military actions.

This two-factor model has illustrated the impact of blue and red force strength on the survivability of the blue forces. Together with the fitting of simulated data by Dockery and Chiatti with the aid of a program developed by Cobb, one result of which is illustrated below, the two-factor model provides an anchor for further investigations (64, 60). Dockery and Chiatti have used this program to analyze the data obtained from COMO III, a complex, event-driven Monte-Carlo type of simulation of a frontal air attack on a forward air defensive region using a range of offensive aircraft and defensive aircraft, missiles, and radars (60) (Figure 2.2.5).

The simulation was performed to analyze the formation of a breakthrough or corridor in the defensive region. However, analysis of such a breakthrough, whether in the air or on the ground, has proven resistant to the more conventional types of analysis using linear equations. In a very real sense, a breakthrough represents a catastrophe for the defenders, an observation that led to the initial attempts to use catastrophe theory as a modeling tool to support the analysis of such breakthroughs. In the results presented in Figure 2.2.5, the statistical procedures are used to determine whether or not the influences acting on the system are orthogonal, and therefore independent. Here the procedures have led to the identification of the axes X1 and X2 (which represent the stockpile of missiles and the number of attacking aircraft, respectively) as almost completely independent variables in the simulation. The behavior variable, which was identified through the use of the statistical procedures employed in this example, is defined as the amount of ordinance delivered per attacker.

The analysis has shown that a significant number of the COMO III replications have catastrophe landscape coordinates which place them within the catastrophe region of the diagram so that they actually appear to exhibit a bimodality of behavior. Under these circumstances, the analysis reveals that some attacking aircraft are successful and deliver a large amount of ordinance while other aircraft are unsuccessful and deliver a relatively small amount of ordinance. Thus, there appear to be two "classes" of aircraft under these conditions. Such bimodal behavior was not even suspected from a conventional type of review of the raw simulation data produced by the COMO III program, and was only revealed as a result of the catastrophe-based analysis.

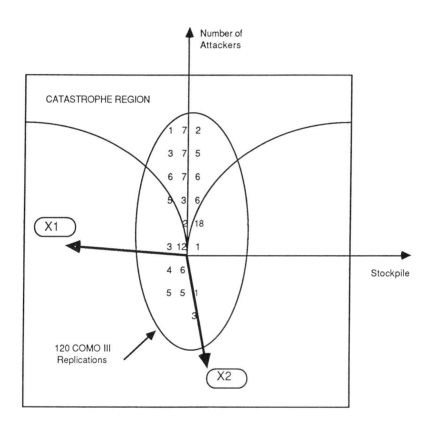

FIG 2.2.5   *Application of catastrophe theory to military analysis (After Dockery and Chiatti (60))*

2.2.3. (iii)   Four Factor Combat Model

The second model (12, 13) describes the impact of red and blue force strength, firepower, and command and control capabilities on the survivability of the blue forces. This model is based on the butterfly catastrophe (Figure 2.2.6) with the folowing identifications being made: Factor 1, called the blue force strength, represents influences which

impose short range order on a defending (or attacking)
(blue) force. Factor 2, called the red force strength,
represents influences which impose short range order on an
attacking (or defending) (red) force. Force 3, called the
firepower balance, represents the relative levels of
firepower of the opposing forces and reflect influences
which impart intermediate range order on these forces.
Factor 4, called the command and control capability
available to the blue forces, represents the influence of
those factors that impose long range order on the blue
forces. The behavior variable represents the survivability
of the blue force.
    In this four-factor model the conflicting factor axes
represent the inherent strengths of the opposing red and
blue forces in terms of their levels of training or group
cohesiveness, but without consideration of the relative
levels of firepower or command and control capabilities or
other long range assets such as helicopter forces. The
crucial thing is that these longer range assets represent
influences external to the forces' inherent strength. In
the illustration (Figure 2.2.6), the relative firepower and
command and control capabilities available to the two
forces are represented by scales with indicator arrows.
The position of the indicator arrow represents the existing
value of the particular control factor and changes in such
values, reflected by a movement of the indicator arrow,
causes a corresponding change in the shape of the manifold.
We track these changes by comparing the changes in the
shape of the "footprint" of the folded region of the
manifold.
    Conditions in which the blue force has a significant
advantage in firepower and command and control capabilities
compared to the red force are illustrated in the model by a
distortion of the manifold surface to produce a relatively
large region that is identified with conditions of high
blue force survivability (Figure 2.2.6). These additional
influences can thus off-set the effect of a relatively low
intrinsic blue force strength. A reduction in the blue
force command and control capability advantage during
combat will lead to a reduction in blue force
survivability. Under these circumstances, it would perhaps
appear to the blue force commander that the "ground" was
falling away from under his feet as the folded region of
the surface moves in response to changes in the level of
command and control capabilities. Here the model
illustrates how a drastic reduction in command and control
capabilities (caused by the destruction of a key command
center, for example) can cause a significant decrease in
the survivability of these forces, an event which can be
represented by the movement of the state point from the
upper (or high survivability) to the lower (or low
survivability) region of the manifold (path a-b,
Figure 2.2.6) in response to a decrease in the level of
blue force command and control capabilities. The indicated
area drawn on the plane in this figure represents those

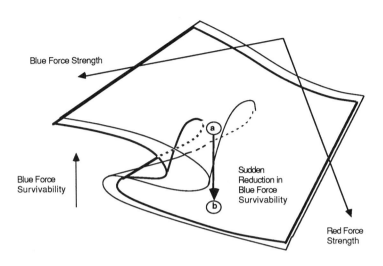

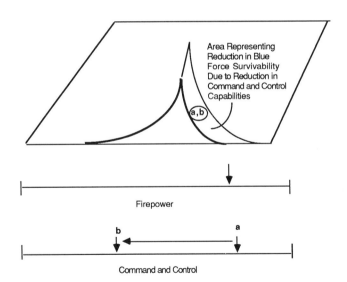

Force balance, firepower, and command and control capabilities
determine military force survivability.

FIG 2.2.6   *A military analysis and problem-solving landscape*

sets of factor values for which such a reduction in force survivability can occur.

2.2.3. (iv)   *A Framework for Generating Lanchester-type Combat Equations*

Catastrophe theory has been used as a framework to generate a series of Lanchester-type combat models (10). Such models consist of a series of time-dependent deterministic differential equations which represent different combat attrition processes (65) (also Taylor (66)). Initially motivated by the need to provide a mathematical justification for the principle of "force concentration" (which can be stated that the best strategy is to keep one's forces concentrated in a particular location) Lanchester's work has subsequently provided the basis for the modern mathematical analysis of the combat process.

The equations for modern warfare are the most widely known equations of the Lanchester-type and can be represented as:

$$dx/dt = - ay \qquad\qquad (2.2.3)$$
$$dy/dt = - bx \qquad\qquad (2.2.4)$$

where coefficients (a) and (b) represent the combat effectiveness of the two opposing forces (y) and (x), respectively.

The initial development and application of Lanchester-type equations has also been driven by the need for a deterministic differential equation that could be integrated. The restriction to deterministic cases has been overcome by the recent developement by Cobb and Harrison (67) of a software package which can be used to integrate stochastic and highly complicated versions of Lanchester-type combat equations. A general framework based on catastrophe theory that generates a wide range of Lanchester-type combat equations such as those described in equations (2.2.3) and (2.2.4) has been developed by Woodcock and Dockery (59).

An important motivation for the activity involving the use of catastrophe theory to generate combat model so the Lanchester type was the realization that, for potential functions of the form V(x,y), the following relationships exist:

$$dx/dt = - \partial V(x,y)/\partial x \qquad\qquad (2.2.5)$$
$$dy/dt = - \partial V(x,y)/\partial y \qquad\qquad (2.2.6)$$

(35), (2). Thus, if the properties (x) and (y) in equations (2.2.5) and (2.2.6) are identified as functions of the strength of two military forces, then the left-hand sides of these equations are equivalent to the left-hand sides of the Lanchester-type of combat equations. The right-hand sides of equations (2.2.5) and (2.2.6) can be derived by the differentiation of an appropriate type of catastrophe theory-related potential function with respect to its (x) and (y) behavior variables.

Woodcock and Dockery have shown that the hyperbolic umbilic catastrophe can be used as a generator or relationships representing Lanchester-type ancient combat and modern warfare equations and that the double cusp catastrophe (which has eight controls, two behavior variables, and therefore is not an elementary catastrophe) can generate a much more extensive list of such equations (59). They have written the following multiple element combat equations involving tactical activities which are based on the double cusp catastrophe function:

$$dx/dt = -2axy^2 - 2bxy - cy^2 - 2dx - fy - g \qquad (2.2.7)$$
$$dy/dt = -2ax^2y - bx^2 - 2cxy - 2ey - fx - h \qquad (2.2.8)$$

Inspection of these equations reveals that the x force can manipulate the (d) and (g) coefficients without influencing the y force and that the y force can manipulate the (e) and (h) coefficients without influencing the x force. However, both forces share access to processes represented by the (a), (b), (c) and (f) coefficients. Thus, if one force establishes the value of one or more of these terms by defining the nature of the combat environment, for example, then this will directly restrict the potential actions of the other force.

Woodcock and Dockery have shown that it is possible to make an extensive series of identifications between Lanchester-type combat relationships on the one hand, and the coefficients of the double cusp catastrophe-based multiple element combat equations on the other (59) (Figure 2.2.7). This figure shows that the multiple element combat equations can describe Lanchester-type ancient combat, modern warfare, and area fire attrition process as well as a range of other attrition processes involving different combinations of firers (F) and targets (T).

This research has led to the first mathematical identification of an attrition process that describes the impact of "smart" weapons on the combat environment. It has also described an attrition process that might represent combined forces combat. The smart weapons attrition process is described by the terms (cy^2) and (bx^2) of equations (2.2.7) and (2.2.8). Under conditions in which smart weapons are being used, it is proposed that the firing of a weapon will depend upon the cooperative interaction between two members of the force that is engaged in firing the weapon. One of these members could employ sensors for target detection and control the trajectory of the weapon while the other member would actually load and fire the weapon, for example.

Thus, while the initial motivation for the use of the catastrophe functions was simply the need to produce a generator of attrition coefficient relationships of the Lanchester type, this work has led to the possible identification of hybrid combat environments in which force

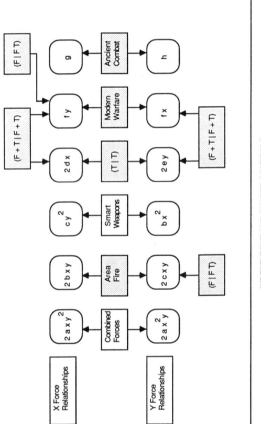

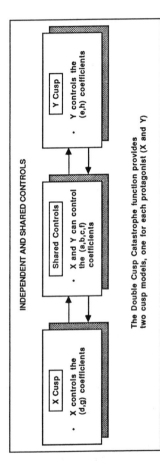

FIG 2.2.7   *The double-cusp catastrophe can serve as a generator of multiple-element Lanchester-type attrition equations (After Woodcock (10))*

attrition may be caused by more than one process. While the original Lanchester-type equations describe situations where only one type of combat takes place at any given time, the catastrophe analysis suggests that particular types of combat attrition process may be interdependent and could occur simultaneously. Thus the catastrophe theory-based analysis may provide new clues to the nature of the elaborate multiforce interactions that can take place on the modern battlefield. Analysis of this possibility is the subject of on-going research.

2.2.4   Force Multipliers Don't Always Act as Force Muiltipliers

Models based on population dynamics have provided an understanding of why factors that act as force multipliers don't always act as such under all conditions. This finding is based on a consideration of force growth and competitive impact models describing the interaction of two military forces (F_1 and F_2) which involve properties identified by Woodcock and Dockery (68) as mobilizaton factors, supply capabilities, and competitive impact parameters.

$$dF_1/dt = (m_1/S_1) \left\{ S_1 - F_1 - \beta_{12}F_2 \right\} F_1 \qquad (2.2.9)$$
$$dF_2/dt = (m_2/S_2) \left\{ S_2 - F_2 - \beta_{21}F_1 \right\} F_2 \qquad (2.2.10)$$

In these equations the symbols F_i, m_i, and S_i represent the force strength, mobilization factor, and supply capability of the ith force (i = 1, 2); and the expressions represent the competitive impacts of force 2 on force 1 and force 1 on force 2 respectively.

The conditions under which the competitive impact of force 1 on force 2 is greater than the ratio of the supply capabilities for force 2 compared with force 1 and where the competitive impact of force 2 on force 1 is greater than the ratio of the supply capabilities for force 1 compared with force 2 can be described by the force trajectories presented in Figure 2.2.8. This figure shows that elements of force 1 will survive for initial force ratios where (F_2/F_1) < 1 while force 2 will be annihilated and, for initial force ratios where (F_2/F_1) > 1, elements of force 2 will survive and force 1 will be annihilated.

These outcomes are sensitive to relatively small changes in the levels of the two opposing forces in force ratio conditions close the separatrix line (A = B). Close to this line small changes in force ratio can have a dramatic impact on the combat outcome. Thus small changes represented by path (a-b), and path (c-d) result in changes in the eventual victor of the combat engagement. By contrast, in regions far from the (A=B) seperatrix, the outcome of the modeled combat is relatively insensitive to small changes in force ratio. For example, changes represented by paths (e-f) and (g-h) lead to no difference in the eventual combat outcome (Figure 2.2.8).

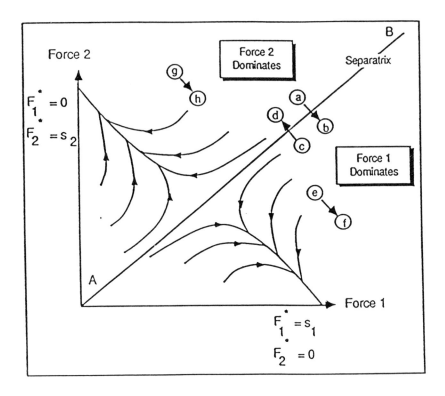

FIG 2.2.8   *Force multipliers don't always act as force multipliers.*
              (After Woodcock (10)).

2.2.5   Population-Dynamical Models of Insurgent Force Strength

A military force-strength model based on population
dynamics can provide a new type of understanding of the
dynamics of insurgent force activities (Woodcock and
Dockery (69)). This model is based on the assumptions that
a society supports the growth of a military force (F_1),
that elements of the force become disaffected and either
join an insurgent force (F_2) or take no further part in
military activity, and that elements of the insurgent force
are destroyed by military action. The model is expressed
in equations (2.2.11) and (2.2.12).

$dF_1/dt = m_1(1-F_1/S_1))F_1 - m_5(1-\exp\{-(m_2F_1)/m_5\})F_2$ (2.2.11)
$dF_2/dt = m_4m_5(1-\exp\{-(m_2F_1)/m_5\})F_2 - m_3F_2$ (2.2.12)

where S_1 is the supply capability of the society for the
military force and the terms $m_1, ..., m_5$ are coefficients
describing various aspects of the force mobilization,
disaffection, recruitment, and attrition processes.

Analysis of these equations shows that the qualitative behavior of the process is critically dependent upon the value of the supply capability (S_1). For low supply capabilities, the levels of the military and insurgent forces reach stationary state values without exhibiting an oscillation, while, for intermediate supply capability values, the force levels undergo a damped oscillation to reach stable stationary state levels. For supply capability values above a critical level, the force levels exhibit sustained oscillations known as limit cycles as the result of a process known as Hopf bifurcation (70) (Figure 2.2.9). This analysis shows that where sustained force strength oscillations take place, both military and insurgent forces can exhibit periods of relative strength and weakness with respect to their adversaries. Such an understanding may provide the basis for the development of new methods for the tactical control of insurgents.

2.2.6   Chaotic Dynamical Systems Models

The combat environment can exhibit extremely erratic and even choatic behavior under appropriate conditions. Many, if not all, combat modeling and decision aiding facilities do not expose the analyst and decision-maker to such erratic or chaotic conditions so that they are often ill-prepared to deal with such conditions when they appear in actual combat. Chaos can represent the degree of uncertainty in the planning process and the emergences of chaotic behavior in a military system can reflect conditions where the controls acting on a system become ineffective.

Mathematical analyses have revealed that the solutions of some very simple equations can exhibit very elaborate patterns of behavior. Thus, as the values of the influences acting on some very simple, deterministic, systems are increased in a linear manner, these systems can exhibit behavior characterized, in turn, by trajectories which form point attractors, limit cycles, and apparently random or chaotic orbits. The concepts of point attractors, limit cycles, and chaotic orbits are part of a new language which is emerging from the study of advanced mathematics and its application to the analysis of complicated systems and can provide a new language for the description of combat. Using this new language has led to the discovery of new and unexpected relationships between military system variables as well as the prediction of new types of military behavior.

Wassermann described catastrophe unfoldings which distinguish between spatial and temporal control factors (31). Based on this analysis Woodcock coined the phrase "space-equivalent and time-equivalent unfoldings" to describe events at fixed spatial locations at different times, and fixed points in time at different spatial locations (55), (56). Dockery and Woodcock (61) have explored the nature of these unfoldings and have

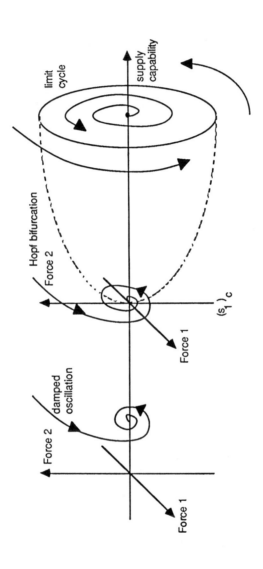

FIG 2.2.9   *Sustained oscillations can occur in some command and control situations (After Guckenheimer and Holmes (2))*

demonstrated that at least some of them can exhibit chaotic behavior under appropriate circumstances.

There are a total of ten cusp-like space- and time-equivalent unfoldings (55), (56). The emergence of chaotic behavior has been demonstrated in at least some of the six space-equivalent catastrophes. One of these catastrophes has the form:

$$V(x,t) = x^4 + ux^2 + t^2x^2 + vx + t^2x + wtx \qquad (2.2.13)$$

where x is the behavior variable and t, u, v, and w are control factors, with the spybol t explicitly respresenting a temporal control factor and the symbols u, v, and w representing spatial control factors.

Fiegenbaum (1), for example, has demonstrated that iteration of an equation of the form:

$$f(x) = 4\mu x(1 - x) \qquad (2.2.14)$$

where μ is a coefficient whose value is in the range 0.0 to 1.0, can exhibit chaotic behavior for values of μ close to unity as shown in Figure 2.2.10 (which was produced by Dockery and Woodcock (61)). For increasing values of μ above 0.73, the plot of f(x) against x appears to be increasingly erratic and becomes chaotic for μ - 0.98, for example.

It is also possible to generate chaotic behavior from at least some of the space equivalent catastrophes. Thus, manipulation of equation (2.2.13) produces the following relationship:

$$f(t) = 4\mu t (1 - t/4\mu) - v \qquad (2.2.15)$$

where w (which is set equal to -4μ) and v are catastrophe control factors. Iteration of f(t) as a function of t can generate chaotic behavior for particular values of the μ and v coefficients (Figure 2.2.11). The graph of equation (2.2.15) for μ = 0.55, v = -0.2 appears to be relatively well behaved while the graph of this equation for μ = 0.55, v = -0.3 is extremely erratic (61).

In other studies, Woodcock (71) has investigated the nature of systems of difference equations which are based on those described earlier by Henon (72). The Henon equations possess very complicated properties which have been described in terms of a "strange attractor" ((72), Civitanovic (73), Ruelle and Takens (74), (9), Campbell and Rose (75), Sparrow (76), for example). This study (71) has revealed that linear changes in system variables can generate very elaborate patterns of behavior. Examples of such behavior are shown in Figures 2.2.12a-c.

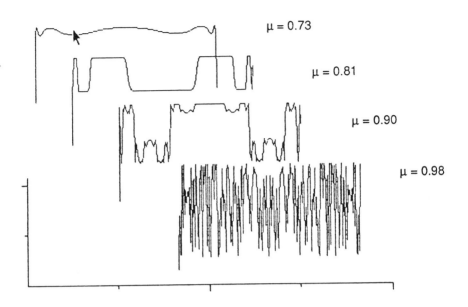

FIG 2.2.10   *Chaotic behavior generated by iteration of the function*
f(x) = 4 μ × (1-x). (After Dockery and Woodcock (61)).
Iteration of the function f(x) = 4 m × (1-x) illustrate a rapid
approach to chaos for values of μ close to unity. Tic marks
on the ordinate are for 0.5 and 1.0, the abcissa runs from 0.0
to 2.0. Tracings are offset by a constant amount for display.

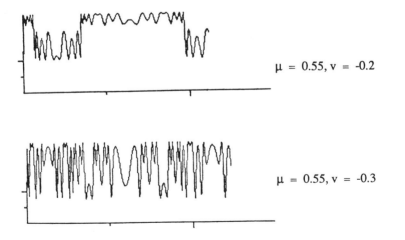

FIG   2.2.11   *Chaotic behavior generated by iteration of a space-*
equivalent catastrophe. (After Dockery and Woodcock (61)).

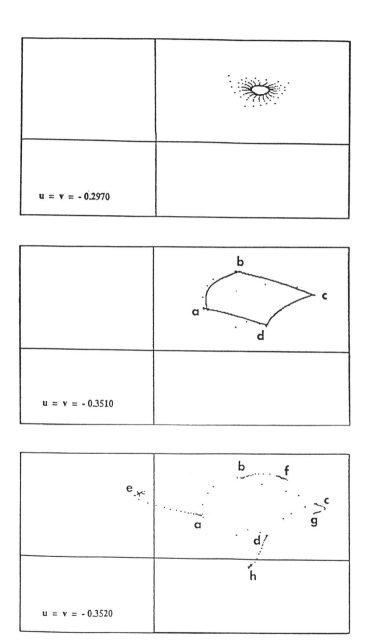

FIG 2.2.12   Chaotic behavior in a simple system. (After Woodcock (71))

For positive values of the variables u and v the system appears to possess a single point attractor with a single transient. Setting u and v both equal to -0.297 produces conditions in which the point attractor has undergone a Hopf bifurcation and a limit cycle trajectory has been created (Figure 2.2.12a). With the variables both set equal to -0.351 (Figure 2.2.12b), the limit cylce is transformed into a "rectangular attractor" (71). Positions (a, b, c, and d) on this attractor act as the sources for transient "arms" at the end of which are located separate attractors with spiral transients (at positions e, f, g and h, respectively) when the values of u and v are changed to -.0.352, for example (Figure 2.2.12c). Further changes in these variables generate even more elaborate patterns of system behavior. The nature of this behavior and its application to military systems is a matter for on-going research.

2.2.7   *Cellular Automata can Stimulate the Combat Environment*

Cellular automata are elemental computing devices which occupy cells on a physical map, and which act independently based on a small set of internal rules. These rules typically prescribe actions to be taken based on the immediate physical environment of the automaton. The theory of cellular automata has been developed over the last thirty years by mathematicians, computer scientists, and biologists to describe the survival, reproduction, and evolution of complex organizational forms with the aid of large numbers of identical, simple, elements which are capable of interaction and change (Farmer et al. (77), Wolfram (78)). They have been used in a number of applications, including models of the properties of physical (Margoulus (79), Toffoli (80), and Vichniac, (81)) and self-organizing systems (Kauffman, (82)). Cellular automata have also been applied to problems in such areas as image processing, logic transforms, and logic processing (Preston and Duff (83) and Preston (84)). They have also been used to provide the basis for new types of computing machine (Hillis (85) and Toffoli (86)).

2.2.7. *(i)   Automata Rules*

The value and excitement of cellular automata lies in finding the simplest body of rules that can both generate nontrivial global combat-like phenomena and provide a new understanding of the combat process itself by squeezing the maximum amount of behavioral complexity from the least complicated set of rules. Woodcock et al. (15) have used cellular automata as part of a research project to find new ways of understanding the nature of the combat environment in terms of spatially and temporally discrete dynamical systems.

While each cell possesses very simple properties, a large ensemble of them can exhibit very elaborate behavior due to the large number of neighbor-neighbor interactions. The imposition of simulated topographical barriers inhibits the movement of simulated forces. Such movement requires an increase in the complexity of the automata rules that compensates for the increase in the complexity of the simulated battlefield. This increase in automata rule complexity can be interpreted as an increase in the command and control capabilities provided to the elements of the simulated forces.

The behavior of each automaton involves performing some form of predetermined response to achieve a defined goal and depends upon the number of its "friendly" and "unfriendly" neighbors and such factors as the presence of barriers to movement. A typical goal could involve the capture of the base camp of one side in a simulated conflict by automata representing combat elements of an adversarial force. Basic cellular automata have only one rule and therefore can perform only one type of task. Enhanced automata have several rules and can perform more elaborate tasks. The interaction of different, and sometimes conflicting, rules can generate very complicated patterns of behavior. In practice each automaton can be provided with a set of rules which permit them to perform tasks which can be described as situation assessment, movement, action, and activity coordination and which appear to be illustrative of at least some aspects of military combat.

The assessment of situations by cellular automata elements involves the use of *assessment rules* to determine whether a given automaton has "friendly" or "unfriendly" neighbors. The movement of cellular automata involves the use of *suppoprt threshold rules*, which can represent the instructions for some form of concerted military movement and provide the basis for determining whether or not each automaton should advance toward or retreat from a specific goal. Cellular automata actions involve the use of *engagement rules*, which control the nature of the interaction of automata representing hostile foreces after situation assessment and movement activities have been performed. Barriers (which can represent a range of topographical and other features) can have a profound and often unexpected impact on the pattern of automata movement and the nature of this impact is defined by a series of *substrate rules* (Woodcock (87)).

2.2.7. (ii)   Combat Activities

In a simple goal-directed automata combat activity characterized as a "capture the flag" engagement, each of two adversarial forces use simple rules in an attempt to occupy and therefore capture the base camp of its opponent. Typical initial force deployment conditions are represented by the arrangement of automata shown in Figure 2.2.13a. A full-scale attack in which elements of each force are engaged along a significant frontal area is illustrated in Figure 2.2.13b. A counter-attack by the blue forces

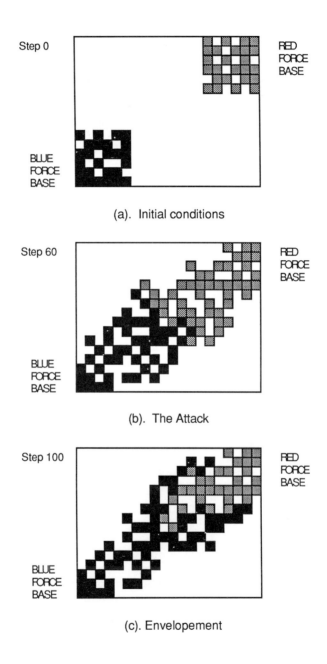

(a). Initial conditions

(b). The Attack

(c). Envelopement

FIG 2.2.13   *Cellular Automata: capture the flag   (After Woodcock et al (15)).*

(Figure 2.2.13c) leads to a repulsing of the red advance and the mounting by the blue forces of a two-pronged enveloping attack involving a combination of frontal and flanking movements against the remaining red forces.
Cellular automata simulations can provide a method both for assessing the fundamental impact of barriers on the behavior of actual military forces, and for determining those conditions under which these barriers can be avoided or circumvented. From the initial deployment of automata illustrated in Figure 2.2.14a, forward movement leads to a condition in some "pioneering" elements of the blue force penetrate the gap between the barriers (Figure 2.2.14b). However, subsequent blue and red force interactions lead to a condition of stalemate where the forces attempt to move around the barriers, but are unsuccessful (Figure 2.2.14c). Under these conditions the barriers slow down the free movement of the forces and these forces are unable to make significant advances without considerable modifications being made to the rules responsible for generating their behavior.
Movement of elements of the opposing forces through the gap between two simulated topographical barriers requires change in the automata rules which can be interpreted as an increase in the command and control capabilities provided to the elements of the simulated forces. Under such circumstances, forward movement of pioneering elements of the blue force permits them to penetrate the gap between the barriers and establish a bridgehead (Figure 2.2.15a). From this bridgehead, elements of the blue force advance in significant numbers, mount an attack (Figure 2.2.15b) and capture the red force base (Figure 2.2.15c).

2.2.8   Summary

The models of military systems described in this section draw on such areas as catastrophe theory, dynamic, stochastic, and chaotic systems including strange attractors, population dynamics, and cellular automata which provide the basis for the development of a new understanding of the modern combat environment. Catastrophe theory organizes information, creates new knowledge, and acts as a starting point for further investigations. Models based on catastrophe theory have been used to illustrate the impact of command and control capabilities, firepower, and force strength on military force survivability. The validity of this approach has been established by the use of sophisticated new statistical procedures to analyze the output from elaborate simulation models of the combat environment. A framework based on catastrophe theory that can generate all the commonly used Lanchester-type of combat attrition equations (such as modern warfare, ancient combat, and area fire) as well as equations representing new types of combat process (such as smart weapons fire) has also been developed.
Models of military behavior motivated by models of population dynamics assume that individual mobilization is

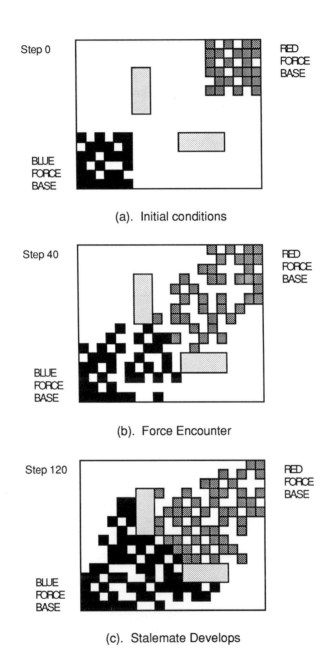

(a). Initial conditions

(b). Force Encounter

(c). Stalemate Develops

FIG 2.2.14   *Cellular Automata: the impact of barriers (After Woodcock et al (15))*

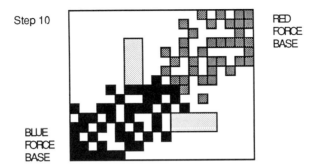

(a). Blue Force Bridgehead Established

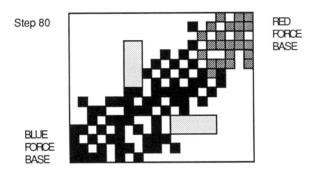

(b). Blue Force Advances in Strength

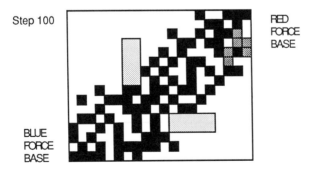

(c). Red Force Base Captured

FIG 2.2.15   *Cellular Automata: the impact of increased command and control capabilities (After Woodcock et al (15))*

responsible for military unit growth, that the support provided by a societal infrastructure can influence this growth, and that competition between opposing forces can lead to the annihilation or coexistence of these forces. Another model provides a new insight into the nature and impact of force multipliers while other models describe how a linear change in the value of a variable identified as the supply capability of a system can result in the emergence of limit cycle oscillations through the process of Hopf bifurcation. Under particular conditions even simple mathematical models can exhibit chaotic behavior. Chaos can represent the degree of uncertainty in the planning process and the emergence of chaotic behavior in a military system can reflect conditions where the controls acting on a system become ineffective. Models of such behavior which are under development are aimed at providing new insights into the causes and effects of such conditions in the military context.

Cellular automata can both generate nontrivial global combat-like phenomena and provide a new understanding of the combat process itself by squeezing the maximum amount of behavioral complexity from the least complicated set of rules. The imposition of simulated topographical barriers inhibits the movement of simulated forces. Such movement requires an increase in the complexity of the automata rules that compensates for the increase in the complexity of the simulated battlefield. This increase in automata rule complexity can be interpreted as an increase in the command and control capabilities provided to the elements of the simulated forces. The development of advanced mathematical models of combat and their hosting within the electronic workbench environment is the subject of on-going research and additional results will be presented elsewhere in due course.

2.2.9   *References*

1. Feigenbaum, M.J., 1982, In 'Order in Chaos', Campbell, D. and Rose, H. (eds). Horth-Holland, Amsterdam and New York.

2. Guckenheimer, J. and Holmes, P., 1983, 'Nonlinear Oscillations, Dynamical Systems, and Bifurcations of Vector Fields', Springer-Verlag, New York.

3. Holden, A.V. (ed)., 1986, 'Chaos', Manchester University Press, Manchester.

4. May, R.M., 1976, *Nature*, 261, 459-461.

5. May, R.M., 1977, *Nature*, 269, 471-477.

6. Prigogine, I., 1980, 'From Being to Becoming'. W.H. Freeman, San Fransisco.

7. Thompson, J.M.T., 1982, 'Instabilities and Catastrophes in Science and Engineering, John Wiley, Chichester.

8. Thompson, J.M.T., and Stewart, H.B., 1986, 'Nonlinear Dynamics and Chaos', John Wiley, Chichester.

9. Velo, G and Wightman, A.S., 1985, 'Regular and Chaotic Motions in Dynamical Systems', Plenum Press, New York and London.

10. Woodcock, A.E.R., 1986, 'An Investigation of Catastrophe Theory as a Command and Control Device', Synetics Corporation, Rome, New York.

11. Woodcock, A.E.R., 1987, In: *'Proceedings of the Second International Conference on C³ Information Technology and Management Information Systems'*, 31-37, The Institution of Electrical Engineers.

12. Woodcock, A.E.R., and Dockery, J.T., 1984, 'Application of Catatrophe Theory to the Analysis of Military Behavior', SHAPE Technical Centre, The Hague, The Netherlands, Consultants Report, STC: *CR-56*.

13. Woodcock, A.E.R., and Dockery, J.T., 1987, *Signal*, April, 43-52

14. Woodcock, A.E.R., 1986, In: *'Proceedings of the Ninth MIT/ONR Workshop on C³ Systems'*, 213-218, MIT, Cambridge, Mass.

15. Woodcock, A.E.R. Cobb, L. and Dockery, J.T., 1988, *Signal*, January, 39-50.

16 Hayes-Roth, F., Waterman, D.A., and Lenat, D.B., 1983, 'Building Expert Systems', Addison-Wesley, Reading Mass.

17. Winston, P.H., 1984, 'Artificial Intelligence', Addison-Wesley, Reading Mass.

18. Barr, A. and Fiegenbaum, E.A., 1981, 'The Handbook of Artifical Intelligence', *1,2,3*, William Kaufmann, Los Altos.

19. Fiegenbaum, E.A., and McCorduck, P., 1983, 'The Fifth Generation', Addison-Wesley, Reading Mass.

20. Ayer, A.J., 1952, 'Language, Truth and Logic', Dover, New York.

21. Boden, M., 1977, 'Artificial Intelligence and Natural Man', Basic Books, New York.

22.   Guyton, A.C., 1981, 'Textbook of Medical Physiology', Saunders, New York.

23.   Marr, D., 1982, 'Vision', W.H. Freeman, San Fransisco.

24.   Nowakowska, M,. 1986, 'Cognitive Sciences', Academic Press, New York.

25.   Popper, K.R., 1983, 'Objective Knowledge', Oxford University Press, Oxford.

26.   Popper, K.R., and Eccles, J.C., 1977, 'The Self and Its Brain', Routledge and Kegan Paul, London.

27.   Shafto, M. (Ed)., 1985, 'How We Know', Harper and Row, New York.

28.   Shepherd, G.M., 1983, 'Neurobiology', Oxford University Press, Oxford.

29.   Williams, P.L., and Warwick, R., 1980, 'Gray's Anatomy', Churchill Livingstone, Edinburgh.

30.   Thompson, D'A.W., 1917, 'On Growth and Form', Cambridge University Press, Cambridge.

31.   Wassermann, G., 1975, *Acta Mathematica*, 135, 57-128.

32.   Thom, R., 1969, *Topology*, 8, 313-335.

33.   Thom, R., 1975, 'Structural Stability and Morphogenesis', W.A. Benjamin, Reading Mass.

34.   Brocker, T. and Lander, L., 1975, 'Differential Germs and Catastrophes', London Mathematical Society Lecture Notes, *17*, Cambridge University Press, Cambridge.

35.   Poston, Tim and Stewart, Ian, 1978, 'Catastrophe Theory and Its Applications', Pitman, London.

36.   Zeeman, E.C., 1977, 'Catastrophe Theory, Selected Papers 1972-1977', Addison Wesley, Reading Mass.

37.   Zeeman, E.C. and Trotman, D., 1976, In: 'Structural Stability, The Theory of Catastrophes and Applications', (Hilton, P. (Ed)). Lecture Notes in Mathematics, *525*, 263-327, Spriner-Verlag, Berlin and New York.

38.   Woodcock, A.E.R., and Poston, T., 1974, 'A Geometrical Study of the Elementary Catastrophes', Lecture Notes in Mathematics, *373*, Springer-Verlag, Berlin and New York.

39.   Arnold, V.I., 1984, 'Catstrophe Theory', (Tr. by R.K. Thomas)., Springer-Verlag, Berlin and New York.

40.   Adelman, I. and Hihn, J.N., 1982, *J. Conflict Resolution*, 26, 592-620.

41.   Beaumont, J.R., 1982, *Int. J. Man-Machine Studies*, 16, 113-145.

42.   Berry, M.V., 1976, *Adv. Phys.*, 25, 1-26.

43.   Cobb., L., 1987, *Behavioral Science*, 23, 360-374.

44.   Cobb., L., 1981, In: 'Statistical Distributions in Scientific Work', Taille, C., et al. (eds), *4*, 67-90.

45.   Gilmore, R., 1981, 'Catastrophe Theory for Scientists and Engineers', Wiley Interscience, New York.

46.   Guastello, S.J., 1987, *J. of Applied Psychology*, 72, 165-182.

47.   Hilton, P. (ed)., 1978, 'Structural Stability, The Theory of Catastrophes and Applications', Lecture Notes in Mathematics, 525, Springer-Verlag, Berlin and New York.

48.   Janich, K., 1974, *Math. Ann.*, 209, 161-180.

49.   Lu, Y.-C., 1980, 'Singularity Theory and an Introduction to Catastrophe Theory', Springer-Verlag, Berlin and New York.

50.   Thompson, J.M.T, and Hunt, G., 1973, 'A General Theory of Elastic Stability', John Wiley, London.

51.   Stewart, I., 1981, *Physica*, 2D, 245-305.

52.   Stewart, I.N., and Woodcock, A.E.R., 1981, *Bulletin of Mathematical Biology*, 43, 279-325.

53.   Stewart, Ian, and Woodcock, Alexander, 1984, *Math. Proc. Camb. Phil. Soc.*, 96, 331-349.

54.   Wilson, A., 1981, 'Catastrophe Theory and Bifurcation Applications to Urban and Regional Systems', Croom-Helm, London.

55.   Woodcock, A.E.R., 1978, *Bulletin of Mathematical Biology*, 40, 1-25.

56.   Woodcock, A.E.R., 1978, *Bulletin of Mathematical Biology*, 41, 101-117.

57.   Woodcock, Alexander and Monte Davis, 1978, 'Catastrophe Theory', E.P. Dutton, New York.

58.   Woodcock, A.E.R., and Dockery, J.T., 1984,. In: 'The
      Use of Artifical Intelligence in the Analysis of
      Command and Control', by Dockery, J.T. and van den
      Driessche, J., SHAPE Technical Centre, The Hague,
      The Netherlands, Technical Report, TM:749.

59.   Woodcock, A.E.R., and Dockery, J.T., 1986). In:
      Woodcock, A.E.R., 1986, 'An Investigation of
      Catastrophe Theory as a Command and Control Device',
      (Appendix A), Synetics Corporation, Rome, New York.

60.   Dockery, J.T., and Chiatti, S., 1986, *European Journal
      of Operations Research, 24*, 46-53.

61.   Dockery, J.T., and Woodcock, A.E.R., 1986, 'Models of
      Combat II: Catastrophe Theory and Chaotics Behavior',
      (Pre-print).

62.   Isnard, C.A. and Zeeman, E.C., 1976, In: *The Use of
      Models in the Social Sciences*, Collins, L., (ed)., 44-100,
      Tavistock Publications, London.

63.   Holt, R.T., Job, B., and Marcus, L., 1978, *Journal of
      Conflict Resolution*, 22, 171-208.

64.   Cobb, L., 1983, 'A Maximum Likelihood Computer
      Program to Fit a Statistical Cusp Hypothesis', SHAPE
      Technical Centre, The Hague, The Netherlands.

65.   Lanchester, F.W., 1914, *Engineering*, 98, 422-423.

66.   Taylor, J.G., 1983, 'Lanchester Models of Warfare', *I,
      II*. Operations Research Society of America,
      Alexandria, Va.

67.   Cobb, L., and Harrison, G., 1985, 'A Computer Program
      to Solve Stochastic Lanchester Equations', The
      Organization of the Joint Chiefs of Staff, The
      Pentagon, Washington, D.C.

68.   Woodcock, A.E.R., and Dockery, J.T., 1986. In:
      Woodcock, A.E.R., 1986, 'An Investigation of
      Catastrophe Theory as a Command and Control Device',
      (Appendix B), Synetics Corporation, Rome, New York.

69.   Woodcock, A.E.R., and Dockery, J.T., 1986, In:
      Woodcock, A.E.R., 1986, 'An Investigation of
      Catastrophe Theory as a Command and Control Device',
      (Appendix B), Synetics Corporation, Rome, New York.

70.   Marsden, J.E., and McCracken, M., 1976, 'The Hopf
      Bifurcation and Its Applications', Springer-Verlag,
      New York.

71. Woodcock, A.E.R., 1987, 'A Strange Attractor', (pre-print).

72. Henon, M., 1976, *Comm. Math. Phys.* 50, 69-77.

73. Civtanovic, P. (ed.), 1984, 'Universality in Chaos', Adam Hilger, Bristol.

74. Ruelle, D., and Takens, F., 1971, *Comms. Math. Phys.*, 20, 167-192.

75. Campbell, D., and Rose, H., 1983, 'Order in Chaos', North-Holland, Amsterdam and New York.

76 Sparrow, C., 1982, 'The Lorenz Equations: Bifurcations, Chaos, and Strange Attractors', Springer-Verlag, New York.

77. Farmer, D., Toffoli, T., and Wolfram, S., (eds.), 1984, 'Cellular Automata', North-Holland, Amsterdam and New York.

78. Wolfram, S., 1984, *Physica*, 10D, 1-35.

79. Margoulis, N., 1984, *Physica*, 10D, 81-95.

80. Toffoli, T., 1984, *Physica*, 10D, 117-127.

81. Vichniac, C.Y., 1984, *Physica*, 10D, 96.

82. Kauffman, S.A., 1984, *Physica*, 10D, 145-156.

83. Preston, K., Jnr., and Duff, M.J.B., 1984, 'Modern Cellular Automata', Plenum Press, New York.

84. Preston, K., Jnr., 1984, *Physica*, 10D, 205-212.

85. Hillis, W.D., 1984, *Physica*, 10D, 213-228.

86. Toffoli, T., 1984, *Physica*, 10D, 195-204.

87. Woodcock, A.E.R., 1987, 'Cellular Automata Rules for Battlefield Simulations', (Pre-print).

Reducing Uncertainty and Ignorance in C2 Systems

C.J. Harris
(Southampton University)

2.3.1   Introduction

Chapter 2.1 addressed the main sources and implications for uncertainty in command and control systems. Reasoning from uncertain, incomplete, and sometimes inaccurate information is necessary whenever the C3 system has to interact in an intelligent manner (through say situation assessment or decision making) with the environment. The perception of the world is achieved through the set of knowledge sources of data fusion (see Chapter 3) produced through partially processed sensory information and intelligence. This information is limited by sensor capabilities (temporal and spatial coverage, resolution, ambiguity rejection, portion of EM spectrum utilised, diversity of features, response times etc) and is inherently *evidential*. This is particularly the case with knowledge based expert systems which have to reason on the basis of evidence generated by multi-sensor integration according to the degree of partial belief associated with each sensor. Even with prior knowledge of a situation in which a knowledge source is observing a portion of the environment, to locate and classify objects within it, by multi-sensor integration is not a simple problem, since this presupposes that each knowledge source partially understands what observables/characteristics can be linked with each type of object.

2.3.1.(i)   Evidential Reasoning

There are essentially three types of evidence:-

(1)   **Uncertain evidence.** A knowledge source probing an environment does not usually reveal exactly what the environment contains, instead it provides or attributes various degrees of belief to several environmental possibilities. The attributed degrees of belief to a proposition reflect the relative strength of the contributing evidence. For example it may have determined from ESM and radar tracks that a sensed aircraft target is

unlikley to be a fighter, but can't determine if
it is a bomber or a transport (EW or AWACS or
other) without other information (such as EO or
ESM).

(2) **Incomplete evidence.** The precise degree of belief
accorded to *every* environmental possibility
generally cannot be determined on the basis of a
single body of evidence, nor indeed is it possible
to know all the possibilities or eventualities
(yet this is the basis for Bayesian statistics).
Any single body of evidence can determine the
degree of belief in a possible outcome, but should
remain uncommitted to another. That is *ignorance*
(as a measured bounded quantity) is an important
component of evidence (or the lack of).
Understanding what remains unknown (and therefore
requires unveiling) is just as important a
component of evidential information as what is
known. For example, an incoming unobserved sea
skimming missile over the radar horizon is of
greater significance than the observed fighter at
60km that deployed it!

(3) **Incorrect evidence.** If a knowledge source's
information is largely correct, except for sensor
resolution or numerical 'noise' errors, then it
contains some 'measurement' errors within its
conclusions. However if the evidence is incorrect
(say detecting an erroneous target), through some
qualitative error or hypothesis, then it contains
gross errors. This is further complicated by
bodies of evidence being correct about some
things, yet incorrect, to varying degrees, about
others.

2.3.2   *Representation of Uncertainty of Evidence*

Since evidence is typically uncertain, something beyond
the purely logical approach is necessary. Boolean
expressions of propositional truth and falsity are
inadequate (so called crisp logic) as they fail to
represent the various degrees of partial beliefs.
Nevertheless, evidence in the context of intelligent aids
to decision making in C² systems, is well expressed in
terms of truths and falsities, therefore whilst Boolean
expressions are inadequate they must be represented, or
included as a subset of a more representative probabilistic
description. Partial beliefs are usually represented by
probability measures and as such have formed the basis of
much work in expert systems.

For a given situation suppose that there are fixed sets
of environmental possibilities:-

$$F = \{q_1, q_2, \cdots q_n\}$$ (2.3.1)

with every proposition of interest either true or false
relative to each possibility. Then every proposition is
completely defined by the subset A of F (A $\subseteq$ F) containing
exactly those q_i for which the proposition is true. For
example F = {Aircraft Target Classes} = {air superior,
multi-role, bomber, transport, helicopter, drone, missile,
other}. A = {Fighter} = {air superior, multi-role} $\subseteq$ F
(Papoulis (1)). The possibility measures, a partial belief
in each q_i, can be expressed through a Bayesian
distribution over F(1). This is achieved by distributing a
unit of belief amongst the elements, q_i, of F based upon
their relative occurrance or likelihood. That is

$$dist : F \rightarrow [0, 1]$$

$$\sum_{q_i \varepsilon F} dist(q_i) = 1 \qquad\qquad (2.3.2)$$

Thus, for all ($\forall$) A $\subseteq$ F, the probability of the
proposition A, P(A) defined on the space F is

$$P(A) = \sum_{q_i \varepsilon A} dist(q_i) \qquad \forall A \subseteq F \qquad\qquad (2.3.3)$$

from which it follows that P(A) = 1 - P($\overline{A}$)   ($\overline{A}$ signifies
the complement or <u>not</u> of A).

Clearly the Bayesian approach requires the evolution of
the probability of every proposition in the space F,
irrespective of the quality of evidence. Given that there
is a wealth of statistical data, this methodology is
appropriate, however when it is impoverished or even
unobtainable, an alternative methodology such as Dempster-
Shafer or Fuzzy sets is necessary. Reasoning based upon
subjective elements of these probabilities is similarly
intractable. Also what is the interpretation of low
probabilities, have we not observed an object and have no
reason to believe its presence, or have strong reasons to
disbelieve its presence? Intuition fails at this level of
detail leading to frequently inconsistent, unjustifiable
and unverifiable models of C^2 systems! Here point
estimates of probabilities are incompatible with the
required level of precision for decision making. In the
following we shall in turn consider the merits of Bayesian
(including learning schematas such as Neural Nets),
Dempster Shafer, and Fuzzy sets to model and reduce the
uncertainty associated with C^2 systems.

2.3.3   *Bayesian Hypothesis Methods in Data Fusion and Decision Making*

Traditional surveillance, communications and pattern
recognition systems have utilised Bayesian hypothesis
testing procedures when the data is corrupted by noise.
Performance can be improved by utilising multiple sensors

or data sources, but straightforward extension of classical Bayesian methods requires some care as the evaluation of detection thresholds of individual sensors is often coupled through the distributed sensor network. Data fusion through the combination of detector decisions via say Bayesian probabilistic methods have used AND logic combiners, AND/OR combiners as well as optimal receiver operator characteristics (Tenney and Sandell, (2)). None of these approaches addresses the derivation of optimal fusion rules (based upon Bayes rule) for distributed sensors whose individual detector decision rules are known. More recently Chair and Varshney (3), have developed a data fusion association or a comparison system of the AND/OR type, for distributed sensors that weights individual decisions according to the uncertainty of each detector.

2.3.3. (i) Bayesian Hypothesis Testing for Multi-Sensor Data Fusion

Consider a binary testing problem - the detection or absence of an airborne target - from an array of n independent sensors, x_i (i = 1, 2, ...n). There are two hypotheses:

H_0: target is present with *apriori* probability $P(H_0) = P_0$
H_1: target is absent, with *apriori* probability $P(H_1) = P_1$

Each detector produces a binary output $z_i = \pm 1$ according to whether H_0 or H_1 is determined by a decision rule $z_i = f_i(x_i) ..., i = 1, 2, ... n.$
The data fusion system has as inputs (see Figure 2.3.1) the individual detector decision, each weighted by the reliability or uncertainty factors, W_i, associated with each detector. The optimal decision rule is given by the likelihood ratio

$$\frac{P(z_1, ...z_n/H_0)}{P(z_1, ...z_n/H_1)} \begin{array}{c} H_0 \\ \gtrless \\ H_1 \end{array} \frac{P_1}{P_0} \qquad (2.3.4)$$

(or by Bayes rule (P(AB) = P(A/B).P(B))

$$\frac{P(H_0/z_1, z_2, ...z_n)}{P(H_1/z_1, z_2, ...z_n)} \begin{array}{c} H_0 \\ \gtrless \\ H_1 \end{array} 1 \qquad (2.3.5)$$

Given that a target has been detected by the ith sensor, there is a probability, P_{fi}, of false alarm, and similarly a probability, P_{mi}, of non-detection. Thus $(1-P_{fi})$ is the probability of correct detection, and $(1-P_{mi})$ is the probability of correct *non-detection* of the target, when the ith sensor produces an output of $z_i = 1$ and -1 respectively. If A_0 is the set of all i for which $z_i = +1$;

A_1 is the set of all i for which $z_i = -1$ (ie set of all detector outputs that decides on the absence of a target), then

$$P(H_0/z_1, z_2, \dots z_n) = \frac{P(H_0, z_1, \dots z_n)}{P(z_1, \dots z_n)}$$

$$= \frac{P_0}{P(z_1, \dots z_n)} \cdot \prod_{A_0} (1 - P_{fi}) \cdot \prod_{A_1} P_{fi} \qquad (2.3.6)$$

Similarly

$$P(H_1/z_1, \dots z_n) = \frac{P_1}{P(z_1, \dots z_n)} \prod_{A_0} P_{mi} \prod_{A_1} (1 - P_{mi}) \qquad (2.3.7)$$

Substituting (2.3.6) and (2.3.7) into the likelihood ratio (2.3.5) and taking logs gives the log-likelihood ratio test for data fusion as

$$log \frac{P(H_0/z_1, \dots z_n)}{P(H_1/z_1, \dots z_n)}$$

$$= log \frac{P_0}{P_1} + \sum_{A_0} log\left(\frac{1 - P_{fi}}{P_{mi}}\right) + \sum_{A_1} log\left(\frac{1 - P_{mi}}{P_{fi}}\right) \underset{H_1}{\overset{H_0}{\gtrless}} 0 \qquad (2.3.8)$$

Hence we have the data fusion system of Figure 2.3.1 where the individual decision weights are determined by sensor reliability and are given by

$$W_0 = log\left(\frac{P_0}{P_1}\right)$$

$$W_i = \begin{cases} log\left(\dfrac{1 - P_{fi}}{P_{mi}}\right) & if \quad z_i = +1 \\[2ex] log\left(\dfrac{1 - P_{mi}}{P_{fi}}\right) & if \quad z_i = -1 \end{cases} \qquad (2.3.9)$$

This optimum log-likelihood binary data fusion system is a feedforward refinement process, which generates a threshold type decision output based upon the weighted sum of current individual decision outputs; no memory or prior experience with similar sensor data patterns is involved. Clearly more intelligent decisioning could be achieved if reward/penalty based feedback from the output to the weighting functions based on successful/unsuccessful target detection, occurs. Finite Stochastic Automata and Neural Nets offer the potential for supervised learning to achieve truly AI based data fusion and decisioning.

2.3.3. (ii)   Supervised Learning

In learning pattern classification, the environment offers the system a sequence of measured vectors or patterns which must be recognised or classified. The learning system adjusts its decision process so as to maximise the probability of misclassification through the matching of patterns/observations to output classes. Most significantly, since the resulting decision rules also apply to *similar* patterns not observed, or in the training sequence, the system performs a generalisation by containing greater knowledge than say just a look up table would (just as humans do in recognising situations/objects by *similar* prior experiences that is learning by example). Supervised learning pattern recognition has been well researched (Duda and Hart (4), and Cohen and Feigenbaum (5)), of the many methods those based upon stochastic approximations Barto and Anandan (6) are most general and can be shown to converge.

Consider again the binary testing problem of the previous section for which there are two class types (H_0, H_1) with *apriori* probabilities P_0, P_1 respectively. For an observed input pattern vector $\underline{x}(k) = (x_1(k), x_2(k), \ldots x_n(k))^T$ or equivalently $\underline{z}_k = (z_1, (k), \ldots z_n(k))^T$ at time k, the data fusion output is $U_k = +1$ or -1 (target detected or absent) by equation (2.3.5) if the Bayesian a posteriori probabilities,

$$P(H_0/\underline{x}_k) - P(H_1/\underline{x}_k) \underset{H_1}{\overset{H_0}{\gtrless}} 0 \qquad (2.3.10)$$

However, $P(H_i/\underline{x}_k)$ are not known, we therefore must find a parameter vector $\underline{a} \varepsilon \ R^n$ such that

$$P(H_0/\underline{x}_k) - P(H_1/\underline{x}_k) \to \underline{a}^T \underline{x}_k \qquad (2.3.11)$$

and the decision process is

$$U_k = \begin{cases} 1 & \text{if } \underline{a}^T \underline{x}_k > 0 \\ -1 & \text{if } \underline{a}^T \underline{x}_k < 0 \end{cases} \qquad (2.3.12)$$

There are a variety of schemes for optimal selection of the parameter $\underline{a}$ for example, the mean squared approximation to the cost functional

$$J(\underline{a}) = E[\{\underline{a}^T \underline{x} - U(k)\}^2]$$

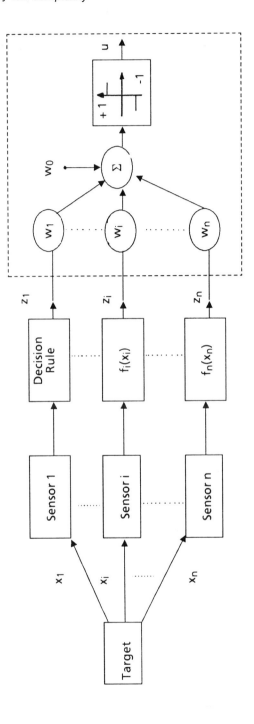

FIG 2.3.1   *Binary data fusion*

But the functional $J(\underline{a})$ is not known, however the observed sample error $(\underline{a}_k^T. \underline{x}_k - U(k))^2$ and sample gradient $\Delta(\underline{a}_k)$ is:-

$$\Delta(\underline{a}_k) = 2(\underline{a}_k^T \underline{x}_k - U(k))\underline{x}_k \qquad (2.3.13)$$

The consequent learning algorithm is of the one step ahead error predictor type (cf Kalman filters, stochastic approximation algorithms etc)

$$\underline{a}_{k+1} = \underline{a}_k - \rho_k [\underline{a}_k^T \underline{x}_k - U(k)]\underline{x}_k \qquad (2.3.14)$$

which converges (Kasyap et al, (7)) to the optimum parameter $\underline{a}^0$ with probability one if the gains ρ_k satisfy the conditions,

$$\rho_k \geq 0, \quad \sum_k \rho_k = \infty, \quad \sum_k \rho_k^2 < \infty$$

This algorithm is directly related to the pseudoinverse of linear operators, regression analysis, and to single level neuron type adaptive elements such as the albus perception (Betz et al (8), Ellison (9)) which have been used for learning control and prediction. Of particular importance to C² systems is the ability of such learning schematas to deal with not only vector patterns to scalar decisions, but also to higher level processes such as vector-to-vector, matrix-to-vector, and matrix-to-matrix that is *networks* of elements implementing learning pattern-classification algorithms. It is unlikely that single element gradient-descent learning algorithms, such as (2.3.14), will cope with a matrix of parameters for networks of elements, owing to the inability to determine local gradients and the multimodality of the cost functional $J(\underline{a})$. What is required in such cases is not just input-output relationships but also input vector patterns to internal states/connections, and internal states to output variables together with assessments of their (at least) collective behaviour under learning. A current popular research area that satisfies these requirements are neural net models.

2.3.3. (iii)   Neural Net C² Systems

Much of the current AI research is directed towards emulating the human parallel processing capability, this processing ability derives from the large number of neurons used (approximately 10^{10} with 10^{14} connections), rather than speed (order of milliseconds for humans compared with nanoseconds for modern Von Neuman Computers). A variety of neural net models have been derived (Albus (9), Forrest et al (10)) for applications including pattern recognition for words and text (Gardner et al, (11)), image processing

(Forrest, (12)) and prediction and control (Betz et al (8)). Whilst they all differ in structure and complexity they share common features.

(i)   'nodes' or 'association cells' are connected such that each node state effects other connected nodes through the strength or weight of connectivity; this in turn determines the network dynamics or output processing of input stimuli

(ii)   The new state of a node is dependent on the output of other neurons.

(iii)   The network training or learning is the process whereby the weights of node connection are modified to achieve the desired output processing for a specific input or training data. In C^2 input data vectors might be a set of measured parameters associated with a target (such as target ESM data (PRF, pulse width), IR signature, range, range rate and contextual data such as relative target size through imaging and intelligence), and output might be target identification and perhaps recommended response/actions. The significant point here, is the potential ability of the neural net to iteratively learn from a position of ignorance, to generalise and classify patterns; whereby the 'teacher' provides corrective feedback information about the desired function or pattern to be learned.

Model neuron behaviour. A neuron, with state s_i, receives a large number of input signals, $\underline{x}$ = (x_1, ...x_n)^T, processes them and produces an output z_i. Let W_{ij} be the *synaptic* weights associated with the input signals (x_j) to the ith neuron, then the total stimulation to the ith neuron is

$$s_i = \sum_j W_{ij} x_j + \theta_i \qquad (2.3.15)$$

where θ_i represents some threshold or resting potential (which we can ignore for practical purposes). Usually the neuron output z_i is a nonlinear function of its state that is

$$z_i = f(s_i(t))$$

which is often of a saturation type (as in the Hopefield net (13) and Bayesian hypothesis testing procedure of Section 2.3.3. (i)).

$$z_i = Sgn(\sum_j W_{ij} x_j + \theta_i) \qquad (2.3.16)$$

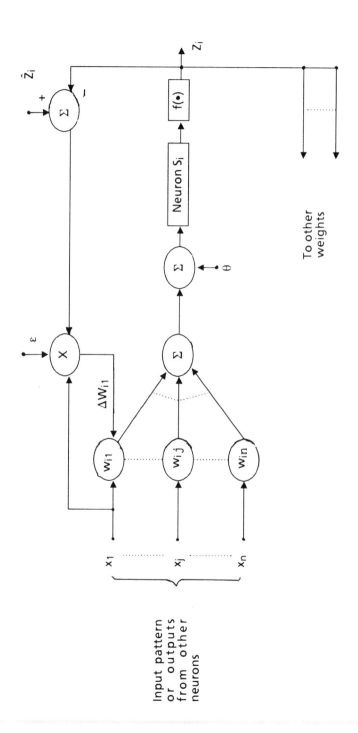

FIG 2.3.2 *Neural net learning models*

Neurons have the ability to modify the synaptic weights vector $\underline{W} = \{W_{ij}\}$ depending upon the input/output signals. For example the *delta rule* computes the error between actual and target output for a given input, and modifies the connection weights W_{ij} to obtain an output closer to the desired target, that is

$$\Delta W_{ij} = \varepsilon(z_i - \hat{z}_i)x_j \qquad (2.3.17)$$

where ε is a constant step size parameter and $\hat{z}_i$ is the desired output. (Figure 2.3.2 illustrates the feedback or learning loop).

It would appear that the whole input sensory space has to be spanned in order to predict all possible outputs, fortunately the *smoothness* properties of neural nets ensures that 'similar' or noisy input vectors lead to similar outputs. Also the generalisation property implies that if we have two input pattern vectors which are measurably close, and one of them has been previously observed (and therefore has an associated pattern weight vector $\underline{W}$), then the neural net can produce an output close to the correct output. Undoubtedly the rapid developments in parallel computer architectures (see Section 1.2), such as SIMD - eg ICL DAP, or MIMD - eg Meiko transputer computer surface, computers, will instigate early real time applications to the areas of data fusion, situation assessment and decision making in C^2 systems.

2.3.4   *The Dempster-Shafer Approach to Sensor Integration*

The fundamental problem with the Bayesian approach is the failure to represent the *incompleteness* of the evidence. However, the principle of indifference is frequently utilised to overcome this shortcoming, whereby *equal* probabilities are ascribed to the various propositions when the available evidence provides no reason for preferring one proposition to another. For example if we have evidence to support the disjunction of mutually exclusive observations A_1 (= fighter), A_2 (= transport A/C), A_3 (= helicopter), A_4 (= missile), as $P(A) = \text{prob}(A_1, \cup A_2 \cup A_3 \cup A_4) = 0.8$, clearly $P(\overline{A}) = 0.2$ (= probability of drone or other aircraft class). The principle of indifference suggests that $P(A_i) = 0.2$, therefore $P(A_i \cup A_j) = 0.4$ for $i, j = 1, 2, 3, 4$. $i \neq j$, which implies that there is a distinct preference for the disjunction of any two propositions over the third. If however the evidence does not provide a preference for these disjunctions over the singletons, there are several incompatible ways in which the principle could be used. Further what if these propositions are themselves disjunctions of other more primitive propositions?

This confusion is avoided in the Dempster-Shafer (DS) theory (Shafer (14)), in which the belief in a proposition A is represented by an *evidential interval* $EI(A) = \{S(A)\ p\ell(A)\}$ of the closed real interval [0, 1]. The lower bound $S(A)$

represents the degree to which the evidence *supports* the propostion, $p\ell(A)$ represents the degree to which the evidence fails to refute the proposition (or for which it is *plausible*). In Bayes theory prob $(A) = S(A) = p\ell(A)$, that is the evidential interval has collapsed to a point – when we have precise likelihood assignment. The principle of indifference applies in D-S theory, but now over intervals instead of probabilities, with singleton propostions and their disjunctions being assigned identical intervals, thus avoiding the dilemma of Bayes approach.

Let F be a set of propositions about the exhaustive and exclusive possiblities of some numerical or symbolic variable x. F is called the *frame of discernment* and 2^F is the set of all subsets of F. Let $m(q)$ (so called basic probability assignment or mass) denote the degree of belief that the true value of x is in a subset $q \subseteq F$, *and* no smaller subset of q. It is useful to think of x as a mass of weight $m(q)$, which is constrained to stay in q, but is otherwise free to move inside q. This freedom represents the noncommittal nature of our belief or ignorance.

Assume that F has subsets q_1, ...q_n (called *focal elements*) – representing the set of knowledge sources propositions such that

$q_i \neq \phi$ (the empty or null set), and $m(q_i) \neq 0$

$$m(\phi) = 0$$
$$0 < m(q_i) \leq 1$$
$$\sum_{i=1}^{n} m(q_i) = 1 \qquad\qquad (2.3.18)$$

That is a knowledge source distributes a unit of belief across the set of propositions or focal elements, q_i, in proportion to its weight (or amount of evidential support). The so called *partial belief* $m(q_i)$ represents the proportion of belief committed to the proposition q_i. $m(q)$ can be interpreted as a segmented/partitioned line of unit length, with the length of each sub segment corresponding to the mass attributed to its focal elements q_i.

$$\underset{0}{\overset{\text{m}(q_1) \quad\quad \text{m}(q_2) \quad\quad\quad\quad \text{m}(q_i) \quad\quad\quad\quad \text{m}(q_n)}{\rule{8cm}{0.4pt}}} \quad 1$$

A *simple* probability mass function $m(q)$, $q \neq \phi$, and $q \neq 0$ is such that

$$m(q) + m(\theta) = 1 \qquad\qquad (2.3.19)$$

A special case is when $m(F) = 1$, and $m(q_i) = 0$ for all $q_i \neq F_j$. This function represents total ignorance, since no proportion of belief is committed to a proposition $q_i \subseteq F$. The definition of a partial belief function establishes an isomorphism between subsets of F and logical propositions. Hence the concepts of conjunction , disjunction, negation and implication are equivalent to the logic forms of intersection, union, complementation and inclusion.

We define the *support* or total belief function $S: 2^F \rightarrow [0, 1]$ as:-

$$S(q_i) = \sum_{q_j \subseteq q_i} m(q_i) \ , \ 1 \le i,j \le n \qquad (2.3.20)$$

this represents the degree or total belief to which the evidence *supports* the proposition q_i (and all its subsets). Note in general:

$$S(q_i) \ + \ S(\overline{q}_i) \ne 1$$

$$\sum_{i=1}^{n} S(q_i) \ne 1 \qquad (2.3.21)$$

(Compare with equations (2.3.18) and (2.3.19)) - this is because some mass may be attributed to propositions that imply neither q_i nor $\overline{q}_i$.

The *plausibility* function $p\ell: 2^F \rightarrow [0, 1]$ is defined by

$$p\ell(q_i) = 1 - S(\overline{q}_i) = 1 - \sum_{q_j \subseteq \overline{q}_i} m(q_j) \qquad (2.3.22)$$

which represents the degree to which the evidence fails to refute the proposition q_i, that is the degree to which it remains *plausible*; $S(\overline{q_i})$ is called the *disbelief function*. The following propositions are possible but not necessary:-

(i) $q_i = F$ for some i , $1 \leqq i \leqq n$

that is one of the focal elements of F can be the entire frame of discernment

(ii) $q_i \cap q_j \ne 0; 1 \leqq i, j \leqq n$

that is the focal elements need not be disjoint (cf probability distributions).

(iii) $\underset{i=1}{\cup} .. \ q_i \ne F$

that is the union of all the focal elements need not cover the entire frame of discernment, that is there is a domain of ignorance or uncertainty.

The *evidential interval*, $EI(q_i)$ or uncertainty of q_i is given by

$$EI(q_i) = p\ell(q_i) - S(q_i) = 1 - S(\overline{q}_i) - S(q_i) \qquad (2.3.23)$$

represents the residual ignorance associated with q_i. Hence complete ignorance is the unit interval $EI(\cdot)$ = [0, 1], that is the proposition is plausible, but there is no evidence to support it. A zero interval represents the Bayes probability assignment to q_i (that is Bayesian probability is a special case of D-S theory); in general

$$S(q_i) \le P(q_i) \le p\ell(q_i) \qquad (2.3.24)$$

   Example 2.3.1: Consider the possible set of hypothetical radar emitter types F = $\{q_1, q_2, q_3\}$, produced by missile systems SA6, SA4, and *other* types. An SA6 uses emitter q_1, $\{SA6 = \{q_1\}\}$, whereas it is known that a SA6 and SA4 use either an emitter q_1 or q_2, $(SA6 \cup SA4 = \{q_1, q_2\})$, also no other missile uses emitter q_1, $(\overline{SA6} = \{q_2, q_3\})$, the probability masses of these propositions are determined as m(< SA6, SA6 $\cup$ SA4, $\overline{SA6}$, θ >) = <0.4, 0.2, 0.3, 0.1> (θ = uncertainty or ignorance). Then the evidential intervals for the above propositions are:

$$EI(SA6) = (0.4, 0.8), EI(SA6 \cup SA4) = (0.7, 1), EI(\overline{SA6}) = (0.2, 0.6)$$

that is there is greatest support and smallest uncertainty for the proposition the missile is of type SA4 or SA6.
   Should the evidential intervals become either $\{0, 0\}$ or $\{1, 1\}$ the corresponding propositions become false and true, and the rules of combining evidential intervals (Lu and Stephanou (15)) reduce to the corresponding rules of propositional calculus. Therefore belief mass functions and the associated propositional inference rules enable a natural transition between probabilistic and deterministic propositional calculus. The primary advantage of the partial belief method of representing knowledge, is that each knowledge source can express itself at the most appropriate level, allowing decisions over one proposition or another to be suspended until further data is available. This representation of ignorance reduces the possiblity of false knowledge source reports. Each knowledge source can represent exactly what it believes without eliciting unsupported statements or speculating about outcomes for which it has little or no supportive data.

2.3.4. (i)   *Consensus of Evidence - Data Fusion*

Dempsters Consensus rule (Shafer (14)), combines multiple bodies of information such as to increase the belief in propositions that are supported by the various bodies of evidence and away from all others. Bayes rule for probabilities is just a special case of Dempsters rule. To derive Dempsters rule, consider two knowledge sources, KS$_1$ and KS$_2$ with respective partial belief functions $\{m_1(q_{1i})\}$ and $\{m_2(q_{2j})\}$; j, i = 1,2, ...n. Construct a square of unit area (representing certainty), with each side representing the partial belief functions of KS$_1$, KS$_2$ respectively.

The horizontal strip of weight $m_1(q_{1i})$ represents the committment by KS$_1$ to q_{1i} whereas the vertical strip $m_2(q_{2j})$ represents the committment by KS$_2$ to q_{2j}. The intersection of these strips commits a belief $m_1(q_{1i})$ $m_2(q_{2j})$ to the combination of propositions $q_r = q_{1i} \cap q_{2j}$; there may of course be other squares (such as $q_{2j} \cap q_{1i}$, $q_r = q_{2j} \cap \theta_1 = \theta_2 \cap q_{1i}$ for θ_1, θ_2 = ignorance in KS$_1$, KS$_2$ respectively) which contributes to this proposition. Therefore the total belief committed to the proposition $q_r = q_{1i} \cap q_{2j} \subseteq F$ is

$$m(q_r) = \sum_{q_r = q_{1i} \cap q_{2j}} m_1(q_{1i}) m_2(q_{2j}) \qquad (2.3.25)$$

Clearly some belief in the *orthogonal* combination of KS$_1$, KS$_2$ (m = m$_1$ $\oplus$ m$_2$) is committed to the proposition $q_{1i} \cap q_{2j}$ = ϕ, the null set. Since the total belief in the combined knowledge source must be unity, then equation (2.3.25) must be normalised by disregarding all squares for which $q_{1i} \cap q_{2j}$ = ϕ, or equivalently multiply (2.3.25) by the correlation factor

$$k = (1 - \sum_{q_{1i} \cap q_{2j} \neq \phi} m_1(q_{1i}) m_2(q_{2j}))^{-1} \qquad (2.3.26)$$

Hence we have Dempsters consensus rule for combining evidence from two orthogonal or *independent* knowledge sources as

$$m(q_r) = k \sum_{q_r = q_{1i} \cap q_{2j}} m_1(q_{1i}) m_2(q_{2j}) \qquad (2.3.27)$$

If k = 0, then m = m$_1$ $\oplus$ m$_2$ does not exist and m$_1$ and m$_2$ are totally contradictory sources of evidence, and as such k is a correlation measure between data sources. Dempsters rule (2.3.27) can be generalised to n-sources of evidence (Lu and Stephanou, (15)) and can also be used to generate the evidential intervals (measures of ignorance) of combined data or knowledge sources. Given propositions A,

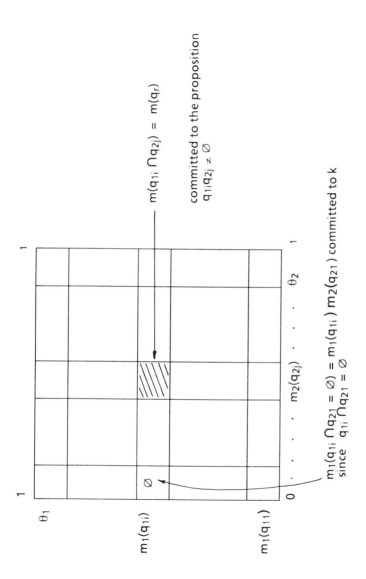

FIG 2.3.3 *Consensus evidence square*

B $\subseteq$ F, with evidential intervals EI(A) = {S(A), pℓ(A)}, EI($\overline{B}$) = {S(B), pℓ(B)}, then evidential interval of their combined knowledge/evidence is given by

$$EI(A) \oplus B) = \{1 - k(1 - S(A))(1 - S(B)), \, k\,p\ell(A)\,p\ell(B))$$

(2.3.28)

where k = $(1-(S(A)S(\overline{B}) + S(\overline{A}) . S(B)))^{-1}$. This formation of the consensus evidential interval is useful since it demonstrates that Dempsters rule is both commutative and associative, that is the grouping and ordering of combinations of evidence, inferencing etc is immaterial. Also if we denote $\ominus$ as the inverse operator to $\oplus$ in Dempsters rule, then we can *decompose* or retract earlier combinations of evidence or inferences by

$$EI(A) \ominus EI(B) =$$

$$\{k^{-1}(1 - S(B))(S(A)\,p\ell(B) - p\ell(A)\,S(B)), \, k^{-1}(1 - S(B)\,p\ell(A)\,p\ell(B) - S(B))\} \quad (2.3.29)$$

where
k = $(1-S(B))(p\ell(B) - p\ell(A)S(B)) - (1-S(A)p\ell(B)(1-p\ell(B))$

This inversion result enables a conclusion of an earlier consensus to be withdrawn without influencing conclusions reached by other mechanisms. Similarly the *conditional* support for a proposition A given that proposition B is true (A, B $\subseteq$ F) can be generated as

$$S(A/B) = \frac{S(A \cup \overline{B}) - S(\overline{B})}{p\ell(B)}$$

(2.3.30)

Note:
(i)   this result should be compared with the Bayes result

$$p(A/B) = \frac{p(A \cap B)}{p(B)}$$

(ii)   also this consensus rule reduces to a singleton probability for the mass function $m_2(A)$ for a proposition A. Hence for all $q_r \varepsilon F$ the equivalent Bayes rules are

$$m(q_r) = k \sum_{A \cap q_{1i} = A} m_1(q_{1i})$$

(2.3.31)

where

$$k = (1 - \sum_{A \cap q_{1i} \neq A} m_1(q_{1i}))$$

and

$$p(B/A) = \sum_{q_r \, \varepsilon B} m(q_r) \quad , \quad \forall B \subseteq F \qquad\qquad (2.3.32)$$

Example 2.3.2: To illustrate D-S theory in the context of C² systems consider the following hypothetical tactical air threat multi-sensor data fusion system. Our model environmental possibilities (eg targets) are classified as aircraft types = (Air superior, multi-role or ground attack, bomber, EW or AWACS, and other types - such as helicopters, drones, missiles, unknown) $\underline{\Delta}$ (AT1, AT2, AT3, AT4, AT5) sensors are deployed and include ESM or target electronic emissions (pulse repetition frequency - PRF, carrier frequency (RF) and pulse width), target Infra-Red signatures, and Optical. Whilst these are directly measured target features they are independent or disparate knowledge sources reflecting different target spectral and spatial characteristics whose joint information or consensus should provide an improved estimate of target class identification with reduced uncertainty. It is assumed that we have prior parameter distributions of the various aircraft classes electronic and IR emission characteristics; typical parameter *distributions* (each of unity area) are shown in Figure 2.3.4 for emitter RF(GHz), pulse width (μsec) and IR wavelength (μm). The receiver has a specific and limited range, or bandwidth of measurement to provide the degree of resolution required; it is assumed in the example that the passive sensor receivers ranges are respectively (7-8)GHz, (0.3-0.4)μsec, (3-4)μm for RF radar carrier and pulse width, and IR wavelength respectively. As with all measurements there are associated measurement errors, noise etc or simply uncertainty; we shall represent these by $\underline{\theta}$ = (θ_{RF}, θ_{PW}, θ_{IR}, θ_0) = (0.13, 0.15, 0.25, 0.2). Overlaying these receiver ranges on the emitter parameter distributions, produces a variable percentage contribution of each emitter aircraft class to each receiver range (see hatched areas). Normalising these areas to unity and multiplying each by (1-θ), where θ = uncertainty in the receiver's measurements, gives the resulting mass functions of

$$M_{RF}(AT_1, AT_2, AT_3, AT_4, AT_5, \theta_{RF}) = \,<0.2, 0.4, 0.12, 0.15, 0, 0.13>$$

$$M_{PW}(AT_1, AT_2, AT_3, AT_4, AT_5, \theta_{PW}) = \,<0.45, 0.05, 0.25, 0.1, 0, 0.15>$$

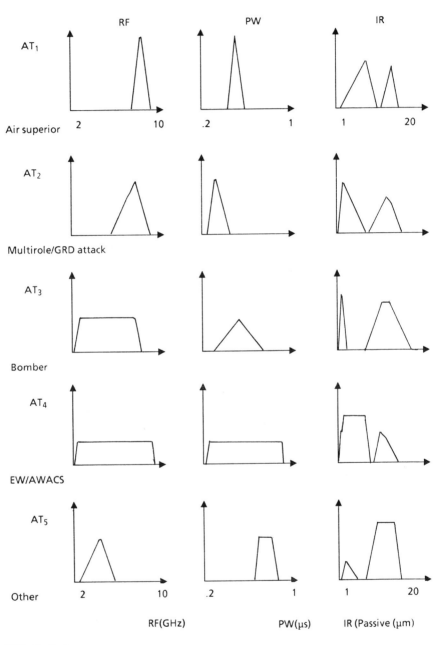

FIG 2.3.4

$$M_{IR}(AT_1, AT_2, AT_3, AT_4, AT_5, \theta_{IR}) = <0.25, 0.3, 0, 0.2, 0, 0.25> \qquad (2.3.33)$$

The optical observations are *known* to be:

$$M_0(\ldots, \theta_0) = <0.4, 0.4, 0, 0, 0, 0.2> \qquad (2.3.34)$$

that is the visual observer considers the aircraft class target to be equally likely an air superior or multi-role fighter, with uncertainty of 20%.

The Dempster consensus square for RF and PW mass functions is shown in Table 2.3.1.

TABLE 2.3.1 *Consensus square for RF and PW mass functions*

RF→	AT_1	AT_2	AT_3	AT_4	AT_5	θ
AT_1	0.09	0.18	0.054	0.0675	0	0.0585
AT_2	0.01	0.02	0.006	0.0075	0	0.0065
AT_3	0.05	0.1	0.03	0.0375	0	0.0325
AT_4	0.02	0.04	0.012	0.015	0	0.013
AT_5	0	0	0	0	0	0
θ	0.03	0.06	0.018	0.0225	0	0.0195
PW ↑						

Given that the aircraft classes are disjoint (that is $AT_i \cap AT_j = \phi$ for $i \neq j$), then from Dempsters rule (2.3.27) the composite mass function for a *correlation* of k = 2.4 is

$$M_{RF \times PW}(AT_1, AT_2, AT_3, AT_4, AT_5, \theta) =$$

$$<0.43, 0.21, 0.19, 0, 0.05> \qquad (2.3.35)$$

and the evidential intervals for the various aircraft classes are:

$$EI_{RF \times PW}(AT_1, AT_2, AT_3, AT_4, AT_5)$$

$$= (\{0.43, 0.48\}, \{0.21, 0.26\}\{0.19, 0.24\}\{0, 0.05\})$$

This information can now be combined with the independent IR mass function knowledge source (2.3.33) by Dempsters rule to give a consensus or composite mass function and evidential intervals for the knowledge sources of RF, PW and IR respectively as

$$M_{RF \times PW \times IR}(AT_1, AT_2, AT_3, AT_4, AT_5, \theta)$$

$$< 0.48, 0.27, 0.1, 0.133, 0, 0.026 >$$

(2.3.36)

$$EI_{RF \times PW \times IR}(AT_1, AT_2, AT_3, AT_4, AT_5)$$

$$= (\{0.48, 0.506\}, \{0.27, 0.296\}, \{0.1, 0.126\}, \{0.133, 0.159\}, \{0, 0.026\})$$

Clearly there has been increased support for AT_1 and AT_2 and a decrease in uncertainty. Finally if we add the observers mass functions (2.3.34) the overall mass functions and evidential intervals are:

$$M_{RF \times PW \times IR \times 0}(AT_1, AT_2, AT_3, AT_4, AT_5) =$$

$$< 0.58, 0.33, 0.03, 0.05, 0, 0.01 >$$

(2.3.37)

$$EI_{RF \times PW \times IR \times 0}(AT_1, AT_2, AT_3, AT_4, AT_5)$$

$$= (\{0.58, 0.59\}, \{0.33, 0.34\}, \{0.03, 0.04\}, \{0.05, 0.06\}, \{0, 0.01\})$$

On the basis of the RF and PW sensor data, the D-S theory leads to three hypotheses AT_1 {0.43, 0.48}, AT_2 {0.21, 0.26} and AT_3 {0.19, 0.25} with 5% uncertainty or ignorance, AT_1 is clearly favoured to AT_2 or AT_3, although there is no distinguishable difference between AT_2 and AT_3. Utilising all sensor data sources indicates hypothesis AT_1 is significantly greater than AT_2 with AT_3 being eliminated - with an uncertainty of only 1%.

The Dempster-Shafer consensus of evidence method has recently been extended by Shenoy and Shafer (16) to propagating belief functions in diagnostic trees (for use in fault diagnosis, inferencing etc), to belief function predictors for learning systems (Harris (17)), and have found increasing applications in C^2 data fusion (Wilson, (18); Waltz and Buede, (19); Bonasso, (20), Garvey et al 21)). The great strength of the Dempster-Shafer approach to evidential reasoning is its ability to deal with limited information from multiple bodies, albeit independent sources. A complementary method of dealing with uncertain data that reflects human decision processes is fuzzy logic.

2.3.5   *Application of Fuzzy Logic to C² Systems*

The problem of dealing with uncertainty of evidence or imprecision in decision making can also be resolved by modelling the system and its probabilities by Fuzzy sets and logic (Zadeh, (22)). The central concept of fuzzy sets is the membership function, $\mu(\cdot)$, which like a probability distribution takes on values between 1 and 0. The membership function is determined *subjectively* via the process of knowledge elicitation, experience or guesswork - no formalised procedure exists for its evaluation (Gaines, (23)); however despite this obvious shortcoming the precise membership distribution shape does not greatly affect the resulting inferences drawn from the fuzzy calculus, indeed it would appear that fuzzy inferencing is very human-like! Small values represent a low degree of membership, whilst high values represent a high degree of membership or belief, or increasing values represent increases in membership of a set.

Let X be a set of points or objects, x, (say target range, or range rate). Then a membership function $\mu_A(x)$ defines all those points, x, that are contained in the subset $A \subset X$ but also assigns to each point a grade of membership - a number in the interval [0, 1]. Such a subset, A, is called a fuzzy set. It can be thought of as a more generalised form of ordinary set, because an ordinary or deterministic set $\mu_A(x)$ takes on only the binary values $\mu_A(x) = 0$ $(x \notin A)$; $\mu_A(x) = 1$, $(x \in A)$. Fuzzy sets can be used to group points which have subjective or imprecise discriminants, eg the range is 'much' greater than 12km, the range is 'close' to 20 km etc (see Figure 2.3.5a and 2.3.5b respectively)

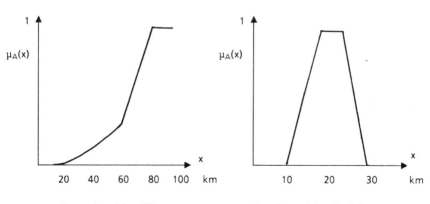

a. Range 'much' > 12km   b. Range 'close' to 20km

FIG 2.3.5   *Fuzzy membership functions*

The calculus of fuzzy sets is based upon a series of propositions that enable us to impute from imprecise inputs, through a model or process, what the imprecision in outputs or conclusions should be:

(i)   **Equal** fuzzy sets A = B: iff $\mu_A(\underline{x}) = \mu_B(x)$ $\forall x$

(ii)   **Complement** of a fuzzy set A is $\bar{A}$ with membership

$$\mu_{\bar{A}}(x) = 1 - \mu_A(x) \ \forall x \qquad (2.3.38)$$

(iii)   **Containment**: $B \subseteq A$ iff $\mu_B(x) \leq \mu_A(x)$ $\forall x$

(iv)   **Union** (the OR operation) of fuzzy sets A, B; is the degree to which x belongs to *either* A OR B is the maximum of their individual membership functions

$$\mu_{A \cup B}(x) = \max_x [\mu_A(x), \mu_B(x)] \qquad (2.3.39)$$

(v)   **Intersection** (the AND operation) of fuzzy sets A, B; is the degree to which x belongs to *both* A AND B, is the minimum of the individual degrees of membership.

$$\mu_{A \cap B}(x) = \min_x [\mu_A(x), \mu_B(x)] \qquad (2.3.40)$$

(vi)   **Composition** applies to bivariate fuzzy relationships. If the fuzzy set A, describes some relationship between X and Y, and B the relationship between Y and Z, with respective membership functions $\mu_A(x,y)$ and $\mu_B(y,z)$ respectively. Then the composition fuzzy set BoA relating X to Z, has a membership function given by

$$\mu_{BoA}(x,z) = \max_y [\min(\mu_A(x,y), \mu_B(y,z))] \qquad (2.3.41)$$

A special case is when we have a functional relationship $y = f(\underline{x})$; between the inputs (say multi-sensor data sources) $\underline{x} = (x_1, x_2, \ldots x_n)$ with associated membership functions $\mu_1(x_1)$, $\ldots \mu_n(x_n)$, and the output y (say the fused picture) as:

$$\mu_0(y) = \max_{y = f(\underline{x})} [\min(\mu_1(x_1), \mu_2(x_2), \ldots, \mu_n(x_n))] \qquad (2.3.42)$$

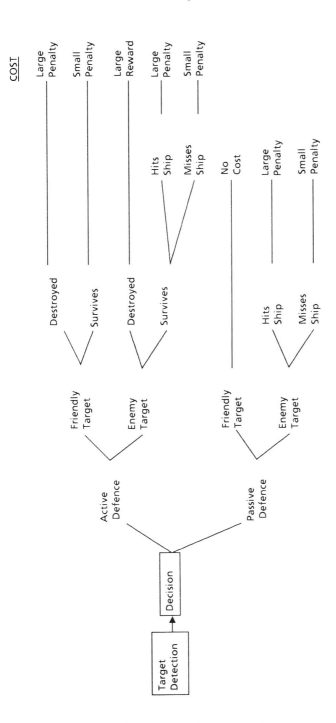

FIG 2.3.6

(vii)   **Implication** A → B; the degree to which some fuzzy proposition A implies another B, is the degree of truth of (either (not A) OR B) that is from:

$$\mu(A \to B) = \mu_{\overline{A} \cup B}(x,y) = max(1 - \mu_A(x), \mu_B(y)) \qquad (2.3.43)$$

This can be generalised, to A and B fuzzy relationships between variables x,y, with membership functions $\mu_A(x,y)$ and $\mu_B(x,y)$, then

$$\mu(A \to B) = \min_{x,y} [max(1 - \mu_A(x,y), \mu_B(x,y))] \qquad (2.3.44)$$

that is A → B, for only as large as the minimum of the levels of implication for each (x,y) over all values of (x,y). Note these definitions of implication are somewhat arbitrary, but are effective for practical purposes in command and control systems.

Of considerable importance in command and control systems are decision trees, with binary splitting or oppportunities that have two decisions or hypothesis H_0, H_1, at each stage and probabilistic or fuzzy measures associated with the tree splits at succeeding stages. An example of this is a small task force Naval Commander who is 'notified' of an unidentified approaching low flying high target, and he has to decide whether or not to actively or passively defend himself. With any decision or action there are associated penalties/rewards or more generally costs which weight or bias the various decisions. For example if he fires at the target, it may be a friendly damaged aircraft, or he may miss it altogether; also if he fails to destroy or decoy away the target, it may be an enemy aircraft that subsequently hits his ship or escorts. A possible simplistic decision tree for this scenario might be seen in Figure 2.3.6.

Associated with each nodal split there are probabilities or likelihoods, for example there is a probability P_1, that the target is friendly (or $(1-P_1)$ that it is enemy); a probability P_2 that given active defence is used the target is destroyed (or $(1-P_2)$ it survives) - irrespective of friendly/enemy type (this is essentially a measure of the ship's weapons protection capability); a probability P_3 that the target hits the ship after active defence has been used (or $(1-P_3)$ it misses after active defence is used); Finally, the probability P_4 that if passive defence is deployed the enemy target hits the ship (or $(1-P_4)$ it misses). Given these probabilities the *Bayesian* probabilistic decision tree is given in Figure 2.3.7.

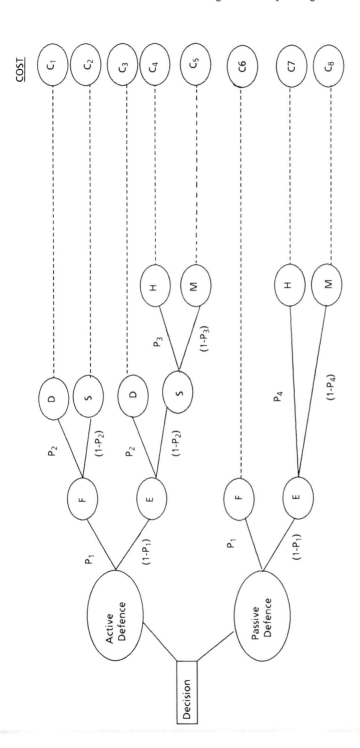

FIG 2.3.7 *Bayesian probabilistic decision tree*
F = Friend, E = Enemy, D = Destroyed, S = Survive, H = Hit, M = Miss, C = Cost

Clearly there are two alternative decisions available, options active defence (AD) or passive defence (PD) with respective averaged costs

$$\widehat{AD} = P_1(P_2 C_1 + (1 - P_2) C_2) + (1 - P_1)(P_2 C_3 + (1 - P_2)(P_3 C_4 + (1 - P_3) C_5)) \quad (2.3.45)$$

$$\widehat{PD} = P_1 C_6 + (1 - P_1)(P_4 C_7 + (1 - P_4) C_8) \quad (2.3.46)$$

Active defence is preferred to passive defence if $\widehat{AD}$ > $\widehat{PD}$, which is readily evaluated if $(P_1 - P_4)$ and $(C_1 - C_8)$ are known with certainty. However the probabilities $(P_1, ..P_4)$ are both time varying, imprecise and situation dependent and can only be realistically represented by their respective fuzzy set membership functions $\mu_1(P_1)$... $\mu_4(P_4)$. In practice the probabilities $P_1, ... P_4$ or their membership functions $\mu_1, ... \mu_4$; are elicited from the user or by post mission analysis. Illustrative membership functions are illustrated in Figure 2.3.8. Given these functions the membership function for the decision variable $s = \widehat{AD} - \widehat{PD}$, can be evaluated from equation (2.3.42) as

$$\mu(s) = \underset{s}{max}[min(\mu_1(P_1), \mu_2(P_2), \mu_3(P_3), \mu_4(P_4))] \quad (2.3.47)$$

Given the membership function which is optimised with respect to the decision variable constraint s, we still have to generate the decision making rule. For binary decision processes, the membership function $\mu_A(x,y)$ for some fuzzy variable/statement/proposition, A, is the extent to which *both* x belongs to the possible set of average costs associated with hypothesis or decision, H_0 *and* y belongs to the possible set of averaged costs associated with the alternative hypothesis H_1; thus from (2.3.39)

$$\mu_A(x,y) = min(\mu_{H_0}(x), \mu_{H_1}(y)) \quad (2.3.48)$$

and the implication of propositions (2.3.44) becomes

$$\mu(A \rightarrow B) = \underset{x,y}{min}[max(1 - min(\mu_{H_0}(x), \mu_{H_1}(y)), \mu_B(x,y)] \quad (2.3.49)$$

In this case the membership function $\mu_B(x,y)$ indicates the preference for the hypothesis or decision H_0 over H_1. Examples include:-

(i) $H_0(H_1)$ is very strongly or strictly preferred to $H_1(H_0)$ if:-

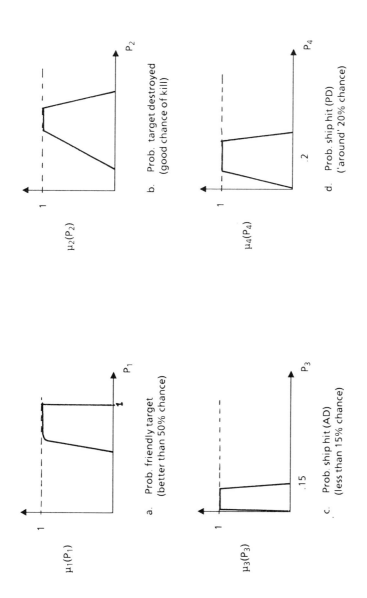

FIG 2.3.8   *Target/operational membership functions*

$$\mu_B(x,y) = \begin{cases} 1 & \textit{If } x - y > 0, (x - y < 0) \\ 0 & \textit{otherwise} \end{cases} \qquad (2.3.50)$$

(ii) H_0 is 'somewhat' preferred to H_1 if:-

$$\mu_B(x,y) = \begin{cases} 1 & \textit{if } (x - y) \geq 2.5 \\ 0.5 + 0.2\,(x - y) & \textit{if } 2.5 \geq (x - y) \geq -2.5 \\ 0 & \textit{if } (x, y) \leq -2.5 \end{cases} \qquad (2.3.51)$$

Note:
(i)   in the context of the above example $x = \hat{AD}$, $y = \hat{PD}$; $s = x - y$.

(ii)   for the strictly preferential hypothesis H_0 of (2.3.50), it can be shown that the membership function (2.3.49) simplifies to

$$\mu(A \to B) = 1 - \max_{x}\,[min\,(\mu_{H_0}(x), \mu_{H_1}(x))] \qquad (2.3.52)$$

Critical to the commander's decision making is the *apriori* requirements of target detection; here uncertainty arises through either false alarms or failure to detect a target; we should therefore include this increased uncertainty prior to the decision process to allocate (or otherwise) resources.   Thence *given* a target has been detected with probability P_0, if P_f is the probability of false alarm with cost C_f, then probability of correct detection is $(1 - P_f)$ with associated cost C_d.   Also if a target is not detected with *apriori* probability P_0', then if P_m is the probability of failing to detect a target or missing it with cost C_m, the probability of correct non-detection of a target is $(1 - P_m)$ with associated cost C_{dm}. The binary target detection process is shown in Figure 2.3.9.   The expected costs of target detection and non-detection are respectively

$$d = P_0((1 - P_f)C_d + P_f C_f) \qquad (2.3.53)$$

$$n = P_0'((1 - P_m)C_{dm} + P_m C_m) \qquad (2.3.54)$$

There are substantial uncertainties associated with the prior probabilities P_0, P_0' (which can be reduced by multi-sensor data fusion); they can for example be represented by the fuzzy membership functions of Figure 2.3.10 - here the probability of target or signal non-detection has been *determined* to be a 'little more likely' than its detection probability P_0.

Similarly the probabilities of false alarm and miss detection are imprecisely known; experience has shown that

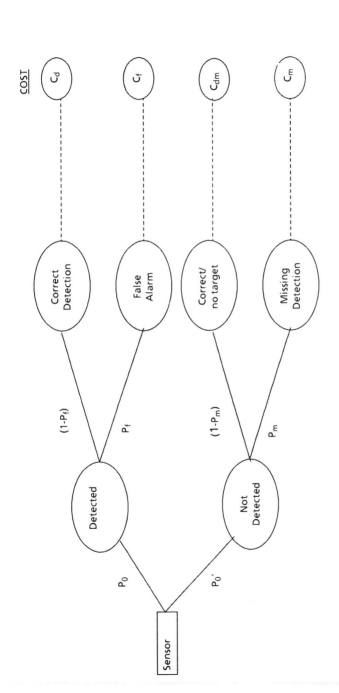

FIG 2.3.9 *Binary sensor detection tree*

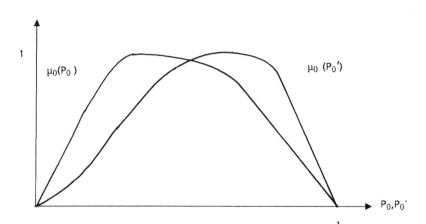

FIG 2.3.10

for illustration the probability of false alarm is 'less
than about 10%' whereas due to EW the probability of miss
detection is 'about 35%' - see Figure 2.3.11.

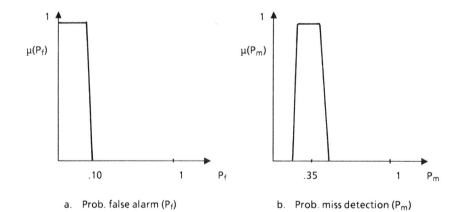

a.   Prob. false alarm (P_f) b.   Prob. miss detection (P_m)

FIG 2.3.11   *Membership functions for detector false alarms and misses*

If we define the detection decision variable as

$$s(P_o, P_0', P_f, P_m) = d(P_0, P_f) - n(P_0', P_m) \qquad (2.3.55)$$

then its membership function is given by equation (2.3.42) as

$$\mu_s(s) = \underset{s}{max} \quad [\underset{P_0, P_0', P_f, P_m}{min} \quad (\mu_0(P_0), \mu_0(P_0'), \mu(P_f), \mu(P_m)] \qquad (2.3.56)$$

subject to the optimising constraint of equations. Given the convex membership functions of figures, the composite output membership function $\mu_s(\bullet)$ is readily evaluated for prescribed cost functions $\underline{C} = (C_d, C_f, C_{dm}, C_m)^T = (+30, -20, +25, -35)^T$ in Figure 2.3.12

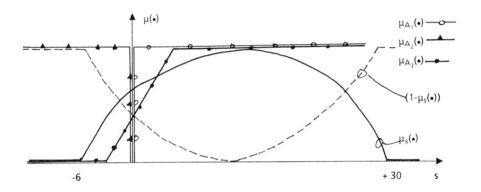

FIG 2.3.12 *Detection composite output and decision membership functions*

The implications of the hypothesis H_0 or H_1 (detection or non-detection respectively) for the membership function $\mu_s(\bullet)$ may be evaluated from equation (2.3.50) by calculating the measure of support for various user defined fuzzy decision propositons (see equations (2.3.51), (2.3.52)). For example proposition:

A₁: It is certainly better to detect (H_0) a target than not to (H_1)

$$\mu_{A_1}(s) = \begin{cases} 1 & If \quad s > 0 \\ 0 & otherwise \end{cases}$$

Hence from Figure 2.3.12 and equation (2.3.12) $\mu(X \to A_1) = 0.33$

A₂: It is certainly better not to detect (H_1) than to detect (H_0):

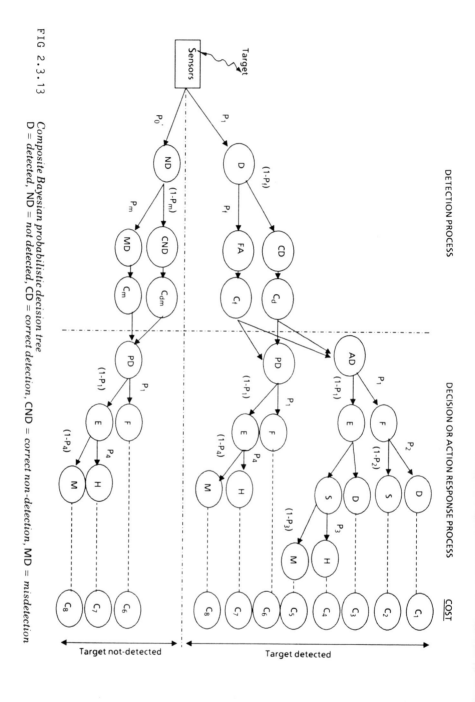

FIG 2.3.13   *Composite Bayesian probabilistic decision tree*
D = detected, ND = not detected, CD = correct detection, CND = correct non-detection, MD = misdetection

$$\mu_{A_2}(s) = \begin{cases} 1 & \textit{If } s < 0 \\ 0 & \textit{otherwise} \end{cases}$$

Hence from Figure 2.3.12 and equation (2.3.12) $\mu(X \rightarrow A_2) = 0$

A3:   Detecting (H$_0$) is better than non-detection (H$_1$):

$$\mu_{A_3}(s) = \begin{cases} 1 & \textit{if } s \geq 2.5 \\ 0.5 + 0.25 & 2.5 \geq s \geq -2.5 \\ 0 & -2.5 \geq s \end{cases}$$

$\mu(X \rightarrow A3) = 0.42$

There is a clear preference (given the prescribed costs) for the target/signal detection hypothesis over non-detection. Should the membership functions for the probabilities change we can either repeat the calculations *a posteriori* or carry out a *apriori* sensitivity analysis to determine the most sensitive probability distributions.

The illustrative composite target detection and defence response system is shown in Figure 2.3.13, it is now possible given the commander's decision propositions are known (see for example equations (2.3.50-51)), to compare the two decision alternatives *Active* Defence/*Passive* Defence.

2.3.6   References

1.   Papoulis, A., 1965, 'Probability, Random Variables and Stochastic Processes', McGraw-Hill, New York.

2.   Tenney, R.R. and Sandell, N.R., 1981, 'Detection with Distributed Sensors', *IEEE Trans AES*, vol. 17, No. 4, pp 501-509.

3.   Chair, Z. and Varshney. P.K., 1986, 'Optimal Data Fusion in Multiple Sensor Detection Systems', *IEEE Trans AES*, vol. 22, No. 1 pp 98-101.

4.   Duda, R.D. and Hart, P.E., 1973, 'Pattern Classification and Scene Analysis', J. Wiley, New York.

5.   Cohen, P.R. and Feigenbaum, E.A., 1982, 'The Handbook of Artificial Intelligence', vol. 3, Los Altos, C.A.: Kauffman.

6.   Barto, A.G. and Anandan, P., 1985, 'Pattern Recognition Stochastic Learning Automata', *IEEE Trans SMC*, vol. 15, No. 3, pp 360-375.

7.   Kasyap, R.L., Blaydon, C.C., and Ku, K.S., 1970, 'Stochastic Approximation' in Adaption, Learning and Pattern Recognition Systems Theory and Applications. Ed. J. Mendel and K.S. Fu. Academic Press New York.

8.   Betz, R.E., Allerton, D., Evans, R.J. and Sathiakumar, S., 1988, 'An AI Based Controller for Dynamic Systems', *Proc 1st IFAC Symposium on Real Time AI Control'*, Swansea (Sept 1988).

9.   Albus, J.S., 1975, 'A New Approach to Manipulator Control: the Cerebellar Model Articulation Controller (CMAC)'. *ASME J. Dynamic Systems, Measurement and Control.* vol. 97, No. 3, pp 220-233.

10.   Forrest, B.M., Rowell, D., Stroud, N., Wallace, D.J. and Wilson, G.V., 1987, 'Neural Network Models', Edinburgh University, Physics Reprint No. 87/419.

11.   Gardner, E., Stroud, N. and Wallace, D.J., 1987, 'Training with Noise: Application to Word and Text Storage', Edinburgh University, Reprint No. 87/425.

12.   Forrest, B.M., 1987, 'Restoration of Binary Images using Networks of Analogue Neurons', Proc. Parallel Architectures and Computer Vision Workshop, Oxford University.

13.   Hopefield, J.J. and Tank, D.W., 1985, 'Neural Computations of Decisions in Optimisation Problems', Bio. Cyt. vol. 52, pp 141-152.

14.   Shafer, G., 1976, 'A Mathematical Theory of Evidence', Princeton University Press, New Jersey.

15.   Lu, S.Y. and Stephanou, H.E., 1984, 'A Set Theoretical Framework for the Processing of Uncertain Knowledge', Proc. Nat. Conf. on AI August 6-10, University of Texas, Austin, USA.

16.   Shenoy. P.P., Shafer, G., 1986, 'Propagating Belief Functions with Local Computations', *IEEE Expert*, Fall Issue 1986, pp 43-51.

17.   Harris, C.J., 1988, 'Some Aspects of the Mathematical Theory on Evidence in Multi-Sensor Data Fusion'. *5th IMA Conference on Control Theory.* Strathclyde University, September 14-16, 1988.

18.   Wilson, G., 1987, 'Multi-sensor Data Fusion in C² Systems' in 'Advances in Command, Control and Communications Systems: Theory and Applications', eds C.J. Harris amd I. White, Peter Peregrinus.

19.   Waltz, E.L., Buede, D.M., 1986, 'Data Fusion and Decision Support for Command and Control', *IEEE Trans SMC*, vol. 16, No. 6, pp 865-879.

20. Bonasso, R.P., 1985, 'Analyst II: A Knowledge Based Intelligence Support Systems', Mitre Corp. Tech. Rept. MTR-84 W00220. April 1985.

21. Garvey, T.D., Lowrance, J.D. and Fischler, M.A. 1981, 'An Inference Technique for Integrating Knowledge from Disparate Sources', *7th Int. Joint Conference on AI*, pp 319-325.

22. Zadeh, L., 1973, 'Outline of a New Approach to the Analysis of Complex Systems and Decision Processes', *IEEE Trans SMC*, vol. 3, pp 28-44.

23. Gaines, B.R., 1976, 'Foundations of Fuzzy Reasoning', *Int. J. Man-Machine Studies*, vol.8, pp 623-668.

Chapter 3
Intelligent data fusion

Toward the Utilization of Certain Elements of AI Technology for Multi-Sensor Fusion

J. Llinas
(Calspan Corp. USA)

3.1.1   Introduction

Technological advances in several fields have resulted in greatly improved performance capabilities for military system sensors. The benefits of very large scale integration (VLSI) and very high speed integrated circuits (VHSIC) in the solid state area, high-precision numerically controlled machines, computer-aided design and computer-aided manufacturing (CAD/CAM), among other design and production improvements, are representative of the means by which modern-day sensors are achieving significant improvements in overall operational proficiency. Representative performance gains include increased resolution, higher detection probabilities at greater ranges, and faster response times. Associated gains in specialized, embedded, and generic digital processors (resulting from essentially the same technology gains described above) have resulted in dramatic potential and actual improvements in sensor data processing power.

Robust exploitation of such improvements through multi-sensor fusion (MSF), however, has to date been confounded by a variety of factors:

-   Most sensors operate in well-defined, and usually narrow portions of the electromagnetic spectrum (i.e., they are "spectrally weak"),
-   amortization costs of technical development, increased costs for associated software, and other economic factors have kept specific sensor system costs relatively high,
-   in spite of significant reductions in size and power requirements, packaging can often be a major obstacle to achieving multi-sensor systems,
-   equivalent gains in the hostile electronic countermeasure systems, driven by advances in the same support technologies as for friendly sensors, have kept hostile capabilities for deception and denial at an equivalent rate of progess.

There are non-technical issues which must also be dealt with if we are to make progress toward the potential benefits of MSF; we must overcome institutional barriers associated with ownership of sensors, sensor platforms, and communications channels as well as service-specific traditions in tactical procedures so that men, processes, and procedures can also aid in achieving the potential benefits of the MSF process.

The spectral narrowness of most sensors keeps constant pressure on technologists and system designers to create new systems to fill spectral niches or exploit ever more detailed subtleties in the observations. Since in many tactical settings there is normally a significant variety of detectable and measurable emissions from an entity of interest, system designers are faced with a difficult tradeoff problem in system design (see Table 3.1.1).

TABLE 3.1.1   *Representative observable-sensor pairings*

Dectectable/Measurable Emissions/Characteristics	Sensors
• RF Emissions	EW sensors (RWR and ESM), COMINT, ELINT
• Infrared Emissions/Contrast	Infrared Imagery, Passive and Augmented
• Acoustic/Seismic Emissions	Acoustic/Seismic Sensors
• Optical Contrast	Television Imagery, Passive and Augmented Direct View Optics, Passive and Augmented Optical Augmentation Sensors
• Radar Cross Section	Radar
• Electro-Optical Emissions	Electro-Optical Sensors
• Mechanical/Structural Vibrations	Laser-Based Sensors
• Hi-Resolution Signatures	NCTR Techniques; MM Wave Radar

Table 3.1.2 (Hofmann (1)) expands on illustrating the difficulties of the multi-sensor system design tradeoff problem by enlarging on the specific attributes of a representative set of sensor types; the table includes operational as well as technical attributes.

TABLE 3.1.2   *Sensor characteristic matrix (Hofmann (1)).*

Sensor Type	Detection Range	Detection Time	Target Identification	Range Measurement	Probability Of Detection	Vulnerability To Detection	Vulnerability To Counter-Measures	All Weather	Twenty-Four Hour	Instantaneous Field-of-Regard
Radar	Long	Moderate	Marginal	Yes	Moderate	High	High	Yes	Yes	Small
IR Imagery – passive – augmented	Moderate Moderate	Moderate to Long	Possible Possible	Relative Only	Low Low	Low High	Moderate Moderate	No No	Yes Yes	Small Small
TV Imagery – passive – augmented	Moderate Moderate	Moderate to Long	Possible	Relative Only	Low Low	Low High	Moderate Moderate	No No	No Yes	Small Small
EW Sensors – RWR – ESM	Short Long	Short Short	Possible Yes	No Possible	High High	No No	High No	Yes Yes	Yes Yes	Large Large
Acoustic/Seismic Sensors	Moderate	Moderate	Possible	Possible	Low	No	Moderate	Yes	Yes	Large
Direct View Optics – passive – augmented	Moderate to Long	Moderate to Long	Possible Possible	Relative Only	Low Low	Low High	Moderate Moderate	No No	No Yes	Small Small
Optical Augmentation Sensors	Moderate	Moderate	Possible	Yes	Moderate	High	Moderate	No	Yes	Small
Passive E-O Sensors – Warning – ESM	Short Long	Short Short	Possible Yes	No Possible	High High	Low Low	Moderate No	No No	Yes Yes	Large Small

It is in part the list of potential benefits resulting from MSF that provides a framework for the resolution of this sensor tradeoff problem. These benefits are shown in Table 3.1.3 (Waltz (2)); system designers must select specific items from this list to establish a basis for the sensor tradeoff.

But this is only one half of the solution to the *sensor* tradeoff problem: the remaining portion is represented by defining the *techniques* for MSF that must be implemented in order to achieve each corresponding benefit. Each technique will impute specific requirements on sensor performance and operational characteristics. One can argue further that such tradeoffs are necessary for solution of the *sensor* portion of the MSF problem but are insufficient for solution of the command and control (C^2) *system* problem, for which yet other issues are introduced. This brings us to a broader discussion of the MSF process in the context of C^2 system architectures - this is presented in some detail in the next section.

There is a special, added dimension to the potential benefits of MSF in the context of C^2 systems: higher levels of inference, at multiple levels of abstraction, are possible by building *not only* on the MSF benefits and information resulting from the "sensor subsystem" but also on the *contextual* information provided by a priori of interactively and recursively established data bases. It is in this context especially that artificial intelligence (AI) technology has special applicability to the MSF process. However, broad-based, multi-spectral MSF or disparate, (i.e., both metric and categorical) data will in fact require the employment of *both* analytically-based and AI techniques.

3.1.2   Multi-Sensor Fusion in the Context of C^2 Systems

Fusion can be defined as a process of integrating information from multiple sources to produce the most *specific* and *comprehensive* unified data about an entity, activity, or event. This definition has some key operative words: specific, comprehensive, and entity. From an information-theoretic point of view, fusion, to be effective as an information processing function, must (at least ideally) increase the specificity and comprehensiveness of the understanding we have about a battlefield entity or else there would be no purpose in performing the function. Such gains are frequently described as "information leverage" or "information multiplication", with fusion described as an "information multiplier" (drawing on analogy to advanced weapons as "force multipliers"). The term "entity" arises as a result of sensor resolution considerations, wherein measured data may be associated with multiple targets or target groups rather than specific, single targets. Hence, "entity" is used in a conservative way to reflect the idea that observations may in fact be related to platform or target sets in the general case.

TABLE 3.1.3   *Benefits of multi-sensor fusion (Waltz (2))*

- Robust Operational Performance

  One sensor can contribute information while others are unavailable, denied (jammed), or lack coverage of a target/event

- Extended Spatial Coverage

  One sensor can look where another cannot.

- Extended Temporal Coverage

  One sensor can detect/measure a target/event when others cannot.

- Increased Confidence

  One or more sensors can confirm the same target/event.

- Reduced Ambiguity

  Joint information from multiple sensors reduces the set of hypotheses about the target/event.

- Improved Detection

  Effective integration of multiple measurements of the target/event increases the assurance of its detection.

- Enhanced Spatial Resolution

  Multiple sensors can geometrically form a synthetic aperture capable of greater resolution than a single sensor can achieve.

- Improved System Reliability

  Multiple sensor suites have an inherent redundancy.

- Increased Dimensionality

  A system employing different sensors to measure various portions of the electromagnetic spectrum is less vulnerable to disruption by enemy action or natural phenomena.

One top-level C^2 functional architecture in which MSF functions are portrayed is shown in Figure 3.1.4 (2). In this view, there are several key functions:

- Data Association - this is the process of assigning observations to targets or entities, i.e., of associating measurements with entities. This is part of the so-called "tracker/correlator" (T/C) process frequently described in the literature.
- Multi-Target Tracking - given the association between measurements (or parameters) and entities, this is the process of estimating moving target tracks or, alternatively, estimating fixed target positions.
- Data Combination - as defined in (2), combination is the process of identity estimation. In other taxonomies, this would be called the classification process.
- Data Reasoning - in this architectural definition, the higher level inference processes are grouped under the generic process of "data reasoning". In this taxonomy, situation assessment estimates are produced by this function.
- Situation Data Base - current and past situation estimates (some researchers call these estimates "snapshots" or "sitmaps" (situation maps)) are stored in and accessed from the situation data base.
- Sensor Management - to complete the C^2 system-level description of MSF as a feedback process, a sensor management function is included.

There are various observations and comments to make regarding this model. One important aspect is that fusion products exist to support the command and control functions - the author entirely agrees with this view. Two comments should be made regarding the sensor-related functions. One is that in certain cases no sensor-specific tracking may take place external to the fusion process (this function is called "sensor tracking" in Figure 3.1.4); in this case, the tracking function would be performed entirely as part of the fusion process in what some (e.g., Reiner (3)) call a "centralized" tracking architecture. As shown in Figure 3.1.4, the multi-target tracking process would necessarily perform *track-to-track* correlation and fusion, which is not the only architectural option possible. The other comment is that in many cases the sensors are not organic to and controlled by the organization performing the fusion process. In such cases the fusion process may generate tasking requests of the sensors but the connection in fact would be a loosely coupled one, and not a closely coupled feedback process as portrayed here.

Figure 3.1.5 provides a somewhat different top-level view of the fusion process, although the general functionality is similar to that shown in Figure 3.1.4.

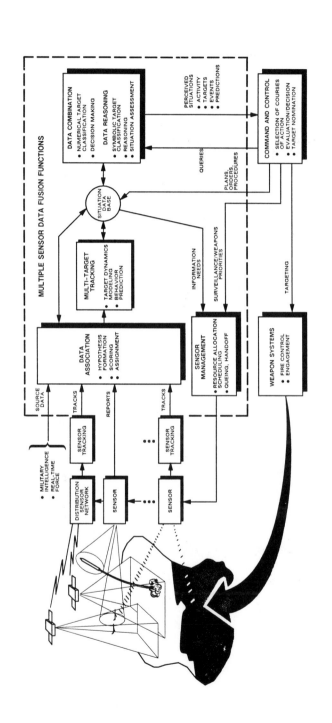

FIG 3.1.4   *Primary fusion functions in the C3I operational model (after Waltz (1)).*

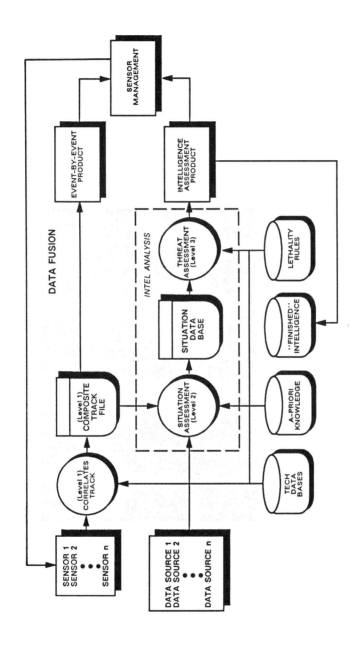

FIG 3.1.5   *Data fusion domain.*

This view is the emerging perspective of the Data Fusion Subpanel of the Technology Panel for C3 (TPC3) of the Joint Directors of Laboratories (JDL), a tri-service government organization in the United States which is supporting standardization, technology exchange, and joint service research in the fusion discipline. One important distinction of this model is the notion of the three "levels" of fusion: position/identity estimation (Level 1), situation assessment (Level 2), and threat assessment (Level 3).

Other top-level insights to the fusion function can be gained from Matthews (4), "Tactical Intelligence/Functional Flow Analysis" produced by the Rome Air Development Center. This document provides Functional Flow Diagrams and Descriptions (F^{2}D^2 charts) of a three-tiered functional architecture for generic Tactical Air Force functions. The process follows a systems engineering approach to functional decomposition and allocation. In the three-tiered description (component-force-unit) of (4), the fusion function is allocated at the force level, and is largely report-driven, with major products being:

- ordnance recommendations
- target nomination products:
  - immediate strike/recce requests
  - changes to fragged missions
- threat alerts
- changes affecting preplanned targets
- requests for information
- dynamic situation data base or order of battle changes

Figure 3.1.6 shows the top-level fusion F^{2}D^2 from (4). In this model, there are two levels of fusion described: situation assessment and threat assessment, with target nomination being a third major activity. Although not shown diagrammatically, this model also includes a position-identity estimation process within the situation asessment function.

One final perspective which will be described here is that derived from (5), "Intelligence Preparation of the Battlefield" ("IPB"). Interestingly, this document does not actually define a fusion function per se but is nevertheless very useful in examining the processes of data integration and analysis, particularly as regards the use of support data.

Figure 3.1.7 shows the top-level view of the "IPB" process which is really a combined situation plus threat assessment process and thereby the document describes two of the major C^2 system level fusion functions. The over-riding analytical framework of IPB is based on "templating" techniques, in which a priori templates or profiles of events, activities, deployments, etc. are prepared and used as a basis for interpreting and comparing the collected dynamic data. Table 3.1.4 shows the template set used in IPB.

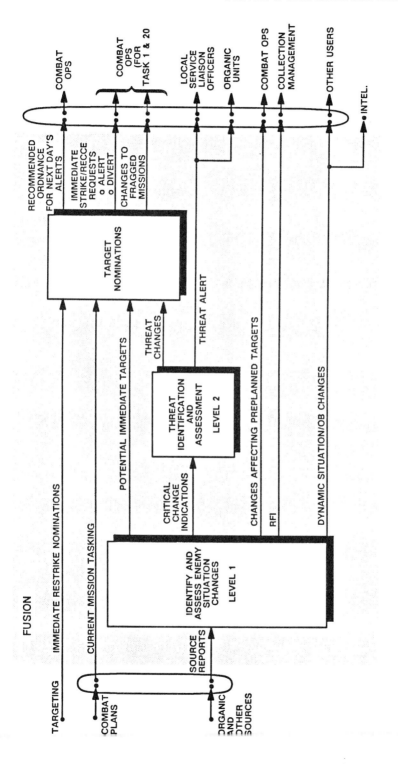

FIG 3.1.6   *Top-level fusion function F²D² (after Matthews (4)).*

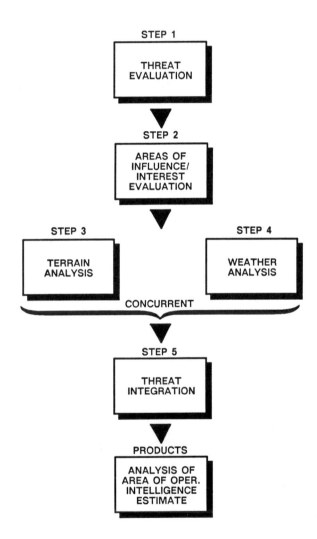

FIG 3.1.7   *Intelligence preparation of the battlefield process (Anon (5))*

Table 3.1.4   *Intelligence preparation of the battlefield templates (Anon (5))*

Template	Description	Purpose	When Prepared
Doctrinal	Enemy doctrinal deployment for various types of operations without constraints imposed by weather and terrain. Composition, formations, frontages, depths, equipment numbers and ratios, and high value targets (HVT) are types of information displayed.	Provides the basis for integrating enemy doctrine with terrain and weather data.	Threat Evaluation
Situation	Depicts how the enemy might deploy and operate within the constraints imposed by the weather and terrain.	Used to identify critical enemy activities and locations. Provides a basis for situation and target development and HVT analysis.	Threat Integration
Event	Depicts locations where critical events and activities are expected to occur and where critical targets will appear.	Used to predict time-related events within critical areas. Provides a basis for collection operations, predicting enemy intentions, and locating and tracking HVT.	Threat Integration
Decision Support	Depicts decision points and target areas of interest keyed to significant events and activities.	Used to provide a guide as to when tactical decisions are required relative to battlefield events.	Threat Integration

3.1.2. (i)   Summary

These top-level perspectives are the starting point from which to fully analyze the C^2 systems-level fusion function. They provide a point of departure for a top-down analysis process to derive system and sensor-specific functional and performance requirements in conjunction with the desired MSF benefits of Table 3.1.3 both at the sensor level and at the multiple-level inferences as just described. These perspectives assert that fusion is a support function to the C^2 function, and they provide guidance for understanding the top-level utility and purpose of, and benefits provided by the fusion function. They also provide a framework for defining the functional interfaces and both the intermediate and final products developed by the function. Accordingly, they also provide guidance for the type of display processing and presentation techniques that can yield the most useful support to the fusion process. A final comment is that the "output boundary" of the C^2-level MSF process concludes with various type *hypotheses* - i.e., MSF is viewed as a hypothesis-generating process. Thus, in the sequential process leading to eventual decisions to take military actions, MSF precedes option generation, plan development, evaluation, and commitment.

3.1.3   Internal Details of the Fusion Process

This section provides additional details and perspectives regarding data fusion processes from an "internalized" view, focusing on the information processes.

The top-level view of Figure 3.1.5 introduced the notion of "levels of fusion":

Level 1: Position/Identity Estimation
Level 2: Situation Assessment
Level 3: Threat Assessment

The definitions and rationales of these levels are as follows: Level 1 is identified as the first category of fusion product because all other interpretations, assessments, and inferences proceed from position/identity estimates of entities in the area of interest. This information is necessary to the initiation of other analysis processes from which higher-level products result. There are various analytical methods employed to generate such estimates, but position estimates are generally based on optimal estimation techniques (Kalman filtering, etc.), and identity estimates are generally based on parameter matching techniques ranging from relatively simple (e.g., majority vote) to more complex, statistical methods (Bayesian, Dempster-Shafer, etc.).

The fusion of positional data first involves choices of how to perform the association process for positional measurements typically without the benefit of related identity information, since identity estimates are most often either a) not available or b) separately processed from the positional data. Thus, association and fusion of observations is usually based on positional data alone, the logic being that position measurements which are "sufficiently close" to one another most likely are associated with the same entity. Since the mathematical association process operates on positional data, most association techniques employ kinematic "gates" or filters to aid in processing by providing a means to reject bad data. Modern methods employed for the tracking function range from constant-coefficient to nearest - neighbor, multiple hypothesis, probabalistic data association and other type filters for handling multi-sensor data coming from multiple targets (see Blackman (6) for example). Some generic tracker/correlator architectures are shown Figure 3.1.8. The actual fused position estimates are computed within the filter cycles for estimating the filtered position and predicting the position of the next measurement sample. Alternatively, for fixed targets, for which the position estimates are often based on multiple imagery sources, the positional closeness measures are usually a variant of the many types of resemblance coefficients used for clustering analysis (e.g., the Mahalanobis distance metric) - see the later discussion on automatic target recognition.

Fusion of identity estimates (often called identity "declarations") from separate sensors is generally performed using either voting or ranking methods or statistical methods ranging from Bayesian to Dempster-Shafer to fuzzy set techniques, among others. The fused identity estimates are usually defined in probabilistic terms, i.e., as probabalities of an unknown entity being of some particular class or as being some specific target.

3.1.3.(i)   Potential Role of AI in Level 1 MSF

However, these traditional methods of classification can certainly can be augmented by expert systems (ES) methods from AI, wherein various types of factual or procedural information can be exploited to aid in identity estimation. Target behaviors consistent with registered flight paths, mission schedules, political boundaries, originating airbase, air corridors, and rules of engagement are amongst the types of logical consistency checks that can be heuristically applied using ES methods. Hierarchies of rule sets can be formulated according to, for example, a hierarchy of hostile mission types.

Contextually-based ES's as described above, which require support data bases of various types, are not the only category of ES method useable for classification. ES methods can also be applied to fuse multi-sensor data by applying rule sets directly to the measurements or derived parameters, as an alternative to the statistical methods. Because many parameters which generally associate with identity are "fuzzy" in nature (e.g., radar cross-section),

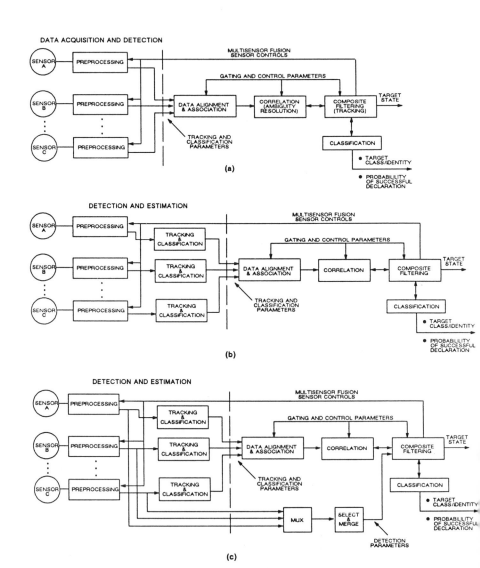

FIG 3.1.8   *Generic tracker/correlator architectures*
a = centralized, b = autonomous, c - hybrid (Reiner (3))

identity-inferencing rules or expert data interpretation guidelines can be as useful or more useful than statistical methods for MSF.

Further, ES methods may also find utility in optimally coupling the classification process with the positional estimation process. While (6) outlines both Bayesian and Dempster-Shafer based approaches, rule-based methods are at least conceptually feasible to guide the synthesis of these processes. Finally, (3) and others have postulated ES concepts for managing the employment of several trackers which would be held in an "algorithm inventory", and employed according to expert rules which would depend on the state of some (undefined) goal function; this concept is shown in Figure 3.1.9 (the algorithm inventory is shown notionally as the "correlation routines" box).

The next level of fusion in this model is called situation assessment, Level 2. The distinctive aspect of developing results at this level is that the analysis is assessing the meaning of the Level 1 Position/Identity results *in the context of some background or supporting data.* It is at this step that the requirement for support data bases can grow significantly, to include terrain, weather, and cartographic data as well as many other types - Figure 3.1.10 shows one possible list of support data base categories. At this level there do not seem to be any formal definitions of the products which have emerged from the military, i.e., the definition of a "situation assessment" has not been solidified although one candidate is as follows:

"A process by which the distributions of fixed and tracked entities are associated with environmental, doctrinal, and performance data."

This definition is a synthesis of the overlay and template definitions of the so-called "Intelligence Preparation of the Battlefield" process (5). Yet another way to understand the situation assessment analysis and its results derives from recent intelligence analyst training materials (7). In this approach, analysts are trained to develop multiple perspectives (called the Red, White, and Blue perspectives) of a given situational data display; this has been termed the "concept of shifting perspectives". The views are defined as follows:

Red View: a view of the data from the point of view
             of the enemy commander, i.e., as if the
             Red war plan were available.
Blue View: the traditional view of the friendly force
             commander i.e., the view in the context of
             the friendly force missions.
White View: the view in the context of the battlefield
             environment and the effects the
             environment may impose on Red or Blue
             options.

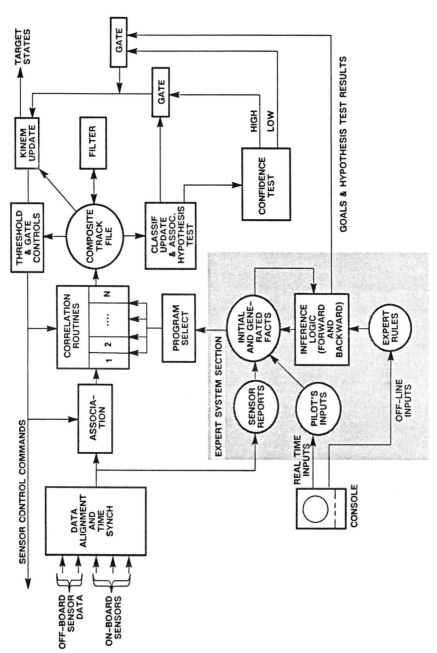

FIG 3.1.9   *Hybrid multisensor fusion data flow (after Reiner (3)).*

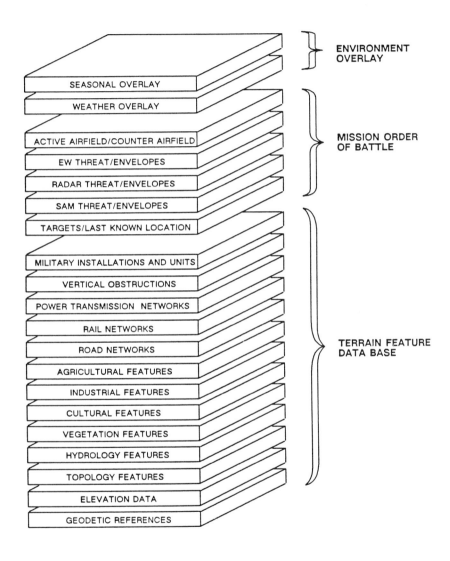

SEASONAL OVERLAY

WEATHER OVERLAY

ACTIVE AIRFIELD/COUNTER AIRFIELD

EW THREAT/ENVELOPES

RADAR THREAT/ENVELOPES

SAM THREAT/ENVELOPES

TARGETS/LAST KNOWN LOCATION

MILITARY INSTALLATIONS AND UNITS

VERTICAL OBSTRUCTIONS

POWER TRANSMISSION NETWORKS

RAIL NETWORKS

ROAD NETWORKS

AGRICULTURAL FEATURES

INDUSTRIAL FEATURES

CULTURAL FEATURES

VEGETATION FEATURES

HYDROLOGY FEATURES

TOPOLOGY FEATURES

ELEVATION DATA

GEODETIC REFERENCES

ENVIRONMENT
OVERLAY

MISSION ORDER
OF BATTLE

TERRAIN FEATURE
DATA BASE

FIG 3.1.10   *Representative list of fusion support data bases*

Figure 3.1.11 portrays the so-called White perspective and its viewpoints focused on the time, space, and environmental context of the battlefield and entities upon it. While the method of developing the White view yields information products consistent with some traditional views of the situation assessment process, this work (i.e., (7)) correctly suggests an expansion in the perspectives from which we define situation assessment. Correspondingly, the associated definition of MSF at this level must take on new meaning, and include additional inference processes derived from the new perspectives.

As denoted in the candidate definition suggested here, the situation assessment process also includes the use of what are generically called "performance" models. What is meant here are those analyses such as:

- vehicle or aircraft mobility and trafficability performance envelope calculations
- sensor/emitter/terrain line of sight calculations
- air corridor analyses

that is, those analyses which involve the use of a model of the performance of an entity. Many other such performance calculations are possible for the support of developing situation estimates.

As previously described, IPB fosters the use of "templating" techniques to actually analyze the overall tactical situation; other researchers have also employed such methods (e.g., Llinas (8)). These template-based techniques revolve about an approach in which *expected patterns of behavior* are described via templates comprised of activities, events, entities, and associated time and distance relationships. As observations are made, various templates are instantiated as being possible; some type of confidence score is usually employed to assess the validity of occurrence of the overall event.

3.1.3. (ii)   Potential Role of AI in Level 2 MSF

At Level 2, there are three basic ways that AI technology can help in generating useful results:

1. By providing methodologies to implement or support the pattern or template-matching functions required to associate battlefield entities and events to an order of battle or mission-level hierarchy; most current implementations have usually employed either rule-based or frame-based techniques within ES constructs. Alternative approaches could employ more traditional pattern-recognition methods (see Section 3.1.4.3).
2. By providing methods of aiding in the interpretation of the results of various performance models (e.g., understanding the tactical implications of sensor line of sight and

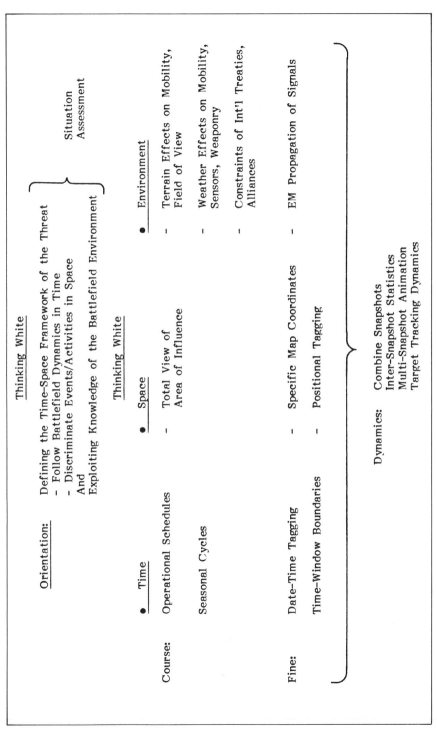

Orientation: Thinking White

Defining the Time-Space Framework of the Threat
- Follow Battlefield Dynamics in Time
- Discriminate Events/Activities in Space
And
Exploiting Knowledge of the Battlefield Environment

Thinking White

● **Time**   ● **Space**   ● **Environment**

Course: Operational Schedules   – Total View of   – Terrain Effects on Mobility,
                                         Area of Influence   Field of View

              Seasonal Cycles   – Weather Effects on Mobility,
                                                                    Sensors, Weaponry

                                                                 – Constraints of Int'l Treaties,
                                                                    Alliances

Fine: Date–Time Tagging   – Specific Map Coordinates – EM Propagation of Signals

              Time-Window Boundaries – Positional Tagging

Dynamics: Combine Snapshots   Situation
                Inter-Snapshot Statistics   Assessment
                Multi-Snapshot Animation
                Target Tracking Dynamics

EIG 3.1.11   *The "White" perspective of intelligence data analysis (according to (Anon (7)).*

terrain masking calculations); such methods would
fall in the category of intelligent assistants.
3. By providing various narrow-domain decision aids
    which   support   the   performance   of   explicit
    functions   comprising   the   overall   situation
    assessment   process.   Numerous   decision   aids,
    covering a wide range of such narrow functions,
    have been developed over the past 5 - 10 years
    using various elements of AI technology (e.g.,
    (9), (10)).

Items (1), (2), and (3) comprise an applications hierarchy
of the employment of AI at this level.
   However, the concepts of employment for AI technologies
described in (1) - (3) above have not typically derived
from an integrated architectural approach. Recent efforts
have taken a fresh look at the situation assessment problem
from the point of view of developing an integrated work
station architecture which would conceivably employ:

-   cooperating expert systems,
-   natural language processing (NLP) for both message
    reception, routing, and construction, and an NLP
    man-machine interface,
-   spatial data base management systems,
-   speech input-output.

These concepts are elevating the overall cognitive
capability of the machine-based support provided to the
situation asessment problem. Future systems will likely
include learning capabilities which would potentially allow
so-called "cold" fusion processing, i.e., fusion processing
without any (or limited) a priori (i.e., data base)
information to be realized.
   Finally, there is the Level 3 - Threat Assessment
fusion product. There are two distinctive characteristics
of this level: quantitative estimates of enemy strengths
are computed, and expected courses of action are assesssed.
Together with the information of Levels 1 and 2, this
integrated perspective defines a threat assessment or
profile. To do this requires additional estimation
processes to be applied, and additional data bases to be
available (especially those which delineate weapon
characteristics of various entities).   Estimating the
expected courses of action requires the fusion of doctrinal
operations and tactics behavior and terrain and unit
mobility or aircraft performance envelope data, among other
factors.   Figure 3.1.12 shows additional factors which
could be accounted for in a detailed enemy course of action
estimation process. It can be seen from this figure that
there is a mission-dependent set of such possible courses;
that is, the course of action estimation process should
asseses courses as a function of likely missions, given the
overall situation. Integrated displays of such information
may look like (at least notionally) Figure 3.1.13 again
taken from (5).   It seems clear that AI techniques or

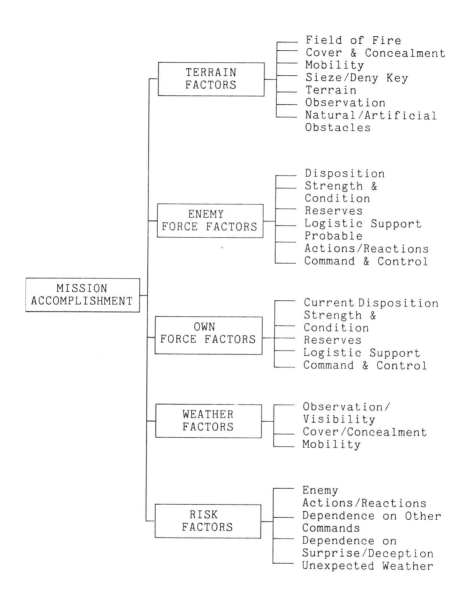

FIG 3.1.12   *Factors involved in course of action estimation*

possibly advanced templating or figure of merit techniques
would be required to fuse and deduce such estimates from
the observations, calculations, and support data base
information.   To date, no integrated AI (or other)
approaches along these lines seem to have been described in
the open literature.   Some decision-aiding work has been

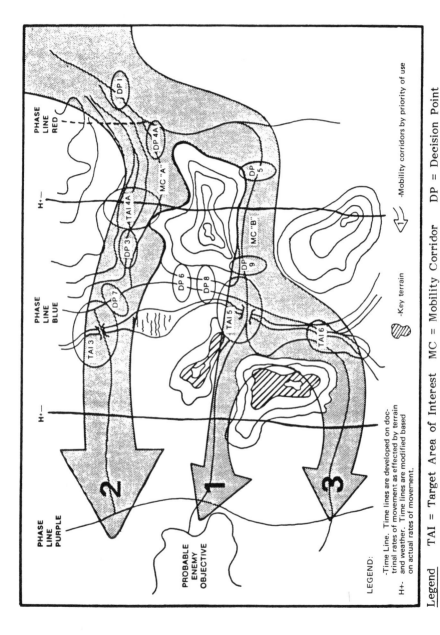

Legend   TAI = Target Area of Interest   MC = Mobility Corridor   DP = Decision Point

FIG 3.1.13   *Notional enemy course of action display (after Anon (5)).*

done associated with component analyses of the overall approach.

The estimation of enemy strength (or, equivalently, the ability of the enemy to inflict quantifiable levels of Blue force losses) obtains from both: 1) knowledge of the quantities and types of equipments and troops the enemy has available, and 2) qualitative information regarding the enemy's patterns of behavior in employing these resources since, frequently, the manner in which an enemy uses his resources can be indicative of the status of those resources.

Estimating the total (and important sub-total) quantities of equipments is itself a separate fusion process wherein the figures are derived from a fusion of e.g.:

- the entity data resulting from Level 1 fusion processing,
- estimates of likely (but not observed) entities based on doctrinal equipment and troop deployment templates,
- battle damage reports,

among other factors, e.g., equipment reliability data, supply line analysis, etc.

Likely quantities of equipments to be employed in a possible action can also be estimated from enemy patterns of behavior. For example, the ability to conduct an aircraft sortie of given strength partly depends on sustainability. Decreased sustainability would result in reduced strength estimates; in turn, decreased sustainability can depend on other behavioral factors as shown below:

Factors such as these could be combined into a hierarchical behavioral model which describes their relationship to basic enemy capabilities, such as their sortie generation capability. In addition, for each behavioral factor, a scale could be developed that permitted an intelligence analyst routinely to translate specific observations into a numerical assessment of the degree of change that has occurred and its effect on equipment counts.

3.1.3. (iii)   Potential Role of AI in Level 3 MSF

The potential use of AI technology at Level 3 is considered very great but various necessary capabilities for achieving useful results have not yet been demonstrated. Correspondingly, meaningful prototypes have not yet been reported on in the open literature. Nevertheless, it is useful to consider the possibilities for application, e.g.:

- the use of cooperating ES's in which the employment of multi-domain knowledge truly achieves a synergistic affect,
- the use of learning systems that can be adaptive to programmed or situation-driven changes in enemy doctrine/behavior (adapting to enemy "war-modes"). Various learning system notions are possible ranging from rote learning, to parameter adjustment, to discovery-based approaches. Implementations may be feasible on neural network-based computers,
- the use of advanced spatial data base management techniques which provide a supporting framework for the higher, Level 3 inference processes.
- the use of hierarchical knowledge structures in which high and mid-level meta-knowledge constructs can be effectively and efficiently employed.

Antony (11) suggests an approach to designing Level 3 fusion systems which relies on a biological system metaphor; Table 3.1.5 shows the suggested equivalency in the system functions.

3.1.4   Issues in the Application of AI Technology to MSF

While the enumerated potential applications of AI technology to MSF described in Section 3.1.3 are considered valid, there are many issues related to implementation of the technology that must be dealt with. If we consider the elements of AI technology to be those shown in Figure 3.1.14, it can be seen that most application areas, e.g., speech understanding, learning, computer vision, among others, are generally immature as regards the breadth of understanding required for proper implementation across a broad range of problem types. That is, current capabilities limit the breadth of application of many of these techniques.

Of the technologies in Figure 3.1.14, those which have been applied with some reasonable frequency in MSF problem domain include expert or knowledge-based methods, techniques from natural language processing, and methods of pattern recognition. In what follows, the issues in applying such technologies to the MSF case will be separately discussed.

TABLE 3.1.5   *Biological system - multisensor fusion system metaphor (after Antony (11))*

Biological Systems	Distributed Fusion Systems
• network of millions of neuron clusters computing relatively simple functions	• network of pattern recognizers
• evolutionary upward compatible architecture	• evolution development potential
• asynchronous, distributed processing	• asynchronous, distributed processing
• Hierarchical organization	• Hierarchical organization
• massively parallel architecture	• high concurrency parallel architecture
• sequential processing	• pipelined architecture
• multiple sensory information fusion	• multiple sensor information fusion
• distributed memory	• functionally /contextually distributed memory
• long term memory	• incremental decision processor knowledge base
• medium term knowledge	• global blackboard
• short term memory	• system states
• memory and processing redundancy	• distributed long term and medium term memory; functionally redundant processing
• dynamic reconfiguration	• modularity supports reconfiguration
• ability to generalize	• generalized deterministic, probablistic or fuzzy pattern recognition

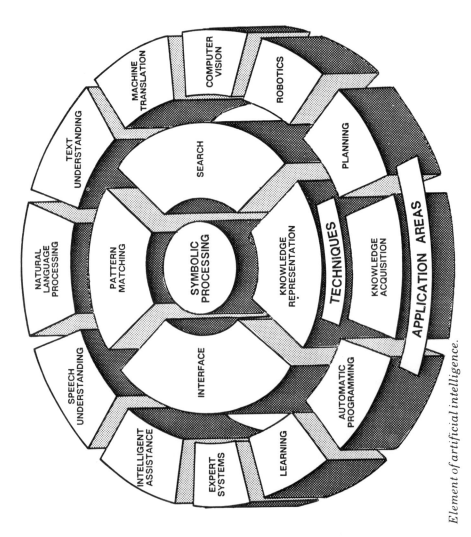

FIG 3.1.14   *Element of artificial intelligence.*

3.1.4. (i)   *Expert or Knowledge-Based Systems (ES/KBS)*

Although ES/KBS applications have certainly dominated the use of AI technologies for military purposes (with varying degrees of success), there remains a list of significant issues to be dealt with before ES/KBS concepts can be reliably and broadly applied to many military problems, including MSF.

ES/KBS techniques are currently performing certain narrow-domain decision making tasks at or near a human expert level. However, automated fusion processing exhibits the following characteristics not generally associated with expert system application domains to data (11):

1   time varying dynamic input states;
2   real time operational requirements;
3   diverse data classes;
4   diverse knowledge classes;
5   processing and message passing delays;
6   spatial distribution of the sensors;
7   lack of ground truth in design and performance evaluation;
8   lack of human expertise in certain subproblem domains;
9   multiple levels of abstraction in the decision process; and
10   very large knowledge bases.

Consider just two of the shortfalls of the conventional production system. First, the time varying aspect of the sensor data, as well as the hierarchical situation assessment itself, demands a form of sequential processing that is not supported by the conventional production rule paradigm. A more general paradigm is required that accommodates both conventional signal processing and rule based system approaches.

Second, in the classic rule based expert system, the conditions for rule firing can be evaluated by simply searching for their existence in the working database. For dynamic, real world applications, condition evaluation generally involves some form of functional processing. As an example, consider the following hypothetical production rule (11):

IF   (Target x is on a secondary road & Target x is a wheeled vehicle & Target x has been following a low-to-moderately concealed route & a path exists from present location of Target x to forward Unit y & the distance between Target x and Unit y is decreasing)

THEN   (Target x is a resupply vehicle for Unit y [Conf C_1] or Target x is a reinforcement vehicle for Unit y [Conf C_2]).

Satisfaction of the above conditions involves: 1) fuzzy intersection of the road knowledge base with Target x track record, 2) target classification, 3) intersection of the track file with the terrain and foliage database, followed by assessment of the level of concealment, 4) generalized path following based on vehicle class, terrain, current weather conditions, doctrine and enemy and friendly order of battle, and 5) generalized metric computation based on track histories of both Target x and Unit y.

Simple flat or even hierarchically organized production systems cannot efficiently deal with the evaluation of a large number of such high level rules in the time evolving battlefield environment. Clearly, a more functionally oriented framework than is offered by a conventional expert system is required.

In (11), Antony has suggested such a framework, describing a generalized fusion model and discussing: issues of knowledge representation; spatial, hierarchical, and temporal reasoning; and implementation issues. This framework is synopsized below, much of which is from (11).

As regards a generalized fusion model, Antony suggests that a data-driven, expectation-based model is more appropriate than conventional AI graph search methods due to the time-varying nature of the fusion problem. He suggests a hierarchical, multi-stage, KBS as shown notionally in Figure 3.1.15. Antony suggests that this architecture supports a broad range of conventional techniques, such as signal procesing, hypothesis-and-test and template match techniques for evidence assessment in support of expectation based observations and production systems.

The blackboard supports cooperative and competitive problem solving by maintaining the current situation assessment that is accessible to all elements of the system. Five stages of the data fusion process model produce the following correlations (in the following, read "x" as "correlated with"):

Stage 1 Local Sequential Processing: (sensor report) x (sensor report history)

Stage 2 Global Sequential Processing: (sensor report history) x (system situation assessment)

Stage 3 Multisensor Fusion (OB = Order of Battle): (single level of abstraction OB) x (single level of abstraction OB)

Stage 4 Multiple Level of Abstraction OB: (single level of abstraction OB) x (hierarchical force structure OB)

Stage 5 Multiple Level of Abstraction Situation Assessment: (event recognition) x (hierarchical situation assessment)

Figure 3.1.16 depicts important classes of domain knowledge appropriate at these various stages in the fusion process.

Figure 3.1.17 expands the view of the interaction between the fusion blocks and the blackboard. The feedback

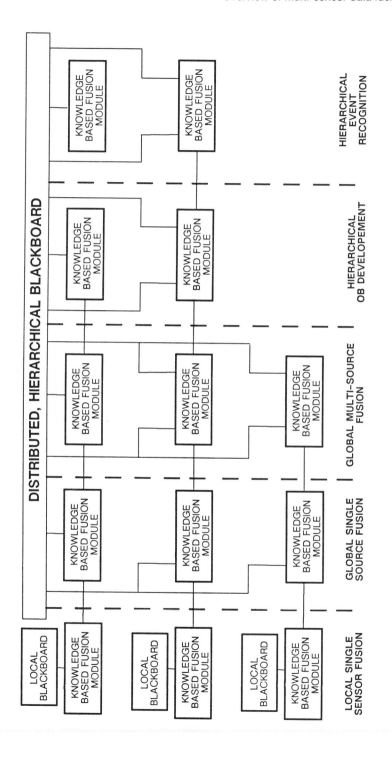

FIG 3.1.15   *Proposed distributed knowledge based fusion system (after Antony(11)).*

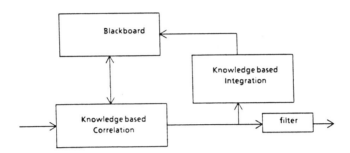

Figure 3.1.16   *Representative knowledge classes for tactical data fusion (after Antony(11))*

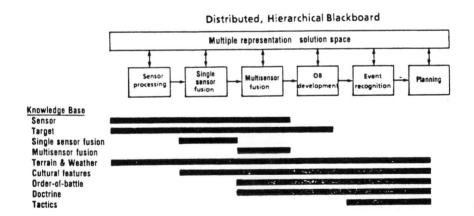

Figure 3.1.17 *Generalized fusion module (after Antony(11)).*

to the blackboard explicitly depicts the update of the
situation assessment that occurs as a result of the
integration process. The filter output supports the
sequential elements of the proposed model. Thus
Figure 3.1.17 is a model of a generic fusion process
containing the two dominant subprocesses of correlation and
integration.

Since the system must maintain multiple lines of
reasoning, the correlation process results in one or more
of the following decisions:

1) one event represents a sequential update of
another event (e.g., track update, redundant
report),
2) one event represents another part of an identical
event (e.g., two distinct track segments of a
single target trajectory),
3) one event represents an alternate view of another
event (e.g., multiple sensor views of a single
target),
4) the event does not correlate with any other
existing event (e.g., new event),
5) the event represents a false report (e.g., error
or spoof).

Antony continues to discuss specifics of knowledge
representation issues, structuring his approach about the
biological metaphor, involving long-term, medium-term, and
short-term knowledge. Long-term knowledge representations
comprise: 1) generalized entity-relationship graph models,
2) spatial knowledge (where he describes the criticality of
a robust spatial data management concept in spatial data
handling) and, 3) procedural knowledge. Medium-term
knowledge, considered to contain the system's current world
view, is represented by the blackboard construct. Short-
term knowledge is reflected in the dynamic state
representations for the system.

Finally, Antony discusses issues in reasoning,
emphasizing the broad range of spatial reasoning classes
(see Table 3.1.6) that support the MSF process.

McCune (12) has examined the applicability of ES/KBS to
military problems in a broader sense, i.e., broader than
solely for MSF processing, and enumerates advantages and
disadvantages of ES/KBS techniques. Using McCune's data, a
list of research and development issues has been
constructed, and is shown in Table 3.1.7.

There is yet another critical development issue: the
test and evaluation process of ES/KBS, for which no
standards have yet been agreed to. Llinas and Rizzi (13)
have recently developed a framework for defining consistent
approaches to the test and evaluation of ES/KBS. Among
other issues, their report discusses such topics as:

-   the need for a "gold standard" or standards of
acceptability for results,

TABLE 3.1.6   *Examples of spatial reasoning capabilities that support battlefield data fusion (after Antony (11))*

Boolean queries
Spatial windowing and search
Target history representation
High level production rule condition satisfaction
Correlation processing
Spatial patterns of targets and events
Distance measure, area, centroid, boundary length
Region intersection
Active spatial windows
Target extrapolation
Target classification
Tactics assessment
Global route planning under spatial (weather, terrain, etc.) constraints
Hierarchical line-of-sight development
Target Tracking

TABLE 3.1.7 *ES/KBS research and development issues (McCune (12))*

(1) -	A standardized, consistent ES/KBS development paradigm has not yet been defined, nor have development matrices been defined and collected.
(2) -	Reliable, easily understood techniques for handling uncertainty in the knowledge bases have not been defined.
(3) -	ES/KBS development remains a costly and largely unpredictable undertaking due to:
	- effects of (1) above,
	- limited tools and understanding associated with knowledge acquisition,
	- slow execution speeds in certain computing environments.
(4) -	Techniques for achieving reliable graceful degradation do not yet exist.

- contrasts between peer-review based or post-mortem based evaluation points of view,
- standards for evaluating evaluators, in the case of peer-review based testing,
- a need for "blind" testing (i.e, wherein human and machine results are indistinguishable in the evaluation) - this is analogous to the "Turing Test".
- domain sensitivity effects on the knowledge bases,
- achieving statistical significance in the results.

Dillard (14) also examined the applicability of ES/KBS techniques to data fusion but includes natural language processing and pattern recognition techniques in her overall assessment. She suggests that "the greatest problem with production systems ... is that there are innumerable nonroutine situations which could occur", suggesting that knowledge base incompleteness may be a non-trival problem in ES/KBS development.

3.1.4. (ii) Natural Language Processing (NLP)

There are generally two ways that NLP techniques are involved in the MSF processes: (1) they are applied to the automatic routing and/or understanding of the fundamental information input in message-based MSF systems, or (2) they are applied in various ways to improve the man-machine interface. In message-based MSF systems (MBMSF), sensor-level data is usually assumed to have been preprocessed by some external function not normally considered part of the fusion system per se in order to derive parametric-type data. Thus, positional and attribute parameters and contextual information is provided, at least partly, in the form of textual messages and data "messages".
A representative message and data input structure generally involved in MBMSF is shown in Figure 3.1.18 from (14). Much of what follows is excerpted from various of Dillard's works. NLP techniques are needed to deal with data in two of the categories shown in Figure 3.1.18: slowly perishing textual information, which is usually in the form of a well-written document, and rapidly perishing textual information, which is typically the comments section of a tactical message. Several NLP approaches have been described in the literature; because of problems with context, many researchers in the area of text understanding by computers frequently use "frames" in their approach to knowledge representation. A frame is a data-structure for representing a situation, and can be thought of as a network of nodes and relations (see e.g., Minsky (15), (16), Winston (17) and Hewitt (18)).
Data fusion applications of a framework approach would include situations that involve a predictable dynamic sequence of events, such as a refueling procedure, a missile attack, a particular kind of training exercise, an infrared flare ejection, and a submarine rising to periscope depth. In such cases, the frame construct acts

like a template, providing an "expectation structure", which, when filled, supports the inference of the occurrence of a given situation. Since the information in components or slots may have come from multiple sensors, the frame construct can be said to provide a basis for MBMSF. Relatively static situations which possible could be represented by frames are: "looking" at a land mass (reference to a unique landmark, for example, could call up other pertinent information about an otherwise unidentified area) and "looking at " a ship's superstructure (enabling reasoning of the type "if its superstructure was badly damaged, its surface-search radar is probably inoperative"). Intelligence reports of various kinds might also be representable by frames. A report that "country x plans to achieve domination of countries y and z by aggressive political efforts and by a threatening show of naval strength in the Gulf of ..." should invoke a frame which recognizes that political efforts and shows of strength are methods of achieving domination, and that there is an increased expectation of country-y's naval units moving in response, to that area.

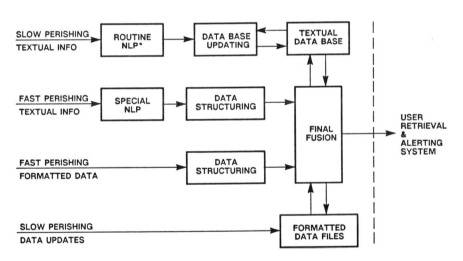

*Natural Language processing

FIG 3.1.18   *Message inputs to fusion processing (after Dillard (14))*

It can be seen that the concept of a frame is closely analogous to that of a template as described for situation assessment. While in situation assessment template components are instantiated by sensor observations, in NLP frame components (called "slots") are instantiated by special word or phrase occurrences in messages or by representations of their interpretations. Generally, the representation of narrative text would require collections of related frames linked together into "frame systems". For visual scene analysis, for example, different frames of a system would represent the scene from different aspects. For nonvisual frames, the links between frames can represent changes of emphasis and attention, or cause-effect relations.

The various frame systems are linked together by an "information retrieval network", which participates in the selection of the frame best-suited for representing a situation (15), (16). The interframe structures also can store additional contextual knowledge useful in understanding textual material about a situation.

Associated with the use of frames in our postulated data fusion system is an additional complexity not shown in Figure 3.1.18. The input of textual information and of formatted data were shown as separate processes in Figure 3.1.18. When the textual data is a comments section on an otherwise formatted message, the two kinds of data really should be processed together. Figure 3.1.19 (from (14)) outlines a procedure for handling messages of this type. The formatted data would play a major part in the selection of frame types and the information from both kinds of data would fill the frames.

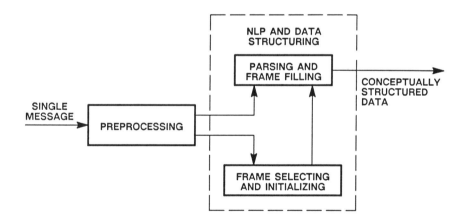

FIG 3.1.19   *Processing a mixture of data types (after Dillard (14))*

It is further conceivable that the filling of a frame would be resumed later as a result of fusion processes that involve the original frame, or that a new frame would replace the original. For example, a later classification of a platform already partly described by a frame would allow use of contextual information about the platform, such as an explanation of intent based on capabilities and behavior i.e., a contextual basis for MSF.

Other researchers have proposed alternative approaches to NLP. Schank and Abelson (19), (20) have proposed and

experimented with a text understanding method that uses
specialized versions of frames. Underlying their frames
are basic constructions called "conceptualizations", which
represent the meaning of sentences. The structures of
these conceptualizations must conform to "Conceptual
Dependency Theory", (20).

Conceptualizations, which are further described in
Schank (21), (22), involve a number of primitive acts.
Among those acts that are applicable to data fusion are
ATRANS (the transfer of an abstract relationship such as
possession, ownership or control), PTRANS (the transfer of
the physical location of an object), PROPEL (the
application of force to an object), MTRANS (the transfer of
mental information), and MBUILD (the construction of new
information from old information).

While Conceptual Dependency representation was designed
to handle single thoughts or sentences, causal chains are
needed to handle the connections among the sentences and
thoughts in a text. As a mechanism for dealing with this
problem in stereotyped situations, (19), (20) introduce the
notion of a "Script", which is defined in Schank (23) as "a
predetermined causal chain of conceptualizations that
describe the normal sequence of things in a familiar
situation". In the fusion of tactical data, for example, a
script for a routine surveillance mission would be useful
for understanding messages received about mission
activities. A script, which is a special version of a
frame, is also a structure made up of slots and of
requirements on what can fill those slots. It describes an
appropriate sequence of events in a particular context.

In (20), Schank and Abelson also introduce a more
general version of a frame, a "Plan", which is a mechanism
used to describe actions in new or unexpected situations
(in MSF applications, perhaps a military operation or an or
of battle).

In order to make sense out of textual material, a text-
understanding system must have a tremendous amount of world
knowledge stored in a suitable conceptual structure. If
the text-understanding system were to be a subsystem of an
automated fusion system, much of its required knowledge
would be the same as that which we would expect to be used
by - the fusion processes. In this and several other
respects, the processing of NL data in a data fusion system
could be considered as an early stage of fusion, and not
just a generator of inputs. If textual material from
several different sources on the same topic are combined
and processed as a single story, then we must certainly
call this processing a kind of MSF. Also, the use of
formatted data in selecting and filling in frames for
messages containing formatted and narrative text
(Figure 3.1.19) would be a form of MSF. However, no NLP-
based methods designed explicitly to perform "multi-message
fusion" have been reported. Concepts involving frame,
script, or plan hierarchies can be imagined but research is
needed to examine the feasibility of direct application of
NLP methods for MSF. Until such feasibility has been

demonstrated, NLP techniques will probably be used in
front-end message processing and input generation to
(other) fusion processes, although some degree of fusion
can be implemented in such front ends. Still, it is
convenient to treat the two as separate processes that must
be appropriately interfaced, while recognizing that some
fusion is involved in NLP and some NLP is involved in
fusion.

A good example of the integration of both production
system and NLP type processing is also reported in another
work by Dillard (24). In this work, Dillard explores the
concepts and details of an NLP front end processor to a
rule-based tactical situation assessment ES called
"STAMMER", basically a MBMSF system. The architectural
concept of this system is shown in Figure 3.1.20; "oracles"
are computational functions for certain relations too
difficult to represent as rules (recall Antony's concerns
on such antecedent issues in Section 3.1.3). While an
apparently detailed design of this concept was carried out,
no performance data have been reported.

The role of NLP in man-machine interface improvement
for military applications has been explored in a variety of
studies. Recently, the Defense Advanced Research Projects
Agency (DARPA) has initiated an "Intelligent Integrated
Interface (I3)" program (Neal et al (25)) which will
greatly improve human interaction with computers by
integrating speech, natural language processing, and
graphics for both input and output; this study will be done
in the context of tactical air control operations. The
solution proposed in this resarch project is based upon a
unified view of language. This unified view will use a multi-
media language, defined by an integrated grammar,
consisting of textual, graphic, and combined text/graphic
symbols in a unified lexicon. Input and output streams
will be treated as compound streams with components
corresponding to different media. This approach is
intended to imitate, to a certain extent, the ability of
humans to simultaneously accept input from different
sensory devices (such as eyes and ears), and to
simultaneously produce output in different media (such as
voice, pointing motions, and drawings).

- In this program, a prototype system as illustrated in
Figure 3.1.21 will be built. This sytem architecture is
based on a Central Reasoning System in the form of an
inference system with access to several knowledge sources.
The concept of an augmented transition network (ATN) from
NLP will be extended and generalized so that it takes a
multi-media input stream and produces a multi-media output
stream. The proposed ATN will be an integral part of the
interface system, functioning under the supervision of the
Central Reasoning System.

3.1.4.(iii)   Pattern Recognition (PR)

The application of pattern recognition techniques to
problems in MSF have until recently been rather limited.

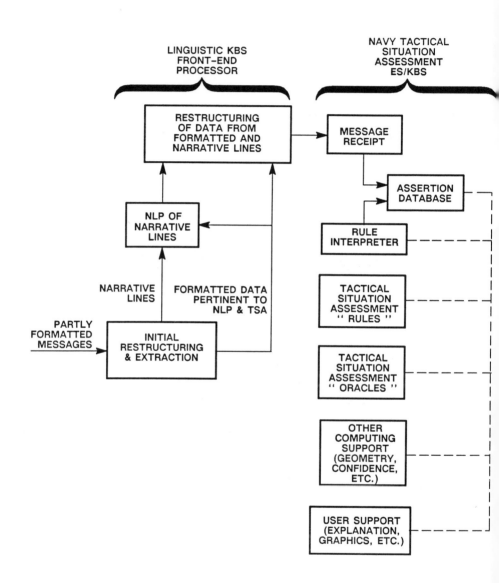

FIG 3.1.20   *Concept of NLP within overall STAMMER design (after Dillard (24)).*

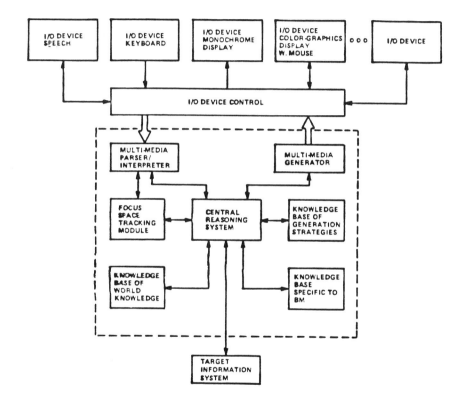

FIG 3.1.21   *Overview of intelligent integrated interface system architecture (after Neal et al (25)).*

The recent efforts that have changed this picture have occurred in the area of automatic target recognition or "ATR" as a result of initiatives in the areas of so-called "smart weapons" and advanced RPV's. These initiatives have, respectively, imposed requirements for (a) improved targeting and aimpoint accuracies, and b) expanded capability in autonomous control. The technological advances discussed in Section 3.3.1 have allowed the integration of multiple sensors into the generally small confines of RPV's and expendable weapons, allowing for the exploration of MSF techniques to satisfy such requirements. The following remarks are largely drawn from the works of Bhanu (26) and Pemberton (27).

Basically, ATR systems involve imaging sensors (among others), and perform automatic target acquisition, identification, and tracking by processing both individual images and image sequences. The algorithmic components of an ATR system can be decomposed into preprocessing, detection, segmentation, feature computation, selection and classification, prioritization, tracking and aimpoint selection. The goal is to perform these functions in real time and to be able to adapt to dynamic tactical situations.

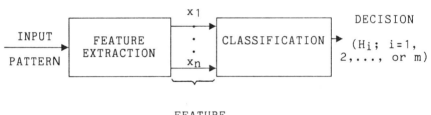

FEATURE
MEASUREMENTS

FIG 3.1.22   *General pattern recognition problem*

Figure 3.1.22 illustrates the two main functions of a pattern recognition system. The vector consisting of the feature measurements x_1, x_2, ..., x_n is called the feature vector or pattern vector. H_i is the hypothesis that the pattern occurs from the ith of m pattern classes. The decision is the conclusion that H_i is true, with i specified. The feature extraction problem, or "characterization" problem, is to find a set of features suitable for use in the classification process. The features selected should be the most informative of the various properties of attributes of the situation or object. Feature selection is generally the most difficult and the most important process in designing a pattern recognition system.

One optimum procedure (for minimizing the probability of misclassification) is to use a Bayes Classifier, which reduces to the maximum likelihood rule when the classes are equally likely to occur. The m decision functions

$$D_i(x) = p(x|H_i) \qquad i = 1,2,\ldots,m$$

are calculated and the maximum $D_i(x)$ corresponds to the decision that H_i is true. One difficulty with this procedure is that we must provide the conditional densities $p(x|H_i)$, and, even when these are known, the calculations can be prohibitively long, an added complication for any real-time situation. There are many applicable near-optimum and suboptimum pattern recognition classification procedures described in the literature that are simpler to implement than the optimum procedure. For the kinds of pattern recognition problems expected in data fusion, the selection and implementation of a suitable decision procedure should be relatively simple compared to the feature extraction task which is an image processing problem. However, the definition and optimization of the feature set is a non-trivial problem, usually involving extensive "training" (i.e., parametric adjustment) in the decision rule. This introduces yet another issue which is the requirement for a large and representative image data base upon which to train and optimize the pattern recognition techniques.

Evaluation of features and their clustering is important in the design of ATR algorithms. Computational efficiency and accuracy of the features and their power to distinguish different targets are also important, since the classification results depend upon the accuracy and reliability of the features. To examine segmentation effects, the features of the segmented target and the true target are compared by measuring the distance between them in feature space and evaluating different features by carrying out a hypothesis test and a variance analysis. To evaluate the clustering of features a clustering fidelity criterion such as $\beta = \text{Fct}(S_B)$. $\text{Fct}(S_W)$, where S_B and S_W are between-cluster and within-cluster scattering matrices, is used. The behavior of β is such that it passes through a maximum at the intrinsic number of clusters. The maximum of β can be determined by incrementing the number of clusters until a decrease is detected. This allows one to obtain the number of clusters inherent in the data. Departure of the number of clusters thus obtained from the known number of clusters tells about the quality of the features. It is also important to determine if the clustering is really present or if it is a statistical artifact because a clustering method always finds clusters, whether or not they are real.

The performance of a classifier is measured by finding the probability of correct classification and the false alarm rate. The probability of classification is given in the form of a confusion matrix and the confidence associated with each classification together with the size of the feature vector and data base. It is usually measured by the well known techniques of partitioning the data set into a training set and a testing set and/or using the leaving-one-out approach. Reliability of a classifier is a function of the clustering quality of the features. It is measured by finding the stability of the feature clustering.

Some of the key reasons for the need for MSF in solving the ATR problem are the nonrepeatability of the target signature, competing clutter objects having the same shape as the actual targets, experience with a very limited data base, obscured target, very little use of available information, related to and present in the image, such as context, structure, range, etc. If use were made of these diverse sources of information, then it is expected that the target signature characteristics would be extracted reliably and the effectiveness of current systems would be improved in both acquisition and classification. Figure 3.1.23 shows some representative MSF performance (false-alarm rate) gains possible by fusing single sensor ATR (e.g., FLIR, mm wave radar) not only with other sensor data (TV or moving target indicator (MTI)) but also with the contextual data provided by a digital map.

Two approaches have generally been used to solve the ATR problem. First is the classical pattern recognition approach, which uses statistical and structural techniques generally categorized as pattern recognition techniques. Such techniques are based on the hypothesis that features of objects from different classes lie in easily separable regions of the multidimensional feature space, while features from the same class cluster together. Figure 3.1.24 shows a representative ATR processing flow diagram for a FLIR sensor. Such an approach has limited knowledge and almost no inteligence and reasoning capability to learn from the dynamic environment and adapt to it. There could be substantial variation due to changing weather conditions, etc., even in a limited geographical area. It is desired that the ATR system be able to learn from the environment and be able to use contextual cues. The other, AI-based, approach provides these capabilities. It not only requires low-level processing, image analysis and pattern recognition methods, but also requires high-level symbolic manipulation.

-The limitations mentioned above have led to the realization that better performance can be achieved by suboptimal ways of handling context rather than by optimal ways of handling the local structure as conventionally accomplished in the pattern recognition approach. The ATR problem is suited for building a knowledge-based system (KBS) for a specific operational environment and geographical area. Recently, attempts have been made to use context (temporal, global, local, and ancillary information, such as map data, sensor data, seasonal, and intelligence information), semantics, and problem domain knowledge to improve the performance of ATR systems (e.g., Refs. (28), Tseng (29), Kim (30), Spiessbach and Gilmore (31), Drazovich (32), and Gilmore (33)). Most of this work

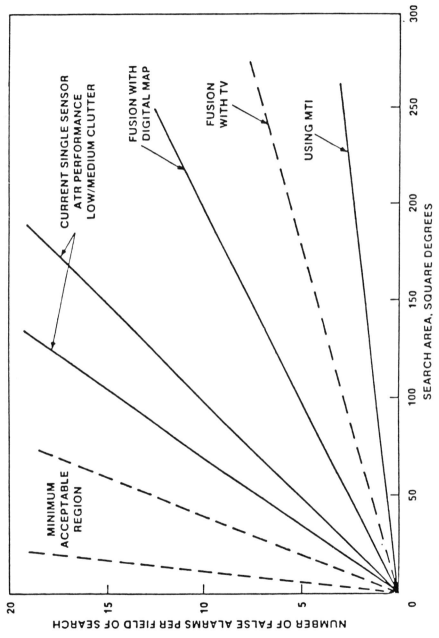

FIG 3.1.23   *False-alarm management with sensor fusion.*

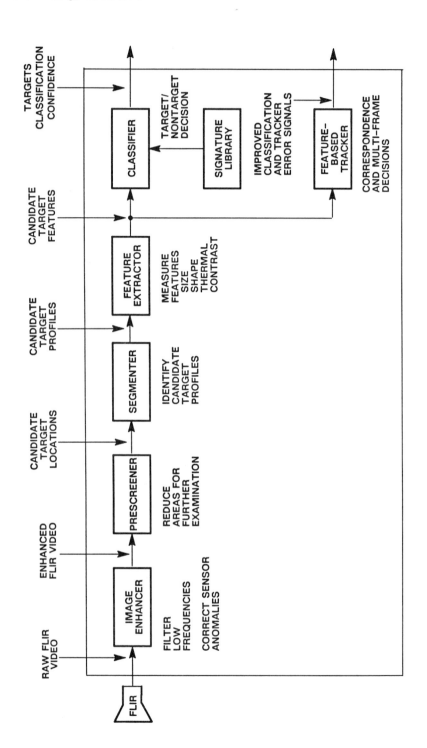

FIG 3.1.24   *Representative ATR processing flow for FLIR sensor.*

has started only in the last few years and the results are
yet to be seen.
     The KBS approach basically has three parts. The first
part   consists   of   the   development   of   low-level   image
analysis techniques and pattern recognition methods, as in
the classical pattern recognition approach.   The second
part includes the techniques for symbolic representation,
strategies to be used for the integration of knowledge,
search and control methods, and the implementation of a
knowledge base so that appropriate knowledge is available
at the right place in the search and decision making
process.   The third part combines the first two parts so
that the system as a whole can be implemented.
     As an example of a KBS system, Figure 3.1.25 shows a
block diagram of a target recognition expert system (28)
which uses a blackboard model.   In this model, all the
information about the properties of objects is stored in
the blackboard.   The "experts" shown in Figure 3.1.25 can
be classified as feature experts, control and decision
making experts, spatial and temporal experts. Each expert
checks with the blackboard for the possible condition of
its activation and it puts the result of processing on the
blackboard.   The individual experts derive their control
from the central control of the blackboard.
     Notice that as yet we have not described any concepts
for MSF; Figures 3.1.24 and 3.1.25 are each reflective of
single-sensor systems.   In performing MSF with imaging
sensors, there are some special issues to be considered.
One of these is associated with sensor look angles to the
target.   If the multiple sensors are not co-boresighted
(which involves various design problems), then some type of
adjustment must be made for dissimilar look angles in the
received images. This can be a non-trivial problem, since
such corrections are usually based on target shape models;
consequently, the correction is dependent on target class.
This represents a dilemma, since target class has not yet
been declared. Because of this situation, most multi-
sensor ATR systems are either co-boresighted or have only
slightly different look angles.   Another problem is that
the error characteristics of the usual sensors employed are
distinctly   different,   and   must   be   accommodated   in   the
processing.   For example, FLIR sensors have poor range
accuracy whereas radar sensors have poor angular accuracy.
     However, the alternative MSF architectures for ATR
systems are not unlike those depicted in Figure 3.1.8 for
non-imaging sensors.   In (27), Pemberton has suggested a
set of MSF ATR concepts as shown in Figure 3.1.26; notice
the close similarity to those architectures suggested by
(3) in Figure 3.1.8.   Figure 3.1.27 shows yet another MSF
architecture for advanced ATR.   This approach is generally
of the feature-based variety (i.e., as architecture (b) in
Figure 3.1.26) but with the process augmented by a KBS-
based MSF classification and tracking process.   Note too
that   this   hypothetical   system   has   two   "dynamic
representation" functions to process, associated with the
real-time data coming from the sensors.   The "mid-level"

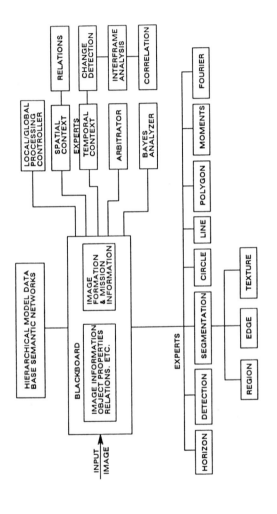

FIG 3.1.25   *Notional block diagram of target recognition expert system (after Bhanu (26)).*

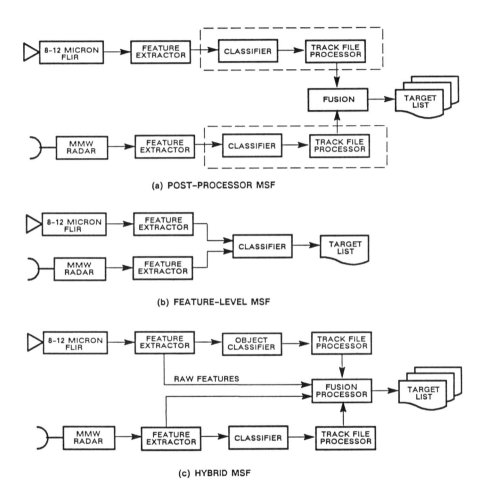

FIG 3.1.26   *Representative MSF ATR architectures (after Pemberton (27)).*

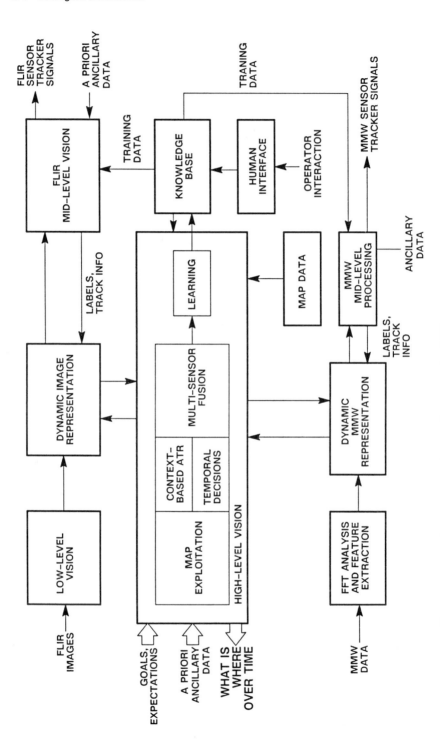

FIG 3.1.27   *Representative fusion processing architecture for ATR.*

processing for each sensor is that based on either dynamic image elements, image features, or mm radar (spectral) features that are processed as data groups or frames, such that short time histories of the data are exploited for classification clues. That is, mid-level processing serves both to buffer the real-time data from the KBS, and to exploit the time dimension of the data for added information.

Pemberton (27) elaborates on the problem of "correspondence processing", which is essentially the association problem mentioned in Section 3.1.2. He suggests an approach which provides for "geometric and classification correspondence" as follows:

• Geometric Correspondence:
  (a) Transforms AZ, EL, R of each target to common reference.
  (b) Groups or nominates targets on the basis of common angular (AZ, EL) position, allowing for angular errors of sensors.
  (c) Groups or nominates targets resulting from (b)-i.e., in common angular space-into common range bins, allowing for range errors of sensors.

This process is shown notionally in Figure 3.1.28. Since this process does not force "deterministic" associations of target pairs (like most tracker/correlator association processes), results can occur wherein some targets from one sensor are paired with more than one target from another sensor. To resolve such ambiguities, Pemberton proposes a "Classification Correspondence" procedure which is rule-based and which scores each target pair, wherein the pair with the highest score is selected as correct. Control is enabled by thresholding the score values. (The analog to this process in the conventional (e.g., radar-based) tracking problem is Bar-Shalom's (34) probabilistic data association filter, wherein measurements are probabilistically assigned to tracks).

Even after applying these processes, target classification ambiguities can remain, and Pemberton chooses to use the Dempster-Shafer method to resolve remaining uncertainties.

Notice that all of this ATR processing has been done at the so-called "Level 1" of MSF, i.e., it has been oriented to producing positional and classification estimates for entities. The use of pattern recognition techiques, however, is conceptually possible at Level 2 and possibly Level 3 as well, since patterns of interest occur in the available data sets. In the recognition of "situations", component patterns, e.g.,

• track history patterns of multiple moving targets (e.g., raid/sortie definition or naval battle group definition),

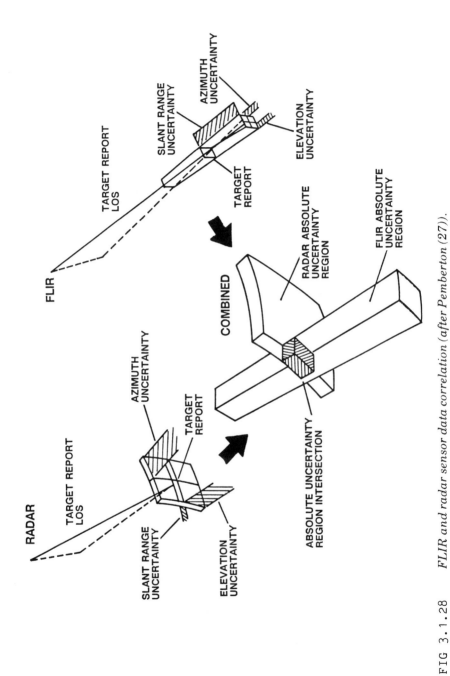

FIG 3.1.28   *FLIR and radar sensor data correlation (after Pemberton (27)).*

- geometric deployment patterns of fixed targets (e.g., SAM regiment doctrinal deployment patterns)

are, of course, of extreme interest. Whether pattern recognition techiques can be applied to the overall situation assesment problem remains to be seen; little work has been done in this area. Further, some researchers (e.g., Druzhinin and Kontoror (35)) assert that there are fundamental differences between situation and pattern recognition that require different methods for solution. In (35), the nature of the difference is elaborated:

> "Situation recognition is a new branch of cybernetics; established terminology and voluminous literature are still lacking; individual publications are narrowly specialized in character. The most closely related field is pattern recognition, but there is a fundamental difference. First, a pattern is static and a situation is dynamic. Second, situation recognition always involves prediction, foresight, and extrapolation, which is usually not the case in pattern recognition. Third, pattern recognition presumes the existence of a classification system, and a basic finite alphabet of patterns established by training. When a new pattern is shown it is necessary to decide to which class it belongs (or to decide that it does not belong to any class). There is no a priori classification in situation recognition, since the number of possible situations is infinite, even though the results have a classification and a finite alphabet. Moreover, various situations may be similar and may even partially overlap in terms of the initial state and character of process. Expressed mathematically, many situations are continuous (i.e., such that a third, intermediate situation can always be found between two others), while many patterns are never continuous. This property of situations is a serious barrier to their recognition".

Presuming this assertion true, then pattern recognition techniques will be generally applicable only to well defined and relatively static situations or pattern-classes, and their use in data fusion most likely would occur as a specialized process (e.g., ATR) embedded in a more general fusion process, i.e., for generating Level 2 and 3 products.

3.1.5   Recapitulation

There seems to be little doubt that the various elements of artificial intelligence technology can and will provide a major contribution toward achieving the significant potential benefits of MSF to emerging military systems. Many useful experiments exploring such applications have been conducted, and some prototypes are being studied under near-operational conditions.

However, much research and development remains to be done. This need is in no small way due to the relative immaturity of both the MSF discipline, as well as many of the elements of AI technology. The MSF community has not yet standardized its vocabulary, nor its methodological and architectural taxonomies. The AI community is in only a little better state regarding these issues but examples of discord remain, e.g., the LISP/PROLOG/ADA debate.

Efforts are under way both in the US and internationally to reconcile many of the technical and professional issues. Some of the MSF concepts discussed here (e.g. those associated with Figure 3.1.5) have in fact been discussed in the UK and FRG. This paper has attempted to present some of the major top-level issues in MSF and its definition as a formal discipline. Once attempting to set these thoughts in place, it has also spoken to the great potential for AI but at the same time raised various concerns which must be dealt with before such potential will be realized.

In essence, this paper is a call for integrated, directed research in MSF to include an appropriate but hopefully robust exploitation of AI. It is asserted that to date there has been no unified research program in MSF that has first developed a formal investigative framework for MSF applications. This is fully true for the particular efforts which have explored the use of AI in MSF, which have been dominated by ES/KBS applications. Only a few of these ES/KBS research efforts have set clear research goals down, dealing, e.g., with the research concerns described in (11) and described in Section 3.1.4.

Table 3.1.8 shows some AI research initiatives considered important to eventually achieving broad MSF capabilities in military systems. The list is not complete but representative of particular research themes, e.g., - achieving real-time or near real-time response, integrating component AI-based subsystems in truly cooperative ways, and understanding a complex, changing problem environment. Coupled to this should be a research initiative in MSF concepts which provides the algorithmic, heuristic or procedural framework for incoporating breakthroughs in AI technology elements within military systems.

A critically important area of research for the current repertoire of MSF techniques is to examine their behavior in the face of countermeasures and/or jamming, and in the face of cover, concealment, and deception (CC&D) techniques employed by hostile forces. Accommodating such actions on the part of an enemy will increase the size of the overall

TABLE 3.1.8 *AI research initiatives essential to achieving robust military MSF systems*

- **Expert System/Knowledge-Based System Elements**

  - Effective, reliable techniques to achieve real-time performance
  - The incorporation of diverse data and knowledge classes
  - Integrated techniques to deal with multiple levels of abstraction
  - Methods for handling "non-stationary" problems (i.e., problems in which the optimal solution changes with time)
  - Rapid methods for knowledge engineering
  - Consensus and standards for test and evaluation techniqes.
  - Achieving true knowledge synergism in cooperating ES's

- **Natural Language Processing Element**

  - Problems in MBMSF systems because of military language ideosyncracies (e.g., ellipsis)
  - Similar problems to those for ES/KBS in understanding a complex, rapidly evolving context
  - Incorporating and/or interfacing MSF processes to NLP processes
  - Research on unified concepts of language and language representation (i.e., beyond text-only representations)

- **Pattern Recognition Element**

  - Achieving real-time processing capability for time-critical systems
  - Achieving acceptably low false-alarm rates in target classification processing
  - Integration of PR techniques with semantic, contextual, structural information, and hierarchical reasoning
  - Research on adaptive PR techniques which can perform beyond their trained boundaries.

---

fusion system, and add to the complexity of designing methods to deal with uncertainty.

TABLE 3.1.9   *Potential uses of AI in Level 1 MSF*

Fundamental MSF Process	AI Technology Element		
	ES/KBS	NLP	PR
Positional/Kinematic MSF	(1) Advanced sensor mgmt. concepts		(1) Advanced tracker/ correlator techniques
	(2) Multi-algorithm tracker management		(2) Basis for flexible, adaptable association methods
	(3) ES/KBS-based maneuver detection		
Attribute MSF	(1) Contextual augmentation of statistically-based classifiers	(1) Same as ES/KBS forMBMSF systems	(1) Improved real time clustering algorithms
	(2) Basis for augmenting trackers with attribute classifier results		
	(3) Basis for accomodating, overcoming counter-measures, CCD techniques		

TABLE 3.1.10   *Potential uses of AI in Level 2, 3 MSF*

Fundamental MSF Process	AI Technology Element		
	ES/KBS	NLP	PR
Situation Assessment (SA) (Level 2)	(1) Template-based implementation concepts for SA (2) Basis for intelligent assistant and cooperating ES/KBS	(1) Direct SA from frame based (or other) NLP, esp. for MBMSF (2) Advanced MMIF	(1) Full or partial SA based on many data patterns available (2) Hierarchical PR systems for multi-mission applications
Threat Assessment (TA) (Level 3)	(1) Same as (2) for SA (2) Expected course of action analysis from spatial data mgmt. systems	(1) Same as (1) for SA (2) Same as (2) for SA	(1) Full or partial TA based on additional data patterns available (weapons, logistical chains, etc.)

The potential uses of AI in MSF are, as mentioned above and in other parts of this paper, numerous. Tables 3.1.9 and 3.1.10 summarize some new and previously mentioned MSF functions and processes at MSF Levels 1-3 which could be effectively performed by elements of AI technology. Realizing this great potential will require solution of basic research issues described above, mapping of complex AI solution techniques into advanced computer architectures, and effective integration concepts and techniques for combining AI and non-AI based software systems into effective and efficient military systems.

3.1.6 *References*

1. Hoffman, C.B., October 1983, "Integrated Sensor Systems", *Journal of Electronic Defense*, 43-46.

2. Waltz, E., 1986, "Data Fusion for C3I Systems", in *The C3I Handbook*, EW Communications, Palo Alto, CA.

3. Reiner, J., 1985, "Applications of Expert Systems to Sensor Fusion", *NAECON* Record.

4. Matthews, C.F., et al, April 1981, "Tactical Intelligence Information/Functional Flow Analysis", *RADC-TR-81-48*, Vol. III.

5. Anon. June, 1983, "IPB-Intelligence Preparation of the Battlefield", *SupR 66000-A*.

6. Blackman, S., 1986, "Multiple-Target Tracking with Radar Applications", Artech House, Dedham, MA.

7. Anon, April 1984, "Tactical Intelligence Analyst Training Circular", (draft), LOGICON Corp., Contract MDA903-82-C-0529.

8. Llinas J., July 1984, "Interactive Processing Program - A Review of the Event Templating Process for Situation Assessment", HRB-Singer, Inc., Internal Memorandum.

9. Armed Forces Communications and Electronics Association (AFCEA), 21-22 May 1985, "Seminar and Exhibition on Artificial Intelligence Applications to the Battlefield", *Proceedings*, Ft. Monmouth, NJ.

10. Anon, 13-15 November 1984, *Proceedings of the Conference on Command and Control Decision Aids*, Rome Air Development Center, Griffiss Air Force Base, New York.

11. Antony, R., June 1987, "A Framework for Automated Tactical Data Fusion", *Proceedings of the First Tri-Service Data Fusion Symposium*, Jt, Directors of Laboratories (Sponsor), Johns Hopkins Univeristy, mD.

12. McCune, B.P., 21-22 May 1985, "A Tutorial on Expert Systems for Battlefield Applications", in *Proc. of a Seminar and Exhibition of AI Applications to the Battlefield*, Ft. Monmouth, NJ (see Ref (9)).

13. Llinas, J., and Rizzi, S., 1987, "The Test and Evaluation Process for Knowledge-Based Systems", SAIC Report to be published as an *RADC Tech. Rep.*

14. Dillard, R.A., September 1978, "New Methodologies for Automated Data Fusion Processing", *Naval Ocean Systems Cntr., Tech. Rpt.* 364.

15. Minsky, M., 1985, "A Framework for Representing Knowledge", in the Psychology of Computer Vision, ed. P.H. Winston, Mc-Graw Hill, 211-2277.

16. Minsky, M., June 19875, "Minsky's Frame Systems Theory", in *Proceedings of the Conference on Theoretical Issues in NLP*, Cambridge, MA, 104-116.

17. Winston, P.H., 1977, "Artificial Intelligence", Addison-Wesley.

18. Hewitt, C., June 1975, "Stereotypes as an ACTOR Approach towards Solving the Problem of Procedural Attachment in FRAME Theories", in *Proceedings of the Conference on Theoretical Issues in NLP*, Cambridge, MA, 94-103.

19. Schank, R.C., and Abelson, R.P., September 1975, "Scripts, Plans and Knowledge", Advanced Papers for the *Proceedings of the Fourth International Joint Conference on Artfical Intelligence*, Tbilisi USSR, 151-157.

20. Schank, R.C., and Abelson, R.P., 1977, Scripts, Plans, Goals and Understanding: An Inquiry into Human Knowledge Structures", Lawrence Erlbaum Associates.

21. Schank, R.C., 1973, "Identification of Conceptualizations Underlying Natural Language", in Computer Models of Thought and Language, ed. R.C. Schank and K.M. Colby, W.H. Freeman and Co., 187-247.

22. Schank, R.C., June 1975, "The Primitive ACTs of Conceptual Dependency", in *Proceedings of the Conference on Theoretical Issues in NLP*, Cambridge MA, 34-37.

23. Schank, R.C., June 1975, "Using Knowledge to Understand", in *Proceedings of the Conference on Theoretical Issues in NLP*, Cambridge, MA, 117-121.

24. Dillard, R.A., October 1981, "Integration of Narrative Processing, Data Fusion, and Database

Updating Techniques in an Automated System", *Naval Ocean Systems Ctr. Tech. Rpt.* 480.

25.   Neal, J.G., Shapiro, S.C., and Smith, Y., June 1987, "Intelligent Integrated Interface Technology", *Proceedings of the First Tri-Service Data Fusion Symposium*, Johns Hopkins University. - Applied Physics Lab.

26.   Bhanu, B., July 1986, "Automatic Target Recognition: State of the Art Survey", *IEEE Transactions on Aerospace and Electronic Systems*, Vol. AES-22, 4.

27.   Pemberton, W., et al, June 1987, "An overview of ATR Fusion Techniques", in *Proc. of the First Tri-Service Data Fusion Symposium*, Jt. Directors of Laboratories (Sponsor), Johns Hopkins University, MD.

28.   Anon. August 1983, "Advanced Antiship Targeting Development", (Technical Appendix), August 1983, Newport Beach, CA: Ford Aerospace & Communications Corp.

29.   Tseng, D.Y., et al, February 1980, "Intelligent Bandwidth Compression", Final *Report to U.S. Army Night Vision and Electro-Optics Lab.*, Fort Belvoir, VA.

30.   Kim, J.H. et al, February 1983, "Investigation in Context Cueing (ICC)", *Report to U.S. Army Night Vision and Electro-Optics Lab.*, Fort Belvoir, VA.

31.   Speissbach, A.J., and Gilmore, J.F., February 1983, "Context Cueing Techniques", *Report to U.S. Army Night Vision and Electro-Optics Lab.*, Fort Belvoir, VA.

32.   Drazovich, R.J., et al, 1981, "Radar Target Classification", in *Proceedings of the IEEE Conference on PRIP*, 496-501.

33.   Applications of Artificial Intelligence", 1984, (J.F. Gilmore, Editor) in *Proceedings of the SPIE*, 485.

34.   Bar-Shalom, Y., and Tse, E., September 1975, "Tracking in a Cluttered Environment Using Probablistic Data Association', *Automatica*, Vol II, 451-460.

35.   Druzhin, V.V., and Kontorov, D.S., 1972, "Concept, Algorithm, Decision", Moscow (Translated and published under the auspices of the U.S. Air Force, Superintendent of Documents, U.S. Government Printing Office).

Application of Expert System Technology to an Information Fusion System

R.B. Woolsey
(Technology for Communications International)

3.2.1　Introduction

　　Expert systems capture in a computer the knowledge which experts possess in a particular field or domain. The purpose of these systems is to allow the computer to draw conclusions as if it were the expert, based on a set of rules or other techniques derived from the knowledge and experience of the expert. We consider here an information fusion system, whose purpose is to correlate, analyse, integrate and present information arising from a variety of remote collection sources. We first provide an overview of the information fusion system and the technologies and techniques of expert systems which apply to the information fusion system. Then we examine an evaluation tool which is used to assess the performance of the technologies, functions and capabilities of the system, and to provide a method for training and understanding the use of the system. This tool drives the system with data that would be similar to a crisis situation in which the system may be used.

　　In describing the information fusion system and the expert system technology it utilizes, we summarize expert systems concepts with an emphasis on those we have selected for the fusion system and we show how to apply these techniques for intelligence analysis. Since the knowledge of experts leads to the best analysis and therefore optimum system performance, the challenge of the fusion system is to capture that knowledge in a machine. We explain the knowledge base that exists in the machine and the knowledge engineering used to capture the experts' skills. Finally, we relate the expert system technologies and concepts directly to the information fusion system.

3.2.2　Techniques Involved

　　Information fusion is a method used to control multiple sensor systems and to combine their data in a way that contributes to the overall intelligence product. There are two types of fusion systems common in the electronic

warfare and intelligence fields.   The first is known as
local or autonomous fusion which involves the collection of
data from multiple sensors on board a single platform which
might, for example, lead to an information display on a
fighter aircraft.   The second is known as global or
regional fusion in which there is the combination and
correlation of data from sensors having wide spatial and
temporal diversity.

There are several areas of application in which one
might see a fusion system for electronic warfare and for
intelligence analysis.   On the left-hand side of
Figure 3.2.1 we see tactical ground support and air
defence, examples of typical local fusion systems.   On the
right-hand side of the figure, we see fleet air defence and
ocean surveillance, typical global fusion systems using
data from multiple sensors.   The information fusion system
we describe here is of the global variety.

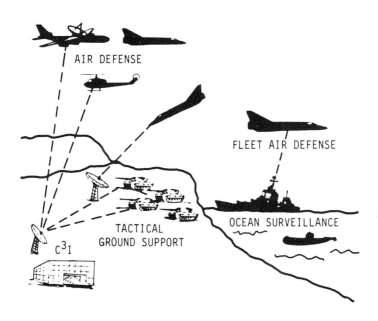

FIG 3.2.1   *Application areas for an information fusion system*

3.2.2. (i)   Generic Function Data Flow

The fusion system itself contains force models, order
of battle information and other data base elements that
describe friendly and hostile forces.   These can be on a
global basis or unique to a particular crisis situation.
Data flow is then as illustrated in Figure 3.2.2.   The
system outputs recommendations for effecting tactical
control, manoeuvres or conducting countermeasures.   It may
output data on alerts, deployments, political response and

overall targeting plans and policies into the threat environment.

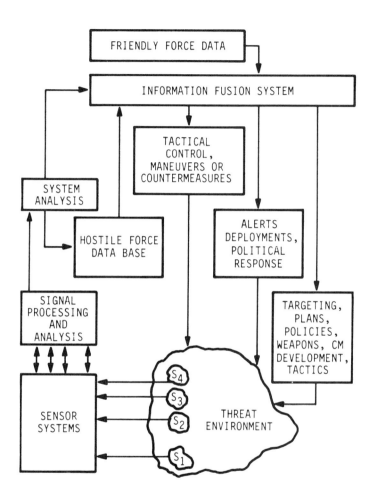

FIG 3.2.2   *Generic functional diagram*

Information on the threat environment then is obtained by sensors tasked by the system. These sensor systems supply data directly into the fusion system or through an intermediate processing system where intitial analysis is conducted closer to the source. This provides a continuous update of information on friendly and hostile forces and situation analysis as it relates to a particular threat. The information fusion system considered here is capable of working on single or multiple threats.

3.2.2. (ii)   *Fusion Elements*

Figure 3.2.3 illustrates overall fusion elements with the four key elements illustrated along the left side. The first is the sense element of the system which provides all raw source data. The second is the element devoted to the classification, tracking and evaluation of sensor input. This element operates on single data sets, as opposed to multiple data sets, to make the most of the raw intelligence received from the sensors. This information then is interfaced to a data base and a knowledge base to be described later. The third function is to identify and analyse the information from the sets of sensors, to combine it to obtain an aggregate of the information. The final element is to report fused data from the system.

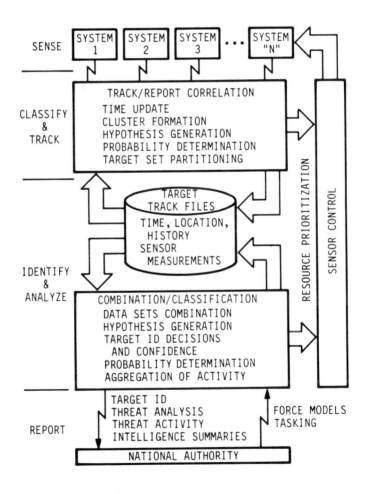

FIG 3.2.3   *Fusion elements*

In the process of classifying and tracking items such as time updates or cluster formation of data from individual sensors, initial hypotheses are formed as to the meaning of the data, probability statistics are applied to the information to assess its validity, and target and set partitioning occurs as it relates to individual tracks and history of targets. The information loaded into the data base represents time and location history as well as sensor measurements. Then the sytem is used to form combinations and classifications of those targets. Data set combinations from COMINT, ELINT, and HUMINT sensors are obtained and hypotheses are revised based on that data.

Any time during this process, it is possible to prioritize resources against the threat being operated upon, control sensors as a result of the other functions and feed information back to the sensors. The fusion elements then operate together to achieve and optimize the available intelligence data.

Finally, a national authority supplies force models and tasking information to the system and general descriptions of threats of interest. Prioritization of threat analysis is input to the system so that the system's resources can be optimized. The answers provided by the system in terms of threat analysis, situation analysis, and event alarms are obtained from the system in the form of target identification, threats, threat activity and intelligence summaries.

3.2.2. (iii)   Overview of Fusion Methods

In order to achieve the fusion elements described above, Figure 3.2.4 illustrates the methods used to fuse the data. A group of sensors is illustrated at the top of the figure. There is a set of probabalistic methods described below which are applied to that sensor data to achieve a level where the system has identified the position, behaviour or activity of the target as viewed in the aggregate by that sensor.

Messages form another source of information for the system. They may be delivered electronically or input to the system through a keyboard. To enable the system to operate on this textual data, a natural language processor has been provided. This processor makes it possible for the machine to read instructions or information in languages such as English by understanding the syntax of text provided to the computer, determining its semantics and assigning a meaning to the text which the computer can understand.

This incoming information is provided to a variety of analysts, each with a specific skill for analyzing COMINT, ELINT, or HUMINT data. These people support the collection of data from the various input sensors and make the ultimate decision regarding the disposition of the collected data. The information resulting from this initial analyis is passed to a threat analyst who has

additional tools, in the form of higher order methods we
describe below, such as templating, scripts, semantic
networks, productions, planning and decision aids that
allow him to make an assessment of the threat from the data
and knowledge bases contained in the system. This provides
the operator with a probabilstic, subjective determination
by the system regarding the likely assessment of the
threat.

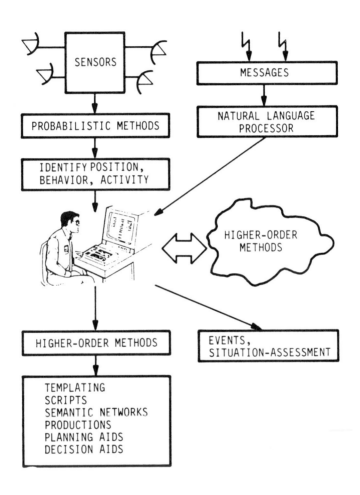

FIG 3.2.4   *Overview of fusion methods*

It is expected that the threat analysts at these
various positions will be expert for the threat environment
that has been tasked on the system. They will evaluate
what has been done by the other analysts as well as that
done in the higher order process by the machine, and

finally provide the best possible assessment of individual events or situations relating to a particular threat.

3.2.2. (iv) Overview of Probabilistic Methods

The major probabilistic methods used to draw conclusions from individual sets of data include the classical interference, Bayesian, Dempster-Shafer, fuzzy set theory, cluster analysis, estimation theory, and entropy. These have been considered in detail by Llinas (1) who examined the kernal process involved, the input-output, the range of application and examples for each method.

Bayesian. This approach provides a decision as to whether data is true or not true and works very well against events that are both well behaved and understood. For example, the modulation parameters measured by a COMINT sensor reliably characterize a transmission. The problem with this method is one of uncertainty; events are never exactly black or white. Most kinds of information that relate to intelligence analysis have some level of uncertainty associated with them resulting from variabilitiy in the data, limitations in sensor measurement of faulty sensor analysis. The desirability of representing this uncertainty has led to the development of the other approaches.

Dempster/Shafer. This approach has very specific boundaries, but it provides the additional capability to characterize an event as being plausible. A confidence factor or credibility interval, also described by Greer (2), is assigned to A or not A as illustrated in Figure 3.2.5. This allows a level of uncertainty to exist between the support and plausibility levels of a piece of data, and provides a method to address objective uncertainty.

Fuzzy Set Theory. This approach represents an extension of classical set analysis in that one describes an object that does not have specific boundaries so that A is represented by one shape and not-A by another, not the complement of the first, as illustrated in Figure 3.2.5. This allows one to define uncertainties, as in shaded areas of the figure, and therefore to treat subjective uncertainty.

Cluster Analysis. In COMINT and ELINT positions there is a requirement to analyse many different parameter sets, and it is desirable to classify those parameter sets as they relate to information in the data base. Cluster analysis has been developed in which parameters are ranked in terms of their importance. A value or a range of values is assigned to each one of the parameters and then the machine takes the set being operated upon and compares them against the data base to determine with which data set these new elements most closely cluster. Provision is made for changing the ranking of individual data elements to allow for identification even when a predominant data element falls outside the cluster range. This is important because while a parameter may rank as number one, the value could be outside some specific range but the particular platform could still be of interest to the COMINT or ELINT position because every other parameter would fall inside the range.

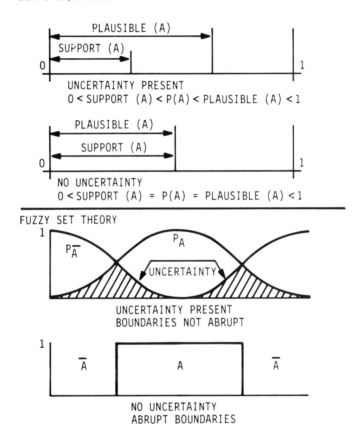

FIG 3.2.5   *Dempster/Shafer and fuzzy set theory approaches to representation of uncertainty*

3.2.2. (iv)   Choice of Probabilistic Methods

We have examined, as have Hall and Llinas (3), the output, or likely output, of various sensors and which of the techniques described above perform best against that output, and have selected for the fusion system three of the techniques listed above. For radar and ELINT sensors, we have used fuzzy set theory for emitter type, location and function analysis for categorizing parameters. In the case of communications intelligence, we have selected cluster analysis for functions that relate to modulation and coding and RF signature. For operation schedules, traffic patterns, functionality of a unit, we have selected fuzzy set theory. In all cases, whether ELINT, COMINT or HUMINT in origin, we use estimation theory against location data.

3.2.2. (v)   *Overview of Higher Order Methods*

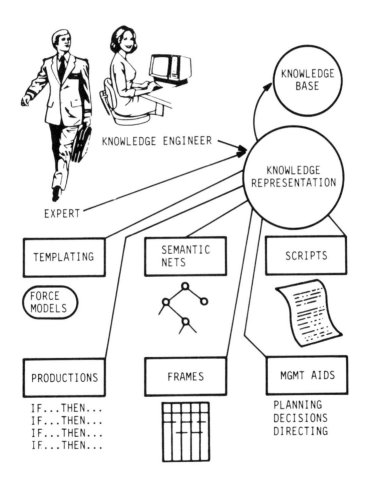

FIG 3.2.6 *Overview of higher order methods*

We have described the functions that are used to operate on individual sets of data that are input to the machine from individual sensors. Once this data has been categorized and classified, the data should be combined in a way that makes sense against a particular threat. The machine needs knowledge of the threat and of ways to combine the information. The system performs best when the threat is well-defined and understood. There is a set of methods to represent knowledge illustrated in Figure 3.2.6.

Knowledge representation can take the form of templating of force model, production of a series of if-then statements, semantic networks relating various facts together to achieve another fact, frames which describe data, scripts, and management aids such as planning and decision tools. This information resides in a knowledge base. The loading of information into the knowledge base requires someone with expertise in the particular field. Thus the expert, who for an information fusion system would be an analyst, passes information to a knowledge engineer who then represents this knowledge in a form readable by the machine. The machine is capable of having knowledge represented in this form. It is also capable of "learning" through the process of going through and assessing new information and updating this knowledge base.

3.2.2. (vi)   *Knowledge Representation by Rules*

Table 3.2.1 represents an example where a set of facts has been organized and a set of rules has been stated such that if all these facts obtain a true state, then the result is a conclusion which should be flashed to the operator, as an "event alarm." It represents knowledge of a situation, an action or a reaction, a premise versus a conclusion and is generally modular and intuitive in nature. The machine also can link these productions together.

As a further example also used in Greer (2), Figure 3.2.7 illustrates the relationship between data, a simple set of facts and the control structure in the machine. The object is to determine the value of A. The knowledge base contains a set of rules which in this particular case represent some simple equations. The control structure then supplies a sequence to that set of rules which ultimately leads to the answer, which is A equals 4. The control structure contains a set of control rules such as not to apply any rules twice. Obviously, the application of Rule No. 2 two times in a row would lead to the wrong answer.

3.2.2. (vii)   *Knowledge Representation by Semantic Networks.*

Figure 3.2.8 is an example of what are known as semantic networks and an individual production that could lead to the fact that the object is a B-1 bomber. In a simple example where we show it is possible to determine, through relationship with other data, that a B-1 bomber, that it is

TABLE I   *Example of knowledge representation by rules*

If

-   Within the last two hours it has been observed that

    --   All organic artillary batteries in the divisional sector DS7 are in place

    --   They are complemented by several non-organic batteries

    --   These batteries are within 1/3 or less of their maximum range behind the flot and in close lateral proximity to several potential key friendly targets

    --   The above information is generated from an imagery sensor of high reliability, and the sensor timeliness factor is less than 30 minutes.

    --   There is an increase in artillary-related communications in DS7

    --   An increase of logistic build-up in DS7 has been detected

Then

- Activate the indicator "artillary is well forward and massed" with high probability

    -   Knowledge represented as

        --   Situation/action

        --   Premise/conclusion

        --   Antecedent/consequent

    -   Modular

    -   Intuitive

    -   Useful for both factual and heuristic knowledge

    -   Useful for reasoning knowledge

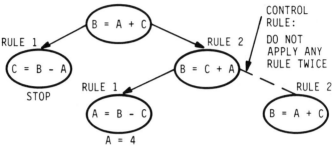

```
FACTS       RULES
B = 10      1. IF X = Y + Z, THEN Z = X - Y
B = A + C   2. IF X = Y + Z, THEN X = Z + Y
C = 6
```

FIG 3.2.7   *Example of knowledge representation by rules*

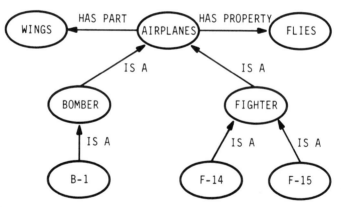

KNOWLEDGE IS ENCODED IN THE LINKS; OBJECTS, CONCEPTS
OR EVENTS ARE ENCODED IN THE NODES

SIMPLIFY CERTAIN DEDUCTIONS BY REFLECTING THEM
DIRECTLY IN A NETWORK STRUCTURE (EXAMPLE: INFERENCES
THROUGH TAXONOMIC RELATIONS)

PROPERTY INHERITANCE

INTUITIVE

GOOD FOR "COMMON SENSE"

TEND TO BE FALLACY GENERATING

FIG 3.2.8   *Example of knowledge representation by semantic networks*

an airplane, that it has parts, and that it has the
property of flight. This is the relationship of non-
related sets of data based on the identification of a
particular target which characterizes that target.

3.2.2. (viii) Use of Domain Knowledge

To summarize, there is a set of sensor information, as
illustrated in Figure 3.2.9, and a sensor interface,
whether it be the natural language processing/message
processing function or the probabilistic methods to operate
on the data. The data is processed and passed through the
control structure in the machinery to the user interface
for the user to operate on. He may choose to update the
knowledge base with a new rule or simply update the data
base as it relates to that particular event. Then higher
order methods are used to operate on the source data using
the rules of the knowledge base and the data of the data
base to generate a hypothesis.

3.2.3   Description of an Information Fusion System

Having described the technique and technologies
involved in the fusion process, we turn to a discussion of
the functionality of a specific information fusion system.
There are several graphics positions with a complete
support set of graphics tools in the system. There is also
a relational data base. Relational data bases are most
useful when random access to multiple sets of data and
relations between sets of data are required, typical of the
fusion system.

The functional positions typically available include a
system supervisor, responsible for the overall management
of the system, and several analysts; a general surveillance
analyst, a communications analyst, a COMINT/ELINT analyst,
a HUMINT analyst and threat analysts.

3.2.3. (i)   Functional Positions

Supervisor. This position establishes the internal tasking
for the system, i.e., given an external set of tasking, the
supervisor determines how the system should operate and
establishes working priorities for the other analysts. He
also handles interfacing with outside sensors and supplies
tasking to other sensor systems. He maintains an awareness
of all activities in the system through the system displays
available on his console. He releases all output messages
to assure that there is a check of data flowing out of the
system.

General surveillance analyst. This analyst assesses all
locational data, whether it is from a human source such as
a simple sightings report, a direction finding report from
an EW system, or the results of a COMINT or ELINT
intercept. All forms of location data are handled by this
general surveillance analyst. He merges information from

the other portions of the system to maintain a general
surveillance data base tracking the actions of particular
threats.   He   establishes   the   area   of   interest   for
surveillance of threats.

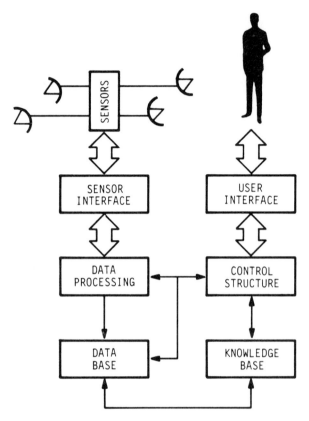

FIG 3.2.9   *Use of domain knowledge*

Threat analyst. These positions, generally more than one in a
typical system, perform the long-term analysis activity.
They are the users of information generated by the COMINT,
HUMINT, and the general surveillance analysts.   They
utilize   the   higher   order   methods   to   use   rules   in   the
knowledge base and data in the data base to combine all the
input   from   multiple   threats   into   an   intelligence
assessment.

Communications analyst.   This   position   extracts   critical
information from COMINT textual data.   The information
could be supplied into the system in several forms, either
electrical, on paper, or by manned machine.   Key COMINT
information as it relates to a particular threat is loaded
into the system through this analyst.

COMINT/ELINT analyst. This analyst develops a COMINT/ELINT library which is capable of supporting both NATO libraries as well as a country-specific library. The ability exists to analyse new hits or new data against that library. The analyst also develops traffic and communications patterns as they apply to relationships between these emitters.

HUMINT analyst. This analyst is responsible for determining the reliability of source input, and maintaining files as they relate to the human data base. He is responsible for summarizing collected HUMINT, alerting other analysts and inserting HUMINT into the data base.

Systems support position. This position is used by maintenance personnel to maintain libraries in the system and exercise other diagnostic functions.

3.2.3. (ii)   System Interfaces

The system accepts manual and automatic inputs from other sensors as illustrated in Figure 3.2.10. It does not matter whether an input is manual or automatic in terms of the processes through which it passes, as all input to the system goes through a parametric validation process. Headers and sources need to be validated and logged into the system so that at all times the systems supervisor has an understanding of what data is coming to the system and how well assigned sensors are responding to tasking. Messages that are valid can be parsed and data inserted in the data base and/or be provided to an operator's input message queue. Provision is made for operator messages as well as supervisor intervention for messages failing input processing. The supervisor identifies the error or source of the message and passes it back into an appropriate queue for analyst processing. In any case where an analyst has a message to release, it goes to the release queue for review by the system supervisor.

In a particular threat assessment, some number of external sensor resources would be required to resolve the threat, to analyse threat related data and to report upon the threat. Tasking would come into the system from a national command authority, and intelligence would be provided to that authority after analysis by the system.

3.2.3. (iii)   Knowledge Base and Knowledge Engineering

The development of the knowledge base in the system requires a combination of effort by the software engineer and the military analyst. Software engineering provides the tools, including the architecture of the environment, and development support system, numerical techniques and the relational data base. For programming, a list processing language, LISP, is often used. The user provides the analyst who has the expertise relative to a particular threat in terms of military organization, rules of engagement, military doctrine, communications, weapons, electronics and other military equipment characteristics or whatever expertise is required to analyse a particular threat. The system combines the tools supplied by the system and the user's expertise in the knowledge base. Scenarios, rules, tree constructs, semantic networks described above, data base design, facts and algorithms to support the system are included in the knowledge base. It is a representation of the knowledge provided by the expert, interpreted and loaded by our engineers into the system. This is the knowledge engineering process, and it is the key to an information fusion system.

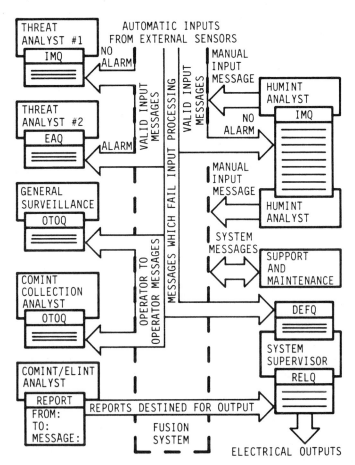

FIG 3.2.10   *Internal interfaces, showing input message, event alarm, operator to operator, default and release queues*

In summary, we must observe that expert knowledge provides the key to the behaviour of the system. The system possesses a very important set of tools and technology but a user can take advantage of these

technologies only if he loads the expertise into the
system. An effort is required to capture and use this
expertise. Furthermore, expert system technology is
relatively new and some of the techniques have not been
tested in a real world environment. There are gaps that
remain in the implementation. The system has the
flexibility and expandability to accept new technologies
and it becomes evident they will improve the system. To
take full advantage of the system, a close relationship
between the user and the developer is required.

3.2.4   *Evaluation Methodology*

A scenario driver has been developed to provide a
vehicle to exercise the system and provide a suitable
training tool. This driver provides messages and input
data to the system similar to the input which would be
obtained from external sensors and human sources during a
crisis situation. The scenarios challenge the user to draw
reasonable conclusions from the available data and to task
appropriate sensors to gather additional data. The
scenario is interactive and users who do not take
appropriate action during the period of the scenario will
fail to fully comprehend scenario events for lack of proper
interpretation of information or for lack of additional
information which could have been acquired by proper
redeployment of sensors.

3.2.4. (i)   *Description of Scenarios*

Existing scenarios consist of a naval scenario which is
typical of an ocean surveillance problem and a ground force
scenario in which an aggressor force and a defending force
are involved. In both cases we have attempted to make
scenario events as realistic as possible and to make them
detectable; we have defined certain actions that would take
place in the scenarios such that they are detectable by a
reasonable set of sensors.
The system must be equipped with the correct set of
sensors to feed data to the system. The driver input
requires analysis, both on data that arrives from
individual sensors and through the use of higher order
methods to obtain the situation assessment required to
produce the intelligence report. Resource tasking back on
the sensors is an interactive part of the scenario. The
driver itself will respond to the tasking received from the
system. Ultimately, reporting is expected. The quantity
and quality of the information contained in the reports is
graded by the driver in such a way that one can determine
how well the analysts have performed and how well the
system has performed in supporting the analyst. The
drivers have been developed to exercise all of the
capability of the system.
As background to the scenario, we have assumed that the
year is 1989, that Egypt is a firm NATO ally, that the
Libyans are allied with the Soviets, that there is tension

between Egypt and Libya and that the Soviet Union in
support of Libya desires to demonstrate a force capability
in the Mediterranean. The naval scenario traces the
formation and deployment of a Soviet amphibious assault
force. It depicts the development of Middle East tensions
with the Soviet Union, Libya and Syria as participants.
The intent is to discover the manner in which the assault
force assembles, actions and movements which take place,
and the defence which is deployed against any aggression.
The object is to ultimately understand the Soviet offenses
and Libyan defences. The ground scenario depicts the
deployment of that assault force on Libyan soil, the Soviet
troop lift, Soviet aircraft deployment in support of that
assault force and the associaton of both PLO and Libyan
forces with the defending force.

3.2.4. (ii)   Operation of Scenarios

The system first informs the intelligence analyst of
the resources available to detect, classify, track,
identify and ultimately produce intelligence reports given
these scenarios. The information fusion system is, of
course, the central resource for this situation and
controls and activity, guides the sensors in their
collection of data and ultimately produces intelligence.
In support of that role, sensors would typically include a
group of HF COMINT collection sensors since it is known
that a large amount of Soviet communications, especially
naval communications, is conducted at HF. A set of mobile
assets, land, sea and air, and HUMINT inputs also would be
utilized. These assets would be described to the analysts
prior to the start of the exercise. They are informed as
to the intent, overall background and location of sensors.
Resident in the system is a knowledge base that relates to
these events. The data base is loaded with files that
target technical information, contain previous copy from
COMINT sensors, and previous parameter inputs from ELINT
and COMINT sensors. This gives the operators the
background to perform the exercise.
In each day of the scenario there are key intelligence
factors which occur. The scenario driver is aware of these
factors, but they would not be specifically drawn to the
attention of the intelligence operators. These overall
intelligence factors manifest themselves in specific
messages or information entering the system from one or
more sensors.

Naval scenario day one. In the first day of the scenario, key
intelligence factors, some of which are illustrated in
Figure 3.2.11, include increased diplomatic communications
between Libyan and Syrian Soviet Embassies and Moscow,
unusual communications between the commanders in Libya and
the MOD in Moscow, unidentified Soviet aircraft flying to
Syria, a Libyan air defence exercise, Libyan air force
close air support tactics, a Soviet ambassador in a
prolonged meeting in Libya and the deployment of Libyan

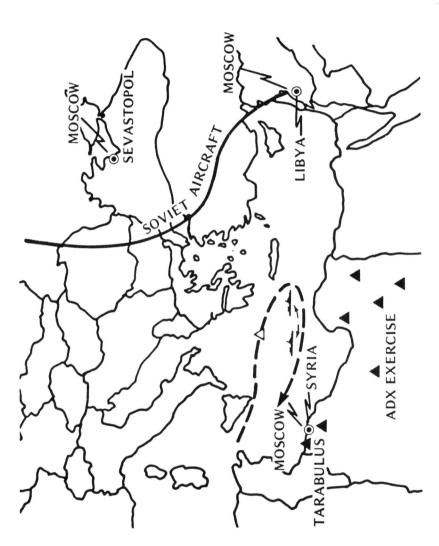

FIG 3.2.11   *Naval Scenario day one*

204 Intelligent data fusion

ground forces in conducting a mobilization exercise. It is important to understand that these events are not obvious to the operator. These are events that reside in the knowledge base of the driver of the system. The system receives certain inputs from its sensors based upon these events.

The system first receives national command authority tasking. The system supervisor sets up and prioritizes resources against the particular threat event and informs the operators of their priorities. On day one inputs from COMINT, ELINT and HUMINT sources become available to the system. The system has a sufficient knowledge base to detect all of these events as a result of correlating information coming from these sensors, i.e., to detect that unusual Soviet diplomatic activity has occurred because the number of messages has increased, to detect the Soviet aircraft deployment, the Libyan air defence exercise, the mobilization of the ground force and unusual Soviet naval communications. These events will be detected, passed to the appropriate analyst, and summarized to the threat analyst.

Resources then must be tasked for the various analysts positions to identify the deployed Soviet aircraft, to determine the subject of the Soviet Ambassador's meeting, to determine the purpose of new Libyan military activity and to exploit any Soviet naval communication. As an example, the COMINT analyst would refer to the target technical data contained in his data base relative to Soviet frequencies of interest for this particular kind of activity and pass it off to the sensors with the appropriate priority on task.

Intelligence reports would be produced by the system based on the events detected for day one, that unusual Libyan and Soviet military activity is in process and that Soviet aircraft are being deployed to Syria. The driver expects within a certain window of time, depending on the overall timeframe defined for this scenario, to see tasking messages returning to the appropriate resources. If the operator fails to take action by responding to the system event analysis, then the driver will provide unrelated messages back into the system, and as time progresses the user may know less and less instead of more and more about what has occurred.

Naval scenario day two. Key intelligence activities on the second day, some of which are illustrated in Figure 3.2.12, include Soviet air activity over the eastern Mediterranean, a set of unusual PLO communications, the continuation of the Libyan air defence exercise, Soviet naval activity near the Bosphorous and Gulf of Hammett, unusual diplomatic traffic and an unidentified Libyan ground force unit in movement. These are the actions again that the driver is aware of in terms of events that will occur in the system which manifest themselves in specific input to the fusion system from the sensors.

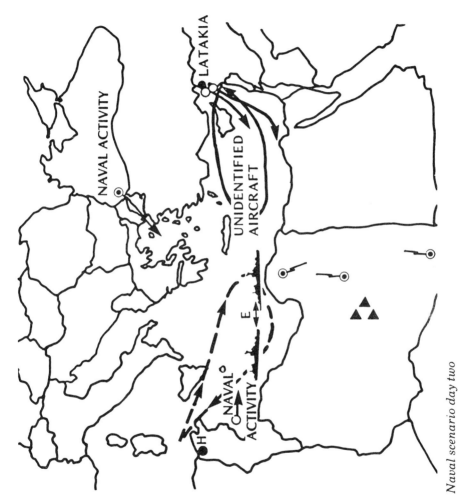

FIG 3.2.12   *Naval scenario day two*

Based on the tasking to the sensors of the activity that occurred, the only new event analysis represented by the data base would have been the recognition of Soviet naval deployment and the recognition of PLO frequencies on the air. The analyst should have recognized, based on the data presented by the system, that a Libyan/Soviet naval exercise is about to take place. He then needs to improve upon his capability to monitor and access that situation and gather additional specific information to better monitor the situation by appropriately tasking the resources.

Intelligence reports would be produced to indicate the movement of Soviet naval ships, the identification of Soviet aircraft in Syria, the continuance of the unusual Soviet diplomatic activity and PLO Libyan cooperation.

Naval scenario day three. On day three the driver would be aware of events illustrated in Figure 3.2.13 including Soviet squadron units conducting an ASW exercise, a Soviet intelligence collection ship departing its normal patrol area, a Soviet tactical C3 multichannel network deployed on the Libyan coast, a Libyan ground force regimental size element in movement, continuation of movement of the Soviet fleet, decrease in Libyan air defence activity and continuation of Soviet diplomatic activity.

In the third day, if the analysts have properly interpreted events and tasked resources, some or all of the following event alarms would occur in the system: the identification of the Soviet ASW exercise would be apparent from both ELINT and COMINT resources, the movement of the Soviet intelligence ship would be noted by COMINT input, the deployment of the Soviet tactical multichannel network via COMINT, the termination of the Libyan air defence exercise by the ELINT deployment and the continuance of Soviet diplomatic ativity both from HUMINT and COMINT resources.

In this case, the system and its operators would make a series of recommendations as to what actions to take over this period of time. Resources should be tasked to determine the purpose and size of the Libyan unit deployment, monitor the Soviet naval activity provide location information on collection assets, determine the purpose of the Soviet naval communication, the purpose of the Soviet aircraft deployment, the nature of the PLO and Libyan cooperation, and monitor the Libyan ground force activity.

Intelligence reports would be issued to indicate the movement of the Soviet intelligence ship, the ASW exercise, movement of Soviet naval communications and the unusual Soviet diplomatic communications. These reports are graded as is the overall output from the system which would occur at the close of the scenario. The operator is expected to provide intelligence summaries that provide situation assessment as developments occur.

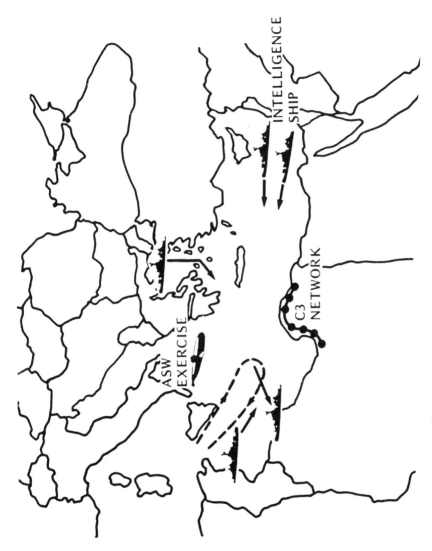

FIG 3.2.13   *Naval scenario day three*

Naval scenario day four.   On day four, events which the driver
simulates with the input it creates, illustrated in
Figure 3.2.14, include the Soviet AWAC aircraft's
deployment to Syria, the Soviet intelligence ship moving to
station off the Egyptian/Libyan coast, the Soviet fifth
squadron units rendezvous to form an amphibious task force,
the termination of Soviet diplomatic communication,
initiation of Soviet air defence activity and increase of
Soviet electronic warfare flights over the Mediterranean.
If the resources are properly deployed, each of these
events should be detectable in the system. The operator
sitting at the threat analyst position would have set up
event alarms in the face of the previous probability
assessment relative to the threat to automatically alarm on
appropriate intelligence indicators.
    The following actions should be taken on day four:
event analysis would identify the Soviet AWACs from ELINT
intercepts, the formation of the Soviet amphibious task
force both by COMINT and HUMINT resources, the location of
the Soviet intelligence ship through HFDF, the
identification of Syrian air defence exercise from ELINT
intercepts and the increased Soviet electronic warfare
flights again from ELINT resources. The tasking would take
place in the manner previously described. Reports on
detected events would be passed out of the system.

Naval scenario final day.   Key intelligence events from the fifth
day shown in Figure 3.2.15 involved the task entering the
Gulf of Sydra, the AWACs active over the Mediterranean,
Libyan TU22 reconnaissance flights, close air support, a
brief Soviet/Libyan naval engagement, mobilization of a
rifle batallion, PLO/Libyan communications, Syrian air
defence activity, Libyan ground force communication, and
the Soviet naval commando force dropping within Libya.
Some of the events would be detectable and some may not be
detectable by the analysts.
    If proper analysis has occurred on earlier data and if
resources were properly deployed, event analysis on the
final day of the scenario will identify the Soviet task
force entering the Gulf of Sydra, the Soviet AWACs
activity, the deployment of Soviet tactical aircraft, the
airlift of Soviet motorized rifle batallion, the increased
Libyan ground forces communication, the Syrian support
activity and the drop of the commando force. Resources
would be tasked to follow this particular event.
    Intelligence reports would be issued to indicate the
location of the Soviet amphibious task force, Soviet AWACs
activity, the increased Libyan ground force activity, the
alert posture of Syrian military forces, and the
cooperation between the PLO and the Libyan military
activity. A summary of the Soviet and Libyan joint
exercise would be the responsibility of the system
supervisor and threat analyst. All activity related to
this particular scenario would be updated in the knowledge
base. For example, the ELINT data base would be updated to
reflect parameter sets supplied as a result of inputs from

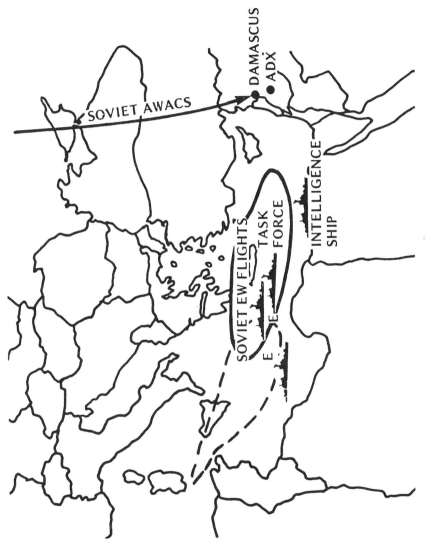

SOVIET AWACS

DAMASCUS
● ADX

INTELLIGENCE
SHIP

TASK FORCE

SOVIET EW FLIGHTS

E

E

FIG 3.2.14   *Naval scenario day four*

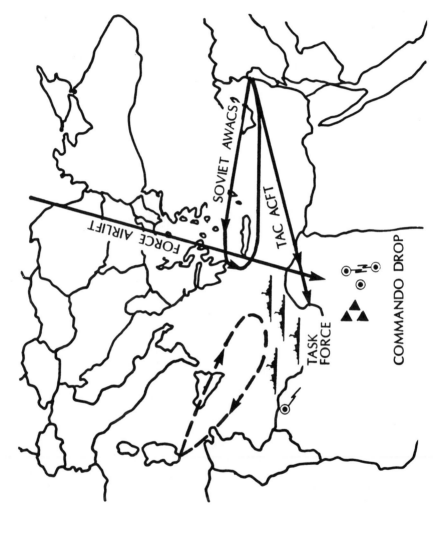

FIG 3.2.15   Naval scenario day five

task resources. The templates and screens, the scripts contained in the system, would have been updated to contain information associated with this particular exercise.

The quality of system and analyst performance would be graded on the basis of the tasking and intelligence reports prepared throughout the scenario plus an assessment of the degree to which the knowledge base has been updated as a result of actions by the analysts during the scenario.

Ground force scenario. This scenario is capable of being run totally independently of the naval exercise or in conjunction with the naval exercise. In the latter case, the data base developed on the naval exercise could be used in support of the ground exercise. Otherwise a strictly ground exercise related data base can be used to support this scenario.

The operation of ground forces scenario is quite similar to the naval exercise described above. For each day there are specific intelligence factors of which the scenario driver is aware but the analysts are not. The system and the analysts receive input from sensors and must identify events and task resources accordingly.

3.2.4. (iii)   Summary of Evaluation Methodology

The scenario driver provides many sensor inputs and messages which simulate typical traffic and observations during periods of potential crisis when an information fusion system would exhibit its value as a national asset to provide intelligence analysis and summaries of events. The scenario driver is a major tool to develop the skill of the operators and analysts as well as to serve as a training vehicle in the use of the fusion system.

3.2.5   References

1.   Llinas, J., section 3.1 this volume.

2.   Greer, T.H., 1969, "Artificial Intelligence: A New Dimension in EW". *Defense Electronics*, October 1985, 106-128.

3.   Hall, D.L. and Llinas, J., 1986, *Course Notes for the DPMA Data Fusion Course*, Data Processing Management Association, EFDPMA Seminars C/O Technology Training Corporation, Dept. DF, P.O. Box 3608, Torrance, CA 90510-3608.

Battlefield Data Fusion

R.T. Naylor (Plessey Defence Systems Ltd), A. Roth (Consultant, QMC Instruments Ltd), P.A. Bromley (University of York), S.N.K. Watt (Plessey Defence Systems Ltd)

3.3.1   Introduction

3.3.1. (i)   The Need For Battlefield Data Fusion

For the highly mobile armies of today the battlefield can extend over many thousands of square kilometers with the combatants equipped with all manner of weapons and means of transport.   To cope with this the command structure has to be able to delegate responsibilities and awareness as much as possible whilst maintaining an appreciation of the evolving operational situation.   In recent years a great deal has been done in the field of Command and Control to improve the facilities for headquarters staff, giving them equipment to assist in information handling and decision making.   The most sophisticated systems are mobile and are distributed through the various command levels of the battlefield.   In addition, considerable efforts have gone into developing facilities for detecting enemy activity and a variety of sources of such data now exist.

The relentless pressure to constrain manpower resources, coupled with the ever increasing capacity to provide information, leads to the need for more powerful tools to process and present that information.   In particular data about the enemy needs to be processed such that the commanders can be provided with a clear understanding of enemy activity.   The task of interpreting Intelligence data is complex, requiring highly skilled personnel.   Automation of elements of the Intelligence Expert's task requires the use of data fusion techniques, and this paper discusses the work being done on the problem within Plessey Defence Systems Ltd (Plessey (1)).

3.3.1. (ii)   Some General Constraints

The approach to the problem has been constrained by a number of general principles which we believe to be important.   The first such principle is that we require a long term Vision of where we want to get to (Naylor (2)).

This Vision can best be described as a fully interactive Intelligence support system, acting in advisory rather than executive capacity (of course), which could be deployed throughout the various levels of command headquarters in the battlefield. The system should be capable of receiving inputs from a number of sources, interpreting these inputs to provide the Intelligence Staff with a consistent best view of enemy activity. Ease of use, particularly as it affects the display of information and the provision of explanations is considered extremely important.

The second constraint is that any system developed must be seen as an evolution of existing Command and Control systems. Whilst it seems obvious that a revolutionary approach of discounting existing systems is not cost effective, there is a great temptation to forget this fact since the use of specialised languages and facilities and the concentration on the domain specific problems is where much of the technical interest lies.

The remaining general factor influencing the work being done is a belief that Data Fusion is a class of problem, with the domain of Military Intelligence being a particularly difficult member of that class. We try therefore to separate the mechanisms we wish to employ in a solution to the problem from the domain specific knowledge required for a full Intelligence system. Such a clean distinction does not come easily in practice, however it seems possible that many of the concepts we are employing could be applied in other domains.

3.3.1. (iii)   Steps Towards A Full Solution

It is clear that there is a considerable complexity inherent in any full solution to the problem of Battlefield Data Fusion. We have therefore attempted to design an approach, based around a general architecture, whereby increasing sophistication can be built into the system. We have called the set of systems ECRES (Enemy Contact Report Expert System). The first experimental system was ECRES-I; this was used primarily to explore ideas and concepts. The full 'Vision' has been christened ECRES-X, and the current work is ECRES-II. The main emphasis of ECRES-II is on the Artificial Intelligence aspects of the probem. The not inconsiderable difficulties of integrating this with more conventional, albeit sophisticated, C3I facilities are left to a later stage.

After discussing some of the attributes of the domain that seem to make it a candidate for solutions which involve techniques from the world of Artificial Intelligence, this paper goes on to describe the architecture being developed for ECRES-II, and to discuss some of the particular problems and our approach to them.

3.3.2   The Domain

It is not always clear that there are good reasons for employing the techniques of Artificial Intelligence when solving problems, however there are a number of characteristics of the domain of ECRES, i.e. Intelligence, Data Fusion and *Threat Assessment*, which indicate that not only are such techniques attractive but conventional algorithmic solutions are not feasible.

To begin with, the data upon which the system operates is governed by uncertainty. Precise observation is difficult, depending upon the nature of the observer as well as on the event observed. Identification of equipments is notoriously difficult with a requirement to be able to convert reported identifications from equipment type to equipment category or to similar equipment types in order to achieve a match with earlier reports. There may be a substantial number of events being observed, some of which are highly significant, others of which convey little important information. There will be many sources of information, some of which will be limited in their facility to clarify or expand upon a report.

The spread of the battlefield and the need to service the different levels of the command hierarchy provide scope for having a number of views of the 'real world'. The enemy is unlikely to co-operate in providing full, accurate information on his movement and intentions, and so the Intelligence staff are attempting to construct a credible real world picture from a number of discrete observations which cannot be assumed to have covered all significant events. Once such a real world picture has been generated there are a number of levels of abstraction that can be applied in infering enemy intentions from this picture. Both inference and abstraction are well established tehniques within Artificial Intelligence.

Finally the useability of a system such as ECRES will depend not only upon the clarity of its Man Machine Interface, but also upon the quality of the explanations it offers in support of a hypothesis about the real world or about the enemy's intentions.

3.3.3   System Components And Architecture

ECRES-II combines a complete *terrain representation* and a comprehensive knowledge of military equipment and formations, with a rigorous approach to data-fusion. The result should demonstrate the utility of both concept and architecture in improving the signal-to-noise ratio of intelligence reaching military decision-makers. This will reduce spurious information, and increase the quality of the data which is presented.

The Terrain Representation will contain details of height and gradient information as well as other terrain attributes. This potentially enables extrapolation of unit positions across the battlefield even though the units may be unobserved.

Detailed *Military Knowledge* will cover equipment
identification and capabilities, which will enable
identities and positions of targets to be confirmed or
inferred, including use of terrain constraints.
Additionally, such knowledge will reflect the underlying
organisation of the forces and their relation to equipment
types and numbers, in order to identify tactical and
possibly strategic movements and intentions.

The ECRES-II system will be based on a *blackboard*
architecture as was ECRES-I, but additional *Knowledge Sources*
will handle many of the clerical tasks perceived to be a
feature of military information processing, and allow the
data-fusion functions to be better specified through a
cleaner separation of concerns.

Figure 3.3.1 outlines the basic architecture of the
whole system. There are four main components:-

i)   User Interface to both Scenario Generator and
       ECRES-II
ii)   Scenario Generator
iii)   The ECRES-II System
iv)   Database (military and terrain information)

Note the clear and logical distinction between ECRES-II
and the scenario generation (or simulation) component (Roth
and Varey (3)). The simulation will be an improved version
of an earlier prototype and will be used to test the
performance of ECRES-II. Without it we would have no tool
by which we could validate the mechanisms and knowledge in
ECRES-II.

Looking within the basic architecture of ECRES-II, it
can be seen to consist of a set of modules arranged around
a blackboard or global data area. Figure 3.3.2 is a
graphical representation of the principal components of
this system and their data dependencies. These are briefly
described below.

3.3.3. (i)   Collection Manager

The collection manager receives all reports from many
sources. These will include enemy contact reports (ECR's),
event reports and higher level military reports. It is
responsible for posting these onto the blackboard via the
blackboard manager.

3.3.3. (ii)   Zone Manager

When a contact report or event is posted onto the
blackboard a zone must be generated for it before any other
processing can continue. This zone will reflect all
possible locations of the equipment even allowing for
slightly inaccurate reporting by the observer. If the unit
or group has not been reported for some time then it might
have advanced unobserved. This module will update the
occurrence associated with the contact report to reflect
the unit's likely current position. An occurrence is a

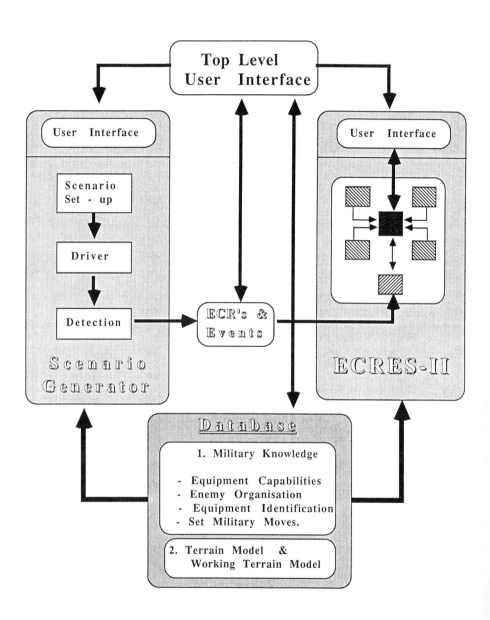

FIG 3.3.1   *ECRES-II System Components*

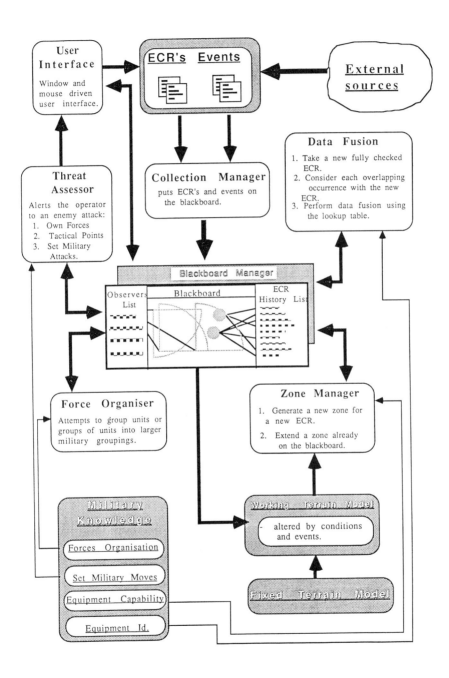

FIG 3.3.2   *ECRES-II Data Dependencies*

postulated enemy position within a hypothesis about the battlefield.

3.3.3. (iii)   Data Fusion

All contact reports already held on the blackboard that might be the same unit or group as a new contact report are checked via a *data fusion* function to see if fusion is justified. If fusion is to take place the module will propose alternative hypotheses to record this decision.

3.3.3. (iv)   Force Organiser

The *force organiser* will search the blackboard and attempt to group a set of units on one level into a single occurrence on a higher blackboard tier. In this way abstraction from detailed, separate events and contacts at a tactical level to summary views at an operational and strategic level are achieved.

3.3.3. (v)   Threat Assessor

The Threat Assessor considers occurrences of units or groups of units at all blackboard levels and attempts to infer when a threat is posed to any indicated strategic locations. Further sophistication will include attempts to match the occurrences within the various levels of the blackboard to pre-defined or user generated military strategies.

3.3.3. (vi)   The Scheduler

The Scheduler is the system component that ensures all the above modules are allocated execution time according to defined rules and priorities. The complexity of this element will be determined to some extent by the actual target hardware. It is clear however that even within a single serial processing environment the scheduler will need to be complex if the best performance in terms of successful fusions and assessments is to be achieved. The scheduler does not appear in the system diagram because it is not involved in data handling.

3.3.3. (vii)   The Blackboard System

An important feature of ECRES-II is the ability to deal with alternative and often mutually exclusive hypotheses about the battlefield situation. The Blackboard System provides the mechanism for managing these alternative sets of beliefs.

Central to the ECRES programme so far has been a blackboard architecture in which several 'expert' modules or Knowledge Sources communicate through a global data area or blackboard (Erman et al. (4), Nii (5), Rice (6), Lakin and Miles (7)). We have extended this concept in ECRES-II and now refer to a 'blackboard system'. This blackboard system consists of a multi-dimensional data structure and a blackboard manager. The blackboard manager is responsible for the maintenance of the blackboard structure.

3.3.4   Knowledge Representation

There are two significant aspects to the knowledge data required by ECRES-II. The Terrain Model describes the battlefield area the system needs to deal with and the Military Knowledge provides the domain information required by zone extension, force organisation and threat assessment.

3.3.4. (i)   Terrain Representation

The requirements for an ECRES-II terrain model include the following:-

Terrain Types - the need to return a set of terrain types for any given area or point of interest.

Field of View - Generation of field of view, line-of-sight and calculation of gradient between 2 points.

Terrain Types. The ECRES-II terrain model can be perceived (though not necessarily implemented) as a series of slices. Each slice represents the battlefield which is divided into areas of the same size. Each area can hold attributes relating to its terrain type. This means that for example in one slice all the areas might hold values representing average height. Other slices might hold imformation regarding the gradient range in each area, or type of terrain.

One purpose of the terrain model will be to support enquiries about the set of terrain properties enclosed in a particular zone or at any given point. Figure 3.3.3 indicates this concept. The three planes are possible slices, perhaps covering terrain gradient, heights, and terrain types. This information is used by the zone manager.

Any area of ground can have more than one attribute, covering roads, rivers, woodland, marsh etc. ECRES-II must be able to take account of all of these different attributes, so that it can always expect the worst and the best of each area. Consider an area that contains both a river and a road running parallel. If a vehicle is on the road at one sighting it does not follow that it will be further down the road at the next, as it could have turned to cross the river. However, it is reasonable to expect it to take longer to cross the river and travel the same distance than it would if simply following the road.

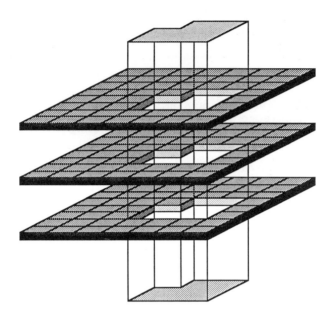

FIG 3.3.3   *Terrain Slices*

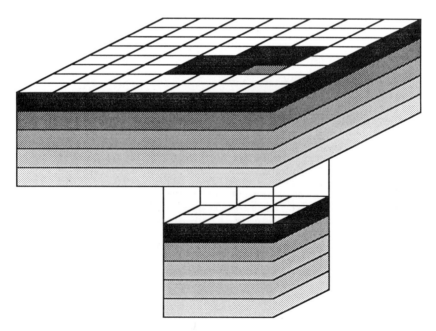

FIG 3.3.4   *Aggregation of Zone Attributes*

Some of the enquiries that will be made of the terrain model will involve zones. The terrain model will be asked for all the different types of terrain enclosed by a particular zone, as depicted in Figure 3.3.4. In this diagram, each different shaded section corresponds to different terrain type. Terrain types are not mutually exclusive on areas, so really they must exist in independent slices as the same area can contain both woodland and open ground. The zone is used to "cut out" a section through the middle of the terrain model. Then, the slices found can be examined to find all the different terrain types enclosed by the zone. After the calculation the model will return a set which can be used to compare with the valid terrain types of the equipment or event. Provided there is one terrain type which is compatible with the vehicle, this is a valid placement.

Generation of Field of View and Calculation of Gradient. The terrain database must include height and gradient information - one need for the height information is to establish or check the observer's field of view. To calculate if the observer's line of sight is possible the intervening units can be interrogated to determine if there are any obstacles. Note that if the heights in the diagram above are taken as averages then the conclusions reached could be incorrect due to small obstacles which do not sufficiently affect the average height.

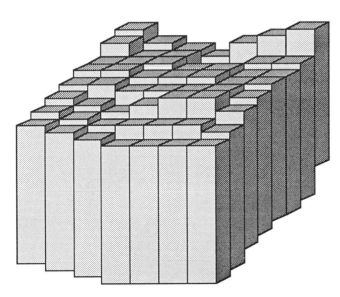

FIG 3.3.5   *Representation of Heights in the Terrain*

Gradients can also be derived from this information, but in practice this will only be the average, not the range of possible gradients in the area. Two areas could differ by considerable heights, leading to the conclusions that the gradient in the areas is steep, but it is also very likely that there are places that are virtually flat. Denying that a wheeled vehicle can be there because the average gradient is steep can be wrong. Conversely an average gradient could mislead ECRES-II to believe the ground was flat when in fact there was an intervening steep sided valley.

Note that no consideration has yet been given to the way the terrain model is stored internally. As far as the user is concerned, there is a simple array of fixed-size which can be queried independently to find their terrain contents.

3.3.4. (ii) Military Knowledge

The knowledge-source for Military Knowledge is called MIL-K. This is knowledge about the structure, make-up and operation of the Enemy's forces.

MIL-K Representation Scheme. A single representation of the components of the Enemy Forces, from individual elements upwards into the structures which aggregate them into functional groups is central to ECRES. The representation will be class-object based, with multiple-inheritance and will support relationships between entities in the complex military type hierarchy.

The representation scheme associates different equipment types with:-

i)   a classification of the actual uses to which those equipments can be put to allow inference of the consequences of detecting those equipments;

ii)   a range of terrain-related mobilities;

iii) the formations or groupings with which this equipment type is associated.

This last association also forms a "unit" at the next level of grouping, with its own mobility-association. Clearly the force organisation structure has been separated from the individual equipment attributes because it is logically different. Within the system the higher level group can inherit the attributes of its components but in the military database the force organisation will suggest all the possible higher level formations within which an equipment type might belong. An inheritance structure linking an army and all its individual equipment types would be too complex and unmanageable.

Equipment Identification. This section is used as an equipment type checker for the Data Fusion module, to determine whether or not two equipment types are in the same generic class even if their actual reported identities are apparently not the same. Equipment data is expected to be reported at the most detailed level possible, starting with category (e.g. APC), subdivided into types (e.g.BMP), and then into variants (e.g. BMP-1, BMP M-1976, BMP-2K).

Using the above example two independent observers may make two reports. One may refer to an APC and the other, a BMP-2K. In this case because a BMP-2K is an APC the case for fusion is much greater than if they had been similar equipments but not of the same generic class.

Equipment Capabilities. This knowledge records the capabilities of the different equipment types with regard to their movement over different types of terrain. This can be correlated with the terrain model to show how fast that equipment can move over particular areas of ground.

The capabilities of each type of equipment can be incorporated into the same data structure as equipment identification, using frame slots for the capabilities of the equipment over the different types of terrain.

Force Organisation. The Force Organisation knowledge will be separate from the equipment information because it relates to equipment groupings rather than individual equipments. Within the system military groups will inherit the attributes of their component equipment types. The knowledge in this module will detail the composition of the different levels of force groups, giving the breakdown of divisions into regiments, battalions, companies, and units.

Set Military Moves. The set military moves component of the military knowledge will contain as many of the standard military actions as possible. It is intended that a Strategy Definition Language be designed and incorporated into ECRES in its later development to enable the Scenario Generator to set up the military movements. This will enable the user to set up realistic scenarios which will define and deploy objects.

The knowledge of set military moves will be used to try to infer the strategies are being employed by means of goal-oriented reasoning.

3.3.5 Uncertain And Incomplete Information

As already noted ECRES needs to be able to reason about a battlefield situation on the basis of information received. This information is often inaccurate, inconsistent and incomplete. Sometimes, as in the case of extreme observer error or enemy 'misinformation' the reports received can be completely erroneous.

Techniques are needed for aggregating, summarising and abstracting useful information at the appropriate level of granularity. In addition there is also a need to detect and resolve conflict due to inconsistencies between information sources, and rank alternative hypotheses or beliefs about the battlefield situation.

A key component will be the ability to cope with uncertainty of information both in terms of the credibility of observers and from the very nature of the contact reports.

We have chosen to use a blackboard architecture which represents the mechanism for displaying alternative and mutually exclusive sets of hypotheses. This is discussed below; we then briefly discuss some aspects of reasoning with uncertainty that we are currently considering.

3.3.5. (i)   The Blackboard System

The blackboard system consists of a data structure and a blackboard manager. The blackboard structure is a multi-dimensional, partitioned, data-area that represents battlefield information at different levels of abstraction. Knowledge Source's co-operate by sharing information and posting hypotheses on this structure. The blackboard manager is responsible for:-

1. The maintenance of the blackboard structure
2. Policing the exchange between Knowledge Source's and the blackboard
3. Keeping track of Knowledge Source execution
4. Hypothesis maintenance.

Figure 3.3.6 is a diagrammatic representation of the blackboard structure. It is organised into a number of separate tiers or levels each representing a certain level of military organisation. Each level contains a set of 'plates' which are graphical representations of hypothetical battlefield situations. Plates are connected within the structure by arcs. Plates connected by such an arc are 'related'. At any one time a particular plate, or set of related plates, will form the Current Best Hypothesis or set of best hypotheses.
The bottom level of the blackboard structure represents alternative battlefield hypotheses at the unit level. The Force Organiser will attempt to group the units on any plate into meaningful military formations which will be placed on a higher blackboard level. The diagram shows only two higher level blackboard tiers. These higher levels hold force organisation and threat assessment plates. Threat assessment will be done only on selected force organisation plates as indicated on the diagram.
The ECRES-II blackboard system will maintain multiple alternative blackboard hypotheses at several levels. It is intended that ECRES-II will be capable of maintaining a number of feasible weaker blackboard hypotheses in addition to the Current Best Hypothesis.
The management and maintenance of hypotheses is undertaken by the Blackboard Manager. Spawning of new hypotheses will occur at 'choice-points' (where more than one interpretation of the battlefield situation is possible). Pruing or de-commissioning out-of-date and less credible hypotheses will keep down the number of hypotheses held (or 'active') at any one time. Much care will be needed to avoid the pruning of information which may later become more credible on the basis of new data. Ideally, the mechanism for maintaining all current feasible hypotheses should ensure that the number maintained is kept to the minimum whilst ensuring that the actual battlefield situation is represented in one of the hypotheses (though

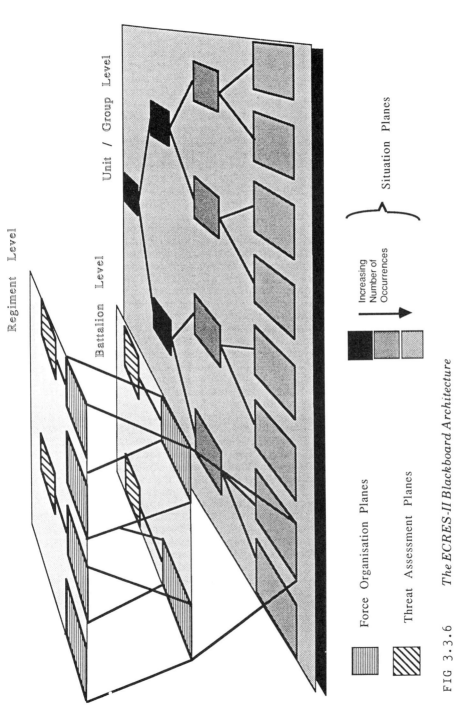

FIG 3.3.6   *The ECRES-II Blackboard Architecture*

not necessarily by the Current Best Hypothesis). The
dynamic domain will give some tolerance to inappropriate
pruning particularly at the lower levels of enemy
hierarchy.

3.3.5. (iii) Uncertainty

Blackboards provide an approach for coping with
uncertainty, but in addition we require techniques within
the blackboard system for ranking alternative hypotheses.
Uncertainty can occur from various sources which for
Bonissone and Brown (8) include "the reliability of
information, the inherent imprecision of the representation
language in which the information is conveyed, the
incompleteness of the information, and the aggregation or
summarization of information from multiple sources."
Many techniques have been suggested which address some
of these problems. Techniques for managing uncertainty
include one-valued, two-valued and fuzzy-valued numerical
approached including Bayes Rule, Modified Bayes Rule,
Shafer/Dempster theory, fuzzy logic etc (see Section 2.3).
Techniques for reasoning with incomplete information have
included non-monotonic logics, truth maintenance and belief
revision systems, e.g. TMS (Doyle (9), McAllester (10 & 11)
and ATMS (De Kleer (12 & 13)). It is not our intention to
examine these approaches here. For a review of current
approaches to these problems see Bonissone and Brown (8).
We have taken a modular approach towards handling
uncertainty and completeness. ECRES-I generated and
assigned simple (one valued) numerical weightings to
represent the degree of belief in a particular hypothesis.
During the development of ECRES-II we will be examining and
experimenting with alternative, and more sophisticated,
techniques.
The code that handles the weighting or credibility
factor of hypotheses will be a very modular piece of code
which is easy to replace with something more sophisticated
later. The intention is to incrementally increase the
sophistication of the uncertainty handling mechanisms by
'plugging in' new software modules. We believe this
approach will serve as a method with which to examine the
relative merits of different approaches to uncertainty.

3.3.6   Data Fusion

The data fusion process involves four stages:-

Detection and Validation
Correlation
Collation
Inference

In the ECRES-II design the operation of the defined
Knowledge Sources combine to achieve data fusion.
Therefore the above four stages have become integrated in
our system approach.

The primary validation of the input data can be
performed by currently available command and control
battlefield systems. We therefore assume for the
development of ECRES-II that such checking has been done.
Within ECRES-II there will be elementary syntactic and
semantic checking before the data enters the system.
    Once ambiguities have been removed all relevant
information coming from the battlefield should be utilised.
If a tank is reported at a certain location and this is
checked and found to be in a river, a validation process
might reject the report or severly reduce its credibility.
Our approach is to acknowledge that the observer probably
did see a tank and made a slight error in estimating its
location. Our conclusion is to accept that a tank exists
in that area somewhere near the reported location. In this
way further validation is effectively performed by
correlation.
    Correlation takes place in most of the ECRES-II
Knowledge Sources. The Zone Manager performs spatial
correlation. This acts as a preprocessor to the Data
Fusion Knowledge Source. The Data Fusion Knowledge Source
itself attempts to relate every new detection event with
all units in the same zone already recorded on the
blackboard.
    The Force Organiser addresses all levels of the
blackboard in order to maintain consistency between them.
Reports will be received about all military organisations.
Therefore the Force Organiser must relate a report of a
large military organisation to its components as well as
correlating each new report of a unit with its formation.
The Threat Assessor uses the military knowledge to attempt
to match the enemies movements to particular stored
military moves.
    Collation is only performed by the Data Fusion module
and the Force Organiser. The Data Fusion module is
responsible for combining two unit reports to indicate that
they are the same unit and they are displayed as such on
the blackboard. The correlation of the data reduces the
number of collation possibilities. This allows blackboard
plates to be created for all collation possibilities
according to Data Fusion rule base.
    The Force Organiser is responsible for higher level
collation. It bases its decisions on the force
organisation military knowledge. This knowledge consists
of the order of battle structure and the position of the
constituent groups in order of march. This is a simpler
basis for collation than the rules required within the Data
Fusion Knowledge Source.
    A certain degree of inference is performed by the Data
Fusion and Force Organiser Knowledge Source's but it is the
Threat Assessor Knowledge Source that will perform the most
sophisiticated inferences. The Threat Assessor will
attempt to infer what the enemy is doing based on
incomplete information provided on all blackboard levels.
It will reason about the enemy's intentions using military
knowledge and will attempt threat predictions. Full

capabilities are part of the 'vision' of ECRES-X. Some elementary threat inference will be included in ECRES-II.

3.3.7   Implementation Issues

In this section we discuss the implications of parallelism and networking for the ECRES programme. In a parallel system the processes are co-operating to achieve a single goal. In contrast, network nodes would be co-operating to achieve different local goals.

3.3.7. (i)   Parallelism

The ECRES-II system as introduced previously consists of a set of software modules or Knowledge Sources arranged around a global data area or blackboard. Since these Knowledge Sources can be considered as independent processes, this structure would appear to benefit from a parallel implementation.

There are however several difficulties with this approach. One such difficulty which is common to many blackboard architectures relates to the limitations imposed by using shared memory. Since no two Knowledge Sources can write to the blackboard simultaneously, a lockout mechanism is required. A solution to this requirement is presented by Ensor & Gabbe (14) in their Transactional Blackboards paper. Their solution describes a mechanism for locking the parts of the blackboard that are being written to, while at the same time allowing many modules to read from the other areas (or partitions) of the blackboard. Although this solution is an improvement upon single blackboard and single access mechanisms it does not provide potential for an adequate degree of parallelism.

Another difficulty specific to the ECRES domain is that the Knowledge Sources are in fact serially dependent. In ECRES-II, the Force Organiser can only operate on detection events that have been processed by the Data Fusion Knowledge Source.

The solution to the first problem is to divide up the blackboard so that more than one Knowledge Source can gain access to the data at once. This approach has been taken by several researchers. In the TRICERO system, Nii (5), the blackboards are functionally separated. There is one blackboard for handling the data from each sensor source. In addition there is a blackboard which is used to correlate the data held on the other blackboards. Alternatively the Lesser and Corkhill (15) approach is to use distributed co-operating blackboards. These architectures still present problems of co-ordination and correlation of the disparate knowledge.

The second approach could be taken with ECRES by partitioning the blackboard into separate units. Each of these partitions could be individually accessible by several Knowledge Sources. A possible enhancement would be to allow Knowledge Source to retask themselves when denied access to a critical resource, This would allow the Knowledge Source to access other blackboard partitions or perform other duties. However, as with the Lesser & Corkhill approach, this leaves two problems unresolved. The first problem is concerned with consistency and the second with the mechanism for establishing the overall system conclusions at a given time.

One effect of solving these problems would be to minimise the communication overheads. The system would then be ideal for placing on a loosely coupled parallel network such as a transputer array [Inmos (16 & 17)]. These ideas are currently being investigated within the ECRES project. However the main drive is to solve the AI software problems because it is our belief that hardware developments are so rapid that the systems needed to run ECRES-II in real time will be available when the system has been written.

3.3.7. (ii) Networking

Networking is an eventual ECRES requirement. The domain on which ECRES is targetted needs multiple co-operating ECRES processors each with multiple user access.

The problems of networking can be divided into the physical and the theoretical. The physical aspects of networking such as communication links and database management have been tackled previously. It is the theoretical problems of distribution and the security implications that present larger problems. This aspect of networking can be subdivided into the following considerations:-

Technically Possible
Organisationally Sensible
Politically Allowable

The technical problems of data handling to allow mobility, survivability and recoverability have already been tackled in currently fielded networked systems.

The organisational problems of handling the ECRES data in a network needs rigorous control. The Brigade, Division and Corps headquarters will all be concerned with different levels of abstraction. In such a network there may be no need for every ECRES node to maintain all the available data. It may be possible for the Corps HQ ECRES to pass on unprocessed data relating to lower organisational levels. It would then only process the data that concerns the military personnel at that HQ. This will reduce the processing loads of each ECRES node. This approach is similar to that used in TRICERO.

The political considerations present major implementation constraints and additional software problems. The implementation constraints include the restrictions on the message passing because of the sensitivity of the data. In software terms this may have to be handled by placing tags on the sensitive data and placing filters in each node. There are also enormous software problems with applying AI techniques to political rules. Such rules will be very difficult to ellicit or encode given the complex interactions in political decision-making.

Although we have focused on a particular domain, any implementation should be adaptable to different domains. Therefore the design will not be rigidly fixed to the military organisational structures. The constraints in this domain are very restrictive. Therefore, if we can solve the problems of this domain then we can hope to apply similar principles to other domains.

3.3.8   Testing

One of the most expensive aspects of the development and delivery of conventional C^3I systems is their testing both against specification and for the removal of implementation bugs. There is no reason to believe that the testing phase of the development of a system such as ECRES will be any simpler. Our approach of developing the system around a basic architecture into which increasing complexity and sophistication can be built is in line with the 'prototyping' approach to development currently much favoured within the industry.

The bugs which may be found in ECRES will be in one of the following three categories (with examples):-

-   A mechanism fault, (A zone fails to expand when it should)
-   A factual fault, (London located in France)
-   An opinion mismatch (Experts disagree on an assessed threat)

The testing strategy will need to distinguish between these types of fault in order to demonstrate the dependability, robustness and quality of the system. To avoid an intense philosophical debate on 'what is reality' we judge 'facts' to be such things that a reasonable man on the standard Clapham Omnibus would accept as true. 'Opinions' are interpretations of such facts, and are essentially dependent upon the rule base by which we judge facts. Testing for mechanism faults is not dependent upon detailed knowledge of the domain, and within ECRES-I we concentrated upon mechanism with no attempt to get accurate domain knowledge into the system. At this level different aspects of the system can be tested and debugged. Tests can concentrate on single functional entities such as Zone Management, Man Machine Interface or Scheduling. Testing for factual errors or unacceptable opinions is entirely dependent upon the domain knowledge held in the system. Indeed the system can only be as good as the knowledge that it contains. There are considerable implications in this for the repeatability of testing and the inherent security and maintenance of a delivered system. The acceptability of ECRES against test criteria will need to be judged in two ways; one is against a human expert and the other is against the original enemy strategy i.e. reality.

For the system to be usable at all it has to be capable of accepting updates to factual data in the field, since this is the very stuff upon which it works. If considered against a conventional database there seems no problem in, for example creating a new equipment type together with its relevant characteristics. If however we look at the rules that the system uses then it becomes more difficult. It seems easy enough to add or amend a relatively self contained rule about equipment behaviour, however the ammendment of rules used for more general things such as scheduling, or threat assessment may have undesirable consequences. If such changes were to be allowed in the field in an uncontrolled manner the system would not only be unreliable but also potentially insecure. The resolution to this dilemma seems to lie in the provision of a suitably trained system manager who has priviledged access to the rule base together with a means of exercising his version of the system before the changes get issued to the operational version (or versions) of the system.

For the testing of ECRES we have developed a Scenario Generator (see Figure 3.3.1) which will increase in sophistication with the increasing complexity of ECRES itself. The idea is to use the Scenario Generator to define enemy deployment and activity, together with data about Observer positions and capabilities. The output from this simulation is a series of contact reports representing reports by the observers on the enemy activity. Heuristics are used to provide a suitably scant and confused picture. These contact reports are then fed into ECRES which processes them in an attempt to reveal the original enemy activity. The benefits of such 'closed loop' testing is repeatability of tests and the speed at which tests can be generated. It would take a considerable amount of effort to generate a sufficient quantity of realistic contact reports by hand. The possible danger in the approach is that both halves of the loop can be consistently wrong. To overcome this the testing strategy must include a phase of subjective evaluation by human experts, leading eventually to direct competition against the experts.

3.3.9   Conclusions

In this paper we have described an architecture with which we are able progressively to develop a system which will address some of the problems of Battlefield Data Fusion. Such a rolling development approach allows us to tackle the many complex design and implementation difficulties inherent in the domain. For each such problem we have been able to see how our current solutions may evolve in terms of effectiveness and sophistication.

There are a number of problems that require more than just technical solutions. An example of the kind of problem that will need to be addressed as the use of reasoning systems on the battlefield becomes a reality is the question of Interoperability. Should systems exchange hypotheses and explanations, or should they exchange only 'factual' data? What level of credibility is required before concern over assessed threats is passed between systems? We have not attempted to address these questions, rather we recognise the prospect of them arising and the enormous difficulties in answering them.

User acceptance of the system will depend upon effective dialogue style, good presentation and, in particular, good explanations. The user attitude to the system will need to be different to that usually encountered with conventional C^3I systems. The conventional system can be considered as a predictable tool whose behaviour, although complex is essentially algorithmic. A system such as ECRES will need to be viewed more like a cold-blooded human expert who is limited in his domain of expertise. In normal human dialogue with experts, one expects to have to have a certain level of understanding and knowledge of the expert's domain to be able to converse intelligently about details in that domain. The implication of this is that users of systems such as ECRES will require to be well trained, not just in the operational mechanics of the system, but importantly in the domain itself. Such systems are not for naive users.

3.3.10   References

1.   Plessey Defence Systems 1987 - Unpublished internal technical papers.

2.   Naylor, R.T. April 1987, 'Battlefield Data Fusion Plessey Defence Systems, U.K', *Proc. IEE 2nd International Conference on Command, Control, Communications and Management Information Systems*.

3.   Roth, A. & Varey, S., 'The Scenario Generator', QMC Instruments on behalf of Plessey Defence Systems.

4.   Erman, L.D., Hayes-Roth, R., Lesser, V.R., & Reddy, D.R., 1980 'The HEARSAY-II Speech Understanding System: Integrating Knowledge to Resolve Uncertainty', *ACM Computing Survey* 12:213-253.

5.   Nii, H.P., Summer 1986 'The Blackboard Model of Problem Solving & the Evolution of Blackboard Architectures', *The AI Magazine*.

6.   Rice, J.P., 'MXA - A Framework for the development of Blackboard Systems', SPL International Advanced Tech. Centre Report.

7.   Lakin, W.L. & Miles, J.A.H., 'A Blackboard System for
      Multi-Sensor Data Fusion', ARE, Portsdown, PO6 4AA,
      UK.

8.   Bonissone, P.P. & Brown, A.L.Jr., 'Expanding the
      Horizons of Expert Systems & Knowledge Engineering',
      Elsevier Science Publishers B.V. (North Holland).

9.   Doyle, J., 'A Truth Maintenance System'. *Artificial
      Intelligence*, Vol. 12, pp. 231-272.

10.   McAllester, D.A., 1978 'A Three-valued Truth
      Maintenance System', S.B. Thesis, Dept of Electrical
      Engineering, MIT, Cambridge, Massachusetts.

11.   McAllester, D.A., 1980, 'An Outlook on Truth
      Maintenance', MIT AI Lab, Cambridge, Massachusetts.

12.   De Kleer, J., 'An Assumption-based TMS', *Artificial
      Intelligence* 28 (1986) 127-162.

13.   De Kleer, J., 1986, 'Extending the ATMS. *Artificial
      Intelligence* 28 163-196.

14.   Ensor, J.R. & Gabbe, J.D., 'Transactional
      Blackboards', *Proceedings of the 9th International Joint
      Conference on Artificial Intelligence.* Los Altos, California.
      340-344.

15.   Lesser, V.R., & Corkhill, D.D., 1983. 'The
      Distributed Vehicle Monitoring Testbed: A Tool For
      Investigation Distributed Problem Solving Networks',
      AI Magazine 4 (3). pp. 15-33.

16.   Inmos Ltd. June 1986, 'The Transputer Family' Inmos
      Productions.

17.   Inmos Ltd. October 1986, 'The Transputer Reference
      Manual' Inmos Productions.

Techniques for Knowledge-Based Data Fusion

J.A.H. Miles
(Admiralty Research Establishment)*

3.4.1　Introduction

The automation of sensors and the provision of high bandwidth data links has resulted in the human resources in command and control being overloaded with data. *Data Fusion* is now the recognised term for the processing needed to convert this data into an up-to-date model of the world-of-interest to the commander (or manager) of resources. Algorithmic processing techniques have been established to solve some specific data fusion problems, usually limited to one or two types of sensor, but the all-source problem in the context of command and control is far more demanding. The use of knowledge-based techniques has been proposed and investigated at several defence establishments. Research at ARE has evaluated some of the reported techniques and has developed new strategies in the context of tactical picture compilation for the naval application. This article discusses some of the more promising techniques discovered and examines the problem domain in some detail.

Data Fusion is a term used quite widely in both military and civil problem domains. Section 3.4.2 attempts to characterise these problem domains, attempts to define the term *data fusion*, and to show where the boundaries of this and related problems lie. Section 3.4.3 discusses the correlation aspect of data fusion and presents a rule-based solution. Following correlation, the data must be combined to infer the parameters of objects of interest. Methods for this data combination process are discussed in Section 3.4.4. A final summary of knowledge-based techniques for data fusion is presented in Section 3.4.5.

3.4.2   *Data Fusion Applications*

3.4.2. (i)   *Definitions*

Taken at its face value the term *data fusion* could apply to any process of assembling or combining data whether from the same source or from different sources and either as a single shot or continuous operation. For example, the common types of expert system used for classification problems, such as medical diagnosis, could even be included. However, the term is most commonly applied to continuous problems of assembling data from a variety of disparate sources. There are many problems of this nature in both the military and civil worlds but before discussing some examples, an attempt will be made to define the term *data fusion*.

Boundaries of Data Fusion. A data fusion system obtains data usually from a variety of sources, very often including sensor systems. There are no well defined boundaries between these sensor systems and what is termed the *data fusion* system. This leads to problems which are on the borders of data fusion being sometimes considered as data fusion and sometimes included in related problems. Two well known problems which are 'close-neighbours' of data fusion are: the tracking problem and the image analysis problem. The tracking problem is simply described as: the association of measurements from one or more sources to form a trajectory or 'track' of an object. Some consider that this problem should be included in data fusion but as it has fairly clear objectives and already has a name, i.e., 'tracking', the author's preference is not to include it under data fusion.

Image analysis is the problem of taking the output of a high-resolution scanning sensor (for example a TV camera, thermal imager, synthetic aperture radar) and deducing from it a 3-dimensional model of the scene viewed. This problem could be seen as data fusion, in the sense that individual elements of the picture have to be associated in order to produce the model. It is again a problem which has very particular, well recognised characteristics and there does not seem much point in subsuming it under data fusion.

Both the tracking and image recognition problems can be considered as sensor data processing problems which come before data fusion in the processing chain. The results of tracking and image recognition would be used as inputs to a data fusion system. Another future form of input processing could be speech recognition and natural language understanding but there is no particular reason to include these under data fusion either.

The output of a data fusion system could be consumed directly by humans or it could feed into a situation assessment level as proposed in Chapter 4.2. Situation assessment is also considered by some to be part of data fusion and indeed the process of forming high level conclusions from the results of fusing the input data is also a fusion process. Deciding whether to subsume situation assessment is probably application dependent but the author's preference is to keep situation assessment as a separate stage. There is no real dispute on the exclusion of resource planning and resource allocation functions; these are clearly outside even the most flexible definition of data fusion.

In this article the term data fusion will be used in the narrower sense outlined above but it is accepted that the term is used in the wider sense to include low level tracking problems and high level situation assessment. See Llinas (Chapter 3.1). Figure 3.4.1 attempts to summarise the two uses of the term data fusion:

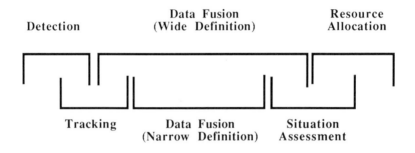

FIG 3.4.1. *Scope of Data Fusion Problem*

The narrow definition of data fusion suggests that the process starts after any single sensor processing e.g., tracking, and finishes when data from all sources has been fused at the most detailed level, usually at the smallest object level resolvable by the sensors.

The wide definition of data fusion spans all processing after detection within sensors up to the highest level of situation assessment just prior to resource allocation.

A Functional Definition of Data Fusion. The purpose of data fusion is to form a picture or model of the system to which the data refer. A simple definition of data fusion could be:

'Data Fusion is the continuous process of assembling a model of the domain of interest from disparate data sources'.

In most cases data fusion is applied to dynamic domains and hence the model is time-varying and must be updated as new data arrives.

Data Fusion is not usually an end in itself but is often an essential step in a control or command and control system. The domain model produced by Data Fusion can be used directly for control or to support situation assessment and decision making processes.

Examples of possible data fusion applications:

(a) Industrial process monitoring e.g., oil production, chemical plants.
(b) Advanced Industrial Robots.
(c) Air Traffic Control
(d) Human monitoring e.g., intensive care patients, stresssful situations.
(e) Global monitoring e.g., weather, crops etc.
(f) Financial systems
(g) Autonomous vehicles e.g., cruise missiles, land vehicles, torpedoes.
(h) Battlefield - ground and air picture compilation
(i) Air defence - air picture compilation
(j) Naval warfare - air, surface and subsurface picture compilation.
(k) Intelligence e.g., ocean surveillance - wide area surface and subsurface pictures.

Industrial process monitoring is an obvious data fusion application involving the assembly of data from many sensors placed around a complex manufacturing plant. The purpose of fusing the data is to identify fault conditions which indirectly cause many of the system states to go out of their operating regions and hence trigger several alarms. The nuclear reactor accident at Three-Mile Island is an example of this monitoring problem. There are also opportunities for applications on oil production platforms where the cost of closing down production when any fault occurs is very high. By identifying the nature of the fault by fusing instrument data it may be possible to rectify the fault on-line.

Industrial robots currently have few, if any, sensors to monitor what they are doing but in future flexible manufacturing systems it may be cost effective to equip each robot with sensors in order to allow them greater freedom of movement and flexiblity of actions. This development is likely to require some data fusion function.

Air Traffic Control mainly uses radar and radio inputs to provide a picture of the air space. At present air traffic controllers cope with this task but as the amount of traffic increases there will be a requirement to automate the picture formation task using data fusion techniques.

Continuous monitoring of the human body is also a possible data fusion application if automated assistance is required.

Monitoring almost anything on a world-wide scale involves data fusion. Weather forecasting for example, draws data from many sources. Monitoring crops from space and ground sensors is another similar problem.

Financial systems within a large company or the economy of a country are monitored by people using many sources of information. This is a data fusion process and there is scope for automated assistance.

Autonomous vehicles for military purposes are self contained systems with their own sensors. They have to operate in real-world environments of varying complexities. For example, simple missiles often rely on a single sensor for each function and therefore no data fusion is required. However, a future autonomous land vehicle, is likely to need several types of sensor just for understanding the complex terrain around it. Stein (1) describes the use of multiple sensors on an experimental autonomous land vehicle. There are obvious similarities bewteen this application and an advanced robot for civil use.

Finally there are the main military applications of data fusion, compiling pictures of battle situations from sensors and other sources of data for use in manned vehicles (ships, submarines, aircraft) on the battlefield and over large areas (oceans, continents and space). Llinas (2) cites 22 systems in the literature covering all military domains.

The experimental work at ARE which uses some of the ideas presented in this article is reported in Lakin and Miles (3-5), and in Byrne, Lakin and Miles (6). These experiments include data fusion and situation assessment for the naval domain. Ocean surveillance data fusion is addressed in Groundwater (7) and in Drazovich (8). A battlefield system is also described in Drazovich (8). Garvey et al (9) describes an approach to integrating multi-sensor data for threat assessment in an aircraft application. This system includes elements of both data fusion and situation assessment. Fusion of Intelligence data is presented in Woolsey (10).

3.4.2. (ii)   Data Fusion Problem Categorisation

This article is mainly concerned with military data fusion problems but it is useful to recognise civil applications because technology developed commercially may be applicable to military systems or vice versa. However there are significant differences between most civil examples of data fusion and that required in tactical warfare. Some differences arise because civil systems operate in 'man-designed worlds' or benign real-worlds whereas tactical systems have to operate in hostile real-worlds.

To illustrate the differences, data fusion problems can be categorised into three types by the characteristics of the problem domain i.e.,

(1) Designed-Worlds. E.g., Industrial Process; Air Traffic Control
   - Known normal or OK state,
   - Reliable, accurate sources of data,
   - Fairly constant data rate.
   - Cooperative domain elements

(2) Benign Real-Worlds. E.g., weather forecasting, patient monitoring.
- Partly known normal state,
- Reliable sources of data but poor coverage,
- Partly variable data rate,
- System unaffected by sensing.

(3) Hostile Real-Worlds. E.g. Military Land, Sea and Air Surveillance; Targetting, Navigation.
- No easily defined 'normal' state,
- Sources of data can be inaccurate, unreliable, subject to interference,
- Highly variable data rate,
- Sensing can significantly affect system,
- Uncooperative domain elements.

The reason for data fusion in a 'designed' system (1) is to monitor that it is behaving correctly. This is possible because the system has been designed to operate with particular parameters and any deviation from those parameters is deemed to be abnormal. In principle it is possible to place highly reliable, specially selected sensors in all vital components in order to detect abnormal operating conditions. Where remote sensing is required, such as in air-traffic-control, the objects being sensed can be made to cooperate to give reliable signals. In practice there is usually considerable tolerance in operating parameters and over a complex system, it is often difficult to assess when unacceptable operating conditions have arisen and what the effects are likely to be. For these reasons it is certainly not a simple problem in spite of being well structured.

Data fusion problems in the real-world (2) are potentially much more difficult because of the inherent complexity of the world and lack of knowledge about its design on which to base models of behaviour. Also it is often impractical to provide sufficient sensors to give complete coverage of the world and sensing is usually remote and therefore prone to errors.

Hostile worlds found in most military applications pose the same difficulties as any real-world problems but with the added disadvantage of deliberate interference and deception by an enemy. Because of this it is not sufficent just to sense the world and fuse the data together but it is also necessary to judge the value of using a sensor and the accuracy of the result. For example in some circumstances the use of a sensor may give away more information to an enemy than give useful data to own forces. The accuracy of data may be in question because of possible interference from the enemy; in this case corroboration of conclusions by data from several different sources is important.

Small and Large Worlds. Having suggested a list of possible application areas for data fusion further discussion will be limited to those of most relevance to

this article i.e., hostile real-world applications, type
(3) above. They can be further categorized as follows:

(1) Small Worlds.   E.g.   Close   range   sensing   for
    targetting or robot navigation.
    - Mainly sensor data,
    - Complete sensor coverage,
    - Accurate up-to-date data,
    - Fast, accurate results,
    - Little manual involvement.

(2) Large Worlds.   E.g. Ground-Air Defence; Sea-Air,
    Surface and Subsurface Defence; Batttlefield; Long
    range targetting.
    - Incomplete sensor coverage,
    - Less accurate, less timely sensor data,
    - Much report data available (Intelligence),
    - Variable response requirement,
    - Requires much world knowledge to get best
      results,
    - Much manual involvment.

    The term *Sensor Integration* is often used for (1) rather
than Data Fusion but it certainly falls within the
definitions given previously.   Autonomous vehicles and
fast-response close-range weapon systems are the main
military applications in this category.
    In large-world applications there are many more factors
to   take   into   account,   not   least   being   the   human
involvement, both in providing some of the input data,
possibly helping with the fusion and interpretation, and
having to understand and use the results. The naval data
fusion problem addressed falls into this category and will
be assumed in all the following discussion.
    Why Knowledge-Based Approach? Automatic processing of
sensor data has become essential in order to cope with the
volume of evidence available in real-time and to support
higher level decision making. Much work has been carried
out on developing algorithmic solutions to combining sensor
data   and   successful   techniques   have   been   demonstrated.
However, these algorithms represent quite simple models of
'world behaviour' and are therefore limited to special
cases.   Their characteristics are:

    -    world mainly in space and time dimensions,
    -    use statistical filtering techniques e.g., Kalman
         Filtering,
    -    require constant supply of data to work usefully –
         not much use with sparse data,
    -    multi-sensor data must overlap in time,
    -    need to incorporate world knowledge but this is
         difficult.

    An illustration of the limitations of simple models and
the need for a knowledge based approach is as follows:

Consider the evidence shown in Figure 3.4.2. We are aboard
a ship at point A with a Radar picture showing five
contacts. A message is received from which the position of
a ship can be plotted for a time one hour ago at point B.
What is the chance that the ship which was at point B is
one of the contacts held on our Radar?

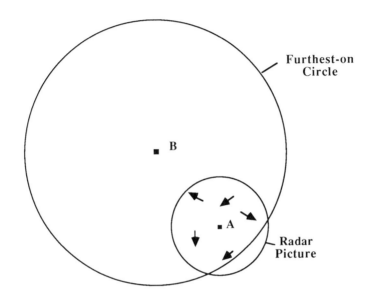

FIG 3.4.2   *Example without knowledge*

Using simple assumptions about the maximum speed of a ship
and allowing for any manoeuvres the ship might have
performed it is possible to draw a circle representing the
area where the ship is likely to be now. Although this
circle overlaps with the Radar picture, the probability of
the ship being any of the Radar tracks is not very high -
it could be any of them or none of them.
     In a real-world example there is usually more useful
knowledge available which a human would find easy to use.
Figure 3.4.3 shows the same situation but with a real-world
context. By adding geographic knowledge and other simple
information a much more useful answer can be given: only
one contact is heading in the right direction and in a
sensible position, i.e the one to the west of own-ship
heading south. Knowledge-based or Expert Systems are an
attempt at allowing such information to be more easily
incorporated into computer systems. They do not, of
course, exclude the use of conventional techniques where
these are appropriate.
     The remainder of this article concentrates on the data
fusion problem and presents a discussion which leads up to
the proposed knowledge-based solution. Firstly the problem
is analysed to reveal the underlying technical problems by

a process of decomposition. This results in a set of
technical requirements which any solution must address.
Finally the proposed solution is described with discussion
and explanation of the knowledge-based techniques adopted.

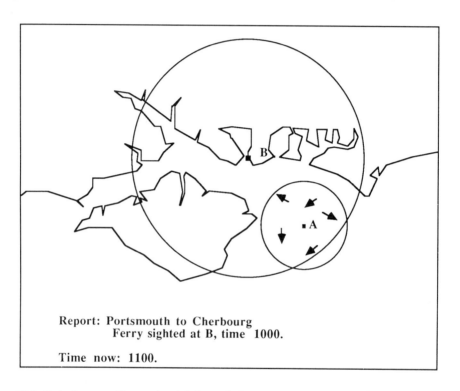

Report: Portsmouth to Cherbourg
Ferry sighted at B, time 1000.

Time now: 1100.

FIG 3.4.3   *Example with knowledge*

3.4.3   *Data Fusion Problem Decomposition*

Data Fusion can be viewed as a two stage process:

Stage 1: Assemble all data which refers to each
individual domain object (e.g. ship,
aircraft, battalion).

Stage 2: Combine assembled data for each domain object
to estimate or infer most likely values for
each object parameter of interest.

Stage 1, which will be referred to as a correlation
process, is only a problem when the accuracy, resolution or
timeliness of the data causes ambiguities to arise. Wide
area surveillance for ground-air defence, a naval task
group or a battlefield are likely to suffer from

correlation ambiguities which will require a great deal of processing to attempt to resolve and in fact may be an insoluble problem some of the time.

Stage 2 is less difficult and has been researched quite widely. Two approaches for combining data to establish parameters seem to have emerged. These methods will be disussed later in Section 3 and an example of the preferred method will be given.

3.4.3. (i)   The Correlation Method

For the purposes of an initial discussion the sources of information shown in Figure 3.4.4 can be considered.

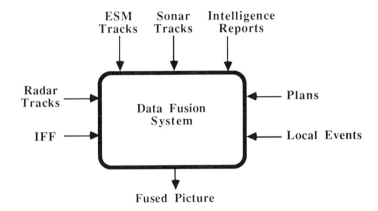

FIG 3.4.4   *Sources of data*

These form a fairly general subset of the many specific sensor, communications and paperwork sources which would be found on a warship. Input data from the sources shown will initially be assumed to have the following characteristics:

* Individual objects: It is assumed that the data will refer to individual objects, e.g. a ship, aircraft or helicopter, rather than to groups, e.g.: the task force, a wave of aircraft. Groups will be discussed later.
* Track data: the data will have the characteristics of what are often called 'tracks', i.e.: a set of contacts over a period of time referring to the same object. This implies, in some cases (e.g. radar), a considerable amount of pre-processing to associate individual measurements of a target to reject spurious data, and to calculate course and speed. This is a reasonable assumption for modern sensors; observations from say an intelligence

source can be similarly regarded, even if there is only one observation.

* No duplication of co-located sensors: this means that if a ship is fitted with, for example, more than one radar, their outputs will be combined before entry into the Data Fusion system. Again this is a reasonable assumption as it is possible to use simple association algorithms to do this reliably without relating to any wider knowledge. It could be done in the Data Fusion system but would be an additional processing burden.
* Timelessness of data: for onboard sensors, minimal delay is assumed between measurement and corresponding input to the Data Fusion system. For other data such as intelligence, delays between observations and data arriving must be allowed for.

None of these assumptions is in fact critical to the strategy adopted, but they help to clarify the following explanations.

3.4.3. (ii)   Correlation Ambiguity Problem

Figure 3.4.5 illustrates some types of input data as a plan view of the world:

* Radar tracks are shown as lines from first detection to present position.
* ESM contacts are shown as bearing lines along which electronic emissions have been detected, giving approximate direction but little idea of range.
* The sectors represent areas in which own units have been ordered to operate.
* The circle indicates the uncertainty of units reported as intelligence from observations made some time ago.

In order to correlate these types of data, the measured parameters must be compared to see if sets of data from different sources could refer to the same real-world object. It can be seen that many of these sources of data are spatially inaccurate and it is possible to assemble the data in several different combinations. This problem is referred to as the correlation ambiguity problem and is the main hurdle to overcome in a data fusion system for the type of problem described.
Correlation ambiguity occurs for the following reasons:

(1) inaccuracy - of both spatial and identity clues
(2) incomplete sensor coverage
(3) delays in receiving data
(5) false alarms
(5) sensor resolution differences

Inaccuracy in the data and incomplete sensor coverage are characteristics of all problems of wide area surveillance using remote sensors. Delays in receiving data from remote sources occur in many systems owing to lack of communication bandwidth and/or manual processing of messages. False alarms are also a characteristic of remote sensing and can be caused by noise, clutter or interference. Sensors cannot always resolve single real-world objects and different types of sensor have different resolution capabilities; this can also cause ambiguities.

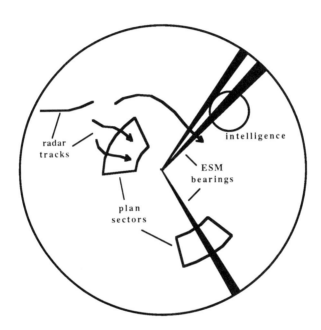

FIG 3.4.5   *Example input data*

Correlation is not confined to dealing with data from different sources. Radar tracks, for example, exhibit breaks when the target goes out of range or into clutter, or the set is jammed. These breaks need to be repaired in order to carry across identity information and to build a more complete picture. This demonstrates the need for correlation in time of data from the same sensor as well as correlation between sensors.

The scenario in Figure 3.4.5 is, of course, much simplified. In reality there could be many hundreds of track segments to deal with over say a 1-hour period, and a very confused picture could result. Hence the importance of asembling all data belonging to each real vehicle so that the picture resembles the real world as closely as possible.

Figure 3.4.6 represents the ideal result of the correlation process: the aggregation of information from tracks and reports of the same vehicle from different sources.

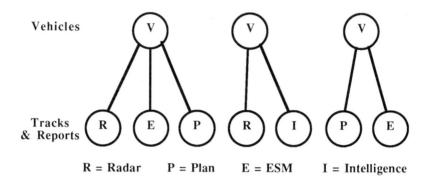

R = Radar   P = Plan   E = ESM   I = Intelligence

Tracks = A set of data over time about a single object from any sensor

FIG 3.4.6   *Ideal result of data fusion*

However, the problem of correlation ambiguity often arises and a simple case is illustrated in Figure 3.4.7. Here, possible interpretations of the data in terms of real-world objects are represented by vehicle hypotheses.

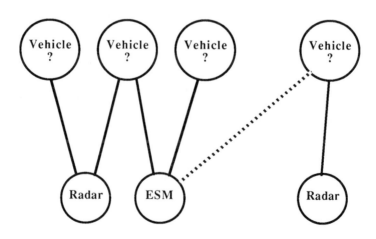

FIG 3.4.7 *Correlation ambiguities*

Even if Radar and ESM contacts on the left of the figure are found to correlate by matching their parameters within pre-defined tolerances, there are still two possibilities:

* Either they are the same object - denoted by the middle vehicle hypotheses,
* Or they are two different objects - demonstrated by the other two vehicle hypotheses.

A single object detected by n sensors will generate $2n-1$ such vehicle hypotheses. As each sensor detects not one but many objects, there is also further ambiguity as to which contacts go together as illustrated by the Radar contact on the right. The inherent inaccuracy of most of the sensor data implies loose correlation rules leading to large number of such ambiguities. The need to process several new contacts per second leads to unmanageable combinatorial difficulties with such an approach.

3.4.3. (iii)   Combinatorial Explosion Problem

There is a further problem illustrated in Figure 3.4.8.

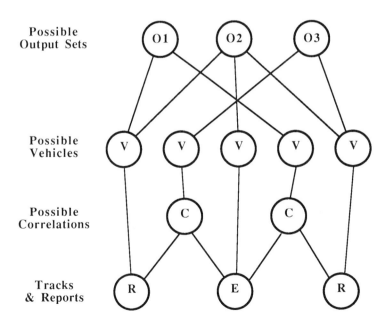

FIG 3.4.8 *Output sets*

Having generated all possible hypotheses to explain the data, it is necessary to decide which ones to output as being the most likely. Attempting to do this by generating every possible consistent output set and then scoring these in some way leads to the output sets shown. For example, taking two Radar tracks either one of which could correlate with an ESM track, there are three possible self-consistent output sets or 'views' of the situation. These are:

* Left-hand correlation is valid   - output set 03
* Right-hand correlation is valid - output set 01
* Neither correlation is valid   - output set 02

This approach is attractive since all consistent sets are represented and, given a satisfactory scoring system, the Current Best View is simply the view with the highest score. Unfortunately the enormous number of views resulting from any realistic scenario renders the approach impractical. For example, even for a single object detected by n sensors, the number of logically consistent views of the situation is given by the so called Bell number B(n) (Sinha (11)). This formula gives the number of possible partitions of a set:

$$B(n) = \sum_{1=0}^{m} \begin{bmatrix} m \\ i \end{bmatrix} B(m-i); \qquad B(0) = 1 \qquad \begin{bmatrix} m \\ i \end{bmatrix} = \frac{m!}{i!\,(m-i)!}$$

where m = n-1.

TABLE 3.4.1   *Bell numbers*

Numbers of sensors	Number of combinations B(n)
1	1
2	2
3	5
4	15
5	52
6	203
7	877
8	4140
9	21147
10	115975

Table 3.4.1 shows how the combinations explode as the number of contributing sensors increases:
The rapid rise in combinations over three sensors is perhaps an indication of the need for a knowledge-based approach with heuristics to limit search in all-source data fusion applications. This statement is rather an over simplification because it also depends on the quality and density of the data but it does demonstrate the need for an approach other than brute force.
Much of the research work on which this article is based has been devoted to creating and validating a solution to this problem. An outline of the solution which is less rigorous but more practical is shown in Figure 3.4.9.

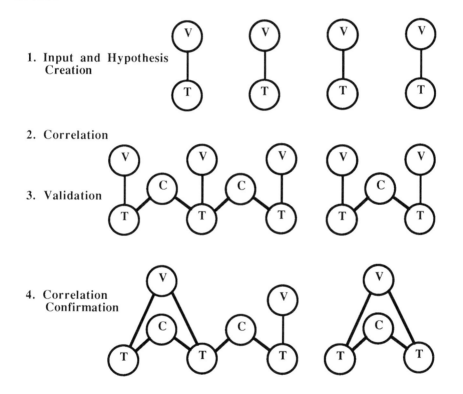

1. Input and Hypothesis Creation

2. Correlation

3. Validation

4. Correlation Confirmation

FIG 3.4.9   *Rule-based data fusion strategy*

This method considers only pairwise correlations and involves 4 distinct steps:

(1) Assume all new contacts are separate and therefore each new contact implies a new vehicle.
(2) Create the possible pairwise correlations between each new track and existing tracks in the system.

(3) Periodically check these correlations to make sure they are still valid; those that fail the check are deleted.

(4) Apply rules to confirm strong correlations and to deny others. Where alternatives are of similar strengths, wait for further evidence.

The correlation decisions are taken in steps 2 and 4. Step 2 requires comparisons between data on new contacts and those already held to determine whether correlation is possible on a pairwise basis. Step 4 is more complicated.

To confirm a correlation, its likelihood must:

* Firstly exceed some absolute threshold,
* Secondly, significantly exceed other possibilities, i.e. be relatively unambiguous,
* Thirdly, the correlation must be part of an allowed set. For example, if A tentatively correlates with B, and B with C, these can only be confirmed if C also correlates with A. In other words, all tracks supporting the same vehicle must mutually correlate on a pairwise basis.

TABLE 3.4.2   *Combinations comparison*

Numbers of sensors	Number of combinations B(n)	Number of pairwise correlations C(n)
1	1	0
2	2	1
3	5	3
4	15	6
5	52	10
6	203	15
7	877	21
8	4140	28
9	21147	36
10	115975	45

By only representing all pairwise correlations of data, the combinatorial problem is much reduced; the number of such correlations C(n) being given by the following formula for comparison with the previous example

$$C(n) = \frac{n(n-1)}{2}$$

Table 3.4.2 compares the pairwise correlations with the Bell numbers.

3.4.3. (iv) Knowledge-based Aspects

In a data fusion problem where the data comes from a variety of disparate sources with different accuracies, resolutions, false alarm rates and transmission delays, a considerable amount of knowledge will be required to perform the task. For this reason, and also to allow for human understanding and interaction, a knowledge-based solution is proposed.

There are two main considerations for any proposed knowledge-based system:

(1) What problem solving model should be adopted?
(2) What forms of knowledge representation are required?

In most experiments involving continuous, real-time problems, researchers have used either the *blackboard model* or a *production system*. They are both rule-based and differ mainly in their control mechanisms. In fact the blackboard model has been used in the experiments related to this work (Lakin and Miles (3-5)) and it will be assumed here. The blackboard model consists of a global data structure 'the blackboard' which is a hierarchical network of hypotheses representing successive levels of reasoning leading to a solution. This data structure is created and modified by sets of rules called knowledge sources.

In a blackboard solution to data fusion, rules will be required for correlation and combination of data, and a data structure will be needed to represent the results. The data structure should ideally be as simple as possible consistent with having clear and clean semantics. This should make it easier to engineer and maintain the knowledge, and make the operation of the system more readily understood by the users.

With a continuous, real-time problem, evidence is collected over a period of time but results must be produced quickly with whatever evidence is available at each stage. Evidence, partial results and current conclusions must all be represented in the data structure. As new evidence arrives, the data structure will be updated and modified by the rules. Because there are ambiguities in the way the evidence correlates, alternative hypotheses must also be represented until there is reasonable proof for selecting or rejecting a particular hypothesis.

The input data represent evidence on many real-world objects so at any time there will be many instances of similar data types to include in the data structure.

The rules which access the data structure need a method of representing the belief in any inference and a method of combining belief measures to apply to higher level inferences. This reasoning system must support explanations so that the chains of inference or lines of reasoning are visible to the user. To summarise, the requirements for a knowledge-based solution are:

- a problem solving model suitable for real-time.
- simple data structure to represent the current state of the solution allowing for multiple hypotheses, multiple instances and with pure semantics.
- sets of rules for correlation and combination of evidence.
- a reasoning method to correlate and combine uncertain evidence in a simple, effective way which can also support explanations.

The *blackboard model* has already been introduced as a suitable model on which to base a real-time data fusion strategy. Blackboard systems are explained and described in (12), (13).

Elements of the data structure have also been introduced. In the blackboard model these elements are called hypotheses. Three generic types of hypotheses are required to support the correlation strategy described:

EVIDENCE - these hypotheses store the input from data sources. They consist of a single time-stamped report or a series of reports over time referring to the same real-world object perceived by the data source. Inferred parameters for correlation purposes will also be stored in these hypotheses.

OBJECT - hypotheses represent the system's model of the domain which it has inferrred from the evidence. Each evidence hypothesis supports exactly one object entity but an object hypothesis may be supported by one or more evidence hypotheses.

CORRELATION hypotheses represent possible correlations between exactly two evidence hypotheses. These have two states: tentative and confirmed.

Rules. The other main component of the solution is the set of rules which create and manipulate that structure. Here is a complete list of rule types required:

INPUT rules update an existing evidence hypothesis or create a new one supporting a new object. They maintain the lowest level of hypotheses on the blackboard including current, historical and statistical information obtained from data sources.

INITIAL INFERENCE rules infer parameters for correlation from evidence. These inferred parameters are added to the evidence hypotheses. Examples could include purely arithmetic rules to convert units and coordinate systems to those used for correlation, prediction rules to provide more up-to-data parameters and inference rules for deducing identity information compatible with other data sources.

CORRELATION rules attempt to correlate a new evidence hypothesis with all existing ones on a pairwise basis. Where the correlation conditions are met, a tentative pairwise correlation hypothesis is created between the two evidence hypotheses concerned.

CORRELATION VALIDATION rules check the validity of existing correlations. If the check fails on a tentative correlation, the correlation hypothesis is deleted. Checks on confirmed correlations which fail cause the object hypothesis to be split and the correlation hypothesis to be deleted.

TRACK REPAIR rules form tentative links between current and past segments of track data. Tracks break because of detection and/or tracking failures in the sensor. These breaks must be repaired in order to produce a complete picture.

REPAIR CONFIRMATION rules attempt to confirm particular track repair links. Once a confirmed repair is established, evidence from past segments of the track can be incorporated into the inferences of object parameters.

CORRELATION CONFIRMATION rules attempt to confirm tentative correlations by considering the absolute likelihood of the correlation, the relative likelihood compared to alternative correlations and whether a consistent set of correlations exist.

PARAMETER INFERENCE rules use the correlated evidence for each object to infer as many of the parameters required as possible. Section 3.4.4. (i) will discuss these rules more fully.

A reasoning system is required to represent the uncertainty in the correlation and combination of evidence; this will be the subject of Section 3.4.4.

This summary covers all the basic mechanisms required but there are still some important issues to resolve when the model is applied to a real situation.

Correlation Time Limit. The description above fails to specify how the amount of evidence will be controlled over a period of time. Obviously the longer the system runs the more input will arrive and the greater the number of evidence hypotheses there will be to consider for correlation. It would be possible to set a time limit for all evidence and discard it when this limit expires. However it would be more flexible if knowledge could be used to discard stale data. This would allow for data to be retained as long as required depending on its importance.

Even assuming such a mechanism there is a problem with allowing new evidence to correlate with stale data. This is because the uncertainty of positional data increases rapidly with time for fast moving objects. Given the position of an aircraft one hour ago and no update since, for example, it could now be anywhere within a radius of several hundered miles. Any new evidence which could possibly be related to an aircraft would be bound to correlate and an explosion of such correlations could result with little hope of resolving all the ambiguitites.

This problem indicates that some time limit should be set for stale data beyond which it is no longer considered for correlation – at least not using the strategy defined above. This limit wil vary depending on the way positional uncertainty increases with time and perhaps the local density of objects; these are the two controlling factors governing the amount of correlation ambiguity.

Sequence of Events. The sequence of outputs from the data fusion system is bound to reflect the sequence of inputs but given the same set of inputs over a period of time, it should eventually produce the same result whatever the order of input. Take, for instance the following example:

(1) Evidence A arrives first.
(2) Evidence B arrives and correlates with A.
(3) Evidence C arrives and correlates tentatively with A.

If C forms a better match with A than B, then the system should switch to correlate A and C. If C had arrived before B this would have been the case anyway.

To ensure consistent results it is necessary to continually re-consider the correlation confirmation decisions already made. The problem is that there is a trade-off between achieving quick results and producing stable results. If decisions are taken quickly they are likely to switch between alternatives several times before a stable result is achieved. Building in some hysteresis will produce a more stable output but it will obviously take longer to correct mistakes. Another alternative is to make the system very cautious about taking any decisions but this may not be useful in practice.

Group Evidence. It is likely that some data sources will have better resolution than others. This will give rise to some evidence referring to groups of real-world objects rather than single objects. In fact in some cases a data source may give more than one set of evidence on the same real-world object. All possible cases must be allowed for in some way.

Where a data source gives more than one set of evidence for a single real-world object it can be dealt with using the same strategy. It is as though there was more than one data source. Care must be taken to ensure that the rules allow for all possible combinations of evidence including combinations of data from the same source. Where a set of evidence refers to a group of real-world objects there are two alternative approaches. Either an attempt can be made to split up the group into a number self-consistent parts or the evidence can be correlated at a higher level in the model where group objects have been created. Each approach has its merits depending on the type of information. For example, a report in text form which itemises the constituents of a group of objects can easily be split up. A much less precise sensor report of a blurred group of contacts where the constituents and even the number of objects are unknown must be retained as a group object. Knowledge representation and rule-based correlation of group evidence need extensions to the strategy discussed.

Multiple Levels. The data fusion strategy has assumed a flat structure for correlating evidence from disparate sources. This may not be appropriate when there are groups of similar sources involved because it may be possible to unambiguously correlate similar sources first in order to reduce the number of combinations. This is illustrated in Figure 3.4.10 with two types of evidence, A and B.

Adding new data of type A to the flat structure requires four correlation attempts in this example whereas adding it to the two level structure only requires two attempts if correlation is successful. Only if unsuccessful need the new evidence be correlated with the full set of evidence from all sources. This subject will be addressed in the next section.

3.4.4   *Multi-Platform Data Fusion*

In a typical naval scenario there will be a number of surface ships with their air assets and perhaps submarines, operating as a group. Assuming that data link and voice communications are available, it will be possible to collect sensor data from other platforms to form a tactical picture over a much wider area than that perceived directly by own ship. There is also the possiblity of combining passive forms of data such as ESM or Passive Sonar, to produce much more accurate track data, for example by triangulation of bearing lines.

In addition to the sensor characteristics, multi-platform data fusion will also depend on the navigation accuracy of the sensor platforms and the characteristics of the data links or voice channels.

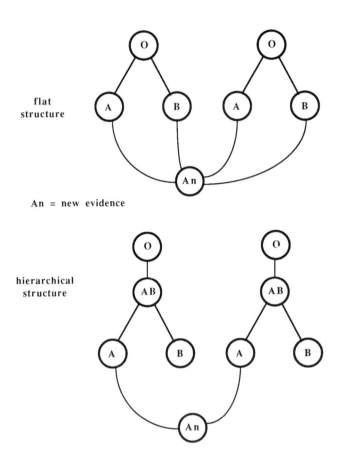

flat
structure

An = new evidence

hierarchical
structure

FIG 3.4.10   *Multiple levels of correlation*

Navigation Accuracy. Accurate sensor platform position is essential for matching the spatial measurements made by sensors on different platforms. Either accurate navigation can be assumed, e.g. using Nav-Star GPS, or some form of accurate relative position estimation will have to be done for each platform prior to using its sensor data; the latter could be achieved for some situations by using Radar measurements of the platforms themselves or commonly held targets.

Data links. Because of the large volume of data produced by active and passive sensors, data links are required to support Multi-Platform Data Fusion. Even with data links, however, the amount of data that can be transferred over a period of time (bandwidth) will be limited.

Given such limitations, it is unlikely that the data received through the data link will be at the same rate as an equivalent on-board sensor. Also only the most important parameters on each track will be transmitted in order to save data bits. As a result of these factors, the status of data link received tracks will not be quite the same as own ship generated tracks and this may affect the organization of the multi-platform data fusion.

Multi-Platform Data Fusion Organization. It was shown above that a multi-level correlation organization is preferred for multi-platform data fusion because it reduces the combinations and hence the processing. There is also the potential advantage that by separating out some stages of processing, these stages might be carried out in parallel.

Figure 3.4.11 illustrates a possible two level correlation hierarchy. It must be borne in mind that in different situations, different sets of sensors will be available so that the structure must not be dependent on any one type for its useful operation; of course lack of some type of sensor will degrade the performance of the data fusion system but it should not render it totally useless.

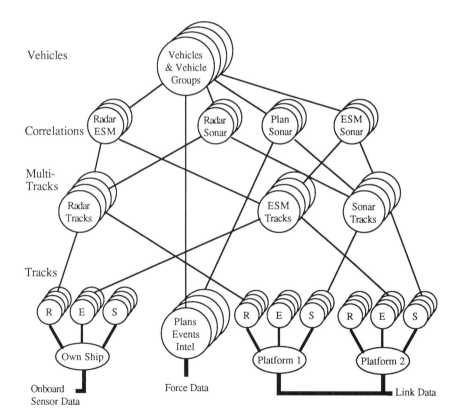

FIG 3.4.11 *Multi-platform data fusion*

The principles adopted in the suggested organization are:

(1) Like sensors on own ship should be combined first - this particularly applies to Radar and its closely associated IFF system.
(2) Radar pictures from different platforms should be combined next to establish a force-wide Radar picture and at the same time, estimate any sensor platform position errors if necessary.
(3) Like passive sensors, such as ESM and passive Sonars should be combined next in order to reduce position uncertainty of contacts as far as possible.
(4) Finally the combined pictures from each type of sensor are fused together using the strategy described.

These principles provide an order for the knowledge to be applied to any particular piece of data but with realistic input, processing at all levels would interleave. Combining like sensors first seems the best choice because like sensors have very similar parameters to compare whereas dissimilar sensors, in general, only have a few parameters in common. This should mean that fewer ambiguities arise in the system as a whole.

3.4.4.(i)   *Combination of Correlated Data*

The result of the correlation stage is a collection of evidence for each vehicle or group of vehicles. The set of evidence might include some of the following:

- position estimates and track history.
- velocity estimates - course and speed, maximum and minimum observed speed, observed manoeuvring behaviour.
- IFF responses.
- emitter characteristics.
- sound signatures.
- Intelligence reports.
- visual sightings
- plan and direct communication details for own platforms.

Given a set of evidence for a particular object the first stage of interpretation is to determine the most likely values for each parameter of interest. the parameters which are required include:

- current or last estimated position and velocities with accuracies
- allegience (friend, netural, hostile)
- identity (basic: e.g., ship, helicopter, aircraft, submarine, missile
  class: e.g., fighter, bomber, frigate aircraft carrier, etc.
  type: tornado, badger, harrier, type 42, seaking, etc.

name or code: e.g., HM Illustrious, F601, etc.)
- base (for aircraft: ship or shore station)
- time on task (for aircraft)
- capabilities (sensors, comms, weapons, max speed, endurance, etc.)
- equipment states (on/off, mode, number of rounds, etc)
- current function (reconnaissance, targetting, attack, jammer etc)

Some parameters may be known exactly, for example the name of a friendly ship, while others will require estimation, such as position, course and speed, or more complex inference, for example the likely mission of an enemy aircraft. The objective must be to build-up a set of data for each object to explain where it came from, what it is, where it is and what is is likely to do in the future. This may not be possible to do entirely on an individual basis so some parameters will be left until the situation assesment stage to be described in Chapter 4.2.

Some evidence will be grouped together either because the sensors cannot resolve the individuals or through the action of clustering rules designed to recognise groups with common properties e.g., velocity, hostility. Evidence about a group of objects can be treated in a similar way to individuals but many of the parameters will be collective and there will be the additional parameters of group size and perhaps shape.

Rules. Knowledge is required for relating each possible clue to infer the parameters required.

Position and Velocity: These rules can only look through all sources of position and velocity estimates to select those with least uncertainty (variance). In some cases it may be possible to narrow the limits of, for example range, by knowing that the object would be picked up on another sensor over part of the unertainty range. Possible rules are:

If up-to-date 3D data from accurate sensor is available then there is no problem.

If up-to-date 2D data from accurate sensor is available then estimate height using range, velocity, identity.

If up-to-date bearing-only data available then estimate range and height by coverage of other sensor not detecting it (if any) and identity.

Allegiance: If exact identity (i.e. name or code) known then this will provide allegiance.

If IFF and/or ESm available athen use to infer allegiance.

Failing that, hostility might be assigned by defaults such as: if aircraft has no flight plan or controller and is not in an airlane then it is probably hostile.

If unknown then use position and trajectory to determine possible allegiance and basic identity e.g., if in airlane and straight track then neutral, if near to other aircraft then military.

Identity: This parameter has a hierarchy of values to cater for the degree to which identity can be determined.

Basic: In the absence of better information from any source, this type can be estimated from track and sensor data.   Clues include position relative to land/sea, range from sensor, sensors held on (e.g., Radar and/or Sonar), velocity and manoeuvring (trajectory): these factors need to be considered over the history of the track.

Class: This level of identity could be obtained from visual sighting, ESM, Intelligence or Plan data.   It seems likely that the type would also be available from such sources in most circumstances and class would then be derived from it.   Although class is a more general level of identity than type it may be a more convenient indicator of function.

Type: Sources mentioned in class would most likely provide this level of identity information.

Name or Code: For friendlies, unique identities will come from plan, event or command data.   Unknown or hostile vehicles will require a visual sighting, ESM or other intelligence for exact identification. Such identification is probably only applicable to ships and submarines.

Base (for aircraft: ship or shore station):   This parameter is of use for aircraft in order to explain their flight path when in transit to or from home and to do calculations based on endurance.   For friendly aircraft the parameter shown be known.   intelligence on hostile aircraft might provide this information and might be used to calculate maximum range and endurance.   Base is the launch ship/aircraft for missiles.

Time on Task: This parameter is relevant to aircraft and helicopters.   It should be known for friendlies and could be assessed for hostiles where flight path is known. Time on task could be used in assessing the capability of patrol aircraft to counter a likely attack or to judge the ability of enemy aircraft to target friendly units in the area of interest.

Capabilities and Equipment States: This knowledge is a combination of fixed information about the equipments fitted to a vehicle and knowledge or observations of their use.

For friendly units all these parameters should be known by in practice may not be owing to lack of communication. IFF operation and ESM data give information about active sensors and communications.

For hostiles, if the type identity of the vehicle is known then some equipments may be known.   ESM will give clues to active sensor operation.   Knowledge of what is or what can be carried by the vehicle comes from plan (friendlies) or Intelligence (hostiles) information.

Function: For friendlies, vehicle function is derived mainly from plan or command information.   For hostiles, an assessment of trajectory, sensor/communications operation, weapon load and group context could give clues to vehicle

function. Multiple functions are possible for ships and some aircraft.
If capabilities are known, it may be possible to infer function and mission from knowledge type of platform. If the vehicle in question is transmitting it may be possible to infer function by type of emissions. Type of trajectory may indicate function and mission e.g., standing-off with radar emissions could be just shadowing with potential of targetting, if closing fast then attacking.
These are illustrations of the kinds of inference required. In some cases the exact information is available in the correlated data with little uncertainty whereas in other cases only very vague clues such as behavioural characteristics will be present and a good deal of uncertainty will exist.
Further inferences on identity, allegiance, function and mission will be assisted by grouping platforms so that collective parameters can be determined and used to assign individual parameters by association; for example, if one aircraft which is hostile forms part of a group then it may be inferred that the group is an air-raid and the other individuals of the group can be taken as hostile by their association with the group. Forming such groups is part of the Situation Assessment function (see Chapter 4.2).

3.4.5   Reasoning with Uncertainty

Many of the early expert systems attempted reasoning with uncertainty. Some used a form of Bayes theorem mixed with logical functions to model the human expert's judgement when reasoning with uncertain evidence (Duda (14)). Such numerical approaches have been widely researched and more complex schemes devised; Dempster-Shafer (Garvey (15)) is a two value system (see also Chapter 2.3) fuzzy logic theoretically uses continuous functions. Not all expert systems, however, use uncertain reasoning; some problems, such as configuring computers - the task of the XCON system (Soloway (16)) do not demand it.
Numerical Uncertainty Schemes. The objective of numerical uncertainty schemes is to use a standard method of representing uncertainty, e.g., probability or a multiple value, and a standard method of combining uncertainty values when conclusions are drawn from the combination of evidence or sub-conclusions. Whether this objective can ever be realised is unknown but experience has shown that numerical schemes are often difficult to apply to real problems and in some cases may not contribute significantly to the result compared to a simple logical approach. There is research still going on in pursuit of a good system.
Using probability as the basic measure with a Bayesian combining rule presents problems of how to set prior probabilities in a domain which is only partly known. Schemes of this sort usually employ strength factors for weighting the uncertainty of sub-conclusions before

combination and coupled with the prior probabilities this leads to a very large set of variables to initialise in a complex inference net. Because many of these variables interact, it can be very difficult to achieve the desired effects, i.e., produce the conclusions which the expert specifies for chosen examples. Even if the system can be tuned to work in the required manner there is no guarantee that it will behave adequately for other examples.

There are perhaps two cases where a numerical approah can be used:

- in problems where the statistics of the input evidence are well known
- for problems where a large number of test examples are available

In the data fusion problem being addressed, a conventional statistical approach could be used for numerical parameters such as position and velocity when statistically known sensor measurements are available.

Another problem with numerical uncertainty is the difficulty of explaining the reasoning to humans. Expressions of uncertainty by humans are usually given in words rather than numerical quantitites. This means that an expert's expression of uncertainty must be converted into numerical form to code his knowledge. Ideally the expert system should convert back into words for the convenience of the user but few systems do this.

Symbolic Uncertainty Schemes.   An alternative to numerical schemes is to retain uncertainty in a symbolic form.   A method for doing this called 'the theory of endorsements' was invented by Cohen and Grinberg (17), Cohen (18, 19).   This theory argues against the commonly used numerical systems for representing uncertainty because these systems tend to obscure the reasons for belief in a hypothesis.   For examle if a hypothesis is assigned a probability of .7 from the support of several lower level hypotheses, there is no way of knowing what contributed to that value; many diferent combinations of support could give rise to the same value.

Cohen and Grinberg suggest a method of inferencing which retains a set of endorsements for each contributing factor to the belief and disbelief in a hypothesis.   These endorsements can then be assessed in different ways by subsequent stages of reasoning and further sets of endorsements produced.   The way the endorsements are combined is entirely rule based specific to each example of inference.   Endorsements translate directly into statements of uncertainty about the hypothesis and thereby provide built-in explanations.   This seems a powerful approach although it might carry memory and processing overheads because of the need to store and process endorsements for each piece of supporting evidence.

Example.   The function of the following simplistic example is to determine the allegiance of a vehicle given various pieces of evidence.   Allegiance is defined as one of the set: (friend, foe, neutral). The evidence is defined by the following factors:

- behaviour
- IFF   identification (friend or foe)
- plan   (whether vehicle follows a known plan)

where

behaviours can be = (threatening, not_threatening)
IFF_states can be = (no_IFF, confirmed_IFF, unconfirmed_IFF)
plan_states can be = (plan_exists, on_neutral_route, no plan)

Given a set of evidence relating to a particular vehicle, the following rules are applied to create some endorsements. These endorsements could be held in a matrix associated with the vehicle hypothesis. Endorsements are statements for believing and disbelieving evidence in this case. Note that for some states of evidence, no positive or negative endorsements can be derived.

RULE using behaviour (derived from track history)
if vehicle_behaviour = threatening then
                         threatening behaviour indicates foe   A
                         behaviour could be misleading
or
if vehicle_behaviour = not_threatening then
                         no endorsements   B

RULE using_IFF
if vehicle_IFF = confirmed_IFF then
                         IFF response indicates friend   C
if vehicle_IFF = no_IFF then
                         lack of IFF indicates foe   D
                         IFF could be faulty
or
if vehicle_IFF = unconfirmed_IF then
                         no endorsements   E

RULE using plan (a flight plan or defence screen plan)
if vehicle plan = plan exists then
                         following plan for friend   F
or
if vehicle plan = on neutral route then
                         trajectory indicates neutral   G
or
if vehicle plan = no plan
                         no plan indicates foe   H
                         could be a mistake

Having set up all the possible endorsements for the available evidence the next stage is to apply rules to derive conclusions and explanations. These rules must allow for all possible combinations of endorsements which could occur. It is difficult to see how any general combining mechanism could be used because each endorsement is specific to the reasoning but Cohen has attempted to generalise the process by using a standard range of statement types. In this example, however, the combining rules simply apply heuristics to the endorsements to generate conclusions with supporting and sometimes conflicting endorsements.

The possible combinations are:

```
ACF     ADF     AEF     BCF     BDF     BEF
ACG     ADG     AEG     BCG     BDG     BEG
ACH     ADH     AEH     BCH     BDH     BEH
```

Even with a simple example the number of combinations is quite large; this is a potential problem with symbolic uncertainty schemes. In this example (and probably in most real examples) some of the endorsements are much stronger than others so that many of the combinations are eliminated. For example the endorsement *IFF response indicates friend* (C) has no negative endorsement, i.e., no uncertainty, and therefore combinations including this can be put together.

```
COMBINING_RULE
       ACF     BCF
if     ACG     BCG        then      IFF response indicates friend
       ACH     BCH
```

This rule has assumed that all other evidence is of no consequence when endorsement C is present but it might be a good idea to include other supportive endorsements to give extra confidence in the conclusion. Endorsement F supports the conclusion so rule could be split thus:

```
COMBINING_RULE_1
if    ACG     BCG        then      IFF response indicates friend
      ACH     BCJ
```

```
COMBINING_RULE_2
if    ACF     BCF        then      IFF response indicates friend
                                   following plan for friend
```

When C is not present F is a strong endorsement compared to the remainder but it is not certain so some uncertainty must be presented. Behavioural indicators are not of much importance in this case but lack of confirmed IFF might be worth including:

COMBINING_RULE_3

if ADF   AEF   then   *following plan for friend*
    BDF   BEF   *could be a mistake*
                             IFF must be faulty

Combinations of A and G are mutually exclusive because a
vehicle following a neutral traffic route should not be
endorsed as having threatening behaviour. This leaves two
combinations which have fairly strong foe endorsements,
strong enough to remove possible negative endorsements:

COMBINING_RULE_4

if ADH   AEH   then   *threatening behaviour indicates foe*
                             no recognisable IFF
                             no plan indicates foe

In the remaining four cases the endorsements are too
weak or conflicting to combine effectively using a cautious
approach to this problem. It may be that in a battle
context weak indicators would be sufficient for some
purposes, for example the combination,

    BDH   =   *lack of IFF indicates foe*
                    IFF could be faulty
                    no plan indicates foe
                    could be a mistake

could be sufficient to endorse as foe for the purpose of
threat assessment. The ability to have different combining
rules for differnt contexts seems a powerful feature of
such a symbolic reasoning scheme.

Summary. The rules for setting up endorsements are fairly
easy to formulate - all they have to do is to set up an
endorsement for any contributions the evidence might impart
to the state of the hypothesis. If there is a lot of
evidence of different types then the number of endorsements
might be rather large.
    Having produced a set of endorsements from the
evidence, further rules are required to derive conclusions.
Different rules may interpret the endorsements differently;
this is a powerful feature of the theory. These rules may
also produce built-in explanations of the conclusions
because they have access to all the factors, i.e.,
endorsements, which are used to derive the conclusions.
    A more significant problem is the generation of
combining rules. These rules have to look at the
endorsements and generate conclusions but if there are many
endorsements, the combination problem arises. Apart from
picking out all the valid patterns these rules also have to
look for conflicting sets of endorsements.

3.4.6   Summary of Techniques for Data Fusion

Data Fusion is firstly a *correlation* problem - in other words a problem of trying to find which pieces of information refer to the same real-world object, and secondly a classification problem - estimating and inferring attributes of the object from the assembled evidence.   Figure 3.4.12 lists knowledge-based techniques under three headings: knowledge representation, control strategy and inference method.

Task	Problem Types	Knowledge Representation	Control Strategy	Inference Method
Data Fusion	Correlation	Algorithms	Imperative	Numerical
	Classification	Hypotheses	Forward/Backward	Symbolic
		Rules	Opportunistic	
		Frames	Do whenever	

FIG 3.4.12   *Knowledge-based techniques*

Knowledge Representation.   Because most of the information has spatial parameters, some algorithms are useful for correlation. Owing to the poor quality or lack of timeliness of much information, considerable ambiguity can occur during the correlation process and therefore a multiple alternative hypothesis technique is appropriate. The conditions for correlation can be conveniently expressed by rules.

The addition of Frames is suggested to provide a more formal schema for representing general domain knowledge and the hypothesis structure in a concise way.   The 'attached procedure' mechanism of frames would be useful for dealing with time-varying attributes of objects.

Once correlation of information has been completed, the identification of real-world objects can begin.   This is a classification problem similar to many problems which have been tackled with Expert Systems.   Classification problems are usually implemented using rules though frames could assist in representing the static knowledge of real-world objects.

Control Strategy.   For control strategy, the blackboard model has proved to be a good framework.   It can support forward and backward reasoning and provides 'opportunistic' control through the use of scheduling meta-knowledge.   An alternative, which has been used in similar applications, is the 'do whenever' strategy of production systems.   This control mechamism is implicit except for the method of choosing which rule to fire from the firable set (the conflict set). Such a strategy is desirable because it removes the control dimension from the concern of the knowledge engineer but there may be penalties in efficiency. The original blackboard mechanism of event-list and rule-based scheduler is more practical but demands more engineering.

Inference. Inference method is the third dimension of knowledge-based techniques and is orthogonal to knowledge representation and control strategy. There are a number of techniques for representing uncertainty numerically and symbolic approaches such as the endorsement scheme described. The main requirement of the reasoning method is that it should be easy to understand and give predictable results for both ease of development and acceptability to the users. Unfortunately some of the probabalistic schemes do not measure up to these requirements. The use of numerical schemes should be confined to reasoning from evidence with known statistics, such as sensor measurements.

When it comes to identification of objects a symbolic method has been shown to have advantages because the uncertainty measures can be kept in a textual form and hence provide good explanation capability. The conclusion for inferencing method is that both numerical and symbolic methods are needed to support the whole data fusion problem.

3.4.7   References

1. Stein, K.J., February 1986. 'Researchers Channel AI Activities Towards Real-World Applications', Technical Survey: Artificial Intelligence, *Aviation Week and Space Technology*.

2. Llinas, J. April 1987, 'A Survey of Techniques for CIS Data Fusion', SAIC, *Proc. IEE C3I Conference*, Bournemouth.

3. Lakin, W.l., and Miles, J.A.H., April 1985. 'IKBS in Multi-Sensor Data Fusion', *Proc. IEE Conference on Advances in C3I*, Publication 247 234-240.

4. Lakin, W.L., and Miles, J.A.H. June 1986. 'Intelligent Data Fusion and Situation Assessment', *MIT/ONR C3I Conference*, Monterey.

5. Lakin, W.L., and Miles, J.A.H., 1987. 'An Approach to Data Fusion and Situation Assessment', Ch 7.3, pp 339-377, Advances in Command, Control and Communication Systems, Peter Peregrinus Ltd., IEE Computing Series 11, ISBN 0 86341 094 4.

6. Byrne, D., Lakin, W.L. and Miles, J.A.H. April 1987 'Intelligent Data Fusion for Naval Command and Control', *Proc. IEE C3I Conference*, Bournemouth.

7. Groundwater, E.H., 1984. 'A Demonstration of an Ocean Surveillance Information Fusion Expert System', SAIC, 1710 Goodridge Drive, McLean, VA 22101.

8. Drazovich, R.J., 'Sensor Fusion in Tactical Warfare, Advanced Decisions Systems', Mountain View, CA.

9. Garvey, T.D. et al, December 1980, *5th Joint Conference on Pattern Recognition*, pp 343-347.

10. Woolsey, R.B., April 1987, 'Applications of Expert System Technology to an Information Fusion System', *Proc. IEE C3I Conference*, Bournemouth.

11. Sinha, B.P., Bhattacharya, B.B., February 1985, 'On the Numerical Complexity of Short-Circuit Faults in Logic Networks', *IEEE Transactions on Computers*, vol C-34, No 2.

12. Nii, H.P., Summer 1986, 'Blackboard Systems: The Blackboard Model of Problem Solving and the Evolution of Blackboard Architectures', *The AI Magazine*.

13. Nii, H.P., August 1986, 'Blackboard Application Systems, Blackboard Systems from a Knowledge Engineering Perspective', *The AI Magazine*.

14. Duda, R., Gashnig, J., Hart, P., 1979, 'Model Design in the Prospector Consultant System for Mineral Exploration', Expert Systems in the Microelectronic Age, Edinburgh University Press, pp 153-167.

15. Garvey, T.D., et al, August 1981, 'An Inference Technique for Integrating Knowledge from Disparate Sources', IJCA 17, vol 1, pp 319-325.

16. Soloway, E., et al, 1987, 'Assessing the Maintainabiality of XCON-in-RIME: Coping with the Problems of a VERY Large Rule-Base', *Proceedings of AAAI-87*, pp 824-829.

17. Cohen, P.R., and Grinberg, M.R., Summer 1983, 'A Theory of Heuristic Reasoning about Uncertainty', Computer Science Department, Stanford University, *The AI Magazine*.

18. Cohen, R., December 1984, 'Progress Report on the Theory of Endorsements: A Heuristic Approach to Reasoning about Uncertainty', Department of Computer and Information Science, University of Massachusetts, MBT 4, *IEEE Workshop on Principles of Reasoning*.

19. Cohen, R., 1985, 'Heuristic Reasoning about Uncertainty: An Artifical Intelligence Approach', ISBN 0-273-08667-7, 1985.

An Object Oriented Approach to Data Fusion

S.L. Rhodes
(Advanced System Architectures Ltd. UK)

3.5.1   Introduction

Naval commanders are facing an escalating problem. Ever improved sensor techniques are being deployed to counter the inevitable increase in sophistication of weapon systems, denser operational environments, and the greater deployment of countermeasures such as ECM, decoys, chaff, and aerosols. The introduction of these sensors and the greater complexity of the threat is leading to a massive increase in the quantity of raw data presented to the ship's operations centre. To understand the progress of battle and exploit any opportunities to gain an advantage, the ship's Command is expected to process and assimilate this data effectively, in real-time. Existing methods for compiling a tactical picture from this plethora of data rely heavily on the expertise of a hierarchy of skilled Sensor Trackers, Picture Compilers and Supervisors. Working in a cramped and often unpleasant environment, these teams are stretched to their limits, and even now are unable to respond as quickly as the tacticians would like. Increased automation of this activity is now generally accepted as essential, to relieve the pressure on the operational staff and to increase the probability-of-survival of ships threatened by modern weapons systems.

A Naval Task Force at sea comprises a number of vessels, surface and subsurface, and supporting aircraft. Such a Task Force is of course a prime target for enemy attack from the air by aircraft or missiles, or from underwater by submarines and torpedoes. Missiles and torpedoes can be launched from long range by aircraft or surface vessels.

To enhance the chance of survival of the fleet, it is vital that the knowledge of all air and sea activity around the fleet is as complete as possible. The region of interest is very large, encompassing an area with a radius of at least one hundred miles. This is to minimise the risk of undetected surveillance craft giving away the location of the task force, and to give the earliest possible warning of an enemy attack so that effective countermeasures can be deployed. To continuously monitor the air/sea activity all of the members of the task force are equipped with sensor systems of various types. These range from highly accurate long range surveillance radars on ships or AEW aircraft, through EW systems such as ESM, to very specialised sensors typified by the dunking sonars carried by helicopters. None of these sensors is capable of giving more than a part of the complete picture, because of their physics of operation, the geometry of the situation, the present state of the environment (weather and propagation conditions), equipment failure or damage, or because tactical considerations e.g. radio silence, prevent the effective use of the systems .

For many years the Western Navies have seen the importance of using the information from more than one sensor to aid in the building up of an air/sea picture, and this led to the early introduction of radio data links, to interchange information between ships. The next stage of natural evolution is to replace the overloaded manual techniques for data fusion with largely automatic systems, with the primary objective of positively identifying uncooperative targets. To achieve this, no opportunity to obtain information about targets operating within range of the task force should be disregarded. Thus an effective data fusion system has to handle a large quantity of information of variable quality. Needless to say, given the short flight-times of present and projected weapons, for the fusion process to be effective it has to function in very near real-time. This gives the task force personnel the opportunity for efficacious tactical reaction. An approach to the design of a data fusion system operating in near real-time, based upon decomposition of the tactical picture into asynchronous objects, is described below.

3.5.2   *The Object Oriented Approach*

The central feature of the data fusion problem is that a rapid flow of data from many independent sources must be processed and correlated to locate and identify a large number of real-world entities. This identification must be as certain as possible, for a given quality of data, within the time constraints allowed. The requirement to operate in real-time, plus the large number of sources and targets involved, suggests taking advantage of any parallelism inherent in the data fusion process by allowing the concurrent investigation of various hypotheses.

The multisensor data fusion problem suggests two possible axes of decomposition. Each track-producing sensor can be treated as a focus, so that some reasoning process can work through a series of observations produced by one sensor, comparing them with information reported simultaneously by other sensors. The advantage of this approach is that the system always remains all-informed, and very low probability hypotheses need never be completely discarded. However, the serial nature of the correlation means that very high speed processors are needed to produce acceptable response times. Furthermore, there is a high risk that the total integration of the system in this way tends to make the design and maintenance of the fusion rules very hard.

An alternative strategy is to divide the picture into objects, one for each of the attested targets. Once the presence of a new target has been recogized, the object representing it within the system is given responsibility for increasing its "self awareness". Each object is given the opportunity to examine incoming data, to determine if it is relevant to it, and if so to use the information to update the status of that target. This approach has three major potential advantages:

a. Highly precise and unambiguous information is processed rapidly, and the effects are seen in the output with minimum delay. On the other hand, in situations when a greater degree of computation is needed, results will only be produced when they are viewed as meaningful.

b. As each object is decoupled from the others, a concurrent process can be set up for each identified target, greatly increasing the potential system throughput. This is because, in most data fusion scenarios, the number of active track producing sensors is much less than the number of targets operating within the area of interest. For example in the scenario of a Naval Task Group in Mid-Atlantic the number of active track producing sensors might be of the order of ten, whereas the number of vehicles, both friendly and hostile, operating in the area of interest could exceed two hundred. It is thus obvious that by far the greatest parallelism can be achieved by decomposing the problem by target rather than by sensor.

c. The object oriented approach holds out the opportunity of producing "clean" rule structures i.e. rules sufficiently restricted in their scope to allow for verification and validation.

To obtain the potential benefits of the object oriented approach, a target computer environment supporting a large number of asynchronous objects is required, with a highly efficient mechanism for passing messages between them. One candidate is the Sofchip Architecture, Coombs et al (1), which has been evolved to support just this type of "loosely-coupled" system. This architecture forms the basis of the performance assessments of the object oriented data fusion system presented at the end of this chapter.

3.5.3   Data Fusion

3.5.3. (i)   General

In order to perform effectively, a ship's command system has to be provided with mechanisms for determining the milieu within which it is operating. Its knowledge of external events is largely built upon information provided by a variety of sensors, each of which can only report on certain aspects of the total picture. Thus to obtain a more complete view, it is essential to combine the information from a number of different sensors (in terms either of operational characteristics or location). The traditional use of triangulation to locate a target is one example of such usage; the combination of electro-optical systems with radar to help in revealing targets masked by chaff is a more recently identified opportunity. This binding together of such information to produce a composite picture of target activity has become commonly known as *data fusion*. [This should not be confused with *situation assessment*, which is a connected, but higher level, activity using the output of the data fusion activity to guide the operation of the overall system.]

3.5.3. (ii)   Problems

Effective fusion of data from disparate sensors on a variety of platforms is inherently very difficult, particularly when attempts are made to overlay such a mechanism on a system containing components which were specified and designed long before modern needs were foreseen. Of the many problems that are encountered in the design of sensor data fusion systems, major issues that need addressing are:-

Real Time Response: The key to effective tactical response in modern naval warfare is the rapid discrimination betwen objects - friend or foe, target and decoy. In principle the data fusion system will produce an identified picture of the environment (air, sea, and subsurface), which is complete and correct at any instant in time. In the limit, this aim can never be fulfilled, but the delay introduced by the fusion activity must be minute in relation to the overall force reaction time, with particular emphasis on the accurate classification of targets.

Sensor Errors: All measurement systems are subject to error. It is vital that the form of these is known, for each type of sensor employed by the fusion system.

Navigation Errors: When sensors are mounted on platforms moving independently, their reported position and heading, relative to the centre of fusion expressed in a given system of coordinates, will contain errors.

Again the form of these has to be known to the fusion system.

Geometrical Ambiguity: There are situations in which the relative position of the sensor systems and the target are such that unambiguous reconciliation of a sensor report with a particular target is impossible. The fusion system has to incorporate a strategy for recognising the possibility of this occurrence, and delaying positive decision until sufficient information has become available to resolve any dichotomy.

Discrimination: There will be times when the discrimination of a sensor system is insufficient to separate targets travelling proximally.   The fusion system has to cope with the correlation of such returns with those from more precise sensors, which are capable of greater resolution.

Time Delay: Reports from some systems will arrive at the centre of fusion significantly delayed from the moment of instigation.   This is likely to be due to failings in the data link, and any intermediate processing involved.

Whilst it is recognized that the above list is not exhaustive, a system which addresses these problems successfully will be highly effective.   The object oriented system architecture described below, has been designed with all these issues in mind.

3.5.3.(iii)   Data Inputs

A basic assumption underlying the system design described here, is that the primary information entered into a data fusion system will be in the form of track reports i.e. time stamped estimates of position (or bearings) which are regularly updated.   Each track report needs to be qualified with some estimate of the likely error, before entry into the fusion system: ideally this should be provided by the sensor system but, in practice, some form of preprocessor may be needed.   It is also assumed that the track extractor (the mechanism within each sensor subsystem, that recognizes that a sequence of plots can be represented as a track) will positively flag the initiation of a new track and allocate it a unique number. However, it is not expected that the track extractor will repair tracks, i.e. realise that an apparently new track is in fact a continuation of one previously terminated. Some forms of sensor produce tracks which are of low accuracy.   These reports are, however, often of considerable value, either because they contain information which can assist in determining the identity of a target or because the physics of their operation is such that they can detect objects that are invisible to more precise sensor systems.   It is also often true that passive systems that can be mounted on a warship i.e. those relying upon emissions from a target, are of lower intrinsic accuracy than those which generate some form of incident energy. Operational circumstances often force the use of such passive systems, to prevent the promulgation of the position of the sensor platform to opposing forces.

Apart from sensor information presented to the fusion system as tracks, there is other data available which can be used as collateral information for the identification assessment. In general such data will be referred to by single plots e.g. visual sightings, or by area e.g. safe lanes. Track plans can be considered as a track in which the position uncertainty increases as time progresses (this allows for the deviation of the actual route and velocity from that originally envisaged). This sort of information cannot in general be used to initiate a track to the fusion process, but can be very valuable as evidence to resolve the identification of a track report from other sensors.

To summarise, it is assumed for current purposes that the input to the fusion system will be:

- Current tracks from sensors tagged with source, and number.
- Historical track data tagged with source, number and time.
- Collateral information presented as plots or areas of note.

3.5.4   Signal Interface

3.5.4 (i)   Purpose

In the approach adopted here, the activities involved in data fusion are divided into two major functional areas: the Signal Interface, and the Tactical Picture. The general relationships between these activities is shown[1] in Figure 3.5.1. Most of the actual processing takes place in the second area, but the Signal[2] Interface plays an important part in the efficiency of the overall process.

In an ideal world all sensors would report in a common basic format, with a coherent scheme for error description. In practical naval systems, sensor equipment of widely different ages and technologies, is employed; the conversion of the information from these sensors to a common internal representation is the responsibility of the data fusion system, in particular the INTERFACE FUNCTION. Each incoming report is converted by this function into a

---

[1] All system structures in this paper are shown using the system design language G. See Hemdal & Reilly (2)

[2] The term signal is used to refer to messages passed between asynchronous objects.

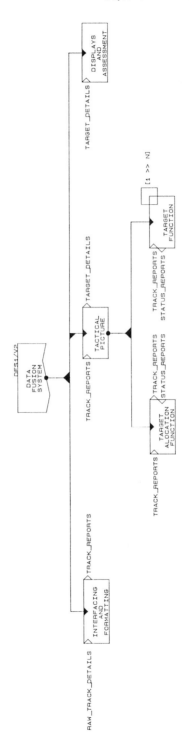

FIG 3.5.1

common signal format which can include any of the following information:

    a. Time of observation.
    b. Error in time of observation.
    c. Target position in range, bearing, and height referred to a plane drawn through the position of the platform containing the fusion system. Not all of these will always be available, e.g ESM generally only produces bearing.
    d. Errors, expressed in an appropriate form.
    e. Target velocity as speed and direction, or as radial and angular velocity relative to the sensor platform. Rate of change of height will be ignored as it is unlikely to be large enough to be of value.
    f. Error, again expressed as appropriate, of the velocity.
    e. Identity - this depends on the source but will include simple allegiance statements (friend, hostile, etc.), description of platform, or detailed SSR or IFF responses.

3.5.4. (ii)   Sensor Errors

One of the most important tasks of the INTERFACE FUNCTION is to reduce the error measurements to a common basis so that realistic correlation can be performed.

All measurement systems produce errors. These come from a wide range of sources ranging from thermal and propagation effects, through to simple mechanical distortion. The accuracy of many sensor systems also depends upon the geometrical relationship between the sensor and the target.

Sensor data fusion aims, by the comparison of common sets of parameters from various sensor systems, to learn more about a target than could be obtained explicitly from a single sensor, relying on one particular combination of physical principles. To make these comparisons it is desirable to have as much detail as possible about the error characteristics of each particular report. In an ideal world each sensor would be calibrated for all combinations of circumstances, to enable appropriate corrections to be made to the measurements. However, despite its serious proposition by some authorities, this is clearly impractical for most military installations.

One point often disregarded is the value of poor quality data to the data fusion process, given that system is aware of the imprecision of the information. Many sensors have the ability to produce such information as a secondary process, and the designers should be encouraged to include such capabilities. Examples are the use of signal amplitude in a radio receiver to determine range, or doppler in a radar to measure radial velocity. Time derivatives of measurements may also be of great value, particularly if the sensor system can produce them as a by-product e.g. as an intermediate result in a Kalman Filter. Sensor systems will, more often than not, be mounted on platforms other than that carrying the fusion system. Reports from these sensors will be spatially referenced, either directly or indirectly, to the position of those platforms. Before such reports can be used, allowance has to be made for the navigation errors of the sensor platforms i.e heading error, and xyz position error.

3.5.5   Object Oriented System Design

3.5.5. (i)   System Structure

The basic structure of the system is shown in the G diagram in Figure 3.5.2. Essentially it is split into two major functional elements; the SIGNAL INTERFACE and the TACTICAL PICTURE. The majority of this discussion is concerned with the structure and operation of the latter, as the algorithms used for signal conditioning are very dependent upon the characteristics of actual sensors systems used and their bearer platforms. We will, however, firstly consider the need for the INTERFACE FUNCTION when looking at system performance and implementation.

3.5.5. (ii)   Interface

The role of the INTERFACE FUNCTION is to convert the incoming data into a common internal signal structure, including a computed value for the uncertainty of the reports, taking into account navigation and sensor inaccuracies. By establishing this function as a separate asynchronous set of processes further parallelism is gained. Benefit is also obtained from the isolation of the tables describing the particular details of possible sensor systems in one place. This ensures that changes due to technology and policy evolution can be introduced easily and controllably. Furthermore, as some of this information may be viewed as sensitive, the data tables may be designated as write only, preventing access to that data by anybody. Risk of compromise arising from captured equipment, or disloyalty, would, therefore, be rendered non-existent.
In addition to its main role of reducing all track reports to a common format, the INTERFACE FUNCTION also acts to prioritize each track signal. The priority level becomes relevant at times of high system load, as correct operation relies upon the preferential processing of most precise information. This is achieved by according the track signals a priority directly related to their expected precision. This means, for example, that track reports from surveillance radars on own ship will be given the highest priority, other radars the next highest priority and so on. The thresholds for this allocation form part of the system knowledge base, although they are physically stored within the INTERFACE FUNCTION. [The system can be

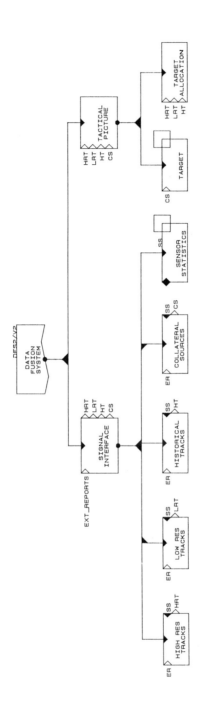

FIG 3.5.2

designed to cope with all incoming signals and thus none will be lost; it is only the order in which they are processed that is adjusted.]

3.5.5. (iii) Track Reports

When the system is started, the tactical picture will show no activity. Signals containing track reports from the sensor systems will now begin to be received by the fusion system. It can be seen from reference to Fig 3.5.2 that these will be passed in turn via the SIGNAL INTERFACE to the functional elements describing the targets i.e. the TARGET FUNCTIONs. This operation is described in detail below.

3.5.6. The Target Function

3.5.6. (i) General

This function forms the basic engine of the fusion system. The structure of this function is shown in Figure 3.5.3. The decomposition chosen means that more of these functions are available than the maximum number of targets expected under the most congested conditions. The functions select relevant information from the plethora of track and collateral data, and hence produce the best possible estimate of the position and identity of the currently adopted target.

3.5.6. (ii) Tracking Initiation

After initialization the TARGET FUNCTIONs remain dormant until a track report is received. Contained within the function are two major data areas; one containing the histories of all tracks found to be relevant to the target being followed, and another containing the description of the Best Fit Track obtained from the selected data. The initialization process resets both these data areas.

The basic mechanism of operation is as follows: The first track received subsequently to initialization must fall into the unknown category. Following the receipt of this track report, the UNKNOWN TRACK function will attempt a correlation with the present Best Fit Track, and must correlate successfully, as at this point no Best Fit track has been stored. This new track accordingly acts as the "seed" track for the target. In most cases, the action of the priority allocation mechanism in the INTERFACE FUNCTION will ensure that a high resolution track is used to "seed" TARGET FUNCTIONs. There will be cases, however, when a low resolution track is accepted as the seed, because, for example, it is beyond radar range or because active emissions are being suppressed.

Tracks which arrive at the function once it has been seeded will all be subjected to correlation against the Best Fit Track. There are three possible outcomes of this assessment:

a. A good correlation with the Best Fit Track.   This track is described as "accepted".
b. A poor correlation with the Best Fit Track.   This track is described as "rejected".
c. There is insufficient information available to assess whether this track is coming from the same target.   This track is then described as "don't know".

The implication of these three conditions are discussed below.

3.5.6.(iii)   Tracking Rejection

A track can only be "accepted" by one target process but it is possible to have a number of processes following updates of a track report in a "don't know" condition.   If the track is rejected then no further action is taken apart from returning it to the TRACK ALLOCATION function by generating a CONTINUE signal (see below).   If the track is accepted it is passed to the ACCEPTED TRACK process which will update the track history table and update the Best Fit Track using this information; this action also locks out any other TARGET FUNCTION from receiving any further information with that identifier (see Track Allocation below).

Unsurprisingly, the "don't know" condition is used to describe the condition when neither of these alternatives can be adopted with any certainty.   As it is possible that the track report belongs to another target, it is returned to the TRACK ALLOCATION function, by the generation of a CONTINUE signal in the same way as a rejected track. [Under some circumstances one track may quite properly belong to several targets, i.e. an ESM system recording a radial raid].   Accordingly, the track report is entered into the track history table so that this data can be used in the event that it is not subsequently claimed by another target and further updates are received.   This data, however is not used to update the best fit track.   [A condition is allowed for called provisional acceptance in which despite the signalling of "don't know" the data is used to update the Best Fit Track.   This is employed when all attempts to determine the true status of a track have failed.   Provisional acceptance also applies to a newly seeded TARGET FUNCTION, until two different sensor sources correlate;   in this situation no CONTINUE signal is generated, despite the fact "accept" or "reject" is not applied.]

3.5.6.(iv)   Track Acceptance

The ACCEPTED TRACK process essentially operates on tracks which have already been accepted by a given target. Thus one of its functions is to update the track history table. It is also responsible for producing the best fit correlation to update the Best Fit Track.

A time will arise when track reports referring to the particular target will apparently cease. This may be because:

a. the target has been destroyed or moved out of sensor range;
b. the sensors are failing to gain adequate response because of physical effects of countermeasures;
c. the sensor platform has gone off-station.

To allow for the occurrence of these conditions a timeout mechanism is provided in the ACCEPTED TRACK function; this acts when no relevant track reports have been received for a predetermined interval. The effect of this mechanism is to extrapolate the various track histories, with an increasing uncertainty, providing a "flywheel" to enable rapid recovery if the target track was only temporarily "broken". However, after a time the uncertainty in the correlation will become so high that the target can no longer be meaningfuly said to exist. At that point the function will reinitialize awaiting a new seed track. The values of the timeout and the reset threshold can be viewed as part of the knowledge base for the function. It is unlikely that optimum values of these thresholds, for a particular system, can be arrived at without experimentation.

3.5.6.(v)   Collateral Data

The final process shown on the diagram in Figure 3.5.3 is connected with the receipt of data from collateral sources, such as intelligence or visual sightings. These will occur at relatively infrequent intervals and will be sent to all currently active target functions. An attempt wil be made to associate this information with the Best Fit Track; if relevant the best fit track will be updated, otherwise the information will be disarded insofar as the TARGET FUNCTION is concerned. This will be a backward inference process, with the initial hypothesis that the collateral data is relevant to the track being rejected if the probability is too low. The rule structure for this activity may become quite complex as a wide range of conditions and events will have to be accommodated. However, the relative infrequency of such inputs means that this process will have limited impact on the overall system performance. In practical terms, it is likely that the rule base for this process will evolve as experience with the overall system is gained. By decomposing the function in the described manner, this evolution can be easily accomodated without prejudicing the other more critical processes.

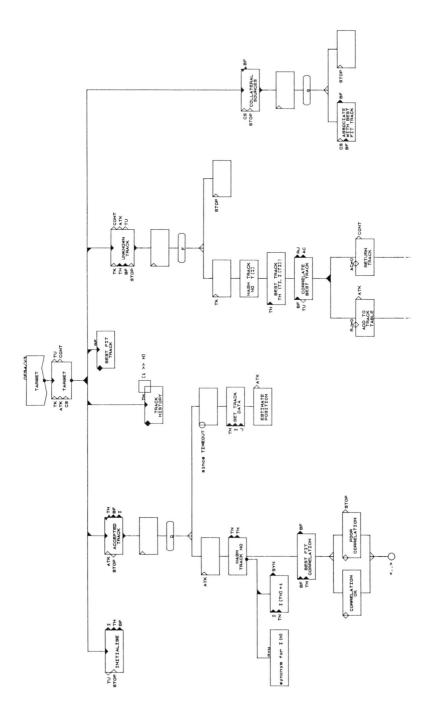

FIG 3.5.3

3.5.7 Target Allocation Function

3.5.7. (i) General

In order to prevent each track report being reassessed by all the TARGET FUNCTIONs each time it is updated, an allocation mechanism is proposed. The functional diagram for this is shown in Figure 3.5.4. The crux of the mechanism shown is a two dimensional array. This is indexed by a number arrived at by hashing the track source "address" (the combination of a sensor source identifier and the allocated track number) and a sequentially incremented target number. Each entry in the array can have three values - reject, accept, and don't know. At initialization all of the array elements are set to "don't know". If any of the TARGET functions are reinitialized due to the disappearance of their target (see above), all of the references to that target are set to "don't know".

3.5.7. (ii) Status Update

After initialization, the TARGET ALLOCATION function waits at the "A" node. At this point the system is awaiting a track report signal from the INTERFACE FUNCTION. To maintain generality three types of track report are shown - high resolution, low resolution, and historical. The fourth type identified on the diagram as "CONTINUE" is generated by the TARGET FUNCTIONs (as detailed above) when a candidate track has proved to be unrelated with other information describing that target. The receipt of a track report signal allows the locus-of-control of the system to move to the STATUS UPDATE NODE after generating the hashed track address. (Note that this hashing algorithm need not be the same as used by the TARGET FUNCTIONs). At this point, the system will normally move down the "else" arm but provision is made to ensure that all the latest updates to the status table have been made before proceeding. This is ensured by giving the track update signal (TU) to the TARGET ALLOCATION function a high priority, and making an input into both waiting nodes A and B (see Figure 3.5.4). Thus at all times a pending update will be serviced before any new allocations are made. The system then indexes through the table by track number (always beginning at 1) until an "accept" or "don't know" entry is found. At this point the track data is dispatched to the appropriate TARGET function.

3.5.7. (iii) Interaction with the TARGET function

The first track received will be automatically dispatched to TARGET FUNCTION number one, as at this point the table only holds "don't know" entries. The next track received will also be routed in the first place to target one for the same reason. However, the function now has to ascertain if the second track could have been produced by

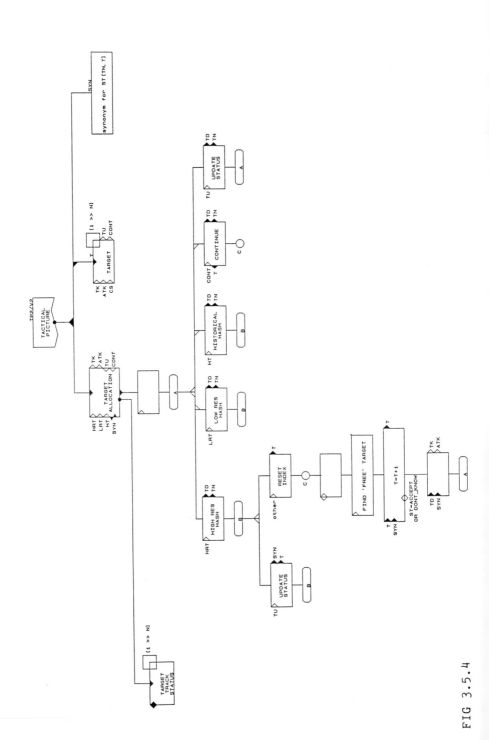

FIG 3.5.4

the same target as the first; it hence attempts to correlate it with the first track. Three outcomes are possible:

a. There is no possiblity that the second track refers to the same target as the first.
b. There is a high probability that both tracks refer to the same target.
c. It is possible that the second track may refer to the same target as the first track but more data will be needed to make a final assessment.

In the first two cases (a and b) a signal (TU) is sent from the UNKNOWN TRACK process to the update status nodes. This leads to the entry in the target track status table being set to "accept" or "reject" as appropriate; this signal is given a high priority to ensure that the table is updated before any new track routing takes place. In the last two cases (b and c) i.e. "reject" or "don't know", a CONTINUE signal is sent to the AWAIT TRACK node as an instruction to pass the track report to another target. The mechanism described above is then repeated, except that the search of the target status table starts at one higher target number than that of the rejecting function.
    If a track report has "rippled" through all active TARGET FUNCTIONs without receiving a positive acceptance, it will finally arrive at an unseeded position. It will thus seed this function, with a provisional acceptance status i.e. collecting new data about that target in parallel with all other functions that have recorded a "don't know". No CONTINUE signal will be generated in the "seed" condition. Acceptance will be triggered by the correlation of an orthogonal set of reports (independent sets of data), which have similarly not been accepted by lower numbered functions. If, prior to this, the track is accepted by another TARGET FUNCTION, no further updates will be given and timeout and reset will occur, freeing the function for reseeding.

3.5.7. (iv)   Correlation Algorithms

The prime aim of this paper is to demonstrate the feasibility of performing real-time data fusion using an object oriented approach. Accordingly, the more complex correlation rules and algorithms applicable in the more marginal cases are not addressed here although much of the research recently performed at ARE Byrne et al (4) is applicable. In addition, it will be noted that no explicit provision has apparently been made for reference to "encyclopaedic" data. Again, this has not been considered in detail here, because such information does not change rapidly and thus reference to it is unlikely to affect the performance of the system. Probably the best place to introduce this type of information is in the ACCEPTED TRACK function by an activity controlled by a timer, in the same way as the position estimators. This ensures that searches of encyclopaedic data are conducted when spare capacity is available, with a primary focus on targets with the greatest level of uncertainty. Such information would be controlled by a separate asynchronous function, and reply directly to an interrogating signal from any of the TARGET functions.

3.5.8.   *Performance*

3.5.8.(i)   *General*

Thus far the discussion has been limited to the functional decomposition of the object oriented data fusion system. In this section, the performance implications of this approach are addressed, assuming the availability of a target computer optimised for message passing.

3.5.8.(ii)   *Track Acceptance*

The effect of the architecture described in the previous sections from the signal passing viewpoint is shown in Figures 3.5.5 and 3.5.6. Figure 3.5.5 shows the process of a track looking for a TARGET FUNCTION willing to adopt it. The track signal (HRT, LRT, or HT), previously unknown to the system, is initially routed to target 1 with signal TK. This target rejects it, sending two signals, TU (to update the Target Track Status table) and CONT (to place the track signal back in the target allocation queue). The track signal is then dispatched to target 2, and so on, until it is finally accepted by target n. Target n indicates its acceptance by sending two signals TU, (as before) and ATK (accepted track signal) to the ACCEPTED TRACK process.

All future occurrences of this track report will now be dispatched directly to that destination i.e. target n. From this analysis, it can be seen that at least $3n$ signals have to be exchanged between various processes to initiate a track.

3.5.8.(iii)   *Poor Quality Tracks*

Figure 3.5.6 depicts the situation when a poor quality track is introduced into the system. Target one places it in the "don't know" category by signalling CONTINUE to the TARGET ALLOCATION function, and at the same time placing it in its track history file. Similarly for target m. Finally the track signal arrives at a TARGET FUNCTION in an initialized state. The incoming track will be provisionally accepted as a seed track, and will not send a CONTINUE signal. This series of events could continue for a number of updates of that track until the TARGET FUNCTIONs 1 or m decide in the light of later data to accept or reject the track. If either of the lower number targets accepts the track it will no longer be sent to target n which in due course will time out and reinitialize itself.

FIG 3.5.5

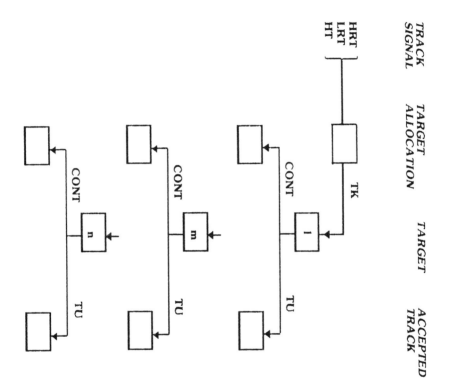

TRACK   TARGET   TARGET   ACCEPTED
SIGNAL   ALLOCATION   TRACK

HRT
LRT
HT

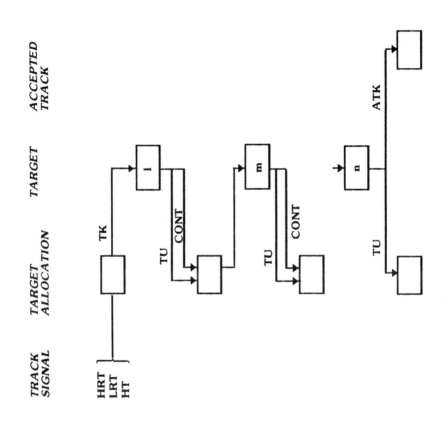

FIG 3.5.6   *Selection of a target with poor data*

[From time to time a false decision will be made and a newly initiated track will be incorrectly terminated. However, the continous checking of the BEST FIT CORRELATION will lead to the divergence of the correlation in the target which claimed the track and hence to the reinitiation of that function]. In this example it can be seen that nine signals will have been generated for a single track report; this shows the extra overhead generated by less certain measurement, and justifies setting signals from lower resolution sensors to a lower priority.

3.5.8. (iv) Scenario Statistics

From examination of the signal flows described above, it will be seen that by far the highest signal passing rate occurs when new targets are being initiated. In order to quantify the size of the computer system required to support a typical application, a scenario, believed typical of a naval task force is used for the calculations set out below. The basic parameters used are:

COMPOSITE TRACK UPDATE RATE   200 sec^{-1}
MAXIMUM TARGET INITIATION RATE   10 sec^{-1}
MAXIMUM COMPOSITE TRACK INITIATION RATE   10 sec^{-1}
MAXIMUM NUMBER OF REAL TARGETS   200

On this basis we will assume a system with provision for handling 200 TARGET FUNCTIONs simultaneously.

3.5.8. (v)   Number of Signals

Assume a situation of maximum activity in which 199 targets are being actively tracked in TARGET functions 1-199. A new target comes into view of the sensor systems and one or more new tracks are initiated. The allocation algorithm will pass this track to targets 1-199 before it is finally provisionally accepted as a seed by the two hundredth. In the analysis of an accept/reject alogrithm given below, it is shown that, under pessimistic circumstances, we may require an additional ten observations of the target each time a newly initiated track is introduced to the system, to reduce the uncertainty to an acceptable level. It is shown that in these circumstances a further sixty invocations of the accept/reject algorithm will take place.
This then means that in the worst case, a total of 260 passes through TARGET ALLOCATION function might be required to confirm final adoption. Thus:

The number of signals per try = 3
Therefore number of signals before acceptance = 230*3
= 780
In the worst case of 10 initiations per second the signal rate would be = 780*10 = 7800 signals/sec.

3.5.8. (vi)   Update

In addition to the track initialization activity there is the task of updating the track histories at the rate of 200 tracks per second. Each track update generates two signals; one from the INTERFACE FUNCTION and the other from the TARGET ALLOCATION function. Thus the total required signal passing capability required is 8200 signals per second.

3.5.9.   Instruction Rate

3.5.9. (i)   General

The other factor controlling the performance of the system is the rate at which the various algorithms can be executed. These fall into several cataegories:

- a.   The external interface.
- b.   The target allocation system and status table update.
- c.   The accept/reject correlation for newly initiated targets.
- d.   The updating of targets with new track reports.

As previously noted the detailed structure of the interface and its performance falls outside this discussion. The other three categories are considered in turn below.

3.5.9. (ii)   Target Allocation

The major processing load in this activity is the searching of the target status table. For any given track reference there would be a maximum of two hundred entries to be searched. Assuming that these entries are evenly distributed, it is reasonable to assume that on average only one hundred will need to be examined before a positive entry is found. [In practice the most frequently accessed tracks will tend to have lower numbers markedly reducing this average]. If we allocate ten instructions for a processor to address the status table, test the contents, and dispatch the track report to the appropriate process, we arrive at a required instruction rate for the target allocation function of:

$$\text{Total Number of tracks per second} \times 10 = 200 * 10 * 100$$
$$= 200,000 \ \text{sec}^{-1}$$

3.5.9. (iii)   Accept/Reject Correlation

Stage 1 Correlation: The accept/reject correlation operates in three stages. The first is primarily aimed at rejecting as many candidate tracks as possible without discarding any which could eventually prove to be pertinent. The selection of the algorithm for this activity will be on the basis of its simplicity rather than its ability to rigorously filter out all unwanted tracks. Methods which could be used include:

a. If the Best Fit Track and the candidate track have dissimilar identities, this can be used as a basis for immediate rejection.

b. Direct comparison of position, range, bearing, height, velocity, angular velocity, radial velocity, heading, and acceleration. Only a subset of these will be available in each case, although to make a reject decision at least two orthogonal sets must be available. The error characteristics of each variable is known (or has been estimated) for both the Best Fit Track and the candidate track, and we know that the measurements are truly independent. Each of the parameters listed above can be considered as orthogonal, hence we may have a reasonable number of tests of the hypothesis that both sets of measurements describe the same target. For each pair of measurements, given we assume a typical error probability density curve such as Gaussian, we can directly calculate the probability that both measurements describe the same target. These calculations can be made very fast by the use of look-up tables. A weighted vote of the outcomes of each pair of comparisons can then be used to arrive at a "reject" decision. For example, one possible strategy is to ensure that all the probability figures for "no match" exceed a certain threshold before signalling "reject".

Stage 2 Correlation: If as a result of the first stage tests the tracks fall unequivocally into the "accept" category or can be rejected with a very low risk of losing a wanted track, the appropriate signal will be sent to the TRACK ALLOCATION function. Otherwise, the track will fall into the "don't know" category and further reports will have to be collected. At some stage, sufficient reports will have been examined to produce a definitive outcome of the correlation of the reports with the Best Fit Track; this result will again fall into one of the three categories.

Stage 3 Correlation: The third stage will only be activated in the marginal cases when, even after stage two has been completed, the status of the track is still "don't know". It will involve the invocation of any encyclopaedic or intelligence data which could help in the resolution of an impasse. [In certain cases insufficient information will be available to make a proper decision. For instance a target travelling along a radial path which is being tracked by radar and ESM on a short base line, may consistently return probability figures which are insufficient to allow a final conclusion to be reached.

These will remain in the provisional aceptance category, in the same way as a seeded track without orthogonal corroboration; the track continues to hold a "don't know" status, but the two sets of data are combined to produce the Best Fit Track. Thus in the case of a raid by a group of targets which can be discriminated by the radar but not by the ESM, the ACCEPTED TRACK routine will accord them all the same identity].

3.5.9.(iv)   Processing Load

To assess the processing load we assume the following figures:
a. The first stage in the correlation will be conducted using a probability look-up table using normalised values. The inputs to the table are a pairs of mean value and error characterisation e.g. standard deviation). The output from the table will be the probability of that target *not* being described by the two sets of input data. It should be possible to do this test with around one hundred instructions.
b. The second phase will only begin after a meaningful history has built up after, say, ten reports. Consider a worst case of two hundred targets distributed evenly around one's own platform. If all of these are giving a positive response to an ESM sensor with an accuracy of twenty degrees we may after the first pass have 200*20/360 = 11 targets in the "don't know" category. The significance of the tests will increase as the square root of the number of independent observations. In the case of ESM correlated against radar we could at best expect three independent observations per track report (comparison of bearing, angular velocity and maybe radial velocity, if the ESM system was equipped with an amplitude discriminator).

Thus the number of "don't know" responses to a new track should reduce as shown in the following table , on the assumption that as the significance increases then so will the number of rejected tracks (regardless of the error distribution of the sensor reports).

Therefore, even given these extreme assumptions we would not expect on average more than two TARGET FUNCTIONs to be considering a newly initiated target. Thus in the worst case set out in the scenario definition, with two hundred targets and a track initiation rate of ten per second we have:

Number of instructions executed in a first pass test on 200 targets = 200*100 = 20,000

The number of subsequent tests on targets which initially respond with "don't know", decay as set out in the table. This gives a total number of test cycles needed to complete the second phase as 40. Again at 100 instructions per pass the total = 40*100 = 4,000.

TRY	NO OF OBSERVATIONS	DON'T KNOWS
1	3	11
2	6	5
3	9	4
4	12	3
5	15	3
6	18	3
7	21	3
8	24	2
9	27	2
10	30	2

38 say 40

The third phase of this operation will be a process implemented as a complex of rules which will evolve with experience. It is thus very difficult to estimate the average path length necessary to conduct this phase in terms of instruction count. However, it would seem unlikely that more than an average of 10,000 instructions would be needed, if reasonably efficient coding was used.

Assume that only half the sensors used are of poor resolution (like ESM) and the remainder are high resolution (such as radar). In the worst case rate of ten tracks initiated every second, only half of the tracks might lead to the invocation of three long correlations; the other half will at worst only invoke one: this gives an average of two long correlations per initiation. Thus the processing load needed to support the phase three correlation process is

= 2*10,000 = 20,000 per initiation

Thus the number of instructions needed by the UNKNOWN TRACK function with a composite track initiation rate of 10 sec^{-1} can be calculated as

(20,000+4000+20,000)*10 = 440,000 instructions sec^{-1}.

Target Update: The ACCEPTED TRACK function adds new data
to the track history table and generates an update of the
Best Fit Track.   As each of the tracks presented to the
data fusion system have already been subjected to some form
of optimal estimation e.g. least squares, the best method
for combining the data is by using Bayesian Inference for
each of the spatial measurements.   If more than one
identification level is present, these will be combined if
possible (i.e. appropriate probability estimates are
available) using Bayes theorem.   However, there is a
problem in the use of Bayesian Inference to combine the
data - it makes the implicit assumption that all the data
is actually describing the same target.   We, therefore,
have to provide an additional test to check for an
incorrectly assigned track.   One technique is to check the
cross correlation of each data element with the Best Fit
Track data each time it is computed.   A rule based
estimator can then assess any increase in doubt of the
relevance of a track to the target and take appropriate
action i.e. either just reject the track or reset the
function.
     The processing load for the Bayesian inference is
relatively light requiring simple linear arithmetic on
readily available variables.   It is considered that 300
instructions should suffice.   The "poor correlation"
watchdog could be more complex depending upon the strategy.
With careful design, however, it should be feasible to keep
the main path down to say, 200 instructions, with the more
complex parts only being called into play when some doubt
exists.   The above analysis thus gives an estimate of 500
instructions for each track update.   Given the scenario of
200 updates per second we therefore have to provide a
processing capability for this function of:

$$200*500 = 100,000 \text{ instructions sec}^{-1}$$

3.5.9.(v)   Total Processing Requirement

     To summarise the above paragraphs the overall
processing requirement can be broken down as follows:

Target Allocation	100,000
Accept/Reject	440,000
Update	100,000
	640,000 Instructions sec^{-1}

Even if we add a contingency of 50% to the above analysis,
it can be seen that the processing load requiring support
is not much more than 1 million instructions per second.

3.5.10. *Implementing the Object Oriented Model*

3.5.10. (i) *General*

The performance analysis conducted above only examines the number of instructions required to execute the application. No account is taken of the overhead required to pass signals between the processes[3], and thence to schedule them. Traditional operating systems and their underlying target hardware are generally acknowledged to be highly inefficient at supporting message passing systems, otherwise known as loosely coupled systems. However, specialised architectures are now evolving to support such systems, of which one example is the Sofchip computer; see Coombs et al(1). A brief description of this architecture is given below.

3.5.10. (ii) *Sofchip Computer*

The Sofchip architecture consists of a bank of Processing Elements which share a common memory, to which they are connected via a Master Control Unit (MCU). Processes, which represent nodes in a graph of processes are represented by their outer level program environments which are kept in the common memory. The reason for keeping the process environments in a common memory is to allow a Context Control Unit within the MCU to allocate any free processing element to any of the processes needing evaluating. In most systems there are greatly more processes then processing elements, and a high degree of latency in the process network. The Sofchip architecture takes advantage of this to provide a much more efficient utilisation of processors than can be achieved by a system which statically allocates processors to processes (e.g. the Connection Machine or a Transputer network programmed in OCCAM).

This dynamic allocation of processing elements is one of the important features of the Sofchip computer, allowing metricable loosely coupled systems to be constructed[4]. A second notable feature is that the processors are potentially any classical microprocessor, or even non-Von Neuman machines such as processor arrays e.g. DAP. The only characterstics of the processing element, mandated by the architecture, is the ability to generate logical addresses, interpret control codes and manipulate data returned via a data bus. This has the very significant advantage of not restricting the user into a proprietary processor; this has been achieved by recognition that the

---

[3] For a definition of process see Rhodes (3).

[4] See Rhodes (3)

only generalised fast way to communicate with a microprocessor is via the memory mapping unit.

The processess communicate entirely by signal passing (NO side effects) by using a protected common buffer pool. Thus signal passing is very much faster than bus oriented packet passing or even dedicated bit serial. This means that the architecture supports fast signal passing between the bank of processors with the good theoretical properties of pure functional programming. A further capability of the architecture is the ability to allocate dedicated ROM and RAM to the processing elements. The ROMs can hold code of commonly occurring subroutines (c.f. machine instructions), which are side effect free, which the processing element can evaluate using the local RAM as workspace; this serves to increase the effective common memory bandwidth.

Each MCU can communicate with any other using exactly the same signal format as that used internally. This means, in principle, that a system design can be dispersed to any required degree. The only caveat is that note has been taken of the time delays and capacity limitations of the chosen interconnecting media.

The Sofchip architecture offers several benefits to the production of the object oriented data fusion system. Functional separation between processes is guaranteed by hardware, thus the propagation of secondary errors is much reduced. There is no shared data because all communication between processes is via signals. The "operating system" of many computer architectures is supplanted by the MCU, thus the whole processing power of the system is devoted to the "application"; the processing "power" of the system is essentially the linear sum of that of the processing elements (subject to memory bandwidth limitations and buffer length). This means that the system can be accurately sized during its early development, and the correct hardware configuration needed to meet the required performance can be selected. As Processing Elements are identical, a high level of reliability can be attained by providing redundant spares. This imposes no extra runtime overheads.

3.5.10.(iii)   Size of Buffer Pool

It was determined above that with the scenario given, a signal passing rate of 7800 signals per second would be sufficient. Therefore, for sizing purposes a signal flow rate of 10,000 sec^{-1} will be used. Similarly it has been projected that our dominant activity, the accept/reject process, will consume around 100 instructions per task: it is thus reasonable to take a figure of 100 instructions as the mean task length of the system. It has also been shown that a processing power of 1 mips should suffice.

In the examples given in Rhodes (3) the characteristics of a number of multiprocessor systems operating with signal driven dynamic parallelism are examined (the Sofchip class of computer). For instance the data fusion design described above could be implemented using three 500 Kips processing elements e.g. 68000, giving an average signal trigger delay of less than 2 mS, and a maximum buffer pool size of 78. This analysis assumes that the signal passing mechanism between processes can support the 10,000 signals per second, and any common resources for the processing elements (e.g. memory bandwidth in the Sofchip Computer) is sufficient for the combined peak processing load.

Such systems have been constructed using standard SSI and MSI components consuming 75 watts and occupying rather less than .25 cubic metres. Implementation of a real time data fusion system based upon the architecture described in this paper appears perfectly feasible, and there is an ongoing project to refine the algorithms presented in outline, with the objective of constructing a demonstration data fusion system.

3.5.11   References

1.   Coombs, C.E., Hemdal, G.A.H., September 1986, 'Sofchip Technology: A New System Architecture of Telecommunications and other Real-Time Systems', *Proc. IEE 6th International Conference on Software Engineering for Telecommunication Switching Systems*, Eindhoven, Netherlands, 7-13.

2.   Hemdal, G.A.H., Reilly, M., September 1987, 'Requirements Analysis and Design Using the Auto-G Tool System', *Proc., Methodologies and Tools for Real Time Systems: IV'*, National Institute for Software Quality and Productivity, Bethesda, USA, Section M.

3.   Rhodes, S.L., September 1987, 'Performance Prediction of Loosely Coupled Systems', *Proc., International Conference on Software Engineering for Real Time Systems*, Cirencester, England, 67-75.

4.   Byrne, D., Lakin, W.L., Miles, J.A.H., April 1987, 'Intelligent Data Fusion for Naval Command and Control', *Proc. IEE Second International Conference on Command, Control, Communications and Management Information Systems*, Bournemouth, England, 101-110.

Chapter 4
Intelligent situation assessment and planning

Expert Systems And The Problems Of Naval Command

D.W. Cruse and W.J. Bingham
(Ferranti Computer Systems)

4.1.1   Introduction

This section is concerned with the application of Knowledge Based System techniques to the problems of Naval Command. This particular naval context is clearly just one example of a C^2 system, and many of the tasks and problems to be described will have a far wider applicability. The job of a naval force commander and the difficulties that he faces will first be described; this will be followed by a discussion of the possible role of expert system techniques. Finally, a specific expert system command aid will be mentioned with which the authors are familiar.

The overall message is an optimistic one. Firstly that I.K.B.S. techniques can provide the key to solving some of the more difficult problems faced by the command function and secondly that they will provide the catalyst for the introduction of computer based assistance in an area that to date has proved somewhat resistant.

4.1.2   The Command Function

The Force Commander at sea is one of the last independent military commanders. With his force of surface ships, submarines and aircraft he may be thousands of miles from his main base and beyond the range of land based air support. The supply ships included in his force provide fuel, ammunition and stores that can enable him to sustain operations independently for days or weeks at a time. His command may even include a force of troops capable of operations ashore.

In these days of sophisticated electronic warfare, he can still remain undetected over large parts of the world's oceans for significant periods. To achieve this, however, he must restrict all types of electronic emissions, and this will severely limit his ability to communicate with his superiors ashore. Increasing sophistication in communications has been matched by more effective countermeasures. The result of this is to make communication from shore headquarters to a force at sea at best intermittent and at worst impossible.

The force commander at sea must therefore be capable of operating on his own for significant periods. To do this effectively he must be capable of making the best possible use of all the information available, however incomplete this may be. He must be able to make from it an assessment of the situation that will enable him to use the resources available to him to the best effect.

Before examining the use of information and resources, it is worth reminding ourselves of the reasons why a force of ships is at sea at all, and what are the responsibilities of the force commander.

Ships are too valuable and scarce a resource to be sent to sea to cruise the oceans in the vague hope of something turning up. In modern war the ocean is a dangerous place. Ships are subject to attack over large areas of it. All groups of ships at sea will have been assembled and despatched to perform a particular mission within a particular time and, as far as they are available, the types and numbers of ships will have been chosen so as to make up a group with the best capability for achieving their task.

The principal responsibilities of the naval force commander can be summarised under five headings:-

(a)   With the forces under his command, to achieve his mission in the time allocated - this may be the safe passage of a convoy, the conduct of an amphibious landing, an offensive strike, clearance of a minefield, or a wide variety of other tasks.

(b)   The safety of the forces under his command, as far as is compatible with achieving his mission. This can also be expressed as achieving the mission with minimum loss to his own forces.

(c)   The destruction of the enemy forces against which he has been ordered to act or which try to obstruct him in the exercise of his mission.

(d)   The administration and logistic support of the forces under his command.

(e)   Keeping other force commanders at sea and headquarters ashore informed of his position, his intentions, the tactical situation in his area, intelligence of enemy forces, and the status of his own forces.

The force commander's problem is summarised in Figure 4.1.1.

To achieve his mission while making best use of his own forces and while imposing the maximum losses on the enemy, the force commander must build up a clear picture of the tactical situation in his area and in the area into which he is moving. Having obtained a view of the situation, he must then assess how this could affect his intentions, how he achieves his mission or even, whether he can achieve it.

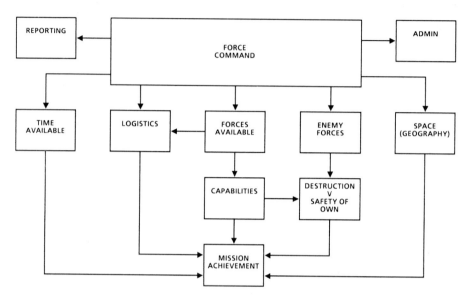

FIG 4.1.1   *The force commander's problem - wartime*

Building up such a tactical picture is not a simple
process. The information available is often fragmentary or
incomplete, is derived at different times and may be
several hours old by the time it reaches the commander at
sea. He may, for example, have a number of reports of
contact with a submarine - from maritime patrol aircraft,
helicopters and other sources. The times and the spacing
of the positions may be such that the reports could
consistently be interpreted as successive contacts with one
submarine, or could be three separate submarines. To make
the correct assessment requires a knowledge of enemy
capabilities, tactical thinking and likely intentions, of
oceanographic conditions and geographical constraints and a
degree of intuition trained by experience.

Individual pieces of information have an effect, not
only on the particular track to which they refer, but also
on previous assessments of other tracks in the vicinity.
Building up the tactical picture is a continuous process
and requires continuous reappraisal of earlier assessments,
if the best appreciation is to be achieved. There is the
danger, ever present, of a commander being driven by
pressure of events, lack of time and tiredness into holding
to an appreciation which subsequent information has made
invalid; into forcing new data to fit the mould, rather
than carrying out the re-assessment that is necessary. The
need for a knowledge-based system to help provide a
consistent appreciation of the situation as new data is
received, whatever the time of day or the other immediate
pressures on the command, is clear.

To dispose his ships and aircraft effectively involves considering the seriousness and directions of the various threats and capabilities of all the units available - a further complex decision.

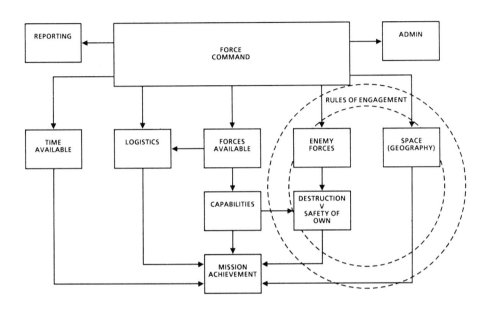

FIG 4.1.2   *The force commander's problem - time of tension*

The problem for the commander, however, is that having carried out all these decision processes, he can never relax in the knowledge that he has reached a final solution. The situation will be continually changing. New information will come to hand. The enemy may not follow the path that earlier assessments suggested. New data may throw doubt on assessments of the tactical picture - for example on how many submarines are operating and where. As his own force moves, the geographical and oceanographical constraints change. The weather will change and so will the logistic state of the force. Weapons and sensors in certain ships may become defective and others that were defective may be repaired. New rules of engagement and new political guidance may be received.

All these factors bear on earlier assessments of the course of action to take, the threat the enemy poses and the best disposition of his own forces. Ideally all changes should be followed by a thorough re-assessment of the tactical picture, of the situation and how it is likely to develop, of the courses of action available and of the disposition of own forces.

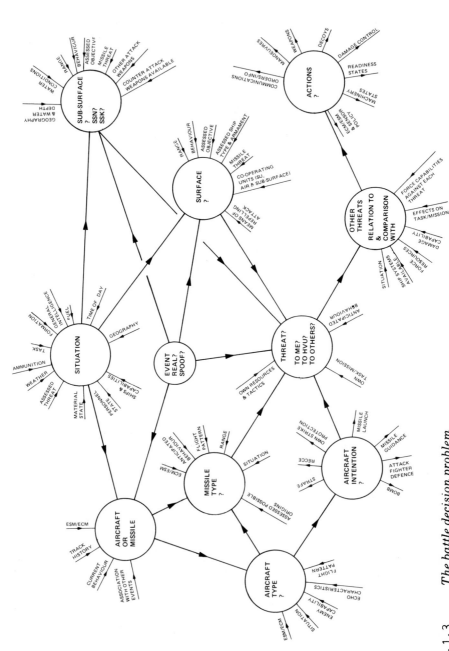

FIG 4.1.3   *The battle decision problem*

From the tactical picture, however it is derived, the commander must assess how the situation is likely to develop and how likely enemy movements may affect his best course of action. To achieve such an assessment he must first apply his knowledge of enemy tactical doctrine. What is the enemy's most likely course of action? Where is the best place for enemy submarines to patrol? How can the enemy expect to do most damage to our own force at least loss to himself?

In the situation short of open war, the possible actions must also be tested against the political situation. What effect on the current state of tension would each move have? Would the effect be in line with the enemy's perceived political aim? Even if it is in line with their aim, is now the moment at which they are likely to want to move politically?

The most likely, and the alternative, enemy actions must then be assessed in relation to the mission of the task force under command. What is the nature of the threat? How serious is it likely to be? Is it within the capability of own forces to overcome it? When is it likely to develop and from what directions?

This brings the force commander to the point at which he must consider the various options for action that are open to him.

How does the threat that he has assessed affect his ability to complete his mission successfully? Is his current course of action the right one? What other options are possibilities that he should consider? Would any of these other options give him a better chance of success? Would any of them contribute more to frustrating the enemy's perceived designs?

In a situation of tension or limited action, the commander must also consider the Rules of Engagement imposed on him by his higher command (see Figure 4.1.2). These often state in considerable detail the limits of action within which the commander may operate. So the commander must assess what he can do within the current rules; whether the current rules enable him to achieve his aim at an acceptable degree of risk; whether he needs to request changes in the rules, what changes he needs and what might be approved.

Clearly, the process through which a commander should go in reaching a decision on what he should do is complex, as illustrated in Figure 4.1.3. It can be time consuming and the time is not always available. This is a second area in which the commander could derive great assistance from a knowledge-based system.

The decision on what he should do - the course of action he should follow - leads the commander to the next phase - the decision on how to dispose the forces available to him. This involves both those he has to protect and also those units whose main contribution is in protecting others. The factors involved in making this decision are derived from the commander's assessment of the situation.

But often the Admiral has a small staff who are overwhelmed by the amount of information available to them, the decisions required from them in a very limited time and the effort required in implementing the decisions (writing signals, working out positions and times etc). Inevitably, assessments are reduced to the bare minimum and over-simplified. Only tactical rules that are clear in an officer's mind are applied. There is no time to look up others. As a result, decisions can be taken on assessments from which vital factors have been omitted, leading to mis-application of the resources available.

The case for assisting the Command is clear. Why has it not been done before? The answer seems to be that it has been too difficult. It has also been a low priority - force commanders are not likely to admit that they cannot cope. However the situation is changing because of the introduction of long range sensors: the towed array, airborne warning and control system (A.W.A.C.S.) and satellite surveillance. Also communications are better, adding to the flow of data being received by the commander. It is probably fair to say that the extent of the problem was not realised until the Falklands War, partly because this was the first war in which naval forces faced a serious missile threat and partly because of the complex logistic problems of supporting an amphibious operation 8000 miles from the nearest main base.

4.1.3   The Role of Expert Systems

The term Expert System is used here to refer to that branch of Artificial Intelligence that deals with the processing of information, inferring new knowledge from existing knowledge and which has the objective of applying computers to tasks that require human skill and experience. Expert systems attempt to incorporate human experience, such as rules of thumb and problem solving strategy skills. For all the applications identified here expert systems are considered from the point of view of providing assistance to the naval command function, carrying out the more routine tasks in an objective manner and allowing the force commander more tactical thinking time. In this context references to Planning will imply an expert system.

Looking more carefully at the force commander's responsibilities, as illustrated in Figure 4.1.4, it is seen that they divide into two categories: Situation Assessment and Resource Allocation. There are five major components to Situation Assessment: Picture Compilation, Vehicle Library, Own Forces, Rules of Engagement and Meteorology and Oceanography.

Picture Compilation is the classic data fusion problem, very complex and difficult. Some advanced form of real-time, Blackboard, expert system is likely to play a crucial role in solving this problem. Work is proceeding at a number of centres and significant progress is being made, e.g. Wilson (1) and Lakin et al (2) [see also Chapter 3]. At present the force commander is presented with a rather

Expert systems and naval command 305

FIG 4.1.4   *Force command - a functional approach*

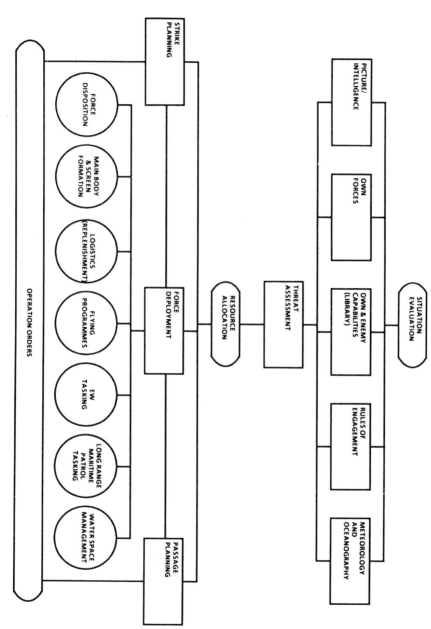

inaccurate, partial picture containing conflicting information, derived from a wide variety of sources of differing accuracy and reliability and interpreted subjectively by staff officers. Computer assistance in collating and combining - or fusing- the data from all these sources and in providing an objective interpretation would be a very major step forward. The ability to archive seemingly-irrelevant information and automatically retrieve it in context would be very valuable. Picture compilation requires a large library of data such as emitter characteristics, missile profiles, e.t.c. to provide identity information.   An intelligent front end to a database may well be used here.

The Vehicle library is a database containing details of both friendly and enemy vehicles, equipment and weapon fits, tactical use, capability etc.

Own forces comprise own and other friendly forces at sea, fixed detection systems and shore based air support including long range maritime reconnaissance A.S.W. aircraft, A.W.A.C.S. and attack aircraft. Some but not all of these are available resources.

Rules of Engagement are available in book form but are very complex and interlocking. A major problem is matching the actual scenario facing the force commander with those described in the R.O.E.   The techniques of the knowledge engineer can be expected to prove valuable here.

Meteorology and Oceanography is mainly database information.   A rule based system may prove useful in merging current and historical data and in interpreting this information.   For example the prediction of oceanographic fronts may be important.

Having, in a manner of speaking, assembled the basic information the force commander now has to make use of it. The first stage is Threat Assessment.

It is necessary to draw inferences about the nature of a likely threat to the force, when it can be expected to manifest itself and how it could be countered. Basically human experience is being used to interprete the tactical picture in the light of the details held in the Vehicle Library.   An Expert System could clearly carry out this role, at least in making the more obvious inferences, allowing the command more time to make a more detailed assessment where this is required.

Turning now to Resource Allocation, Figure 4.1.4 shows that there are three aspects to be considered: Passage Planning, Strike Planning and Force Deployment.

In order to carry out his mission the force commander will need to carry out Passage Planning - to find an optimum route to his destination which for example, avoids the enemy.   Other constraints may be the need to stay beyond the range of hostile aircrafts always stay within reach of shore based support, to make optimum use of meteorological and oceanographic information, pre-disposed support facilities such as oil tankers and use minimum fuel.   There may also be restrictions on submarine operating areas and the need to adopt diversionary tactics, for example to mislead or avoid satellite surveillance. Clearly this is a complex planning problem. As new information becomes available there is a replanning problem with the added constraint of minimum disturbance to the original plan.

Strike Planning applies when a threat is posed to the success of the mission. If the ROE permit, it may be necessary to consider eliminating an enemy force. This is an important planning problem in which some form of Expert System could play a major role. For example it will be necessary to determine the optimum strike opportunity, where and how to deploy own force for maximum effectiveness and minimum retaliation. The state of readiness and capability of each ship and weapon system must be considered as well as the capability of the enemy force.

Finally Force Deployment, a term which covers a whole host of activities. Under this heading we can group:

(a)   Screen disposition - the allocation of ships to stations to form a defensive screen. An expert system for tackling this problem is described in section 4.1.4.

(b)   Replenishment logistics - the supply of fuel, provisions and munitions to each vessel, and the consequent adjustment of screening stations. A difficult allocation and scheduling planning problem subject to a relatively large number of constraints.

(c)   Flying programmes - planning flight schedules for helicopter and fixed wing aircraft. Essentially an allocation problem subject to several constraints.

(d)   Electronic warfare (E.W.) tasking - allocation of frequency bands and duties to the E.W. equipments of the force.

(e)   Water space management - allocation of patrol areas to the submarines of the force to prevent friendly-friendly conflicts.

(f)   The overall disposition of several groups of ships, submarines and aircraft over a large operating area.

There is clearly plenty of scope for the application of expert system techniques to most of these tasks. Research and development work is certainly taking place, for example see Gadsden (3) and Gadsden et al (4), (see also Sections 4.2 and 4.3) and it is likely that expert systems for these individual tasks will become available in the next few years. A truly integrated command aid in this area is, however, a more formidable undertaking.

Before proceeding further it is worthwhile to emphasise the fact that expert systems may only play a small role in these applications, but that role could well be crucial for their successful realisation.

4.1.4   Naval Command Aid

The problem of screen disposition has been used as the starting point for a Command Aid based on expert systems techniques. This particular application has been under development since 1983 and has now passed beyond the prototype phase to become a mature system product.

Viewed as a planning problem screen disposition is relatively simple with little in the way of constraints except for finding a 'best' solution; the search space, although potentially large, is in practice of a size that can be exhaustively searched by efficient algorithms. However it has proved a worthwhile and interesting project and is an important example of I.K.B.S. techniques being successfully applied to a non-trivial problem.

The composition of a naval task force can be considered to consist of two parts: the Main Body and the Screen, as shown in Figure 4.1.5. The main body is the central core of the force, usually high value units, which require protection. The screen is those units (ships, submarines, helicopters and maritime patrol aircraft) whose primary function is to afford protection to the main body.

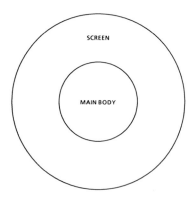

FIG 4.1.5   *Naval task force composition*

The force commander has the very complex task of deploying his assets as effectively as possible against the perceived threats to his mission. To do this he and his staff have to consider the following factors:

(i)   certainty of threat
(ii)   severity of threat
(iii)   effect of threat on mission
(iv)   capability of own units
(v)   acceptable defence compromise

amongst others.

The disposition of the main body and defensive screen is a time consuming task that requires constant attention and modification as circumstances alter. Each vessel in the force has a different capability against different types of threat and the requirement is to produce a defensive screen that is optimum against the various different threats arising from any or all of subsurface, surface and air environments.

The perceived threats are considered in terms of certainty and severity factors as well as direction or sector (see Figure 4.1.6.). Multi-threat situations can occur as well as 360 degree all-round threats.

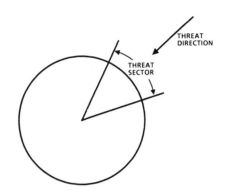

- TYPE OF THREAT

- CERTAINTY

- SEVERITY

- DIRECTION OR SECTOR

FIG 4.1.6   *Threat parameters*

The stationing of the units in a screen is governed by a relatively large number of rules, each stated in terms of a single threat environment, sub-surface, surface and air. In practice a naval force would be acting in a multi-threat environment. The commander and his staff have to apply tactical doctrine enshrined in a variety of publications and have to sort out conflicting priorities between, for example, air defence and anti-submarine warfare in working out how to deploy their assets. This tactical doctrine has been interpreted by naval experts to produce the knowledge base of an expert system.

The first step is to calculate the station positions in the defensive screen, to which ships have to be allocated. A simple approach would be to have stations equally spaced in azimuth over 360 degrees. However a more sophisticated scheme has been implemented where the station positions depend upon a measure of threat "density". Figure 4.1.7 illustrates these two cases. The number of station positions is of course normalised to the number of available ships in the task force.

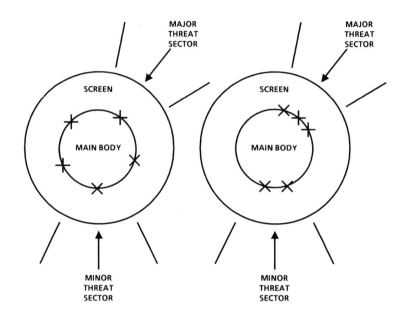

Station Positions Devnoted by ✗

(a) Equally Spaced in Azimuth   (b) Proportional to Threat "Density"

FIG 4.1.7   *Station positioning*

To determine an optimum matching of ships to stations, the expert system, using its knowledge bases and the perceived threats, first examines each station position in the screen to determine the optimum list of equipment needed by a vessel allocated to that position. It then scores each vessel in the force against each station in terms of equipment actually possessed compared to the ideal requirement and in this way, builds up a score matrix of ships versus stations. Figure 4.1.8 shows an example score matrix. This matrix is then searched for all best solutions, the highest score, since in general there will be more than one best solution. The example of Figure 4.1.8 has two best solutions. This is potentially an N! combinational search problem, where N is the number of ships in the screen, but techniques exist to reduce this search space (it is also naturally bounded by the practical size of a naval task force!). Having found a set of best solutions a further search is made using additional rules covering the flexibility of the screen and the minimal overlap of sector coverage to produce a recommended solution.

STATION NUMBER

	1	2	3	4	5	6	7
1	45	55	74	85	67	35	35
2	15	20	41	55	51	40	40
3	35	30	43	50	36	25	25
4	15	5	13	20	20	30	30
5	25	40	53	60	49	20	20
6	10	15	15	15	15	10	10
7	60	90	111	125	99	40	40

SHIP NUMBER

TWO EQUALLY GOOD SOLUTIONS

SHIP 1 ALLOCATED TO STATION 3	SHIP 1 ALLOCATED TO STATION 3
SHIP 2 ALLOCATED TO STATION 7	SHIP 2 ALLOCATED TO STATION 6
SHIP 3 ALLOCATED TO STATION 1	SHIP 3 ALLOCATED TO STATION 1
SHIP 4 ALLOCATED TO STATION 6	SHIP 4 ALLOCATED TO STATION 7
SHIP 5 ALLOCATED TO STATION 5	SHIP 5 ALLOCATED TO STATION 5
SHIP 6 ALLOCATED TO STATION 2	SHIP 6 ALLOCATED TO STATION 2
SHIP 7 ALLOCATED TO STATION 4	SHIP 7 ALLOCATED TO STATION 4

FIG 4.1.8   *Score matrix of ships versus stations*

The facility is provided for the command to change the given solution to take account of any additional facts unknown to the system: on each change the expert system will inform him of what equipment in each ship becomes better or worse placed in respect of the threats being faced.

An important feature is that the screen disposition is presented in a graphical form in a format that has been deliberately chosen to be already familiar to naval command staff. An example of a screen solution is given in Figure 4.1.9. This shows some additional features that are treated algorithmically and do not form part of the expert system solution, such as helicopter stations and patrol sectors. In fact a patrol sector can only be calculated after a ship has been allocated to a station since its size will depend, amongst other things, on the characteristics of the ship. Note also that ship patrol areas are not necessarily contiguous in azimuth.

There are a variety of circumstances in which replanning is required, some examples of which are:

(a)   a ship is added to the screen

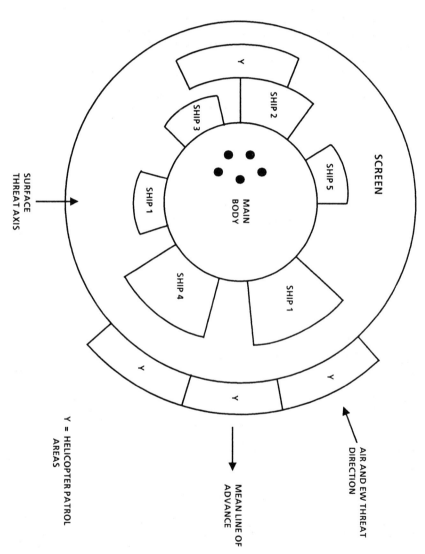

FIG 4.1.9   Example of screen disposition solution

SURFACE
THREAT AXIS

SCREEN

MAIN
BODY

SHIP 2

SHIP 3

SHIP 5

SHIP 1

SHIP 4

SHIP 1

Y

Y

Y

Y

AIR AND EW THREAT
DIRECTION

MEAN LINE OF
ADVANCE

Y = HELICOPTER PATROL
AREAS

(b)   a ship is deleted from the screen
(c)   an item of equipment becomes defective
(d)   the task force changes course
(e)   one or more threats change

The new constraint here is that the new plan should differ as little as possible from the existing plan. This can be achieved by modifying the score matrix to take account of the distance a ship has to travel from its existing station to a new one; the greater the distance the lower the value in the matrix score.

The expert system used is custom built for this application and is written in FORTRAN. It uses two knowledge sources, one being a domain rulebase determining what equipment is needed where, and the second a database of ship equipment fits. For efficiency reasons the rulebase is partitioned into three parts, each containing about 100 rules. Experts in naval tactics have been used to draw up the rules, using their knowledge and experience to interpret written single environment threat rules. Backward chaining is used, the need for each type of equipment being postulated in turn and a check made back through the rules to see if all conditions are satisfied.

The domain rulebase is quite a complicated structure but a typical example is: "If this station is a goalkeeper station and all point defence missile systems have been allocated then this station will require a close-in weapon system".

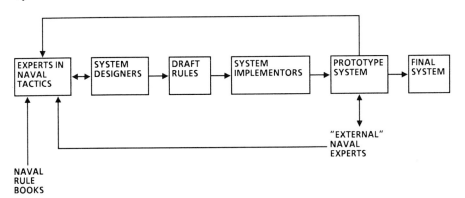

FIG 4.1.10   *Knowledge elicitation process*

The system provides a degree of explanation to help the force commander and his staff understand and thus gain confidence in the recommended screen disposition solution. For example any station can be examined to see a list of required equipment, each item being annotated with a measure of its importance, in six steps ranging from essential through to marginally useful. In addition the score matrix of ships versus stations can be displayed. Finally, as has already been mentioned, in assessing the consequences of any modification (ship exchanges or ship moves) to the recommended solution, the system reports on those major items of equipment better or worse placed to meet the perceived threats.

It is important to emphasise the fact that this application is a hybrid system, a mixture of algorithmic and expert system techniques where each is used in the area to which it is most applicable.

Finally Figure 4.1.10 shows diagrammatically the knowledge elicitation process that was used in producing this system.

4.1.5   References

1.   Wilson G.B., 1987, 'Some aspects of data fusion', 'Advances in Command, Control and Communication Systems', Peter Peregrinus Ltd, London, England, 321-338.

2.   Lakin W.L. and Miles J.A.H., 1987, 'An AI approach to data fusion and situation assessment', 'Advances in Command, Control and Communication Systems', Peter Peregrinus Ltd, London, England, 339-377.

3.   Gadsden J.A., 1984, 'Expert system for evaluating electronic warfare tasking plans for the Royal Navy', *IEEE proceeding 1st conference on AI applications*.

4.   Gadsden J.A. and Lakin W.A., 1986, 'FLYPAST - an intelligent system for naval resource allocation', 9th MIT/ONR workshop on C3 systems, Monterey.

Knowledge-Based Techniques for Tactical Situation Assessment

J.A.H. Miles (Admiralty Research Establishment)*, E.M. England,
H.C. Faulkner, S.P. Frampton (Ferranti Computer Systems Ltd)

4.2.1   Introduction

As part of a research programme to establish knowledge-based technology for naval command and control, the Admiralty Research Establishment, Portsmouth, England is building prototypes for evaluation in the laboratory and later at sea. A *Situation Assessment* function is the subject of one of these prototypes. This article reviews possible knowledge-based techniques for situation assessment and presents a case study of the first prototype system.

Sections 4.4.2 - 4.4.7 provide a detailed discussion of knowledge-based techniques which could be applied to the *situation assessment* problem. Because the term situation assessment is used rather loosely in the literature, the introductory statement includes discussion of the definition used here. This is followed by a statement of possible requirements for a naval situation assessment function and discussions of three strategies for designing a knowledge-based solution. Although not part of the situation assessment function, a section is included on resource allocation to show how the two functions relate and to compare the knowlege-based techniques which are applicable. The techniques discussion is completed with a summary and notes on other reported work.

Sections 4.4.8 - 4.4.11 of this article are a case study of the work undertaken to build a prototype knowledge-based situation assessment system. It describes the formal approach adopted for acquiring the knowledge from a naval expert and the implementation using a blackboard framework and window-based graphics system.

The article concludes with some observations on the success of the work so far and directions for the future.

4.2.2   Introduction to Techniques

Situation Assessment Definition. The scope of the term
situation assessment is discussed in relation to data fusion in
Chapter 3.4 but an attempt will be made to define it more
accurately here. A definition which scopes it in relation
to neighbouring problems is suggested as follows:

'the inference of statements to support resource
allocation decisions from the domain model created by
the data fusion process'.

Whereas data fusion can be seen as a data-defined
process, that is it creates a model of the domain at a
level implied by the input data, situation assessment is
goal defined; there is a definite level of output to be
achieved. Thus the situation assessment problem will
depend on the application; in some cases it may be trivial
because the result of data fusion may be directly usable by
the decision making process, in other cases there may be
considerable transformation to do in order to produce the
level of output required.
The definition above is not very satisfying from an
intuitive point of view because if relies on the concepts
of data fusion and it assumes that the output is directly
related to the decision making or resource allocation
process.
A looser definition might be:

'the inference of a current, high level description of
the problem domain'.

This more general definition is certainly implied by
some practitioners even to the exent of subsuming data
fusion under the heading of situation assessment. A more
specific definition relating to a particular application
will be given in Sections 4.2.8 - 4.2.11.
As far as this research is concerned, situation
assessment is the function which sits between data fusion
and resource allocation. The input to situation assessment
will be the result of the data fusion process which is a
model of the world of interest based on physical objects,
their position, movement and identity, where these
parameters can be inferred from the available data. In
some circumstances this model may be easy to assimilate and
use for decision making but in general, to perform the
naval command and control task, the model must be extended
to produce a more concise higher-level statement of what is
really happening.
Knowledge-Based Situation Assessment. Situation
assessment is the stage in command and control where expert
judgements are really brought to bear and it should
therefore be a fruitful subject for the application of
knowledge-based techniques. This is borne out by the
literature.

Bechtel (1) and McCall (2) describe an early attempt at situation assessment for the Naval domain. Spain, Levitt (3) and Laskowski (4) describe battlefeld systems. Several researchers have focussed on the threat assessment function including Garvey (5) - an aircraft application - Vittal (6), and Babcock (7). More detailed comments on these and other references are given after discussion of specific knowledge-based techniques.

4.2.3 Situation Assessment Problem

A number of assessments can be included under the heading of situation assessment, for example:

(1) Threat Assessment
(2) Defence Assessment
(3) Mission Assessment
(4) Outcome of Actions
(5) Weapon System Geometries
(6) Rules of Engagement
(7) Sensor and Weapon Coverage and Status
(8) Plan Monitoring
(9) Surveillance

Threat Assessment. Threats can be classified as direct, indirect or potential. Direct threats are observed hostile units in the act of attacking; indirect threats are estimates of the attacks which observed hostile units are likely to make based on intelligence about the weapons they carry; potential threats are an assessment of threats which might be encountered based on intelligence only. Assessment of both direct and indirect threats would be a useful function for an advisory system to carry out because a large amount of knowledge is required and many feasibility calculations have to be performed in a short timescale. Potential threats can be assessed on a much longer timescale and there is less need for machine-based reasoning.
Knowledge for a threat assessment will merge the currently perceived deployment of enemy units with encyclopaedic intelligence data on enemy systems and tactics to generate possible attack scenarios. Parameters to be estimated include: type of attack, how soon it could be mounted, number of units involved, likely targets, etc.
Defence Assessment. One of the major objectives of any task group must be to set up an effective defence screen against a number of different types of threat. The objective of the defence assesesment would be to monitor the effectiveness of all aspects of this screen under the constantly changing tactical environment. Its aim would be to alert the command as soon as possible to any weak areas such as might be caused by units changing station, equipment failures and losses during action.
Defence assessment is required to make a useful statement regarding the effectiveness of the defence screen against the possible attack scenarios identified in the

threat assessment. It should attempt to define likely targets for each possible attack and point out any weak points in the screen.

Assesssment of the defensive position will require contributions from some of the more specific assessments outlined below, for example, sensor and weapon coverage.

Mission Assessment. This is a longer term assessment against the objectives of the mission. One approach to this assessment is to compare the current position with the mission plan and note whether the position is as expected. If the objectives are only generally stated then the extent to which each objective has been fulfilled will have to be worked out. Mission assessment for a naval task group is a fairly long timescale activity and is not of great interest to the real-time problems being addressed.

Outcome of Actions. The outcome of any action is of great importance to a commander because it may determine the next course of action. During a battle, such an assessment must be produced very rapidly to be of any use. For example, to conserve missiles an air-defence ship needs to know as soon as all the attacking missiles are destroyed or otherwise rendered harmless. Unfortunately the information on which this type of assessment could be based is often difficult to obtain in the required timescale. Where direct evidence is unavailable, changes of behaviour may be detectable which could be used to make the required assessment.

Weapon System Geometries. This assessment would consider possible conflicts arising from the positioning of various weapon systems in relation to one another. It would periodically examine the weapon arcs and produce alerts if conflicts or dangerous situations which might cause accidents were discovered. There may be difficulties with obtaining accurate information to do this assessment for remote platforms but it may be possible to achieve some results by restricting the assessment to activities on own ship and/or to do checks between, say, friendly aircraft movements and shipboard anti-air missile systems.

Rules of Engagement. When and how to respond to a threat is a very important decision in which Rules Of Engagement (ROE) play a crucial part. The ROE are precise but the perception of the tactical situation and in particular the present threat are imprecise. Well informed judgements must be made, often rapidly, which could be assisted by explicit application of expert knowledge to alert and explain the situtation in relation to ROE.

Sensor and Weapon Coverage and Status. Sensor and weapon coverage estimation would be useful assessments for modifying defence screen and emission control plans. For example, it could assist the problem of deciding which radars, if any, to use in a task group to give the required cover or where to place a ship with surface-to-air missiles to protect other units. For passive sensors the assessment could help to modify unit dispositions for better ranging of threats from given directions.

Calculation of sensor and weapon coverage is not easy because many factors have to be taken into account, some of which can only be estimated. The results might also be difficult to represent for a reasonable set of target objects. The status of sensor and weapon coverage is not easy because many factors have to be taken into account, some of which can only be estimated. The results might also be difficult to represent for a reasonable set of target objects.

The status of sensor and weapon systems including operating condition, operating mode and number of rounds is useful information at ship or group command level. An assessment of this kind could be derived from signal traffic between units.

Plan Monitoring. The idea of this assessment is to monitor constantly whether the plans made are being followed, and if not, to alert the command to the discrepancies.

For groups of friendly units there will generally be detailed plans against which the sensed picture can be assessed. One function will therefore be to judge how well the plan is being followed and to what extent the plan can be confirmed as being the actual situation. Any discrepancies between the observed situation and the planned one can form the basis of a set of alerts to the users.

Groups of neutrals can also be assesed for adherence to expected routes such as air lanes or shipping lanes. Uncharacteristic behaviour such as close spacing between apparently civil aircraft or deviations from expected routes could also be used to alert the command or invoke a reassessment of identity and mission.

Hostile groups, it must be assumed, are probably acting in consort to achieve their goals and must therefore be assessed as a whole. Rules are required here to attempt to deduce what their most likely plan is and to judge when changes in behaviour occur, perhaps indicating a change of mode from just surveillance to intrusion, provocation or attack, for example.

Surveillance. This assessment is an attempt to estimate the extent of our knowledge of the enemy forces and the enemy's knowledge of our forces. The former will be based on the volume swept by our sensors against a background of intelligence information about hostiles known or likely to be operating in the area. The latter will be a judgement based on known enemy surveillance systems either purely from intelligence data or a combination of intelligence and recently observed enemy surveillance.

Unless enemy surveillance units have been or are being observed then assessment of what the enemy knows about own force must be based on intelligence information. Where shadowing aircraft, ships or submarines have been detected then some estimate of knowledge based on observed active sensors and assumed passive sensors could be made.

The outcome of this assessment might assist judgements of whether to use active sensors which might give away more information to the enemy than provide information to own forces. Of the above list of assessments (5) - Weapon System Geometries - and (7) - Sensor and Weapon Coverage and Status - involve calculations based on own force information; providing status information is available there is no particular difficulty in doing these assessments. Also the assessments are relatively slowly changing so real-time implications are less severe. Threat assessment (1) and defence screen assessment (2) require real-time assessments to be made from the current tactical picture produced by data fusion. The remaining assessments (3), (4), (6), (8) and (9) all rely on the existence of good threat and defence assessments and it can therefore be seen that these two assessements are the key to the situation assessment problem. The following technical discussion concentrates on the objectives of producing an informed picture of own force's defence position and the threats posed by an enemy; hereafter the term situation assessment can be taken to refer to these objectives.

4.2.3. (i)   *Decomposition of Situation Assessment*

The problem of situation assessment can be characterised by considering what is required and what is available:

Requirement:
'A complete, high-level description of what is happening now relative to my present position and a prediction of what is likely to happen in the near future'.

Available:
'An incomplete, detailed-level picture of the current position'.

Three complementary strategies are suggested to bridge the gap between these two levels of knowledge. They can be labelled as:

(1) Group formation.
(2) Plan recognition.
(3) Prediction.

Group formation views situation assessment as an extension of the data fusion process; that is, additional layers of hypotheses are added to the data structure to represent tactically significant groups of objects. The aim of the process is to create a higher level view of the tatical picture than is provided by the detailed picture of individual objects resulting from data fusion. Clustering processes are required to form and maintain the groups. Membership of groups would be defined by spatial and functional attributes. A structure based on this idea is presented in Section 4.2.4. Group formation is essentially a data-driven or forward-inferencing process, it works by applying knowledge to the available data to see what results.

An alternative method is to attempt to match the data available to a set of stored patterns in order to recognise known behaviours. This is a goal-driven or backward-inferencing process. Behaviour patterns in this application would represent military tactics or mission plans. The 'plan recognition' strategy is expanded in Section 4.2.5.

Situation assessment is not just a statement of the current position, it must also include prediction of likely future events as a prelude to the decision making process of resource allocation. Methods for achieving useful predictions are also discussed in Section 4.2.5 as these follow on naturally from the plan recognition process.

4.2.4 *Situation Assessment by Group Formation*

The primary objective of this strategy is to group the available data to reveal relationships which may help to determine co-ordinated functions and hence explain the behaviour of all elements within the volume of interest. It is essentially a forward-inferencing process which establishes a higher level description of the problem domain but it also provides two other important functions.

Firstly, it enables feedback into the data fusion process to fill in missing information. By taking a wider view it is possible to infer some of the details; for example, if one aircraft in a closely-spaced group is identified as hostile, then it is likely that all the group members are hostile. This feedback into the lower levels may seem unnecessary since situation assessment is trying to achieve a higher level of description. But in a command and control application it is important to keep as complete a model as possible in order to to check continually the inferences made. If a value has been assigned from a high-level inference and new data arrives giving a different value then the conflict can be detected immediately and the former conclusions reviewed.

Secondly, the formation of groups facilitates the correlation of group evidence; for example a report giving the location of a surface action group without details of individual units.

4.2.4. *(i)* *Knowledge-Based Approach*

The group formation process requies a hierarchical data structure to represent the significant groupings of domain elements (vehicles) and a means to specify the construction and membership criteria for the groups. An appropriate knowledge-based technique for this type of problem is the blackboard model (Nii (8), (9)). This model has been shown to be suitable for the data fusion problem (Chapter 3.4) which has similar characteristics to the group-formation problem being considered here. In a blackboard model the groups are represented by hypotheses at one or more levels. The knowledge for creating and maintaining the groups is held in *knowledge-sources* in the form of rules.

The group structure is supported by the vehicle hypotheses. It should be noted that some vehicles will already be grouped owing to the evidence being group information e.g., following a raid report. Figure 4.2.1 shows pictorally the levels, which are about to be described, built onto the data fusion levels.

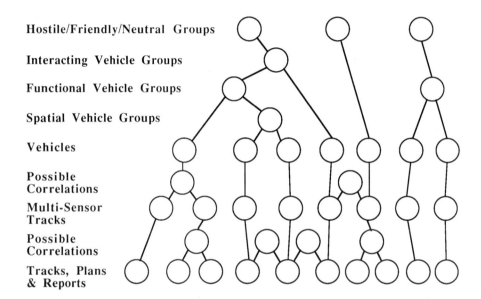

Hostile/Friendly/Neutral Groups

Interacting Vehicle Groups

Functional Vehicle Groups

Spatial Vehicle Groups

Vehicles

Possible Correlations

Multi-Sensor Tracks

Possible Correlations

Tracks, Plans & Reports

FIG 4.2.1   *Data fusion and situation assessment hierarchy*

The following levels of groups, ordered from lowest to highest, have been defined:

Spatial Groups (SG's)	–	groups of vehicles formed by spatial cluster analysis in one or more dimensions.
Functional Groups (FG's)	–	groups of vehicles and/or spatial groups carrying out similar functions.
Interacting Groups (IG's)	–	groups of functional groups which have similar objectives, e.g. attacking/defending the same target.

| Own/Enemy/Neutral Groups (OG, EG, NG) | - | OG is the group of all friendly IG's, and EG is the group of all hostile IG's. NG is the group of all neutral vehicles. |
| Tactical World State | - | ties OG and EG together. |

Spatial Groups. Spatial clustering serves a number of purposes such as enabling groups of track data to be correlated where individuals cannot be resolved. Also it groups together vehicles which are obviously related because of their close proximity and similar behaviour.

Forming spatial groups is conceptually simple, i.e., assigning a vehicle to a group if it is within some defined distance of the centroid of that group. In practice, however, groups will vary considerably in spatial extent depending on the type of vehicle involved and the function the vehicles are performing. For example, aircraft spaced 20 miles apart may not be considered as a group whereas a group of ships might extend over 50 miles. What humans consider to be groups often depends on the scale of the area being viewed. A concept of average spacing could be used to scale the group-defining parameter but this would entail a considerable amount of processing and it is not clear whether the groups formed would have any useful significance. It might only be practical to restrict this form of group just to the most closely spaced cases and rely on functional grouping to provide the most tactically important groups.

With spatial groups there is also the question of how should vehicles be assigned to groups: just spatially; spatially and by allegiance; or spatially, by allegiance and by one or more levels of identity? Another possibility is to group in several different ways, but this would complicate the structure considerably. The most cautious approach is to group in as many parameters as there are available to avoid groups with mixed membership which may not be of any tactical significance. In the naval application it is suggested that allegiance and basic vehicle type are included if available.

Spatial groups could have the following parameters:

- type of cluster i.e., dimensionality (bearing only, range and bearing, allegiance, basic vehicle type)
- number of vehicles
- extent of group in clustered dimensions
- typical vehicle parameters for each type observed (where there is no individual vehicle support)

The main function of spatial groups is to identify obvious associations between vehicles as a means of feeding back common attributes to the vehicle level and to provide a basis for forming functional groups.

Functional Groups. These groups are the first real level of situation assesment because they aim to identify the common functions of related groups of vehicles. The idea is to group together vehicles of similar type which are carrying out the same function. In some cases these groups will be the same as the spatial groups because the function requires the vehicles to be close to each other but in other cases the vehicles may be widely spearated in order, for example, to provide surveillance over a large area.

Each vehicle will not necessarily belong to just one functional group. Ships, particularly, and some aircraft can carry out several function simultaneously and will therefore be members of two or more groups. The definition of functional groups must be chosen to reflect important components of the tactics being carried out.

Parameters of functional groups might be:

- type of vehicle
- number of vehicles
- function
- allegiance
- centroid position and spatial extent of group
- mean line of movement
- membership of group

Functional groups provide a higher level description of the tactical situation but there is a need for further groups to be formed because overall tactics are often a combination of several functions, for example, surveillance, targetting and weapon delivery. The next higher level of groups to represent the groups of tactically related functional groups will be called interacting groups.

Interacting Groups. If two or more functional groups can be seen to be part of a common objective such that they are dependent on each other, then they can be formed into an interacting group. Such interacting groups should be the focus for explaining the major tactical components of the situation.

There are two important categories of interacting groups: defensive groups and attack groups. Defence groups are intended to represent the defence screens operated by subsets of friendly/hostile units. There might be, for example, an Anti-Submarine screen, and Anti-Air screen and an electronic surveillance screen etc. Warships may support all three groups whereas helciopters may only be concerned with Anti-Submarine Warfare.

There should be no difficulty in constructing the friendly defence groupings from vehicle data given access to all the plan information. The system could ask the operator for any information that is missing (indicated by unassigned friendly vehicles or vehicle groups).

Possible defence group parameters are:

- type of defence group e.g., ASW, AAW
- composition of group (obtainable from supporting functional groups)
- mean line of advance (MLA)

- mode of operation (surveillance, defending, counter-attacking, etc)
- sensor coverage
- weapon coverage

Attack groups will be subsets of the set of hostile/friendly vehicles obtained by considering spatial and function parameters. For example, a group of hostile aircraft closely spaced in bearing would form a group and the set of hostile submarines might form another group. Possible attack group parameters :

- type of attack group e.g., surface, air
- objective of the group
- direction
- phase of operation
- probable targets.

Own, Enemy and Neutral Groups. In some situations the formation of interacting groups may provide adequate description of own force and enemy tactics. Circumstances could be envisaged, however, where more than one interacting group was required on each side and a higher level grouping would be useful to show any relationships between the major tactical elements being applied. It is suggested that this next level is simply the groups of all own force and enemy interacting groups. The neutral group is also included as a means of collecting together all the neutral vehicles so that they can be excluded from the tactical situation when necessary.

Fields for OG and EG might include:

- type of mission (e.g., intelligence gathering, shippping escort, convoy protection, amphibious assault)
- mission objectives
- stage of mission
- plan of events and actions
- state of alert (OG only)

Tactical World State Hypothesis. If it is required to infer anything about the overall state of a conflict situation then these inferences could be placed in a 'Tactical World State Hypothesis' supported by own force and enemy groups. This hypothesis represents the overall state of the world in terms of how the Own Group and Enemy Group are interacting i.e. the state of conflict or enagement in the volume of interest.

The levels of hypothesis described have been chosen to represent what appears to be a natural hierarchy of groupings. It would be possible to define far more specific group types but the resulting structure might be too complex for attaching the knowledge in a convenient way. Alternatively fewer levels could be used. This is certainly arguable as in many situations there will be very little difference between spatial groups and functional groups, and between functional groups and interacting groups. A more detailed knowledge engineering exercise will show whether the proposed structure is the best compromise for this application.

4.2.4.(ii)   Group Formation Rules

Rules are required for:

(1) Forming and maintaining groups.
(2) Correlating group evidence.
(3) Inferring group parameters and propagating to individuals.

Grouping vehicles according to a given set of conditions could be performed periodically or incrementally. Periodic grouping could impose a very high processing load through having to start from scratch each time and might give rise to large step changes. An incremental approach is preferred and fits in with the rule-based method proposed. Rules for incremental creation and maintenance of groups could be formulated as follows:

- New vehicles - add to existing groups or create new groups
- Updated vehicles - check that group membership is still valid (this could be done periodically or on each update)

Group functional groups of same allegiance and mission to form interacting groups.

Having established groups, group evidence can be correlated with them. It is not anticipated that much ambiguity is likely to occur with these correlations because the groups used are chosen specifically to avoid the ambiguity which can arise at more detailed levels so it could be done on a 'best fit' basis. It is also possible that two groups could be merged.

Rules required are:

Correlate group evidence with groups on best fit basis. Attempt to merge groups - periodic checks of all groups of each type could allow for this.

Lastly, rules are required to determine paramters of the group and propagate any useful inferences on identity and function to the individual vehicles involved. Rules are:

Calculate numeric paramters of group e.g., size, position centroid (if spatial) and mean velocity of group.
Estimate function of group when necessary from identities and activities of individuals.

Propagate allegiance, identity and other parameters of group to individuals where appropriate.

The idea of grouping related vehicles together as a means of situation assessment is conceptually simple. All the interesting types of group can be defined and rules formulated to create and maintain them. Implementation of such rules is likely to be complex because they operate on parts of a highly interconnected hierarchical data structure where a change at one level will affect other levels. Some ideas for mechanisms to assist in the control of this process are discussed later in Section 4.2.7.

4.2.5   Plan Recognition and Prediction

The group formation method of situation assessment described has one important limitation; it relies on the available data to form the assessment. If there is some data available on all the vehicles of interest to the situation then this is not a serious limitation. In general, however, the set of vehicle data formed by fusing data from all sources will be incomplete and therefore the attempt to form all the functional and interacting groups of interest will not be entirely successful.

Group formation as described is a forward-inferencing or data-driven process; that is, rules are applied to the available data to generate a hypothesis structure of possible inferences. Having reached the limit of this technique it is appropriate to consider a goal-driven approach to see if the problem of incompleteness can be overcome in a useful way.

Goals in an interpretation problem can be described as 'expected patterns'. The idea is to form descriptions of patterns which are expected to exist and then to match those patterns against the data available. If a good match can be found, then details of the pattern which are not present in the data can be inferred with some confidence. In any particular application the questions are whether such patterns really exist and whether the knowledge to describe them can be acquired.

For situation assessment in a military application, we are interested in the behaviour patterns of forces. These behaviour patterns in military terms are referred to as tactics. In AI terms they can be considered as 'plans' or perhaps 'scripts' assuming that they are fairly fixed. Unfortunately, some tactics may evolve quite rapidly and this does pose rapid learning and development problems for a knowledge-based system. Many tactics are constrained by the equipments involved so it is hoped that this concept of plan recognition technique can be usefully applied.

4.2.5. (i)   Knowledge Representation for Plans

Given the plethora of equipment types which could be used by military forces to defend or attack, there are potentially a very large number of possible plans to recognise. A simplistic approach of attempting to embed all possible plans in specific rules would firstly lead to a very large and unstructured rule-base and secondly cause a control problem when only vague data about a plan was available; a very large number of possible plans might be instantiated.

The obvious approach is to use generic forms of plan to which specific equipment knowledge can be attached. Figure 4.2.2 illustrates plans for air attack represented by a high level generic plan with four stages and two example plans which contain specific equipments.

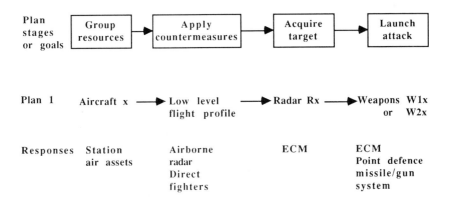

FIG 4.2.2 *Example air attack plans*

The dependencies shown are functional and indicate sequence but in general, spatial and temporal dependencies must also be included to predict the likely position and timing of events. A combination of these constraints will, as far as possible, make sure that only valid combinations are considered. If for example, a particular radar is detected then only vehicles which carry that equipment should be considered; this may also cut down the possibilities in other stages of the plan.

In practice there will be many possible combinations of aircraft and equipments. Different plans using some of the same equipment should be represented as a single plan with options or sub-plans to avoid a proliferation of similar plans all of which would match when the particular equipment was detected.

Context information will also play a part in selecting possible plans. For example, if ships are using radars then an attacker may be able to use passive sensors to gain target information. In fact this indicates the possible extension of plan-based reasoning for deciding on courses of action. This topic will be briefly discussed under resource allocation in Section 4.2.6.

4.2.5.(ii)   Prediction Methods

The techniques discussed so far address the problem of forming an accurate statement of the current position. As a further aid to decision taking, the next step is to predict what is likely to happen in the near future. Accurate predictions will allow measures to be taken to counteract any threat as soon as possible. The earlier accurate predictions can be made, the more time there will be to consider alternative actions and the greater the chances of making good decisions. Prediction can also form the basis of the so-alled 'what-if' facility much desired by commanders.

As before there are two principal methods which can be applied:

- goal driven using stored patterns
- data driven using simulation.

The goal driven approach follows on directly from the plan recognition technique. Assuming that a plan has been recognised at an early stage, the structure of the plan can be used to predict later stages. This process is a vital component in any prediction since plans are the only available models to explain behaviour in a tactical situation. Their limitation, however, is that they must be mainly context independent in order to bound the number of plans stored.

Plans will also be subject to change during execution as it is unlikely that intelligent military forces would pursue a plan come what may. Any interaction between opposing forces will inevitably cause plan modifications even if it is only to select between pre-planned options. The plan recognition technique will obviously fail when behaviours occur which are outside the scope of the plans stored. When this happens the system will have to rely on the forward inferencing techniques described earlier.

Prediction by simulation. Given the current tactical picture, accurate plans for own force actions and possible plans for opposing forces, it would, in principle, be possible to predict future events by playing through the actions on both sides starting from the current position. What is required is a simulation process to step through the scenario in time to discover any interactions between the vehicles involved. These interactions can be used to predict the likely alternatives in less certain stages of the plan and hence indicate changes to own force plans which may be required. This method is analogous to the search techniques used in computer chess programs but, because there is a strong time element in the tactical domain a simulation approach is more appropriate.

To determine whether these methods of prediction are feasible to implement requires experiments with real knowledge and data. Some initial experiments with plan recognition have been reported (Azarewicz (10), (11)) but the usefulness of the approach will only be demonstrated when they are used under realistic conditions. The problem may be that when humans perform the task they do not rely much on stored plans but have enough general knowledge to create likely plans dynamically from the constraints imposed by the equipments employed. Countering this is the fact that much training goes on using set doctrines. However, this is speculation and it is well worth attempting to use stored generic plans as a technqiue for modelling situations and performing predictions.

There are some obvious practical implementation problems:

- can the plans be represented in a way which captures the knowledge without it becoming too complex to maintain? Rapid updating of the stored plans would inevitably be required during a conflict.
- can the reasoning be controlled so that not too many possibilities result but likely cases are not overlooked? The system would be of little value if it produced a large number of possiblities; it should rather delay until a few possibilities are apparent.
- could the simulation form of prediction be implemented to run much faster than real-time? Obviously it would be of little value if it predicted equal-to or slower-than real-time.

The 'grain' of the assessment and prediction is also a problem because in a situation where there are few vehicles involved the reasoning grain needs to be fine but in complex situations with hundreds of objects a coarser grain is demanded for reasoning about collections of objects and to achieve quicker answers, assuming there are processing limitations.

4.2.6   *Resource Allocation*

The topic of resource allocation has wide interest and several prototype systems using knowledge-based techniques have been built. However, very few have tackled the time-critical problems found in command and control. It is not intended to cover resource allocation in any depth because the techniques will be addressed by future research, but a short discussion of possible techniques for time-critical applications will be given.

Resource allocation in current command and control systems divides into two activities with different timescales (perhaps owing to the fact that it is mainly a manual function at present). These will be referred to as:

- Pre-planning resource allocation
- Reactive resource allocation.

Much effort is expended on planning the use of resources some time in advance. This is obviously important because military forces take time to prepare and deploy. Pre-planning resources is not a particularly time-critical exercise which is just as well because planning the deployment of a complex set of disparate resources is very time consuming. The problem is to match the set of resources available to a set of requirements. Although the search space can be very large, heuristic techniques have been used to produce acceptable resource planning systems for both civil and military applications.

More complex problems start to arise in pre-planning resources when requirements change or failures occur during the execution of the plan. This is frequently the case in military situations because unforeseen requirements may arise and equipments may become unservicable. The requirement to change a plan during its execution is often referred to as the 're-planning problem'.

Re-planning is more time-critical than the initial plan generation because the plan is already in operation, but there are also other constraints to consider. Obviously a new plan cannot be generated from scratch because many resources will already be deployed. Also the original plan may have been communicated to many units and it may be important to minimise disruption and communication. The problem of re-planning is being actively pursued in the resource planning research community.

The second dimension to resource allocation is best described by the term reactive resource allocation; that is, in order to be most flexible in the response to a situation, some decisions are left until a specific situation arises. An example would be the direction of fighter aircraft to engage a specific threat; the fighter may already be stationed in a particular area but a decision still has to be taken to direct it to a specific target. Such decisions are usually beyond the scope of pre-planning and must be handled in real-time. This is the most time-critical form of resource allocation and in some cases demands almost instant decisions.

If as much pre-planning as possible has been done then the reactive resourcing decisions should be fairly simple; resources should already be in place and all that is required is to choose from a small number of etablished options by calculating the feasibility of each. Assuming this is the case, then such options could use stored plan segments for the particular resources in question. Pre-stored plan segments of this kind would represent the response tactics to various threats and they could be stored in the same manner as the plans for situation assessement described earlier.

In fact, the response plans could be attached to the same plan structure, a simple example is shown in Figure 4.2.3. Once again some generic form of plan is required because the same kind of response might be used against different elements of an overall threat plan; for example fighter aircraft might be deployed against surveillance aircraft or against missile launchers.

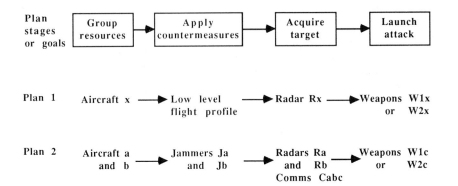

FIG 4.2.3   *Example plan with responses*

The figure lists possible responses at each stage in the plan. In order to generate a set of options, each response must be evaluated using the current status of appropriate assets. For example, the availability and position of fighter aircraft will determine whether the attacking aircraft can be intercepted at a useful range. Choice of which option(s) to take may be left to the commanders who may have other factors to take into account. Some indication of effectiveness might be given if probabilities of countering the threat can be assigned. Options must be tested for conflicts so that only possible alternatives are presented.

If the knowledge for reactive resource allocation can be captured in the way suggested then it can be applied by finding the options available and assessing the merit of each option by plugging in values for the variables and using a cost function. The amount of computation should be largely pre-determined and implementation can be designed for the required response time.

The worrying aspect of the proposed method is that it would appear to have a fixed response to any given situation and would therefore be predictable; not a desirable behaviour in any tactical system. Also, generic responses to all situations must be encapsulated to ensure performance; this could be difficult to construct. The alternative to stored plans is to use plan-generation techniques which attempt to search for a solution using heuristics or constraints to define the search space. These techniques are much more difficult to control as far as response time is concerned because of the unpredictable size of the search space. Their use in time-critical situations would therefore pose other problems.

The above discussion has tended to suggest that the total resource allocation activity consists of non-time-critical pre-planning phase folowed by a plan execution phase during which reactive resource allocation occurs to 'finish off' the details of the plan. In practice, the action of the reactive resourcing process will inevitably disrupt the overall plan because resources will be used up. A re-planning activity is thus required to maintain the overall resource allocation plan. Feedback from the reactive resourcing process will be necessary to allow this re-planning activity to perform its task. Chapter 4.3 explains a configuration for planning and resource allocation modules.

4.2.7   *Summary of Techniques*

Figure 4.2.4 summarises the knowledge-based techniques for situation assessment and resource allocation. The two problems are characterised by a number of problem types and techniques. The techniques are listed under the headings: knowledge representation, control strategy and inference.

Task Levels	Problem Types	Knowledge Representation	Control Strategy	Inference
Situation Assessment	Group Formation	Clustering rules Set definitions	Forward	Logical Heuristic
	Plan Recognition	Rules Plans/Scripts	Backward Pattern Match	
	Prediction	Rules Objects	Time-Step Messages	
Resource Allocation	Pre-Planning Reactive	Rules/Constraints Plans/Scripts	Forward Backward	Logical

Fig 4.2.4   *Techniques for situation assessment and resource allocation*

4.2.7. *(i)*   *Situation Assessment*

Situation Assessment can be performed using a combination of three strategies: group formation, plan recognition and prediction.
Knowledge Representation. Group formation is essentially a forward inferencing process. The objective is to form groups of spatially and/or functionally related vehicles. Rules could be used to form amd maintain these

groups although the actual knowledge to define the groups might be lost in the complexities of housekeeping. For this reason a more powerful mechanism for dynamic set formation is suggested. The idea would be to produce a generic set of rules for set creation and maintenance. These rules would use a list of set definitions to form the specific groups required. This would neatly separate the knowledge for describing specific types of groups from the general housekeeping required to form and maintain groups.

To implement 'plan recognition', plan elements must be stored in a convenient way for both updating and access by the matching functions. Plans/scripts can easily be represented using a frame-based system. For discussion of plans and scripts see Shank (12). Some simple elements of plans might be easier to represent with rules.

Prediction can also use stored plans/scripts to represent expected patterns for a goal-driven strategy. The simulation approach discussed earlier could use an object-oriented representation scheme as these have proved effective for simulation systems.

Control Strategies. Forward chaining is probably most appropriate for group formation and backward chaining might be used for plan recognition although a more powerful pattern-match strategy would be better. Control of prediction, if it relates to simulation as suggested, requires time-step control in order to ensure that correct interaction between objects is maintained.

Inference. In trying to generate interpretations of tactical situations it is suggested that a symbolic uncertainty reasoning scheme, such as that described in Chapter 3.4 would be preferred to the more commonly used numerical schemes. Because the assessments are based on such complex sets of data, it is essential to maintain high visibility of the reasoning in a readily understandable form.

4.2.7.(ii)   Resource Allocation

This term covers the pre-planning, re-planning and reactive resource allocation functions described earlier.

Knowledge Representation. Planning systems have been built using rule-based and script-based techniques but the use of constraints is becoming popular because it is a natural way to specify the search space. Constraint-based planners are also believed to be suitable for the more difficult re-planning function.

A simple method of reactive resource allocation is to have an outline plan for each type of response and, having selected the appropriate plan, fill in the various slots by the most suitable free resource: 'most suitable' in this case might mean the nearest, cheapest, most effective, etc. or some combination governed by heuristics. Plans/scripts are the obvious way to store the possible skeletal plans. Any heuristics associated with the selection and preference of resources could be expressed as rules. Such heuristics can also be viewed as constraints. If there is a need to make trade-offs to achieve a balanced effect in a resource-limited situation, then explicit constraint representation may be favoured so that when planning fails to offer a solution, softer constraints can be relaxed.

Control Strategies. Forward and backward search strategies are used in planning systems. For reactive resource allocation using plans, backward chaining control may be the basic mechanism for picking the most appropriate skeletal plan and filling the plan slots. Some explicit forward search procedure may also be required for finding the best resource available in the dynamically changing tactical situation.

Inference. Resources under command and control sometimes have probabilistic measures of success and some weighting of these measures will be required in order to decide the best course of action. However, many decisions of resource selection will be purely logical, so a combination of uncertain and logical inference will be necessary. It is likely that several possible courses of action may be valid in a particular tactical situation but it is debatable whether there is much point in trying to attach numerical values to their overall effectiveness. Again a symbolic approach is preferred so that the reasoning is clearly visible to the commanders who will usually have to make the final decisions.

4.2.7. (iii)   *Literature Notes on Situation Assessment*

The literature on situation assessment is confused by the lack of an agreed definition of the term. Many authors apply the term more widely than here and include aspects of data fusion while others describe components of situation assessment, particularly threat assessment, without using the term at all.

Some of the specific techniques for situation assessment described have been tried by other researchers for similar problem domains. The 'group formation' approach is particularly evident in the battlefield applications described by Spain (13), and Levitt (14) because of the hierarchical nature of land forces.

More recently the 'plan recognition' approach has been pursued as reported by Azarewicz (10), (11), in a naval context and by Laskowski (15) and Benoit (16) for the battlefield.

Vittal (6) suggests the use of 'simulative inferencing' for prediction and the use of simulation is mentioned briefly by Babcock (7) for 'what-if' reasoning. No experimental work appears to have been reported on this approach.

Other contributors to the subject who deal with specific projects or architectural issues are: Bechtel (1), Ben-Basset (17), Dillard (18), Ferranti (14), Garvey (5), Laskowski (4), Levitt (14), McCall (2) and Wesson (20).

For the resource allocation problems discussed, Gadsden (21) describes a planning system for aircraft missions and Mott (22) describes the extension of this application to provide a re-planning capability. Another example is in Slagle (24) which describes a planning system for allocating weapons to targets. Masui (24) describes a rule-based system for assisting with time-critical decisions for the launch and recovery of aircraft on an aircraft carrier; this is, to some extent, a reactive resourcing problem.

4.2.8   Naval Situational Assessment Case Study

The work described in this case study forms part of a long term research programme in progress at the Admiralty Research Establishment (ARE) investigating the application of Artifical Intelligence techniques to naval command and control. In this context Command and Control describes the processes of information gathering, interpreting that information so as to derive a perception of the world and making decisions on how to respond to that perception. The simple model of a command, control and communcations system shown in Figure 4.2.5 suffices to place the programme items in context.

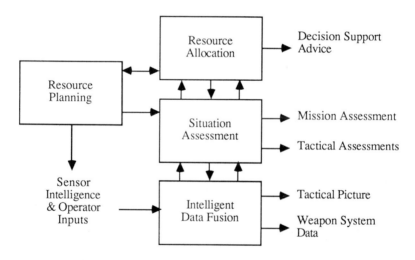

FIG 4.2.5   *Command and control system*

Initial work was focussed in two areas:

- construction of a single ship, and later task force, multi sensor data fusion demonstrator (MSDF) using a blackboard expert system tool Multiple Expert Architecture (MXA) (25). Picture Compilation, the data fusion process, is currently a heavy user of Royal Navy resources and offers an attractive route to reduce Operations Room manning if increased automation proves possible.

- development of a scheduling system for allocating
  fixed wing aircraft and helicopters to flying
  requirements (FlyPAST) (Gadsden and Lakin (21)).
  This system is an example of Resource Planning, a
  non-real-time activity.

An extensive infrastructure, including a capability to
process both real and simulated data and construct colour
graphic displays, has been constructed to enable the
development, application and evaluation of techniques in
the laboratory.

The next step in the overall research programme; the
construction of a Situation Assessment and Threat
Evaluation (SATE) demonstrator which has been undertaken by
Ferranti Computer Systems Ltd (FCSL) on behalf of ARE is
described in this Case Study. The C^3 diagram illustrates
that such a function monitors and interprets the tactical
picture in order to provide prompts and information to the
reaction systems. The work was organised into two distinct
phases, an initial Definition Study, which was viewed as a
prototyping activity, and subsequent construction of a
Demonstrator. This account briefly relates the benefits
and experiences gained from the Definition Study before
describing the Knowledge Acquisition method adopted and
subsequent implementation phase of the Demonstrator. The
presentation of the SATE output in relation to the Data
Fusion system is also considered. In addition to a
description of the Knowledge-Based architecture selected,
the experiences of the team are outlined and some
observations offered with respect to the Life Cycle of a
Knowledge-Based System (KBS) project.

4.2.8. (i) Definition Study

In September 1985, ARE selected FCSL to undertake
Definition Studies on aspects of the application of
advanced technology to problems, including Situation
Assessment, in naval command, control and communications.
The use of advanced programming techniques including
Knowledge-Based Systems which would lead to the
construction of a Demonstrator was a stipulation of the
Statement of Requirement. The initial time-scale of the
Definition Study did not permit prototyping of the
Demonstrator however FCSL elected to use the Definition
Study as a paper prototype exercise with emphasis on three
selected aspects of the development process:

- identification of the scope and role of Situation
  Assessment and Threat Evaluation within the C^3
  system and for a Demonstrator
- determinaton of an appropriate approach to
  producing the Demonstrator
- consideration of the implementation route with
  particular regard to existing ARE prototype
  systems.

Scope and Role of SATE Demonstrator. The Assessment function directly interfaces to two other major C3 components, Data Fusion and Resource Allocation. The relationship of the SATE system to the Data Fusion system is relatively clear cut. The Tactical Picture is constructed by the latter process and forms the principal input to the assessement system; the main concern therefore is the quality and quantity of information required by SATE. However a Situation Assessment and Threat Evaluation Demonstrator implies some activity in the Response phase and defining a clean interface between SATE and the rest of the response system is not so straightforward. Although a SATE function might be capable of initiating pre-planned responses such as autonomous missile deployment where the time-scale of action is seconds rather than minutes, it had to be borne in mind that the intention was to produce an aid to a human operator rather than a replacement automatic function. It was decided to adopt a pragmatic approach and bearing in mind the financial and temporal constraints the following decisions were made:

- effort was to be concentrated on functions (1) and (2) described in Section 4.2.3.
- the Threat Evaluation part of the demonstrator would be limited to merely identifying any threats
- the system would represent SA as undertaken by a Task Group commander typically responsible for half a dozen platforms
- certain areas of knowledge, such as Rules of Engagement, would be ignored initially

As part of defining the scope the following definition was produced:

'Situation Assessment is the process of interpreting the Tactical picture in terms of the deployment, capability and effectiveness of the forces involved'.

It can be seen therefore that the SA process involves assessment of Own Force attributes in addition to other detected entities and covers not only defensive reaction but also execution of own mission.

Approach to Producing Demonstrator. Acquisition and encapsulation into rules of the complete body of knowledge required for a fully comprehensive situation assessment system of course represents a major task. Since the impetus was to produce a Demonstrator rather than pure research the approach selected, although not strictly speaking prototyping, provided for an incremental development. Two, thirty minute scenarios were developed, constrained by the decisions listed above, on which work would be focussed. The scenarios chosen are not intended to be either definitive or complete but representative of an operational environment under warfare conditions. They combine the principal constituents of task group configurations and their defences with typical attack conditions and they highlight various aspects of the assessment process; for example the sub-surface environment tends to develop considerably slower than the air and thus an assessment function must cope with differing time-scales.

For each scenario time-lines of significant events were specified, such as the appearance of a new hostile platform on the Tactical Picture or the receipt of further information on an existing platform, and these enabled an assessment to be built up over a short period. An expert, who has substantial expertise in this area, and one Knowledge Engineer were able to quickly build up initial appreciations of the situation at each time-line providing indications of the information required, the strategy adopted and initial high level rules.

Implementation Route for Demonstrator. The output from the high level knowledge acquisition process described above indicated that the expert formed hypotheses describing possible relationships, both spatial and functional, between platforms with constant reference to the output from the Data Fusion model. The blackboard architecture seemed therefore singularly appropriate for the generation and maintenance of such hypotheses over time. The question then arose as to whether the demonstrator should be linked to the existing Data Fusion system in some way or implemented on a different machine or in a different form and a communication channel constructed. MXA is a blackboard real-time expert system tool, certainly capable of supporting more than the three levels of hypotheses constituting the Data Fusion model. It was decided that the number of levels would be expanded in the vertical dimension to represent the assessment task thus providing 'instant' access to the Tactical Picture data and reducing one potential area of risk. The impact of such an expansion could also from the basis for study and improvement of the scheduling mechanism.

4.2.9 Knowledge Acquisition

Method. As a result of the Definition Study it was decided to extend the existing Data Fusion demonstrator using the MXA tool. This decision influenced the choice of Knowledge Acquisition method. A technique previously used within FCSL was adopted involving a core team of three personnel, an experienced ex-naval officer who acted as the expert and two Knowledge Engineers (KE) although as explained below three KEs actually undertook the Implementation.

Briefly, as described elsewhere (Jackson (26)), the first KE interviewd the expert using the developed scenarios as a focus, asking the expert to assess each time-line as it was played over the desk. Comprehensive information representing the situation at the start of the scenario was available to the expert, describing Own Force mission, weather conditions and so on. The expert provided an assessment of each time-line, typically a paragraph in length, developing it 'aloud' and supplementing it in a directed manner controlled by the KE. The KE took notes of the process which were later transcribed into an implementation independent form. This transcription process was manual and several attempts were needed before a satisfactory method was found; the adopted method links English texts by arrows expressing relationships; it did not prove possible to develop a form of pseudo-English due to the variety of the subject. A clear distinction between the strategy adopted by the expert, that is the order in which Knowledge Sources would be activated, and the rules themselves were preserved. The aim of documenting the knowledge in an independent form was to enable alternative implementations to be used if later programme developments required it.

The second KE took the above notes and designed the corresponding new and amended Knowledge Sources. Additionally, data required by the rules, either from the Data Fusion system or elsewhere was identified. It was expected that not all the knowledge gained would be suitable for the Demonstrator and the second KE would therefore have to select a subset for immediate use.

The principal reason for adopting this technique is that MXA, unlike more recent toolkits such as ART[1], supports a limited range of knowledge representation. By distancing the expert from the implementation it was hoped to avoid any bias in his assessment, that is 'unconscious constraints' arising from knowledge of MXA limitations.

4.2.10   Implementation

4.2.10.(i)   General

The Situation Assessment and Threat Evaluation system (SATE) was developed on a DEC Vax[2] 11/780 running the VMS[2] Operating System, using the tool MXA and suppported by PASCAL. The graphics displays have been implemented on SIGMEX Colour Terminals with user interaction to the SATE model from a VT100. There are problems inherent in such a multi-user environment; in particular it has not been possible to obtain exact performance statistics.

As described above, the first KE prepared the input to the implementation phase as documented independent knowledge which was then implemented by two further engineers. One was the second KE mentioned above who took the implementation independent knowledge (in the form described), selected the subset to be used and designed the rules and associated routines. The third engineer coded and tested this design. Ideally, neither of these implementation engineers should discuss the programming

---

1   ART is held under licence by Ferranti Computer Systems
2   VAX and VMS are trademarks of the Digital Equipment Corporation

details with the expert; all communication was to be
through the first KE to avoid any bias introduced by the
expert 'tailoring' the knowledge to fit the expert system
tool. However, practical considerations such as time
constraints led to the first implementation engineer having
to clarify some points of the knowledge with the expert
directly during the design phase.

It was decided that the design should follow the time-
lines of the scenarios in the same way as the knowledge
acquired from the expert. The output from the second
engineer was thus a document for each time-line of the
scenario; these described how the chosen subset of the
knowledge was to be implemented. This documentation
performed two functions; it was to be used by the third
engineer when coding the rules; it was also to serve as a
record of the knowledge which had been implemented. The
latter proved particularly useful, giving an account of
each rule in English.

Similarly, the coding followed the time-lines. This
meant that the knowledge base was built up incrementally
and new knowledge was only added when required by the next
time-line in the scenario. As knowledge for each
significant event was added to the system, it was tested
before proceeding to the next time line.

To aid the testing, an MXA testbed was developed. This
consisted of a basic MXA system; that is the input routine
and mandatory knowledge sources. It was used to test the
individual knowledge sources with test inputs and only the
variables, functions and procedures which were absolutely
necessary. Once components of the new knowledge had been
tested individually, they were all incorporated into a full
system and this was run to the appropriate time-line in the
scenario; the output was tested against the expected
results as defined in both sets of documented knowledge.

4.2.10.(ii)   Details of Implementation

Five aspects of implementation are considered below:-

- the hypothesis structure
- global data
- the knowledge sources and rules
- functions and procedures used by the rules
- scheduling

The hypothesis structure and overall strategy were
designed before any of the knowledge for individual time-
lines was implemented. Each of the other areas was
considered for each time-line and appropriate enhancements
made.

Hypothesis Structure. In order to undertake SATE, it
was necessary to extend the number of levels of hypotheses
on the blackboard. The Knowledge Acquisition process
revealed that the expert concentrates on four principal
tasks:

- consideration of threats
- execution of Own Mission
- relationships between platforms
- enemy knowledge of Own Force

These do not occur in any fixed sequence but rather in an iterative manner. The Data Fusion system has three levels; namely tracks, multi-tracks and vehicles. It was finally decided that three more levels above this would suffice (Figure 4.2.6); these specified functional groups, interacting groups and allegiance groups. Spatial groups were not included since the proximity of vehicles does not necessarily indicate a common function in the scenarios considered.

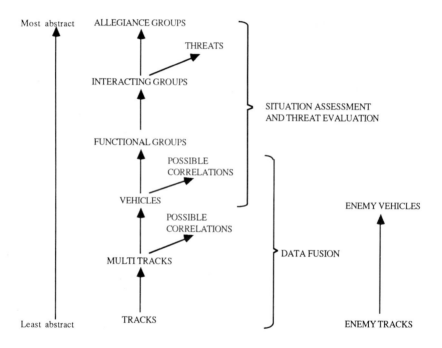

FIG 4.2.6   *Blackboard hypothesis structure*

The basic inputs to SATE are the vehicle hypotheses. From these, groups of functionally related platforms of the same hostility are created; for example hostile ships performing an anti-surface role. Interactions between different groups such as a reconnaissance aircraft providing targetting data for anti-surface ship, are represented by hypotheses at the next level. Finally, groups of vehicles of the same hostility are created; these readily show the allegiance of platforms without having to search the fields of the vehicle hypotheses. Support for hypotheses at a particular level comes from groups at the preceding level. This strategy is discussed in detail in Section 4.2.4.

The primary output from the assessment process is a list of threats; these are stored as hypotheses on the blackboard at an intermediate level above interacting groups which provide both the launch vehicle and the targetting platform (if different).

The assessment of the knowledge which the enemy may have acquired on own force is also held as hypotheses. These follow a similar structure, with the exception of the multi track hypotheses, to those used by the Data Fusion Model and are parallel to such hypotheses.

Global Data. Situation Assessment requires encyclopaedic information such as sensor and weapon fits and weapon parameters. In addition it requires 'current data' such as emission policy, weather, and so on. Since no database of this information which could easily be interfaced to SATE exists it was necessary to 'hard-code' the required data into the system. This was the main use of global data, that is data which is accessible to all parts of the system but which is not held as hypotheses on the blackboard. It is envisaged that this must eventually be replaced by one or more databases. A second use of global data is for those parts of the asessment which cannot be suitably stored as hypotheses on the blackboard; for example the list of priorities of the threats.

All these data areas have been designed and coded so that they can easily be removed if a database becomes available for use with SATE.

Knowledge Sources and Rules. At the time of writing, only the knowledge for the first scenario developed under the definition study has been implemented. However, the rules have been designed so as to allow for easy expansion for further assessments.

SATE currently contains approximately twenty knowledge sources, each containing an average of three rules. Many people assess the size and complexity of expert systems by examining the number of rules which they contain. However, this is a very loose definition of size and is particularly impractical when applied to MXA systems since the rules tend to be large and complex.

The rules in SATE can broadly be divided as follows:-

Assessment of possible functions of vehicles (and thus groupings)
Assessment of likelihoods of possible functions
Assessment of possible interactions between function groups
Assessment of likelihoods of possible interactions
Determination of threats (including prioritisation)
Determination of options for action
Assessment of enemy knowledge

Each rule deals with one type of hypothesis; for example, assessment of the possible functions of hostile aircraft which have just been detected, or assessment of the likelihoods for anti-surface warfare groups.

As each time-line was designed and coded, more rules were added and in some cases existing rules (introduced for a previous time-line) were extended. It was therefore imperative to design the rules so that they were flexible. As mentioned above, only the knowledge gained from the expert for one scenario has so far been implemented but it is envisaged that new rules and enhancements required for other scenarios can be easily added to the knowledge base.

Functions and Procedures. As mentioned above, the rules tend to be large and complex. Therefore in many cases, procedures and functions have been used not only to eliminate duplication of code but to make the rules more readable.

The MXA language is based on Pascal and is precompiled to Pascal before the Vax Pascal computer is invoked. It was therefore possible to write some of the routines in Pascal and link them in after the compilation; however, these routines could not access or modify the MXA blackboard and the number of external functions and procedures is correspondingly small.

Scheduling. For the scheduling of the new SATE knowledge sources, it was decided that initially, until software development was complete, the design used by the Data Fusion Model should be followed. Therefore, most of the knowledge sources are invoked in a round robin method, although a few are scheduled on a priority basis.

4.2.10. (iii)   The Human Interface to Situation Assessment

The command of a ship or force resides in a human who is held responsible for the decisions taken within and actions of his organisation. It is therefore important that the commander, and his staff, should be able to interact with those automatic systems supporting the command process (Figure 4.2.7.) so as to:

- view the products of the automated process and the reasoning
- monitor the quality of the data available to the process
- input data which may not be available from direct sources
- test parameters
- approve or veto the assessment products

In line with the Data Fusion Model only the first two of these capabilities are currently present and are discussed below.

The assessment process really starts from knowledge of own force disposition and capabilities with a progressive build-up of knowledge of the situation outside own force, including activity by friendly, hostile, neutral or unknown entities. The human operator therefore needs to have confidence that the automated processes supporting him are developing a recognised tactical picture with which he concurs, as the baseline environment on which the automated assessment process can work. A description of the Data Fusion model which supports the SATE model appears elsewhere (Lakin and Miles (25)); the operator may have some indication of position, movement, allegiance and platform type depending on the sources of data available to the fusion process and the quality of the relational database supporting the system.

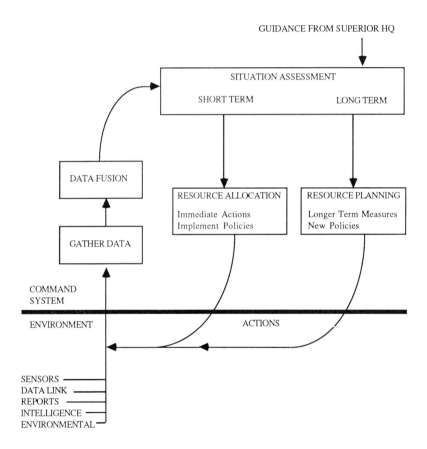

FIG 4.2.7   *The command cycle*

The assessment process provides the essential data for command decision making, either for defence against a threat or for offensive action in execution of the force or ship mission. The operator therefore needs to be able to see the hypotheses developed by the assessment process in order to appreciate the reasoning behind the products. The method chosen to display the hypotheses is a geographic display with vehicle symbols, colour coded for allegiance, annotated for the functional group hypothesis and showing the links of the interacting group hypothesis; separate windows display the threat, options for action and interacting group details, the latter linked to the Data Fusion vehicle window.

The information in the options for action table acts as a trigger to the Resource Allocation function, matching threat database material against revised countermeasures or to confirm that existing measures are satisfactory in the changed situation.

In the SATE demonstrator model facilities have been provided to enable the user to select and manipulate an initial set of parameters such as threat weapons for allocation to vehicles or changes in the weapon attributes in the database. The operator can also call for furthest-on-circles or impose a dead-reckoned course and speed if desired.

Situation Assessment Displays. In common with the Data Fusion model, the output from SATE is displayed in a number of windows under the user's control. Four display windows (Figures 4.2.8 and 4.2.9) support the SATE model:

- Two windows, each showing the results of the assessment in a tabular form, containing the Threat Priority List (TPL) and Options for Action (OA) lists.
- A window containing a textual display of the relationships between groups, referred to as the Interacting Group Table (IGT).
- A window, called the Assessment Graphical Display (AGD), showing graphically the assessed relationships between the air, surface and subsurface vehicles in the commander's area of interest.

Threat Priority List. This window shows the main product of the expert system assessment; the threat priority list (TPL), in tabular form.

A maximum of six threats are ranked in order of severity with the following fields displayed:

priority	ranked in order of severity
platform	this field displays the function code of the principal weapon platform of an interacting group. In the event that the threat is from an interacting group with only one member such as a reconnaissance aircraft then that function code is shown.
weapon type	threat weapon code relevant to the interacting or functional group.
range	boolean values in/out indicate whether own forces are in hostile weapon range.
direction	bearing of threat in degrees, typically a sector indicated by a left and right bearing limit.

```
┌─────────────────────────────────────────────────────────────┐
│                        THREAT TABLE                            │
├─────────────────────────────────────────────────────────────┤
│  PRIORITY     PLATFORM      WEAPON TYPE    RGE    DIRN/SECTOR  │
│     1         REC              M2          OUT     340-060     │
│     2                                                          │
│     3                                                          │
│     4                                                          │
│     5                                                          │
│     6                                                          │
└─────────────────────────────────────────────────────────────┘
```

THREAT PRIORITY LIST

```
┌─────────────────────────────────────────────────────────────┐
│              OPTIONS FOR ACTION    : REVIEW                    │
├─────────────────────────────────────────────────────────────┤
│  STATIONS :              ASW   AAD                             │
│  EMCON POLICY :          AAD                                   │
│                                                                │
│  ECM / DECOY POLICY :    AAD                                   │
│  ESM TASKING :           AAD                                   │
│                                                                │
│  ORGANIC AIR TASK / READINESS :     AAD                        │
│  EXTERNAL SUPPORT REQUEST :                  ALL               │
└─────────────────────────────────────────────────────────────┘
```

OPTIONS FOR ACTION

```
┌─────────────────────────────────────────────────────────────┐
│         INTERACTING GROUP    THREAT DETAILS                    │
├─────────────────────────────────────────────────────────────┤
│   TPL : 1                                                      │
│   PLATFORM IDENTIFIER : BEAR D   FUNCTION        REC           │
│   WEAPON TYPE : M2     RANGE ___    HOMING___   _____          │
│   NUMBER ___                                                   │
└─────────────────────────────────────────────────────────────┘
```

INTERACTING GROUP TABLE

FIG 4.2.8   *AGD tabular displays*

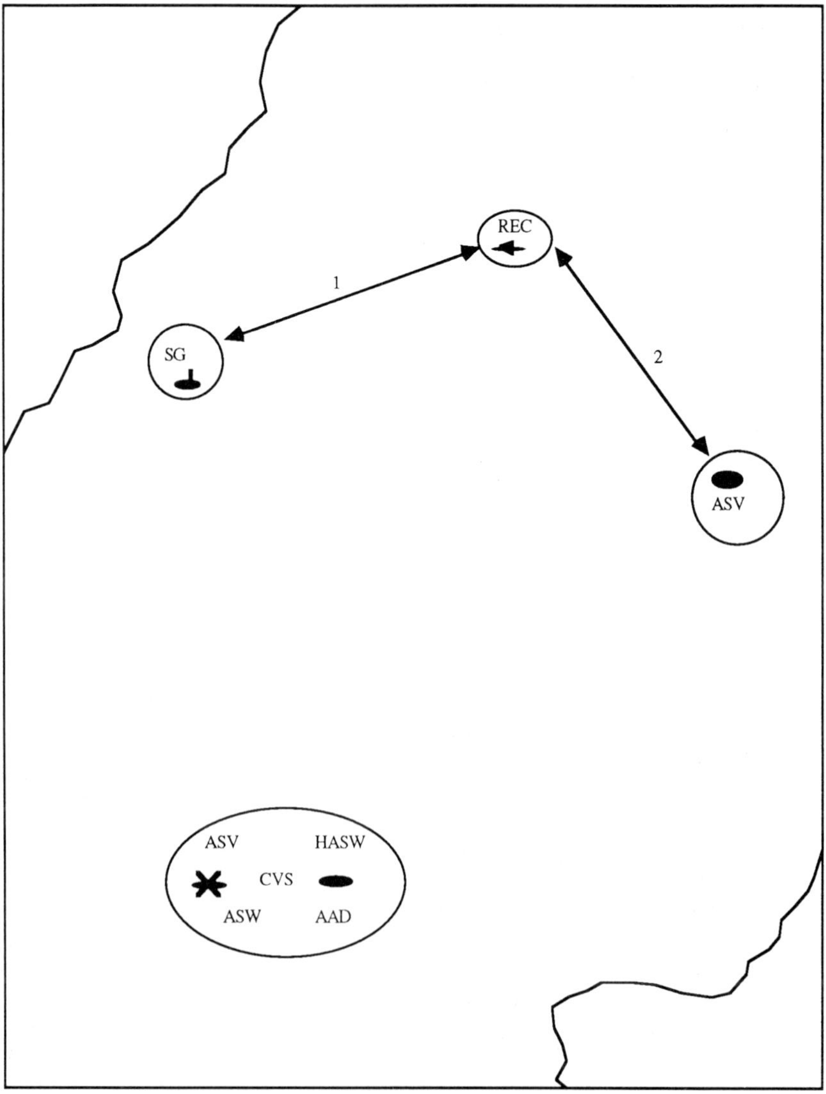

FIG 4.2.9   *Example of two interacting groups*

Options for Action. This table lists a maximum of six check-off factors to be considered in determining the command responses to the threats in the TPL. The assessment function selects factors from a menu of actions such as review asset allocation which are relevant to any threat environment air, surface, subsurface. The field for each factor consists of two parts:

descriptive string of text
parameter code - environment to be considered; either one, two or all three.

Interacting Group Table. A third window (IGT) enables the user to see details of the platforms in the hostile functional groups comprising an interacting group in textual form. The following details are displayed:

TPL Number   selected TPL entry

For each weapon carrying platform in a functional group:

platform identifier
function
weapon type
range   nautical miles
homing   code from weapon homing system lists
number   hostile weapons associated with threat

Assessment Graphical Display (AGD). The AGD shows the products of the assessment in geographical plan form without cluttering the fused tactical picture. The display shows the interacting groups derived in the assessment, identified by functional group symbology and linked to each other, with the relevant TPL number shown alongside the link. The display also shows those parameters the command has selected, either to appreciate assessment factors drawn from the database or to test 'what if' options.
Man Machine Interface (MMI). The MMI already in use for the MSDF model was extended to meet the requirements of the SATE demonstrator so that demonstrations of the fused tactical picture and SATE can now take place simultaneously. The function keys for display are shown (Figure 4.2.9) and are largely self explanatory. The EXPLAIN function has to date only been developed for the MSDF model.

CREATE   -   enables the user to call up and position the different windows as described above.
MODIFY   -   enables selection of scale, range rings and in the case of SATE, interacting groups of interest and access to AGD parameter selection (Figures 4.2.10 and 4.2.11) menu which provides the assessment database or 'what if' parameters for the

command to apply as desired to groups
displayed.

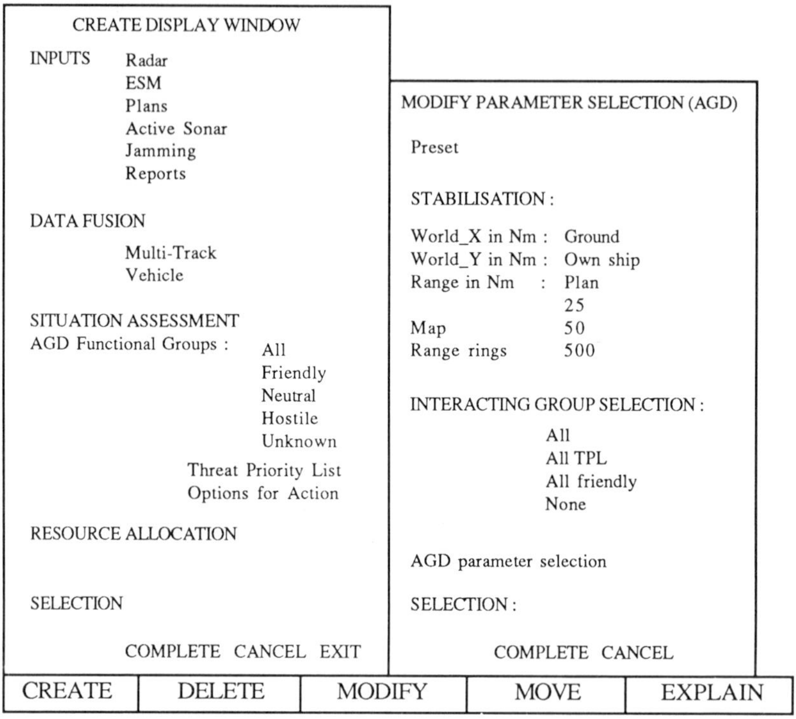

```
┌──────────────────────────────────────────────────────────────────────────┐
│  CREATE DISPLAY WINDOW                                                     │
│                                                                            │
│  INPUTS       Radar                                                        │
│               ESM                                                          │
│               Plans              MODIFY PARAMETER SELECTION (AGD)          │
│               Active Sonar                                                 │
│               Jamming            Preset                                    │
│               Reports                                                      │
│                                  STABILISATION :                           │
│  DATA FUSION                                                               │
│                                  World_X in Nm :  Ground                   │
│               Multi-Track        World_Y in Nm :  Own ship                 │
│               Vehicle            Range in Nm   :  Plan                     │
│                                                   25                       │
│  SITUATION ASSESSMENT            Map              50                        │
│  AGD Functional Groups :  All    Range rings      500                      │
│                           Friendly                                         │
│                           Neutral    INTERACTING GROUP SELECTION :         │
│                           Hostile                                          │
│                           Unknown         All                             │
│                     Threat Priority List  All TPL                          │
│                     Options for Action    All friendly                     │
│                                           None                             │
│  RESOURCE ALLOCATION                                                       │
│                                  AGD parameter selection                   │
│                                                                            │
│  SELECTION                       SELECTION :                               │
│                                                                            │
│        COMPLETE  CANCEL  EXIT          COMPLETE  CANCEL                     │
├───────────────┬──────────────┬─────────────┬──────────────┬───────────────┤
│   CREATE      │   DELETE     │   MODIFY    │    MOVE      │   EXPLAIN     │
└───────────────┴──────────────┴─────────────┴──────────────┴───────────────┘
```

FIG 4.2.10   *Display selection menus*

4.2.11   Discussion

The short three month Definition Study identified a
development path leading to the required Demonstrator. The
paper prototyping activity worked well, highlighting the
principal problem solving methods of the human expert and
the information accessed. In particular, the scope of
several Knowledge Sources were detailed and the output
specified at a high level. Undoubtedly, a physical
prototyping phase would have been extremely valuable, but
it would have had to have been of a reasonable length to
expose the difficulties later encountered.

The method for knowledge acquisition worked well but
during the implementation phase it was found that a link
back from the second Knowledge Engineer to the expert was
required for desk-top verification of the rules designed by
that engineer. This was because of time constraints and it
was found to be not always productive to restrict
communication to being via the first KE.

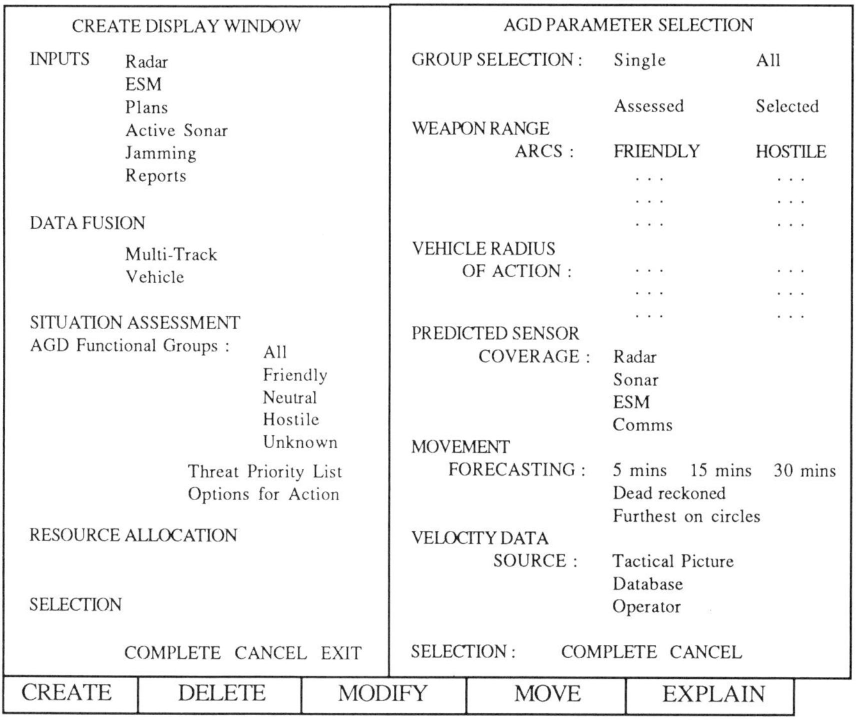

CREATE DISPLAY WINDOW	AGD PARAMETER SELECTION		
INPUTS Radar	GROUP SELECTION :	Single	All
ESM			
Plans		Assessed	Selected
Active Sonar	WEAPON RANGE		
Jamming	ARCS :	FRIENDLY	HOSTILE
Reports		. . .	. . .
		. . .	. . .
DATA FUSION		. . .	. . .
Multi-Track	VEHICLE RADIUS		
Vehicle	OF ACTION :	. . .	. . .
		. . .	. . .
SITUATION ASSESSMENT		. . .	. . .
AGD Functional Groups : All	PREDICTED SENSOR		
Friendly	COVERAGE :	Radar	
Neutral		Sonar	
Hostile		ESM	
Unknown		Comms	
Threat Priority List	MOVEMENT		
Options for Action	FORECASTING :	5 mins 15 mins 30 mins	
		Dead reckoned	
RESOURCE ALLOCATION		Furthest on circles	
	VELOCITY DATA		
	SOURCE :	Tactical Picture	
		Database	
SELECTION		Operator	
COMPLETE CANCEL EXIT	SELECTION : COMPLETE CANCEL		

CREATE	DELETE	MODIFY	MOVE	EXPLAIN

FIG 4.2.11   *AGD parameter selection menu*

In general the use of time-lines to define milestones in the implementation worked very well. It led to clearly visible codable units and greatly eased the testing. However the following points should be borne in mind when following this method:-

- the knowledge base must not be allowed to become specific to the scenario; each time-line would be thought of as introducing a new type of situation to be assessed and not as a specific significant event
- if there are 10 time-lines defined in the scenario, the design, code and test of one cannot be considered to represent 10% of the implementation phase; the first few time-lines require much more effort than those later in the scenario since there are generally a lot of rules

required to maintain the hypothesis structure and deal with correlations etc.

- consideration must be given to events between time-lines; for example, one time-line may introduce a new contact, but before the next time-line this contact may be lost and it will be necessary for the system to deal with the loss of this information.

- if possible the expert should be asked to examine the scenario after each time-line has been completed since these are being used as testing points; this may be impractical if the development of the MMI and displays is not in line with the progress of the knowledge base.

Although its use in the Data Fusion Model made it logical to use MXA, it was found that MXA was very cumbersome to use since it did not support incremental compilations. As the model grew larger, more time was spent building a model for testing than actually testing it; this greatly increased the development time. It became very difficult to balance the amount of code added in between compilations with the time taken to trace faults if an error occurred. This was obviously very frustrating for the programmer and led to a reduction in the time spent on testing. On reflection, for this reason alone it may have been better to implement SATE on either a different machine or as a separate MXA process.

As mentioned above, the time allocated to testing had to be reduced due to problems with MXA. The initial testing of rules and routines was done by comparison of the the results with the design documentation; this was in order to avoid forcing the implementation constraints on the expert. However, as discussed above, there could have been some benefits in having the expert more closely involved at each stage of the implementation with each addition or enhancement to the knowledge base being verified before coding of the next time-line began.

This is a first attempt at displaying the automated threat assessment factors which need to be taken into account in feeding the resource allocation process. Factors such as the warning time required to deploy the Combat Air Patrol against an air threat, have been included in the assessment but are not immediately available for display - although they could be. Other relevant data for resource allocation, such as environmental and system status factors, will be drawn from other sources and these could also be presented on the AGD. There is, however then a danger that the display will become too busy. At this stage it is considered that a separate resource allocation display should be available for that process.

At this stage of development the process develops a cumulative list of Options for Action, rather than relating them to specific items on the TPL. Also at this stage it is not possible to cancel OA's until a threat has been removed, whereas they should be cancelled after due

consideration such as when resource allocation has been
determined in the form of revised policies or deployments.
The MMI is easy to use in the laboratory environment
and is user friendly. However a mouse is not the best
choice in a ship's operations room where ship motion in
heavy weather must be considered. A touch screen MMI is
considered the preferred solution for an afloat system.
In conclusion, the experience gained during the above
Case Study emphasises:

- Incremental development/prototyping is a valuable
  approach but it must be supported by tools with
  adequate capabilities. It was not the constraints
  imposed by limited knowledge representation
  capabilities within MXA which caused problems but
  the manner in which the model had to be compiled
  'en masse' after each upgrade. The LISP machines
  and other similar KBS tools with incremental
  compilers are essential.
  The experts' knowledge must be tapped at each
  stage of the Life Cycle. This means not only the
  initial Acquisition phase but also actively during
  the testing phases of incremental development.

4.2.12   References

1.   Bechtel, R.J. et al, May 1979. STAMMER: System for
      Tactical Assessment of Multisource Messages, Even
      Radar, NOSC, San Diego, California, NOSC-TD-252.

2.   McCall, D.C. et al, October 1987. STAMMER 2:
      Production System for Tactical Situation Assessment,
      NOSC, San Diego, California, NOSC-TD-298, vols 1 & 2.

3.   Levitt, T.S. et al, April 1985. 'A Model-Based
      System for Force Structure Analysis', *Applications of
      Artificial Intelligence II*, vol 548, Los Angeles, CA, ADS,
      Mountain View.

4.   Laskowski, S.J. et al, December 1985. ANALYST II: A
      Knowledge-Based Intelligence Support System, The
      MITRE Corporation, C3I AI Center, 7525 Colshire
      Drive, McLean, Virginia 22102-3481, *Second IEEE
      Conference on AI Applications*, pp 552-563.

5.   Garvey T.D. et al, December 1980. 'The Integration
      of Multi-Sensor Data Fusion for Threat Assessment',
      5th Joint Conference on Pattern Recognition, pp 343-
      347.

6.   Vittal, J.R., January 1981. 'Using AI Techniques for
      Threat Display and Projection, Including Tactical
      Deception Indication', Bolt Beranek and Newman Inc,
      Cambridge, Massachusetts, AD-A 106 801.

7. Babcock, D.F., January 1984. 'An Architecture for the Application of Artificial Intelligence Techniques to Threat Warning', SRI International, AD003027, pp 117-123. *Proceedings of the ARMY Conference of Applications of AI*.

8. Nii, H. Penny, Summer 1986. 'Blackboard Systems: The Blackboard Model of Problem Solving and the Evolution of Blackboard Architectures', *The AI Magazine*.

9. Nii, H. Penny, August 1986. 'Blackboard Application Systems; Blackboard Systems from a Knowledge Engineering Perspective', *The AI Magazine*.

10. Azarewicz, J. et al, 1986. 'Plan Recognition for Airborne Tactical Decision Making', Naval Air Development Centre, Warminster, PA 18974, AAAI.

11. Azarewicz, J. et al, October 1987. 'Multi-Agent Plan Recognition in an Adversarial Domain', Naval Air Development Centre, Warminster, PA 18974, Expert Systems in Government Conference.

12. Shank, R.C. et al, September 1975. 'Scripts, Plans and Knowledge', *4th IJCAI*, pp 151-157.

13. Spain, D.S., 1983. 'Applications of Artificial Intelligence to Tactical Situation Assessment', Advanced Decision Systems, Mountain View, California.

14. Levitt, T.S., May 1985. 'Evidential Reasoning in Situation Understanding', Proceedings of the Society for General Systems Research International Conference, Los Angeles, CA, ADS, Mountain View.

15. Laskowski, S.J., Hofmann, E.J., August 1987. 'Script-Based Reasoning for Situation Monitoring', The MITRE Corporation, C3I AI Center, 7525 Colshire Drive, McLean, Virginia 22102-31481, AAAI-87.

16. Benoit, J.W. et al, October 1987. 'Integrating Plans and Scripts: An Expert System for Plan Recognition', The MITRE Corporation, C3I AI Center, McLean, Virginia. Expert Systems in Government Conference.

17. Ben-Bassat, M. et al, July 1982. 'Knowledge Requirements and Management in Expert Decision Support Systems for (Military) Situation Assessment, *IEEE Transactions of Systems, Man and Cybernetics*, vol SMC-12, issue 4, pp 479-489.

18. Dillard, R.A., May 1986. 'Multisite Situation Assessment: Knowledge-Based Interaction, Reconstruction, and Post Analysis', NOSC, San Diego, California, NOSC TD 903.

19. Ferranti, J.P., March 1981. 'Evaluation of the Artificial Intelligence Program STAMMER 2 in the Tactical Situation Assessment Problem', Naval Post Graduate School MS Thesis.

20. Wesson, R., January 1981. 'Network Structures for Distributed Situation Assessment', *IEEE Transactions on Systems, Man and Cybernetics* vol SMC-11, issue 01, pp 5-23, 0018-9472/81/0100-0005 IEEE.

21. Gadsden, J.A., Lakin, W.L., June 1986. 'FlyPAST: An Intelligent System for Naval Resource Allocation', Admiralty Research Establishment, Portsmouth, England. Presented at 9th MIT/ONR Workshop on C^3 Systems, Monterey.

22. Mott, D.H., Gadsden, J.A., September-October 1987. 'Constraint-Based Reasoning for Planning and Replanning Flying Programmes', Mil Comp, London.

23. Slagle, J.R., Hamburger, H., September 1985. 'An Expert System for a Resource Allocation Problem', *Communications of the ACM*, vol 28, No 9.

24. Masui, S., et al, 1983. 'Decision-Making in Time-Critical Situations', *IJCAI*.

25. Lakin, W.L., and Miles, J.A.H., 1987. 'An AI Approach to Data Fusion and Situation Assessment, Ch 7, pp 339-377, Advances in Command, Control & Communication Systems, Peter Peregrinus, IEE Computing Series 11.

26. Jackson, A., December 1983. 'The design and Development of an Expert System to Assist in the Analysis of Crash Dumps', *Proceedings of BCS '83*, Cambridge.

Intelligent Systems for Naval Resource Planning

J.A. Gadsden and W.L. Lakin
(Admiralty Research Establishment)*

4.3.1 Introduction

A substantial programme of research has been underway for some five years within the Admiralty Research Establishment (Portsdown) on the application of knowledge-based programming techniques to problems in naval command and control. One of the areas addressed is that of Resource Planning. This article, an extended version of a paper presented at the Fourth IEEE Conference on Artificial Intelligence Applications, San Diego (1988), discusses some general issues regarding the use of knowledge-based systems (KBS) technology within the Royal Navy. It addresses in particular the problems of generating plans for the future allocation and deployment of resources, and it reports on the progress of ARE's research into one specific application - that of naval flight scheduling. This is described in the context of the FlyPAST (Flying Programme Assignment Support Tool) demonstrator.

4.3.2 Information Management

It has long been recognized that one of the key factors contributing to the effectiveness of a military commander is the quality of the information at his disposal. Good information requires good information management; this may be somewhat simplistically expressed as the ability to provide the right information at the right time, to the right person in the right form for him to assimilate and, it is hoped, to make the right decision.

Such a capability is easier to advocate than to provide. The information management problems facing, for example, a naval commander at sea are considerable: the basic incoming data has a tendency to be inaccurate, incomplete and inconsistent, as well as being subject to deliberate degradation and deception by an enemy.

Particularly in the time-critical domain of reactive response, the sheer volume of data derived from a wide range of sources can, at times, overwhelm the existing organization of men and machines tasked to deal with it. In the future, more powerful sensing devices and the need to extend the volume of interest for both tactical operations and strategic planning will imply yet greater volumes of data received via an increasing number and variety of data channels. Set against this increase to what is already an overload to our processing and cognitive capability, is the need to reduce naval manning levels in the interests of cost and efficiency.

The above analysis might suggest that, given perfect input data, unlimited computing resources and no time constraints, the problem is soluble. There are however other factors to take into account: as well as being unreliable, the data which feeds the information management process varies across a wide range of types from reasonably structured local and remote sensor data, encyclopaedic data, geographic data etc, to highly unstructured data types such as Intelligence, voice reports and political data. Information is also required from other components of the command and control organization; this includes details of current tactical plans, procedures and actions, and is needed to provide context for a shorter-term situation appreciation function. As well as the input data, the command and control domain is itself notoriously unstructured. Substantial resources have been expended in the search for a 'command and control model'. In the absence of a sufficiently accurate and detailed mathematical, logical or data-processing model, conventional data-processing methods used in isolation are unlikely to make substantial impact on the problem.

4.3.3   Demonstrator Approach

Like many others of its kind, the ARE programme seeks to test the assertion that an inadequately understood problem domain - that of command and control - may be successfully addressed using an equally imperfect technology - that of knowledge-based programming. Our primary criterion for assessing the viability of using these two 'wrongs' to make a 'right' is whether or not we can build something that will actually work. This is the motivation behind the so-called demonstrator approach.

However, the introduction of computers into naval command systems over the past two decades has taught us the vivid lesson that *expected functionality* is not the only important criterion by which to judge the effectiveness of new technology. Issues of **usability, reliability, maintainability, vulnerability, ease of modification, expansion capability, specification, acceptance, validation** and **complexity** conspired to bring about a degradation, as opposed to an enhancement, in the overall performance of naval information systems when a computer was included. The introduction of a technology as radically different as knowledge-based programming is likely to have an equally traumatic effect unless all of the issues listed above are thoroughly understood prior to that introduction. Unfortunately many of those issues, such as **validation** and **acceptance**, are as alien to the knowledge-based system (KBS) practitioner of today as they were to the programmer of twenty years ago. The term 'KBS practitioner' was chosen with care; only when the above problems have been successfully addressed and KBSs are the subject of a viable and mature engineering discipline, can the terms **knowledge engineer** or **information engineer** be used with confidence. In theory, a demonstrator programme, commencing in the laboratory and evolving through shore-based operational environments to large-scale sea-going technology demonstrators, could provide a suitable vehicle for tackling many of these issues. Such long-term and expensive programmes are essential if the perceived benefits of knowledge-based systems are to be realized. However, at present, there would appear to be no organization capable of resourcing such large-scale risk-reduction activities, and no indication that this is likely to change in the foreseeable future.

Demonstrators also serve another purpose. When attempting to specify the requirements for a future system based on new technology of unknown capability, what does the operational user take as the upper and lower bounds for his aspirations? His lower bound is usually taken as that which exists now - albeit with a few improvements to overcome known faults and deficiencies. His upper bound is virtually non-existent. Operational analysis may establish some of the more tangible requirements in terms of threat scenarios and weapon and sensor capabilities, but these represent an almost negligible subset of what needs to be defined. Of the three thousand user-specified functions identified in a recent activity to define a command and control system, about two thirds emanated from the users' preconception of how the system might look based on their experience of earlier systems using obsolete technology. In the operations room of a surface warship, most of the twenty or more operators are not receiving support from the computer but are providing support to it, by feeding it with information or by providing an interface for the real end-user. Their skills are not those of tactics or battle management, but of harnessing the powers of a complex and uncompromising assembly of data-processing hardware and software. The advances in the capability of the machine and the degree to which these are exploited in a new system could radically change the organisation and structure of a command system, with the possible elimination of a whole class of operator. The requirement is likely to change beyond recognition, and certainly beyond the perception of the naval user who is trained intensively in current practice, and cannot be expected to extrapolate that requirement to encompass technology not yet understood even by the scientists and engineers.

It is hardly surprising therefore that requirements specification is a problem area, but the demonstrator offers a potential solution by providing a focus to enable the research and development staff to gain an understanding of the problem domain, and the user to gain an appreciation of the technology's capabilities and shortfalls. Thereby the requirement and the effective application of the technology may be evolved together. But again the organization is not yet geared to this kind of working.

4.3.4   Knowledged-Based System Attributes

The preceeding discussion has attempted to outline part of the rationale for proposing knowledge-based solutions to some existing and predicted problems in naval command and control, along with an indication of the many difficulties which will be encountered and the substantial amount of cost and effort necessary to make those solutions viable. It is important to consider what are the specific benefits of a KBS approach, and whether or not those benefits are likely to justify the level of commitment required in order to exploit them.

It is argued above that, particularly in the time-critical areas of naval command and control, many of the demands placed upon the existing semi-manual systems are not only far beyond the capabilities of those systems, but also, as a result of the complex and unstructured nature of the domain, well beyond the capabilities of conventional data-processing techniques. Knowledge-based systems, through their ability to represent and to reason with a much richer spectrum of knowledge than conventional algorithmic solutions, can, in theory, address much more unstructured problem domains, thus forming the primary justification for the approach. It can be argued that the viability of the surface navy is dependent upon its ability to make complex and timely command and control decisions, which in turn depend on the quality and timeliness of the information management processes which provide the basis for those decisions. A knowledge-based solution to some of those information management requirements should not be regarded necessarily as low risk, but currently there exists no alternative approach to some of the more critical problems which holds out any probability of success. Thus the development of knowledge-based solutions could be regarded as of paramount importance, depending on the individual's perception of the criticality of these information management issues to the command and control process, and the contribution which effective command and control is likely to make to the performance and viability of the surface navy.

However, the potential to address unstructured and hitherto intractable problem domains is not the only attribute of knowledge-based systems of relevance to the Royal Navy. A capability to represent a system's knowledge as a coherent entity, separate from the control structure of the program and in a form approximating to natural language, should enable the authority responsible for the system specification, ie the naval user, to comprehend, amend and validate that knowledge. This offers considerable advantages over knowledge encoded as an obscure algorithm embedded in a complex procedural program coded in a typical computer language. This property of a knowledge-based system currently appears to be more of an aspiration than reality, as the knowledge representations offered by the available AI (artificial intelligence) toolkits are incomprehensible to most people.

A third attribute of knowledge-based methods, of particular relevance to the Royal Navy, is the provision of **explanations** to convey to the user the reasoning process invoked in arriving at a particular result. Extensive analyses of the command and control process as practised at sea during naval exercises have demonstrated that a large percentage of poor decisions have resulted from lack of confidence in the supporting computer equipment. An equipment needs to give an erroneous or misleading answer very few times for it to be switched off permanently. The fact that the answer resulted from misuse of the system or incorrect input data provided by the same or by a different operator does not serve to exonerate the system if there is no mechanism whereby that explanation can be made known. An *explanation* capability would appear to be an essential attribute of an advanced decision-support system, in order to clarify misunderstandings by the user and to identify deficiencies in the knowledge base. However, the explanation mechanisms even of static diagnosis/classification systems are relatively unsophisticated; the provision of explanations within a real-time system for use in the rapidly changing environment typical of surface-ship command and control requires a major research activity addressing both human-factors and technological aspects.

In summary, a substantial programme of work is needed if knowledge-based programming methods are to generate viable solutions to problems in naval command and control, but the potential goals are of great importance, in the context of the future needs of the Royal Navy. The argument that the technology is not yet sufficiently mature to be risked in an operational system is valid; the argument that it is insufficiently mature for investigation in an applied research context or demonstrator environment is self-defeating. The military environment is particularly demanding, and imposes specific requirements on its technology base. Only through applied research can the shortfalls in that technology base be usefully identified and reported back to the foundation programmes; only through substantial applied research can that foundation work be driven in directions relevant to the military or, more specifically, the naval domain; only through applied research can we learn what aspects of the technology to apply to which facets of the problem, and how this may be achieved at acceptable risk.

4.3.5   What is Planning?

The word 'planning' is used very loosely by the AI community (and others) to cover a range of problem types. Historically, 'planning' has referred to activity planning as exemplified by the 'blocks-world' problem. In the 'blocks-world' domain, an initial set of stacks of blocks must be transformed into a goal state consisting of another set of stacks, moving only one block at a time. In addition, a block may only be moved if it has no others on top of it. In activity planning of this kind, the solution is usually in the form of a partially-ordered sequence of actions which transform the initial state into the goal state. The output is often in the form of a PERT-type network (possibly showing the critical path through the process).

However, 'planning' also covers a number of other problem-solving activities which include such domains as scheduling and resource allocation. It is important to classify these areas more closely because experience tells us that different solution strategies are appropriate to different classes of problem. One taxonomy of the planning process, developed by a group of AI researchers at a UK Alvey Workshop in 1986 breaks down the problem-types into **basic resource allocation, resource allocation with a fixed sequence, scheduling** and **design** (Alvey (1)).

Basic resource allocation is exemplified by a simple allocation of resources to a fixed collection of tasks. An example is "Given a set of artillery stations and a set of targets, allocate weapons to targets to maximise target destruction". Here there is *no* sequencing implied; there is no intention that one weapon should fire before another or that order of firing is important. What is produced is a world state which does not refer to time.

The category of **resource allocation with a fixed sequence** was introduced to cover resource allocation problems which *appeared* to produce a schedule. Often there is a fixed schedule which is given as an input to a resource allocation problem. Because this schedule then appears as an output in the solution, it is easy to think that the problem is one of scheduling. An example of this is "Given a set of nurses and a rota system of early, late and night shifts, extending over a week, allocate nurses to their shifts". Here the *sequence* is fixed; the tasks have been prearranged to three shifts per day for seven days. All we must do is allocate nurses to shifts, we do not have to produce the sequencing as part of the problem solving. This distinction is important in the domain described later in this chapter; what appeared to be a scheduling problem was later recast as resource allocation with fixed sequence, with a consequent clarification of the knowledge representation.

Scheduling was defined by the Workshop in Alvey (1) as the selection and sequencing of resources over time to perform a collection of desired tasks. For example, "Given raw materials, and a set of machines to perform the tasks

necessary to process the raw materials, produce a set of
end products". Here we have to work out the sequence as
well as allocating resources. The essential aspect is that
the tasks will have some partial ordering to them
(otherwise it would be straight resource allocation).

For **design** we took a definition from John McDermott
(used in a Tutorial given at the First IEEE Conference on
AI Applications in December 1984): "the creation of an
object whose components are arranged in a way that
satisfies placement constraints and whose components have
been selected to facilitate placement". A typical example
of this is VLSI design. Here we have no time constraints
or time orderings but there are spatial considerations in
deciding which components to put next to each other to
produce the most efficient functional design.

The Royal Navy obviously have scheduling and design
problems but the rest of this chapter will concentrate on
resource allocation as defined above (including that which
involves fixed sequences). The word 'planning' from here
on is used with its domain-specialist meaning rather than
that implied by AI researchers. The next section attempts
to clarify the terminology used in the naval domain
compared with that used by AI researchers.

4.3.6   *Planning in Command and Control*

Planning within naval command and control can usefully
be divided into four categories according to the timescale
of the validity of the plans (Figure 4.3.1).

FIG 4.3.1   *Planning in naval command and control*

Plans which cater for weeks and months ahead are
produced in preparation for missions and exercises; this is
known as **strategic mission planning**. **Tactical resource
planning** is done on a daily basis and produces plans that
are valid for hours or days. **Reactive resource direction**
forms the system's response to real-world events. At the
shortest timescale, the planning involved in **autonomous
weapon/sensor direction** allows no time for the man to be
involved in the decision process (except in a veto role and
inasmuch as his expertise is encoded into an automatic
system).

Each of these categories of naval command and control
planning may well include tasks of all four types
identified in Section 1: resource allocation with and

without fixed sequences, scheduling and design. However, the most common problem types are the two forms of resource allocation and the research programme at ARE has chosen to study the areas of resource allocation (with and without sequences) within tactical resource planning and reactive resource direction as shown in Figure 4.3.2.

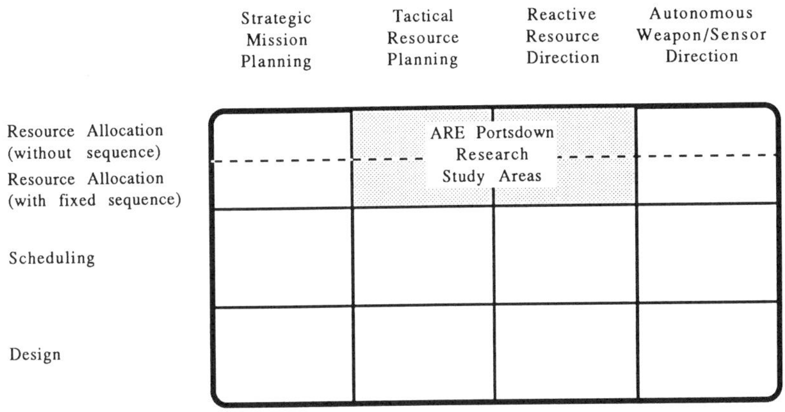

	Strategic Mission Planning	Tactical Resource Planning	Reactive Resource Direction	Autonomous Weapon/Sensor Direction
Resource Allocation (without sequence) Resource Allocation (with fixed sequence)		ARE Portsdown Research Study Areas		
Scheduling				
Design				

FIG 4.3.2   *Research programme study areas*

Here the knowledge is less abstract than that involved in mission planning, while the real-time requirements are not so stringent as those for autonomous systems. Also the fact that the man is still in the decision loop poses some interesting research questions about the role of decision-support systems and the human-computer interaction. Tactical resource planning and reactive resource direction are linked in that the former provides a framework for the latter. One of our domain experts said that the only reason the navy makes plans is so that they can change them! This is actually a serious statement. Although detailed tactical plans are produced regularly, they are destined to be radically changed during their execution as a result of changing requirements and changing resources. An example of this is given later in the chapter.

A further discussion of reactive resource direction is given in Chapter 4.2. The relationship between the concepts in that chapter and those described here are explained by the planning cycle shown in Figure 4.3.3. An initial situation assessment gives rise to a set of requirements and the resources available to fulfil those requirements. These are used as inputs to the tactical resource planning process. As is described later in this chapter, the output of this process is a **knowledge-rich** plan; this includes not only *what* to do but also *why* it is being done. Also stored in this plan representation will be the dependencies of one requirement or event on another. This tactical plan is then fed to the plan execution process which gives rise to world events. A continuing situation assessment process (which is obviously related to the initial situation assessment process) then monitors world events in order to detect changing situations and failing plans. An additional input to situation assessment is the tactical plan with its knowledge-rich representation. Upon detection of events not going according to plan, the situation assessment process either alerts the replanning process or - if time is critical - invokes reactive resource direction to cope with the new state of the world. As is explained in Chapter 4.2 (where the term reactive resource allocation is used), this is a real-time process which is carried out within the framework of the existing tactical plan as far as is possible. The reactive resource direction process is a combination of planning and direction (whereas the plan execution process does not include any aspect of planning). Because of the time constraints on the situation, it is necessary to make quick decisions about what to do in the immediate future; there is no time for a fully-considered replan. Reactive resource direction thus provides a short-cut through the planning cycle in order to cope with real-time reaction to real-world events. This process not only gives rise to new world events but will also have knock-on effects on the original tactical plan. These new events are fed back into the planning cycle, together with their rationale; the tactical resource replanning process will then attempt to amend the existing tactical plan in the light of these new events with as little disruption as possible to pre-planned activities.

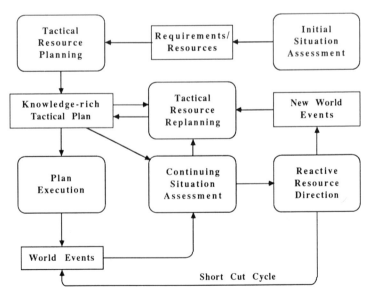

FIG 4.3.3 *The planning circle*

The remainder of this chapter discusses in detail the tactical resource planning and replanning processes. It is explained why they are different processes and why the tactical plan must be stored in a knowledge-rich representation.

4.3.7   Domain Examples

Within tactical resource planning for naval command and control there are a number of different resource categories which need to be allocated. These include:

- the disposition of ships and aircraft to provide a defensive screen around high-value units;
- the allocation of electro-magnetic frequencies to radars and communication equipments on various ships in order to reduce mutual interference;
- the allocation of aircraft to missions, and launch and recovery times for flights;
- the design of a strategy for replenishment of stores at sea.

All but the last of these come in the category of resource allocation as defined in Section 4.3.5; replenishment at sea also involves a scheduling problem. The allocation of aircraft to missions has been chosen for detailed study within the research programme; this is the domain that has schedules 'hidden' within it but is actually a resource allocation problem.

All of the above problems have similar characteristics:

- Although the production of an initial plan is important, it is recognised that the vital area is that of replanning the use of resources to cope with the changing situation and real-world events.
- There is a need for interactive plan development by man and machine (it would be impossible to build all the expertise into a knowledge-based system).
- There is a need for rapid - and 'intelligent' - plan repair. It is not enough to totally replan to cope with a changing situation once the plan has been promulgated; this approach implies too much disruption to a large organisation.
- Possibly the only meaningful measure of effectiveness is that a good plan allows for flexibility of response when the inevitable changes occur.
- They are all over-constrained problems; if there were enough resources you would not have a problem.

4.3.8   Why a Knowledge-Based Approach?

The importance of automated support for these tasks revolves around:

- freeing men for more creative tasks;
- keeping track of multiple, complex constraints;
- offering support in timely replanning (what-if planning and knock-on effects);
- generating multiple solutions and options for action;
- assisting in the development of new approaches to planning (with the current manual methods too much time is devoted to producing *any* solution to allow concentration on producing *better* solutions).

Given the need for automation, why are we advocating a knowledge-based approach? Some automated support could be given in these domains by the use of traditional operations-research techniques. However, these approaches cannot, in general, cope with some of the essential characteristics of our problem types. Some of the disadvantages of dynamic programming identified by a fellow researcher are listed here:

- Dynamic programming is computationally expensive, particularly for multiple criteria.
- There is limited scope for representing complex scenarios.
- There is no user access to the solution process.
- It concentrates on the generation of optimal rather than feasible solutions.
- There are no facilities for plan repair.
- The representation is difficult to modify to cope with changing solution processes.

In contrast the perceived advantages of a knowledge-based approach include:

- Heuristic search techniques can control the search of very large search spaces.
- It is possible to represent complex, interacting and relaxable constraints.
- Solutions will generally be found by cooperative, interactive planning between man and machine. A knowledge-based approach makes it more likely that the user will have access to the solution process. An understanding of this process is also important when constraints need to be relaxed under user control.
- It is possible to generate multiple, feasible solutions which are useful in a 'what-if' approach to planning.
- The importance of replanning in the military domain necessitates the storage of implicit information at plan generation time in order to facilitate the 'intelligent' and timely repair of plans (rather than total replanning).
- The use of an object-oriented representation of constraints not only gives the user easier access

to the problem representation but also should allow easier modification of the representation to meet changing tactical doctrines.

These criteria imply the need for a **clear** and **knowledge-rich** representation of the problem and this *can* be provided by a knowledge-based approach. The emphasis in the last sentence on possibility rather than likelihood is a result of the authors' experience of seeing many obscure knowledge-based representations of problems which seem to negate one of the main advantages of a knowledge-based approach.
The remainder of this chapter describes an experimental knowledge-based system for one domain of naval resource planning/direction (as defined in Figure 4.3.1). It is anticipated that the techniques developed could be generally applied to other naval operational domains (as outlined above) and thus provide the way forward for a generic resource planning workstation for naval command and control.

4.3.9 Flying Programme Generation

The domain chosen for implementation as a laboratory demonstrator was that of designing flying programmes for a task force. This is an example of tactical resource planning (as shown in Figure 4.3.1) that occurs on a daily basis. The objective of the planning process is to allocate aircraft to missions, together with launch and recovery times for each flight. The inputs to the problem are the missions to be flown (each mission consisting generally of several flights) and the resources available to the task force (fixed- and rotary-wing aircraft together with their crews). The constraints on the solution include:

- limitations on flying hours for men and aircraft,
- provision of turnaround times between successive flights (sometimes requiring different equipment fits),
- limited use of deck space for launch and recovery,
- mission priorities.

A more detailed description of the domain is given in Gadsden (2).
Figure 4.3.4 shows part of a typical flying programme from HMS Ark Royal during an exercise in 1986. This programme was produced manually by Ark Royal for the task force and shows the programme as it was designed (probably the day before). It shows the planned activities of various squadrons of aircraft, each flight being indicated by a solid arrow; the dashed arrows indicate aircraft kept at alert status ready to be launched at short notice. The alerts are evidence of predicted replanning on the part of the Operations Officer as these aircraft are likely to be launched in response to expected events. (Currently the

FIG 4.3.4   A flying programme

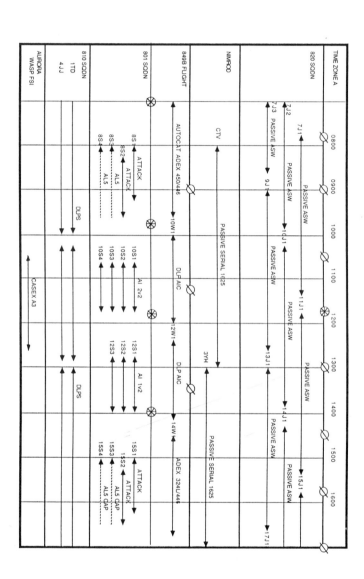

flying programmes are drawn up by hand; the figures in this chapter were taken from Ark Royal's handwritten flying programmes and drawn up using a graphics package for the sake of clarity)   The flying programme shows the period from 0700 to 1700 for squadrons of Harriers (801), Sea King helicopters (820 and 849), Nimrod airborne early warning aircraft, Lynx (810) and Wasp helicopters.   The duty for each flight is shown above the arrow with the flight name, e.g. 7j1, to the left.

Figure 4.3.5 shows the same flying programme at the end of the day after all the plan changes had taken place.   In total, alterations were made to around 25 flights.   These were caused by changes in mission requirements (in response to the changing tactical situation) and changes in the availability of aircraft (usually preceded by an aircraft returning early from a flight in need of unscheduled maintenance).   It is not sufficient to do a complete replan to meet the new situation as this would result in excessive disruption to the flying programme which was already being executed.   In fact, small adjustments are made to the missions and constraints may be relaxed to provide what is termed plan repair rather than complete replanning.   (For example, in the Falklands Campaign, the constraints on flying hours were relaxed to meet the operational need; the crews flying for three times the hours that were laid down in the rule books (HMSO (6)).)   The numbers in circles indicate the identification numbers of the actual aircraft allocated to a particular flight.

This, then, shows the scale of the replanning problem inherent in the generation of flying programmes and in every aspect of naval tactical planning.   The fact that the emphasis of the planning process is so heavily on the replanning phase gives rise to a particular knowledge-based solution.   The need for replanning implies that a great deal of implicit information about the plan must be stored at plan-generation time.   The output from the initial planning process is **not** just the flying programme for the day;   implicit output consists of dependencies between flights and missions so that knock-on effects can be calculated during the replanning phase.

As part of a research programme called FlyPAST (Flying Programme Assignment Support Tool), several knowledge-based planning systems have been built in the laboratory to support the naval officer in the planning and replanning of flying programmes.   Two of these prototypes are based on ART^{TM}* (Automated Reasoning Tool) and are described in Gadsden (2) and Oliver (3).   The remainder of this chapter describes a third system based on a different design approach (which is described in greater technical detail in Mott (4 and 5)).   The chapter ends with an outline of the plans for transition of the research programme through sea-

---

* ART^{TM} is a trademark of Interference Corporation.

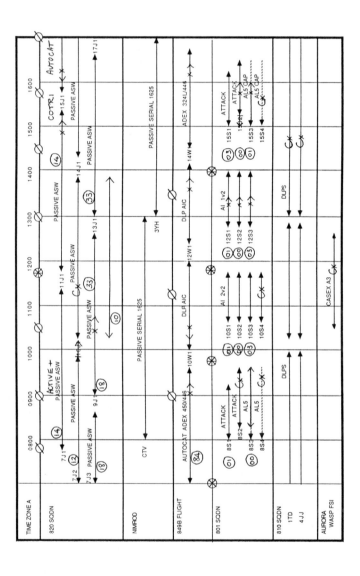

FIG 4.3.5   *An amended flying programme*

trails to operational use, together with some of the problems involved.

4.3.10   The Planning Problem

The missions to be flown are usually specified by giving time and duration together with type of aircraft and number of aircraft to be on task at one time.   Thus we might be asked to provide four Harriers on Combat Air Patrol for six hours from 1100.   From this a certain amount of information can be deduced automatically.   There is no leeway in the timings of the missions so the start-time is fixed.   From the type of aircraft and mission the weapon/equipment fit can be deduced; from this the endurance of the aircraft can be calculated.   Heuristics have been developed by naval officers for planning common types of mission and these have become part of the official tactical doctrine.   These heuristics take the form of templates or patterns of flights and vary for fixed- and rotary-wing aircraft.   Examples of these templates can be seen in Figure 4.3.4 for 820 and 801 Squadrons (which are Sea King helicopters and Harrier aircraft respectively).   These heuristics are used by the planning system both to cut down the search space and to ensure that the solutions proposed are recognisable to the naval officer.   The task that remains, therefore, for the planning system is to allocate the resources to the individual flights while keeping track of the constraints.   For this reason, this particular domain consists of resource allocation although the problem solution actually contains schedules for individual aircraft and crews.

The full scale of the flying programme domain includes many constraints; for the purpose of demonstrating the feasibility of the chosen knowledge-based approach, a number of these constraints were chosen as being representative.   These included:

- aircraft may not fly two flights simultaneously (an obvious statement but one that must be included);
- there must be enough time between flights to "turnaround" the aircraft from one duty to another and to refuel;
- aircraft must be regularly maintained;
- endurance of the aircraft must be taken into account;
- there must be sufficient crews qualified for day- and night-time flying;
- there are time windows when aircraft cannot fly from particular ships.

Many of the more complex constraints on the problem are handled by the human planner by being compiled into a simpler form.   This transformation is of use when building a knowledge-based system to support the planning task.   For example, aircraft maintenance requirements are very complex, being based partially on calendar time and partially on flying hours. It is impossible, organisationally, for the Operations Officer producing the flying programme to take into account every nuance of the maintenance process, over which he has little or no control. Consequently, the maintenance constraints are compiled by the squadrons into a simple statement of aircraft availability as a percentage of total aircraft numbers. This 'rule of thumb' works in most general cases; its failure is one of the reasons for replanning. Similarly, the management of deck space, where Harriers and helicopters share the same launch and recovery areas, is a planning problem in its own right Robinson (7). It is currently handled within the Royal Navy by being compiled into rules of thumb about how long it usually takes to launch and recover certain combinations of aircraft in given weather conditions. Again, these rules can go wrong, which gives rise to the need for rapid, real-time replanning on the part of the officer running the flight deck.

Of course, as these related planning tasks are themselves given automated support, it should be feasible to handle their associated constraints more directly, with independent planning systems cooperating to produce an overall plan. However, the subject of cooperating planning systems is still very much a research issue and will not be addressed here.

4.3.11   The Interactive Planner

The initial statement of the flying programme problem for our interactive planning system is encoded as a network of objects, such as flights, and simple constraints between the objects generated from the constraints identified above. For example, the turnaround constraint is converted into a simple constraint between pairs of flights, stating that the aircraft allocated to the flights cannot be the same, although the flights do not overlap, as there is not sufficient time to prepare the aircraft for the second flight.

Once the patterns of flights have been generated, together with the associated constraints, the resource allocation task continues as follows. The system generates a plan by allocating aircraft to each flight, whilst ensuring that all of the constraints in the network are satisfied. During plan generation, each flight that has not been allocated an aircraft has a list of possible aircraft which *could* be used; this list is called the choice set. Initially, choice sets are derived from constraints of crew requirements, aircraft type and time windows. As choices of aircraft are made for flights, either by the operator or by the system, choice sets for other flights may be reduced because of the turnaround and overlapping flight constraints. The planning algorithm consists of two mechanisms: the selection of an aircraft to allocate to a flight, and the generation of new choice sets for other flights which are related to the allocated flight via the constraints.

The system can then be used to modify the plan when resources or requirements change. During plan generation, assumptions are made about which aircraft is to be allocated to each flight, which aircraft are available and which constraints are relevant. Whilst these may appear to be *facts*, they are stored as *assumptions* so that they may later be changed. From any given set of assumptions, a number of consequent facts may be derived. For example, that an aircraft is not a possible choice for a flight will have been derived because of the existence of some constraints and from allocations made to other flights. by using an Assumption-Based Truth Maintenance System (ATMS) (de Kleer(8)), such derivations are recorded as logical dependencies between the facts and the assumptions made. It is then possible to determine what facts remain valid and what facts are no longer valid if the assumptions are changed. In order to replan, the user changes some assumptions, such as the availability of an aircraft, the system retains those facts that are independent of these assumptions and completes the plan. In a given partial plan, it may be impossible to allocate any aircraft to a particular flight. If so, the set of assumptions that led to the plan is said to be inconsistent. The system removes allocations until the plan is consistent, and then continues with the allocation process. In some situations there is no possible allocation that satisfies the user requirements, i.e. the inconsistency is *independent* of any assumptions. The system can then be used as a guide as to which constraints could usefully be relaxed in order to produce a consistent plan.

4.3.12   User Interaction

The interactive planner, using a constraint-network generator plus ATMS, has been implemented in Common Lisp on a Symbolics. A graphics interface based on the current manual methods has been built in Flavors™* on the Symbolics to interface to various versions of demonstration planning systems. The user interface appears much as shown in Figures 4.3.5 and 4.3.6 with mouse-sensitive areas to allow interaction. User interaction with knowledge-based decision-support systems requires further investigation and is the subject of a proposed research programme at ARE (Portsdown). Our intention is to prototype the interface and user interaction at the same time as prototyping the planning system. The commands that are available to the user are:

-    Generate a plan given a set of requirements.

* Flavors™ is a trademark of Symbolics.

- Replan after a change in the requirements.
- Cancel a flight (resulting in the removal of the constraints attached to that flight and the deallocation of resources for the flight).
- Add new constraints between flights (resulting in the deallocation of the two flights).
- Make a resource unavailable.
- Display the current choice set for a flight (showing which aircraft are definitely unavailable and those which may be available given the current state of knowledge).
- Request reasons for ruling out aircraft from a choice set (in terms of the constraints involved and the conflicting allocations).

A test-case taken from the scenario from Ark Royal (as is shown in Figures 4.3.4 and 4.3.5) was run through the system to test its replanning functionality. The system was able to produce an initial plan based on the requirements and resources available, taking into account allocations previously specified by the user. In all cases it was able to give constructive assistance to the user in the replanning actions which were required on that day. (Further details of these interactions are given in Mott (4).) This support included:

- Calculating the knock-on effects of aircraft becoming unavailable for duty; making suggestions for new aircraft to fulfil the outstanding missions.
- Recognising that requirements can no longer be fulfilled when certain aircraft become unavailable. In this case, the system informs the user of the conflicting constraints and allows the user to relax one. The user in fact chose to cancel some of the flights; the system was then able to replan the remaining missions.
- Recognising the knock-on effects of the late arrival of a flight.
- Indicating choice sets for flights and why certain aircraft are disallowed. For example, when some Harrier flights were cancelled, the system stated that there was only one aircraft available for a remaining flight. When the user asked 'why?' the system explained what the conflicting constraints were.

Test cases were run which included operational scenarios from naval exercises as well as pathological cases designed to test particular parts of the system's reasoning process. In all the test cases run, the knock-on effects were limited to the squadron in which the change was made. It may therefore appear that it is only necessary to consider each squadron in isolation. However, this is only because there are currently no contraints included which operate across squadrons. There *are* constraints which link the squadrons, such as the use of common deck-space and its associated management problems. Once these are introduced, which they must be for an operational system, a full analysis of dependencies will be essential to determine the knock-on effects. There is no reason why the current mechanisms should not be able to cope with this requirement.

4.3.13   Future Programme

All the work described so far has taken place in the laboratory. However, as described in Section 4.3.3, this represents only the first step in a substantial risk-reduction exercise, and we have now reached the stage where the feasibility demonstrator must be engineered for use as an operational prototype. This presents us with the severe problems, identified in Section 4.3.3, of resourcing such an exercise and of establishing the necessary level of user commitment. Assuming that these can be overcome, some of the technical issues which need to be addressed are as follows:

Is there a role for specialist AI hardware in an operational environment? The concerns of standardisation (to reduce spares holding) and robustness to the military environment imply we should attempt to use more conventional computers than those we use in the laboratory. It is likely that sea trials for the programme described here will take place on a conventional, but powerful, commercial colour-graphics workstation which gives access to compilers for most AI and non-AI languages; thus offering flexibility in the choice of implementation. Although not meeting specific military ruggedisation standards, it is expected that the workstation will survive the naval environment without special modification.

Is there a need for special-purpose knowledge-based system toolkits? Other work on this project has been developed using ART^{TM} (Gadsden (2), Oliver (3)); the approach described here (and in more detail in Mott (4 and 5)) has been based on Common Lisp. The reason for the two parallel approaches was to determine the costs and benefits of using a sophisticated (an expensive) knowledge-based toolkit. The building of two prototype systems using ART^{TM} certainly brought about a detailed understanding of the problem domain and the suitability of various knowledge-based techniques for its representation. While there is no doubt that FlyPAST *can* be implemented using ART^{TM}, the decision must be made as to whether such an approach for a *delivery* system is necessary. For the simplest of knowledge-based systems, an expensive and sophisticated solution may not be cost-beneficial; for a complex problem, such a solution may be justifiable. The question remains as to where the cut-off point comes. A growing trend is to keep knowledge representations as simple as possible as this will ease both understanding and later modification of the system. It also eases the problems of transportation to more conventional computer hardware for use in well-

established domain environments. Although there is no such
thing as a general-purpose problem-solver, for a particular
class of problems, such as those identified as resource
allocation for naval command and control, there may be a
case for a domain-independent, but class-dependent, layer
providing a problem-solver which is optimised for those
problems (Figure 4.3.6). This will then enable a domain-
dependent layer for each particular problem in that class
to be added on top. This is the approach that is currently
favoured by the FlyPAST team. It remains to be decided
whether the domain-independent layer providing the basic
constraint language, problem solver and truth-maintenance
system should be based on a knowledge-based toolkit or not.

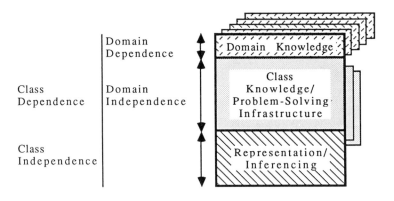

FIG 4.3.6   *Class-dependent problem solving*

The 'standard' route for development of knowledge-based
systems is through prototyping. It is assumed that one of
the reasons for using the knowledge-based approach is
because a solution cannot be specified at the start of the
project and that several prototype iterations will be
needed. In the work described in this chapter, this has
been successful so far because it is still research; if we
are to take this any further, we must enter an engineering
phase. Any future development will therefore come under
the traditional procurement methods of the Ministry of
Defence. As these are based on firm specifications and
fixed-price contracts, it is difficult to see how the
prototyping approach can be accommodated. There is also a
difficulty in ensuring that end-users take the right
attitude to prototypes. If a prototype is too good there
is a danger that it will be seen as 'the answer' and
further development is thwarted. If it is not good enough
there will be little constructive feedback from the end-
user which will aid further development (they are more
likely to throw the equipment over the side!).
     **How do you specify, validate and accept knowledge-based
systems?** Several attempts have been made in the FlyPAST
project to produce a specification of the system. As these

have been carried out within a research environment, it has not mattered too much that we have not necessarily got the specifications (or the means of defining them) right. As we move towards operational systems, the role of a specification as the legal statement of requirements demands a more rigorous approach. One practical method advocated by people who are building 'real' systems is that based on an example-oriented approach concentrating on the user interactions that define the sytem functionality. However, designing to meet specified scenarios and interaction sequences is fraught with dangers of losing generality and building a very fragile system. Another increasingly popular approach involves the development of a taxonomy of problem-solving models. This allows the requirements specifier to build on experience of how similar problems have been represented previously. The existence of a model allows issues of consistency and completeness to be addressed. It is also important that the representation of the requirements specification should be independent of the eventual implementation in order to avoid any pre-judgement on knowledge representation and functionality. (For example, see Lane (9) and Hayward (10)). The validation and acceptance of such systems depends, of course, on having a good specification to measure against. References to treating the acceptance of a knowledge-based system as you would the acceptance of a human doing the task are invalidated when you realise how much we depend on the human's ability to use common-sense and to learn from experience. Although both these attributes are the subject of continuing research, they have not yet reached the stage where they can absolve us of the responsiblity for validation and acceptance.

The above questions are all being addressed in the context of transitioning our laboratory-based research work via sea-trials through to operational use. The work described here will be engineered for shore- and sea-trials with the aim of installing a single-domain system on suitable hardware during the next two years. Research work will continue to ensure the applicability of the representations to other domains mentioned above with the aim of engineering a generic resource-planning workstation for operational use in the mid 1990's. This workstation will also need to be integrated with the rest of the naval command and control system. Of particular interest in this respect is the complementary work of the ARE (Portsdown) AI Group on knowledge-based approaches to real-time data fusion and situation assessment as described in Lakin (11 and 12).

4.3.14   Conclusions

The ARE work on resource planning has demonstrated that knowledge-based methods can be successfully employed to provide automated support for a particular activity in naval resource allocation, namely the generation of fleet flying programmes. It has shown also the need to undertake a significant amount of applied research in order to achieve this, even using the most sophisticated AI toolkits. The work has provided sufficient insight into the planning process to enable a new constraint-based approach to be formulated using an assumption-based truth maintenance system (ATMS). This approach suggests a number of potential benefits. Firstly it provides a knowledge representation which should be able to support not only the initial planning activity but also the more demanding, and more important, replanning function. Secondly, it shows generic attributes relevant to related planning domains in naval command decision support, and shows the potential to encompass both the resource allocation and the scheduling aspects of these related applications. Thirdly it may be implementable as a domain-independent resource planning support layer, at the same time obviating the need for a large and expensive AI toolkit. Whether or not an application based on these principles can be deployed in response to a specific operational need, and whether or not such a capability can be built in the context of the many engineering and procurement constraints outlined in this chapter, depend upon the outcome of a much more substantial programme of research and risk reduction which the current organisation would be hard pressed to resource.

The overall ARE programme on the application of KBS principles to problems in naval command and control, of which this resource planning activity is a subset, has brought to light a number of much more fundamental issues. It has brought to our attention the magnitude of the information management problems facing naval command and control in the future and, even though our objectives have focussed almost exclusively on finding solutions to those problems as opposed to experimenting with a specific technological approach, it has highlighted the lack of any other viable solution strategy. We have learned also that the process of deploying this technology effectively will require substantial resources and some refinement of the existing organizational structure. Whether or not these can be justified by the potential benefits depends on our perception of the importance of effective information management to the surface navy.

4.3.15   References

1.   Alvey IKBS Special Interest Group Report, March 1986, 'IKBS Planning Workshop No.5', IEE, PO Box 26, Hitchin, Hertfordshire SG6 1SA, UK.

2.   Gadsden J.A. and Lakin W.L., 2-5 June 1986, 'FlyPAST: An Intelligent System for Naval Resource Allocation', *9th MIT/ONR Workshop on C3 Systems*, Monterey, California.

3.   Oliver A.E.M. and Gadsden J.A., 21-23 September 1987, 'Use of Multiple Layer Contexts for Flight Planning', IDEX87, Brighton, UK.

4. Mott D.H., Cunningham J., Kelleher G. and Gadsden J.A., 'Constraint-Based Reasoning for Generating Naval Flying Programmes', (to be published in *'Expert Systems: The International Journal of Knowledge Engineering'*, Learned Information Systems, 1988).

5. Mott D.H. and Gadsden J.A., 29 September - 1 October 1987, 'Constraint-Based Reasoning for Planning and Replanning Flying Programmes', *MilComp 87*, Wembley Conference Centre, London.

6. HMSO, December 1982, 'The Falkland Campaign: The Lessons', Cmnd. 8758, London, para. 224.

7. Robinson A., Wilkins D., November 1982 ,'Man-Machine Cooperation for Action Planning', AI Center, SRI International, 333 Ravenswood Avenue, Menlo Park, Ca 94025.

8. De Kleer J., March 1986, 'An Assumption-Based Truth Maintenance System', *AI Journal*, Volume 28 Number 2.

9. Lane R., 29 September - 1 October 1987, 'Requirements Analysis for KBS Development', Milcomp, Wembley Conference Centre, London.

10. Hayward S.A., August 1987, 'How to Build Knowledge-Based Systems: Techniques, Tools and Case Studies', Esprit Special Session at IJCAI-87, Milan.

11. Lakin W.L. and Miles J.A.H., 2-5 June 1986, 'Intelligent Data Fusion and Situation Assessment', *9th MIT/ONR Workshop on C3 Systems*, Monterey, California.

12 Lakin W.L., Miles J.A.H. and Byrne C.D., 1-3 April 1987, 'Intelligent Data Fusion for Naval Command and Control', in 'Blackboard Systems' ed. B. Engelmore and T. Morgan (to be published by Addison-Wesley 1988) (also *2nd IEE Conference on C3 and MIS*, Bournemouth, UK).

Navigating through Complex Databases: A Case Study

B.I. Blum, R.D. Semmel and V.G. Sigillito
(The Johns Hopkins University)

4.4.1   Introduction

A Command and Control system must provide access to two categories of data. First, and perhaps most important, it must manage the timely capture, integration and display of data that are highly dependent upon their temporal context. Such data are perishable, and are of little value once outside some temporal window. Examples include active electronic emissions from hostile assets and near term weather predictions. In both cases, in a matter of hours or days the data will be useful only for ex post facto analyses.

The second category of data is relatively static; it retains its value over considerably longer periods of time. Such data can be stored as a permanent database to be referenced as required. Because these data degrade relatively slowly, it is possible to expend moderate resources on their collection and validation. Moreover, because these data represent an investment, their effective use requires the sharing of common files. Examples here include descriptive information about military equipment and statistical information regarding climate.

While there is a great deal of subjectivity in assigning data to these categories, there are distinctly different technologies used to manage each. The highly temporal data are collected on site, processing requires high bandwidths and realtime computation, and their systems often rely on offline recording to reduce the processing burden. On the other hand, systems for the more static data utilize large databases, they transfer relatively little data per request, and they benefit from the economies of a centralized (or single distributed) architecture.

For highly perishable data, the chief concern is the capture and transmission of the appropriate data in a timely fashion. For static data, the major challenge is the identification and integration of the appropriate information. In this article, we shall consider only the second category of data. We begin with a brief overview of database technology, and then describe an exploratory application under development for the United States Army.

4.4.2   Database Technology

A database is a collection of data, stored in some permanent media, and designed to be maintained and used in support of some organizational objectives. Early databases were structured as uniform collections of data called files. Database management systems (DBMS) were introduced in the 1960's to facilitate the integration of physical files and their access via logical views. In essence, the DBMS provides a higher level representation of the database and presents its contents from the perspective of the user (Weiderhold (1) and Ullman (2)).

Three types of user are identified. The database administrator (DBA) is concerned with the entire database (both physical and logical views); he develops and maintains what is variously called the data model, schema or scheme. The application programmer has a narrower viewpoint that is limited to programs of immediate interest; this view is called a subscheme. Finally, the end user has an even shallower understanding of the scheme. He too uses subscheme views, and frequently their use implies programmer level knowledge, something that we would like to avoid.

There are several different structures used to model a database logically. The earliest DBM's used networks and hierarchies to describe the data stored in the files. In the late 1970's, commercial DBMS's were available to support the relational model; these are the current systems of choice. In the relational model, the logical contents of the database is independent of the file structures chosen to physically store the data. For the purpose of understanding how the end user interacts with a DBMS, it will suffice to consider only the logical level of a relational DBMS.

The relational DBMS models the scheme in the form of relations, i.e., ordered n-tuples. The relations often are called tables, and the relation attributes are considered to be the table headings. The tuples (or "records") in a relation are then thought of as the table rows. Thus, the concept of a table/relation has a strong intuitive foundation. There is also a strong mathematical basis for the relational model. All relations are sets, and the classical set operators can be used with them. In addition, two special relational operators have been identified. The join combines two relations to create a new relation, and the projection forms a relation containing ony the specified attributes from a relation. Most of these mathematical formalisms are hidden from the end user by the DBMS query language.

One final property of the relational model needs to be discussed. We have stated that the "columns" in the table are called attributes. Some of these attributes uniquely define the row (tuple). These are called the key

attributes; the remaining attributes, if any, are called
the nonkey attributes. In the standard notation, one lists
all tuple attributes in parentheses and underlines the key
attributes. For example, EMPL-ID is the key to the
EMPLOYEE relation shown below:

EMPLOYEE(<u>EMPL-ID</u>,EMPL-NAME,EMPL-ADR)

Each tuple in this relation must have a unique value for
EMPL-ID; however, several employees may have the same name
or live at the same address.

We have stated already that the table representation of
the data model has a strong intuitive foundation. Clearly,
it is more comprehensible than equivalent representations
that require knowledge of how the database is stored.

However, we must recognize that the scheme is the
result of a design activity that abstracts and reduces what
is known about the target environment. The goal is to
produce an efficient system implementation that will meet
selected anticipated needs. As long as the database
application is used within the context of its design
intent, this scheme may be satisfactory. Yet, as one
identifies needs on the boundary of those design
parameters, additional information is required. Inasmuch
as this chapter is devoted to the use of AI in database
retrieval, it will be useful to explore briefly the
knowledge used in deriving a specific relational scheme.

Semantic data modeling is concerned with the analysis
of real world needs to formalize a database scheme for
implementation. The process sometimes is called conceptual
modeling, and the result is termed the conceptual model
(Brodie et al (3)). However, some consider the conceptual
model to be a mathematically normalized model that becomes
the basis for the implementation design (Kent (4)).
Because we are concerned with capturing as much knowledge
about the application domain as possible, we shall use the
first definition.

There are several approaches to semantic data modeling.
One of the most commonly used techniques is based on the
Entity-Relationship Model (Chen (5)). In this technique,
one identifies the entities to be represented in the
database (e.g., employees and departments) and the
relationships among them (e.g., employees are assigned to
departments). The E-R model is supported by a diagramming
convention and a method to reduce the diagrams to an
implementable scheme. Notice that this approach is
concerned with identifying the objects and their
dependencies. The relationships are dependencies among the
entities, and the unique entity identifiers are the key
attributes that define a functional dependency for the
entity's nonkey attributes. This dependency information is
reduced to a normalized form that eliminates many-to-many
relationships and transitive functional dependencies. In
the reduction process, some semantic information may be
lost.

The E-R approach is used widely, and it has the advantage of being independent of the implementation environment. Most of the other semantic data modelling approaches attempt to capture the semantic information in a frame-like structure. They rely upon inheritance to define the associations, are built within their own processing environment, and are not concerned with the transition to a relational scheme (Hammer and McLeod (6)).

In what follows, we assume that we have access to all dependency information that was used in creating the implemented scheme, e.g., the knowledge that a department has many employees and that an employee may be assigned to more than one department at one time. We also assume that we can append preconditions to a relation that limit its range. For example, the ACTIVE-JOBS relation has the precondition STATUS not equal "COMPLETE". When integrated with the implementation scheme, one may consider this "predesign" information to be a knowledge base that can aid in the processing of a query. That is, an AI-based system should be able to use this knowledge base to translate an end user statement of need into a formal DBMS query statement. In the example to be described, we call this an Intelligent Navigational Assistant (INA) because it allows a casual user, with little or no data processing experience, to navigate through the database.

Before explaining how the INA is implemented, it will be helpful if we first justify its need. Briefly, there are three modes for retrieval from a database. The first relies upon a procedural description that details how the information should be retrieved and output. For example, given

EMPL(<u>NAME</u>,MANAGER,SALARY)

one could define a procedure to list all employees who make more money than their managers:

```
For all NAMEs in EMPL
      Get the MANAGER and SALARY (as SALARY1)
      Get the SALARY (as SALARY2) for MANAGER's NAME
      If SALARY1 > SALARY2 write NAME
      End
```

The disadvantages of such a procedural approach are that it requires a deeper understanding of the scheme and will have to be modified if the scheme is altered.

One avoids these problems when using a declarative, or nonprocedural, approach. In this case, one states only the formal intent without specifying how that intent should be carried out. The Structured Query Language (SQL) is becoming the standard query language for the relational model, and in this case the query statement might be as follows:

```
Select EMPLOYEE.NAME
From   EMPL EMPLOYEE, EMPL MNGR
```

```
Where EMPLOYEE.SALARY > MNGR.SALARY AND
      EMPLOYEE.MANAGER = MNGR.NAME
```

In this case, the declarative model still requires knowledge of the scheme and the SQL syntax, but it is more compact and more closely tied to the data model definition than the procedural example.

For the casual end user, database access normally is supported by the procedural approach when standard reports are referenced and by the declarative method when ad hoc queries are processed. For the former, a "friendly" interface is provided by the application developer to facilitate request selection. The user is offered access to a set of outputs and options designed to meet most of his needs. The interface is designed for these specified needs; it does not have the flexibility to satisfy unanticipated requests.

On the other hand, the declarative technique is designed to support request processing as needs are identified. Often used reports become the standard because they are used frequently. This approach requires the user to get help from the database designers or to learn the database scheme. Either alternative is easier than waiting for a new application to be programmed. Most Fourth Generation Languages are based upon this model.

Yet both of these approaches fall short of the needs of the infrequent user who must quickly access a large and complex database without the assistance of trained data processing people. One tool for these users is a Natural Language Processing (NLP) interface that allows the user to state the query in English. This natural language statement then is translated into an SQL statement (Tennant (7)). There are commercially available NLP systems that have proven to be very effective in helping casual users access a database, e.g., INTELLECT is a product with a broad user base. However, for very complex queries and data models, it is not clear how effective these tools are. We know, for example, that English is not a good specification language. Therefore, an NLP interface may provide an incorrect but plausible response to a poorly stated query. One way of overcoming the dangers of natural language is to structure the query interface so that only reasonable queries can be formed; NLMENU is an example of this approach (Thompson et al (8)). The direction that we have taken is quite different from these natural language processing examples. We describe it in the following section.

4.4.3   The Intelligent Navigational Assistant

The case study to be described in this section is the result of a project involving artificial intelligence techniques for a database application. The immediate goal is to facilitate access to the Department of the Army Headquarters Decision Resource Database (DRD). The DRD, which contains snapshots from the databases of several dynamic production systems, is to be used for decision making and the analysis of high level problems that cross functional boundaries. To utilize the DRD effectively, there is a need to provide an "expressive" interface that allows users with little data processing experience (but considerable domain understanding) to formulate reasonable and accurate queries. Moreover, the interface must be able to recognize potential differences among the segments of the database. For example, data to be combined in a join may represent the state of functional systems recorded at different times. While such a join might be syntactically valid, there could be grave semantic consequences if these temporal differences went undetected.

The project began with an analysis of the users' needs. Subsequently, a functional architecture of an AI interface to meet these needs was defined (Semmel et al (9)). To gain a better understanding of the problem, we then implemented a prototype of that portion of the system designed to provide the user with query assistance: the Intelligent Navigational Assistant (INA). This prototype currently is being evaluated by the Army, and it is the subject for what follows (Blum et al (10)). We first describe the INA from the perspective of the users, and then we examine how it has been implemented.

4.4.3. (i)   Overview of the INA Operation

The INA is intended to serve as the primary interface for users of the DRD. The DRD is being implemented as a relational database with SQL as the data manipulation language. Experienced users naturally will have access to SQL and its associated tools. Casual DRD users will require explanation of what data exist in the DRD, assistance in accessing those data, and guidance in the formulation of a valid query.

The INA interface is presented after the user is identified. A user profile is retrieved that establishes the default for interaction style, terminal characteristics, etc. The user then is presented with a screen from which he can select the following options:

1. Tutorial. A short online tutorial is provided to orient the user to the DRD objective and explain the conventions of INA use.
2. Vocabulary structure. A sparse thesaurus of the DRD contents is available. It allows the user to view the contents of the database from several perspectives.
3. Query formulation. This is the main use of the INA; the mode of query processing is discussed below in greater detail.
4. Query selection. Previous queries are retained and may be rerun as the DRD is updated or edited to satisfy other needs.
5. Profile modification. The user may modify his profile or augment it with specially defined terms that may be utilized in subsequent queries. For example, M-Force

can be defined as FORCE-ID="M", and subsequent query
references to M-Force will be replaced by the condition
that the element FORCE-ID be equal to "M".

6. Feedback. A facility will be provided for the user to
report on his experience that relate to frustration or
confusion. Within the limits of the prototype
implementation effort, the feedback facility will be
available at the touch of a function key.

When the user indicates that a query is to be
constructed, he is allowed to build the query one term at a
time. The INA assumes that terms will be joined by
conjunction, and facilities for parenthesizing groups of
terms are provided. (We expect that this interface will be
very flexible for casual users. At the same time we hope
that it will be expressive enough to support complex
requests. Operational experience will be required before
these expectations can be evaluated).

Given this "term-at-a-time" flow, the user chooses
terms to be listed (i.e., the attributes in the SQL
"select" clause) and the constraint criteria (i.e., the
qualifiers in the SQL "where" clause). In choosing terms,
the following modes are available:

1. A database attribute name may be used, e.g., FORCE-ID.
2. A term in the user's vocabulary may be entered. The
user enters only the initial letters and then selects
from the dictionary of available terms. Only defined
terms will be accepted; the feedback utility can be
used to identify useful but missing terms.
3. The vocabulary structure may be used to provide a
framework for identifying the desired term. One may
select a term from the structure directly, or go from
the structure to the vocabulary and navigate within the
vocabulary until the desired term has been identified.

To facilitate navigating through the vocabulary of
terms, they are placed in a network (described in greater
detail in the next subsection). The network provides links
between broader and narrower terms as well as similar
terms. Not all terms in the vocabulary directly map onto
attributes in the data model; some terms are provided only
to assist the user in finding the desired attribute.

To illustrate how the vocabulary navigation is
supported, note that in the Force Accounting System, one
functional source for the DRD, there are two terms that
relate to officers: AUOFF (Authorized Officers) and STOFF
(Structured Officers). To a casual user, a request of
"Officers" may seem sufficient. However, in this case the
selection of Officers would show the presence of two
narrower terms (Authorized Officers and Structured
Officers), each of which is associated with a database
attribute. The user also could arrive at the selection
from the vocabulary structure. Here he might choose
"personnel" from the structure. The position of each
structure term also can be shown in the context of the

vocabulary network. In this case, Officer might be listed as one of the narrower terms of Personnel. If Officer was selected as the term, then the selection of the previous paragraph would follow. (Naturally, the display for Officers would list Personnel as a broader term. Thus, one can navigate from the bottom up as well as from the top down).

Once a term is selected, it is processed as follows. If the term is used only to decribe an attribute to be included in the output, then processing is complete. If the term represents a defined condition, then processing also is complete. Examples of defined conditions are the encoding of attribute domains (e.g., for location code (LOCCO) one might include the domain in the vocabulary by defining Antigua as LOCCO="AC", Afghanistan as LOCCO="AF", etc.), the encoding of commonly used concepts or defaults (e.g., Current as FY="88"), and user defined terms such as the "M-Force" example previously given. If a term is a retrieval condition that is not already defined, then the user is asked to specify the condition (e.g., = < > >=) and parameters. The input parameters are type checked and syntactic validation criteria are confirmed. For more complex queries, the user may define terms (similar to the M-Force example) to be used only during the current query session.

As query items are entered, the current active query items are listed in a window. Once the user is satisfied that the desired query has been entered, a request to process is initiated. This processing converts the list of items into a valid SQL statement. The approach for accomplishing this transformation is discussed below; in this section we consider only the user's view of the process.

A query request that seems complete to the user may not be satisfiable. The request may not make syntactic sense, e.g., it may require the join of two non-joinable relations. Alternatively, the request may not make semantic sense, e.g., it may request data elements that are a function of FORCE-ID without specifying a constraint on the value of FORCE-ID. (The list of all FORCE-ID values for a given set of attribute values is meaningless). Finally, a valid request may have been entered, but the query resolution mechanism may not be powerful enough to translate it.

Even when a valid request has been entered, there may be a need for INA feedback. For example, a request may involve a join of relations that represent different temporal states, or there may be knowledge of cross-functional boundary inconsistencies that might bias the query results. In these cases, the INA reports its knowledge to the DRD and allows the user to continue or modify the current query.

Once a valid SQL query has been produced, the interpreted results are shown to the user. Two formats will be available in the final system: one in an English form and the other in SQL. The user profile will determine the desired format. Once the request is accepted, it is forwarded to the mainframe for processing. The query results may be viewed from the INA, downline loaded to another computer (e.g., the INA PC host), or printed.

4.4.2. (ii)   *Overview of the INA Implementation*

The prototype INA consists of three functional units:

1. The User Interface Manager controls user interactions and translates the inputs into valid queries to be processed by the DRD system.
2. The Data Model Manager maintains the knowledge base used to define and resolve queries.
3. Tha Ancillary Function Manager provides the support required to make the INA prototype system complete, e.g., management of the user profiles.

Of these three units, we discuss only the first two; we begin with the Data Model Manager.

In one sense the INA may be viewed as an expert system that allows the user to enter terms recorded in its knowledge base, utilizes its knowledge base to guide the selection of terms, transforms the user's inputs into an SQL statement based upon its knowledge of the DRD data model, and reviews the SQL statement in the context of domain constraints. In this view the data model with its extended sematics is the INA knowledge base. It is the function of the Data Model Manager to create and maintain this knowledge base.

As previously discussed, the INA provides a user vocabulary (called the external vocabulary) that maps into the users' domain concepts. Some of those vocabulary terms are organized in a structure, some are free of the structure. All are linked in a network, which we now define as a "tangle", that links terms to broader, narrower and similar terms as well as to DRD attribute names. (We use the term tangle, taken from its use in tangled hierarchy, to indicate that, despite the lack of an overall structure, there are well understood local mappings).

The following observations should be made about the tangle. There is a symmetry between broader and narrower terms as well as with two terms having a similar relationship. However, two similar terms need not share identical or broader or narrower terms. For example, Authorized Forces is a broader term than Authorized Officers but not broader than the similar term Structured Officers. Moreover, there may be many vocabulary terms that map onto the same DRD attribute. For example, the synonymous terms "Authorized Officers" and "Officers, Authorized" map onto the attribute AUOFF. Because the goal is to aid the user in stating his request, redundancy is desirable. (Instrumentation of the INA to record term utilization provides a mechanism for identifying unused terms).

There also may be a many-to-one map between a vocabulary term and a database attribute. In the trivial case, this can be an alias where the identical element has different names for different views. In the DRD, however, more complex mappings may result from having elements drawn from several operational functional systems. These functional systems have long implementation histories and frequently adapt data elements to meet their particular needs. Thus, the data model must be able to accommodate variations that result from the dynamics of existing operational systems.

To understand this better, consider the following example. The Force Accounting System treats the Standard Requirement Code as a 14 character field while the Tables of Organization and Equipment system limits it to 9 characters. From the perspective of the user, these are identical conceptual objects. The DRD designers may be able to transform the two elements into a single instance; in this event, there will be only one attribute for the Standard Requirement Code. (In fact, this is the case for the current DRD data model). However, if such a merger is not practical, then it is necessary to introduce an extra level into the model, which we call the generic element. In this case, Standard Requirement Code would map onto the generic element SRC that maps onto one or more specific attribute names.

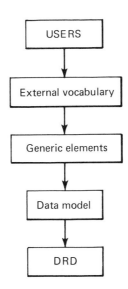

FIG 4.4.1   *INA links between the user and DRD*

To summarize, we now see that there are three levels of terminology. The external vocabulary contains terms, organized as a tangle, that provide links to generic elements. These generic terms are linked to the database attribute names; in general, this is a one-to-one map, but it may be one-to-many. In the case of one-to-many maps, one of the mapped attributes is identified as the primary element. All elements linked to the same generic element inherit the primary element's characteristics such as its format and description; there also are provisions to override the inherited defaults. This three level organization is shown in Figure 4.4.1.

The database attribute names, which we simply call elements, are embedded in relations. Thus the data model must manage the relations together with any special domain considerations. The relations are organized by views, and each relation is defined syntactically and semantically. The syntactic definition includes the elements in a relation and their use as a key or nonkey attribute. Because the DRD designers explicitly identify foreign keys in a relation, the Data Model Manager also supports this use of elements; however, the identification of relationships among the relations (entities) can be computed from the knowledge of the key and nonkey roles.

The semantic definitions augment (and must be consistent with) the syntactic definitions. For example, it is possible to compute relationships among relations and even determine if they are 1:1 or 1:m, but it is not possible to know if the relationship is mandatory or optional. Moreover, for optional relationships, it may be helpful to employ a predicate that determines when the relationship exists. It also would be useful to know when a relation defines a domain (e.g., a relation called SRC that defines all valid Standard Requirement Codes), and when a relation contains only a subset of the valid key instances (e.g., a relation formed by satisfying the selection criteria of an earlier query). Finally, it is necessary to identify all implicit relationships within the data model; for example, in the relation (A,B,C,D,E) there may be an implicit (hierarchical) relationship between A and B such that a value of B will have no meaning unless the value of A is known. To clarify this last notion, consider the attributes BUILDING and ROOM-NUMBER which together constitute a composite key; clearly, a value for ROOM-NUMBER alone has no meaning without the context provided by a specific value for BUILDING.

We call the above the inter-relation constraints. They provide information about how the entities in the data model relate to each other. There also are intra-relation constraints that detail conditions on the attributes necessary to create well formed tuples. For example, an element may be required or optional in a tuple. In a more complex case, the value of one element may establish constraints on other elements, e.g., a value of "O" for the element TYPE may imply that a non-null value for OFFICER is required and the value for ENLISTED must be null.

The elements also must be defined. Validation criteria and descriptive help messages are required by the user interface. Most of this information is available in the data model implementation. However, additional domain specific information may be required. To illustrate, assume that there is a relation with the composite key (FORCE-ID, EDATE). The DBA may have determined that no query of this table will be valid unless FORCE-ID is defined, and a query that gives only FORCE-ID should default to EDATE values that are greater than the current date. Here two "rules" would be associated with the elements FORCE-ID and EDATE (perhaps linked to a specific table); the first would request a value for FORCE-ID if not given, and the second would establish the default condition on EDATE if null.

A hierarchical organization of the objects in the data model is shown in Figure 4.4.2. It is structured as a semantic network with relations such as the following:

```
Is-a-Key-in(ELEMENT,RELATION)
Has-Relationship-with(RELATION1,RELATION2)
Is-Constrained-by(ELEMENT,CONSTRAINT)
Generic-Attribute-Link(GENERIC,TERM)
Generic-Term-Link(GENERIC,TERM)
Broader-Than(TERM1,TERM2)
```

The Data Model Manager maintains the knowledge base just described. It has tools for DBA data modeling and for capturing the post-implementation domain information required by the User Interface Manager.

The User Interface Manager is subdivided into the following modules:

1. The User Interface Control Module supports the user's navigation through the external vocabulary and the selection and validation of inputs. It has tools to process the vocabulary tangle and test the input syntax.
2. The Query Resolution module transforms a set of terms and associated conditions into an SQL statement. For the prototype INA, there are limits placed on the use of aggregation operators (e.g., AVERAGE) and formatting commands (e.g., ORDER BY).
3. The Query Feedback Module takes the output from the Query Resolution Module and forms requests to be processed by the User Interace Control Modules. For example, if a request was made that required a definition of the FORCE-ID value, then this module would organize that request.
4. The Post-Query Analysis Module processes the results of a query and provides assistance to the user in interpreting the results and/or reformulating the query.
5. The Query-Results Management Module manages the output produced by a query and, if defined by the user profile, routes the data to another computer.

Of these modules we will discuss only the Query Resolution
Module.

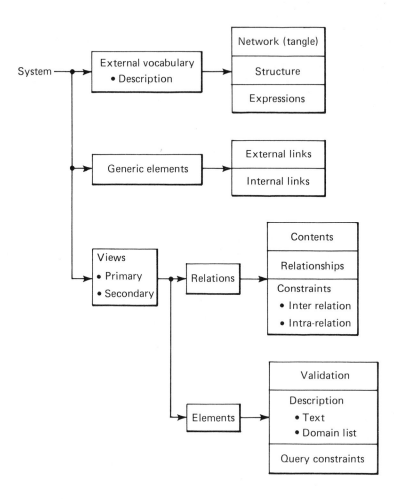

FIG 4.4.2   *Hierachical view of Data Model Manager objects*

The design of the query resolution module is based upon
the following assumptions:

1. There is a complete knowledge base available of the
    data model that contains both syntactic and semantic
    information.
2. The most complex queries will be processed by SQL by
    the experienced users.
3. The user will be available at the terminal to supply
    additional information as required to resolve the
    query.

Even with these assumptions, our near-term goal is limited
to being able to resolve only two-thirds of the queries
entered by the casual users. Building upon this
experience, we will enrich the knowledge base and widen the
range of requests that may be processed. Of course, this
is the standard expert system development paradigm; one
learns by doing.

The Query Resolution Module is initiated after the user
has entered a set of vocabulary terms that map onto generic
elements. Some of these terms also define selection
criteria, and they are accompanied by operators and values.
The first phase of processing considers what relations and
attributes should be used to form the query. Subsequent
phases organize the information into SELECT and WHERE
clauses that use the operators and values.

Processing begins by transforming the generic elements
into attribute names in the data model. For the sake of
simplicity, the following discussion assumes that there is
a 1:1 mapping between the generic elements and the
attribute names (elements). It is known that the selected
elements must be contained in the SQL statement. However,
it also is necessary to associate these elements with
relations in the data model. Lists of all relations and
roles (i.e., key or nonkey) for each element are available
in the INA knowledge base, and the Query Resolution Module
uses this knowledge to transform the request into an SQL
statement. First the functional dependencies are used to
produce a reasonable search path that satisfies the query;
then this path is evaluated using the additional semantic
information available.

The technique is illustrated by way of a simple
example. Assume that the user requested the elements A,B
and E for a database with the following scheme:

    R1($\underline{A}$,B)
    R2($\underline{\overline{A}}$,$\underline{\overline{B}}$,C,D)
    R3($\underline{\overline{C}}$,$\overline{E}$,F)
    R4($\underline{\overline{G}}$,F)

(Note that R2 violates second normal form; however, the
approach does not require normalization beyond first normal
form). In this case, A and B can be obtained from one of
two tables, R1 and R2, and E can be obtained from only one
table, R3. It follows that the SQL statement will require
a reference to R3.E. It also is recognized that, for each
instance that provides a value of E, associated values for
C and F will be known. Moreover, to find E, the key to the
R3 relation must first be found. Thus, C is added to our
list of items to be found: A,B,C and E. Eliminating the
relation R3, which we now know must be retrieved, we again
look to see if a desired element exists in only one
relation. We find that C exists only in R2. To find a
value for C, values for A and B are required. Therefore,
the condition R2.C=R3.C is added and it is seen that a join
of those two relations will provide the desired results.

Next, the module examines the semantic knowledge. For example, if no selection criteria were given for the element A, would it be semantically meaningful to report on all values of A? Or should the user be instructed to supply some restriction on the values for A?

If the example is modified by requesting A,B, and F, then the resolution becomes a little more difficult and may require backtracking to arrive at an almost identical solution. Of course, as the number of relations grows, the complexity of the resolution task increases. We have built a query/report generator using the techniques just described (Blum (11)) and have experimented with the semantics of this type of data model in a program generation context (Blum and Sigillito (12)). Based upon that experience, we are confident that this approach is viable and can be scaled up to support a varied set of users. It will require experience with operational feedback to refine the technique and validate our approach.

4.4.4   Conclusions

In this paper we have described a prototype Intelligent Navigational Assistant currently under development for use with the U.S. Army Headquarters DRD. The approach adopted is to provide a natural user vocabulary for the casual users of the system, allow them to select from this vocabulary the items that they wish retrieved, and then transform their request into an SQL statement to be processed by the DRD computer system. The emphasis in this application has been on the ease of use by "computer naive" domain specialists. A secondary objective is the semantic validation of syntactically correct query statements.

In an earlier section, we addressed the issue of how one could create queries such as "list all persons who make more money than their managers". The INA interface can formulate this type of query, but it is not straightforward. In fact, the INA user could request this query only if he were experienced enough to use SQL. Thus, the major advantages of the INA is not that it provides a better alternative to the available declarative query languages; rather, its benefit derives from its ability to represent knowledge about a database and apply it to potential queries.

As we have seen, the key to the query resolution technique is its organization as an expert system that uses an extended data model as its knowledge base. This data model definition includes three levels of knowledge.

1. The syntactic views that define how each database is implemented.
2. The semantic data that augment each syntactic view. This is formulated during the design analysis that precedes the implementation, e.g., a determination if a relationship between two relations is mandatory or optional.

3. The extended semantics that correlate data definitions across system views and specify implicit constraints, e.g., the fact that key values for the element FORCE-ID always must be supplied.

All of the first and some of the second level knowledge is available in the operational DBMS data model. However, the remaining knowledge always is expressed procedurally in the implementation. One contribution of the INA is that it provides a uniform representation for all three levels.
    If this approach is successful in the DRD application, then it may be extended to the more general domain, in which it is necessary to integrate information in the databases of many independent, operational systems. Modern distributed systems assume an adherence to uniform standards; in effect, they address the issues of syntactic integration. Semantic data modelling, on the other hand, focuses on the design of independent applications. During implementation, however, optimization issues result in the transformation of much of the semantic information into procedural statements.
    The INA suggests one way in which the information collected during the design process can be organized to both facilitate design (using the Data Model Manager) and support queries (with the User Interface Manager). Clearly, as we consider our existing database resources, we note that the different operational systems contain conceptual boundaries that serve as barriers to the ad hoc integration of the common data. Yet modern Command and Control systems must have access to these databases. We hope that our continuing experience with this application will provide insights into this much larger problem of integrating data views across independent systems.

4.4.5   *References*

1. Wiederhold, G., 1983, 'Database Design', 2nd ed., McGraw Hill, New York.

2. Ullman, J.D., 1982, 'Principles of Database Systems', 2nd ed., Computer Science Presse, Rockville, MD, 1982.

3. Brodie, M.L., Mylopoulos, J. and Schmidt, J.W., (eds.), 1984, 'On Conceptual Modelling', Springer-Verlag, New York.

4. Kent, W., 1983, *'Communications of the ACM*, 26:2, pp.120-125.

5. Chen, P.P., 1976, *ACM TODS, 1*, pp.9-36.

6. Hammer, M. and McLeod, D., 1978, 'The Semantic Data Model: A Modeling Mechanism for Database Applications', *Proc. ACM SIGMOD*.

7.   Tennant, H., 1981, 'Natural Language Processing', Petrocelli Books, Inc., New York.

8.   Thompson, C.W., Kolts, J., and Ross, K.M., 1985, 'A Toolkit for Building "Menu-Based Natural Language" Interfaces', 1985 *ACM Annual Conference*.

9.   Semmel, R.D., Lynch, P.G., Blum, B.I., and Weiss, R.O., 1987, 'A Functional Architecture for an AI Interface to the HQDA Corporate Database', Presentations from the U.S. Army Information Systems Engineering Command Technology Strategies '87.

10. Blum, B.I., Diamond, S.D., and Semmel, R.D., 1987, 'Functional Architecture for a Prototype Intelligent Navigational Assistant', JHU/APL Research Center Report RMI-87-007.

11. Blum. B.I., 1985, 'TEQUILA: An Intoxicating Query System', *Proceedings of the 14th MUG*, pp. 87-94.

12. Blum, B.I. and Sigillito, V.G., 1985, 'Some Philosophic Foundations for an Environment for System Building', *Proc. of the ACM* 1985, pp. 516-523.

Index

Accept/reject correlation, 290
Acceptance, 358
Action estimation, 147
  outcomes, 318
Ancilliary function manager, 386
Analysts, 198
Artificial intelligence, 1
  in multi-sensor fusion, 179
Assessment graphical display, 349
Assumption-Based-Truth-Maintenance, 373
Automata rules, 78
Autonomous fusion, 186

Basic resource allocation, 361
Battlefield data fusion, 212
  templates, 137
Bayes classifier, 166, 191
  rule, 105, 226
Bayesian distribution 92
  hypothesis, 92, 139
Bell numbers, 226
Belief function, 101
Biological systems for data fusion, 151
Binary testing, 93
Bingham, W. J., 298
Blackboard systems, 10, 171, 215, 226, 252
Blum, B. I., 380
Bromley, P. A., 212

Catastrophes, 55
Catastrophe theory, 59, 81
Causes of uncertainty, 39
Cellular automata, 78, 81
Chaos, 55
Chaotic dynamic models, 73
Classification, 166
Cluster analysis, 191
Collateral data, 281
Collection managers, 215
Combat models, 55
Combination of correlated data, 258
Combinatorial explosion, 247
COMINT sensors, 189
C3 model, 38, 187
Commander, 298
Conditional support, 105
Consensus of evidence, 104
Control strategy, 265, 333
Correlation algorithms, 285
  ambiguity, 234
  methods, 233
  time limits, 243
Cruse, D. W., 298

Databases, 380
Data association, 131
  driven models, 154
  inputs, 273
  links, 246

manipulation, 385
model manager, 386
reasoning, 131
Data fusion, 92, 185, 212, 226, 234, 271
  applications, 235
  definition, 236
  knowledge based approach, 251
  performance, 287
  problem categorisation, 238
  problem decomposition, 242
  rule based, 249
Decision resource database, 384
  making, 92, 117
Defence assessment, 317
Dempster-Shafer, 92, 98, 139, 174, 191, 226
Dempsters consensus rule, 104
  correlation, 108
Development bottlenecks, 11
Description of scenarios, 201
Disbelief function, 101
Domain examples, 365
  knowledge, 197

ELINT sensors, 189
Enemy Contact Report Expert System (ECRES), 213
England, E. M., 315
Entity relationship model, 382
Evidential hypotheses, 253
  intervals, 100, 102
  reasoning, 90
Exceptions, 21
Expert systems, 7, 19, 139, 153, 185, 304
  applications, 8
  research, 158

Faulkner, H. C., 315
Feature extraction, 166
Finite stochastic automata, 95
Flying programme demonstrator, 367

Force deployment, 323
  multiplier, 71
  organiser, 218
Four factor combat models, 65
Frame of discernment, 100
Frampton, S. P., 37, 315
Frames, 159, 194, 266
Functions and procedures, 344
Functional flow diagrams, 134
  groups, 322
  positions, 197
Fusion elements, 129
  methods, 130
Fuzzy Logic, 110
  membership functions, 110
  sets, 92, 111, 191

Gadsden, J. A., 356
Game playing, 4
Global data, 343
Group evidence, 254
  formation, 320
  rules, 326

Hardware link, 20
Harris, C. J., 90
Hopf bifurcation, 78
Human interface to situation assessment, 344
HUMINT sensors, 189

Ignorance, 91
Incomplete evidence, 91
Incorrect evidence, 91
Inference engine, 9, 266
  net, 8
Information fusion, 185
  retrieval, 161
Instruction rate, 290
Intelligence data, 189
  preparation, 134
Intelligent integrated interface, 163
  navigation assistant, 384
  systems, 356

Interactive intelligence support, 213
  planner, 372
Interacting groups, 324
Interface, 274

Kalman filters, 96, 227
Knowledge acquisition, 11, 339
Knowledge based systems, 7, 153, 171,
  189, 321
  life cycle, 336
  situation assessment, 316, 321
Knowledge elicitation, 331
  representation, 5, 18, 218, 266, 333,
    365
  rich plans, 363
  sources, 215, 343
  source brittleness, 12
  by rules, 194
  by semantic networks, 194

Lakin, W. L., 356
Lanchester type combat equations, 50
Learning, 4
LISP, 6
Llinas, J., 126

Marker systems, 20
Marriette, J. P., 37
Meta knowledge sources, 10
Miles, J. A. H., 1, 234, 315
Military knowledge, 222
Mission assessment, 318
Model neuron behaviour, 97
Moon, J. R., 37
Multiplatform data fusion, 255
  organisation, 257
Multiple levels, 254
Multi-sensor data fusion, 93, 212
  benefits, 130
  biological metaphor, 151
Multi-sensor integration, 90

Naked nautilus, 29
Natural language, 2

Natural language processing, 159, 384
Naval command aid, 308
Naylor, R. T., 212
NELT, 20
Network ambiguity, 24
Networking, 229
Neural functions, 59
  nets, 95
  in C^2 systems, 96
Numerical uncertainty schemes, 261

Object orientated data fusion, 269
  model implementation, 296
  system design, 278
Own, enemy and neutral groups, 325

Parallel computer architectures, 98
  processors, 18
Partial beliefs, 91, 100
Pattern recognition, 159, 163
Picture compilation, 38, 46, 321
Plan monitoring, 319
  prediction, 329
  recognition, 30
  strategic, 362
  tactical, 362
Planning, 361, 371
  passage, 306
  strike, 306
Platform equipment fits, 44
Population dynamical models, 72
Position/identity estimation, 138
Preplanning resource allocation, 330
Problem solving, 3
Processing load, 292
Production systems, 251
PROLOG, 6
Prototypes, 14
Prototyping, 353, 376

Reactive resource allocation, 330
  direction, 364
Reasoning with uncertainty, 261
Relational databases, 197, 381

Resource allocation, 304, 330, 361
Resource planning, 356
    planning demonstrator, 357
Response, 38, 48
    uncertainties, 45
Rhodes, S. L., 269
Roth, A., 212
Rules in data fusion, 252, 259
Rules of Engagement (ROE), 303, 318

SATE, 315
Scenario descriptions, 201
    operations, 202
    statistics, 289
Scheduler, 218, 344, 361
Scripts, 31, 194
Semantic networks, 23, 194
Sensor coverage, 318
    errors, 276
    integration, 98, 240
    management, 131
Semmel, R. D., 380
Sharma, S., 18
Sigillito, V. G., 380
Signal interface, 275
Situation assessment, 38, 47, 134, 141,
    138, 141, 304, 315
    case study, 336
    decomposition, 320
    definition, 316
    displays, 346
    group formation, 321
    spatial groups, 322
    uncertainties, 43
Sofchip computer, 295
Specification, 14
Spracklen, T., 18
Stochastic approximation, 96
Supervised learning, 95
Support function, 101

Surveillance, 197, 319
Symbolic uncertainty, 262
Synaptic weights, 97
System interfaces, 199

Tactical world states, 325
Target allocation function, 283
    function, 279, 283
Terrain representation, 214, 218
Testing, 230, 374
Theory of endorsements, 262
Threat assessment, 138, 214, 218, 317
    fusion product, 146
    parameters, 309
    priority list, 387
Track acceptance, 280
    reports, 273, 279
    rejection, 280
Two factor combat models, 62

Uncertainty, 37, 90, 214, 226, 261
Uncertain evidence, 90
    information, 223
Uncertainties in position, 40
    picture compilation, 39, 44
    situation assessment, 43
User interaction, 373
User vocabulary, 386

Validation, 358, 376
Vision systems, 3

Watt, S. N. K., 212
Weapon coverage, 318
    system geometries, 318
Woodcock, A. E. R., 55
Woolsey, R. B., 185

Zone managers, 215